NORTHERN
CHARACTER

The North's Civil War
Andrew L. Slap, series editor

Northern Character

College-Educated New Englanders, Honor, Nationalism, and Leadership in the Civil War Era

Kanisorn Wongsrichanalai

FORDHAM UNIVERSITY PRESS
NEW YORK   2016

Copyright © 2016 Fordham University Press

All rights reserved. No part of this publication may be reproduced, stored in a retrieval system, or transmitted in any form or by any means—electronic, mechanical, photocopy, recording, or any other—except for brief quotations in printed reviews, without the prior permission of the publisher.

Fordham University Press has no responsibility for the persistence or accuracy of URLs for external or third-party Internet websites referred to in this publication and does not guarantee that any content on such websites is, or will remain, accurate or appropriate.

Fordham University Press also publishes its books in a variety of electronic formats. Some content that appears in print may not be available in electronic books.

Visit us online at www.fordhampress.com.

Library of Congress Cataloging-in-Publication Data

Names: Wongsrichanalai, Kanisorn, author.
Title: Northern character : college-educated New Englanders, honor, nationalism, and leadership in the Civil War era / Kanisorn Wongsrichanalai.
Description: New York : Fordham University Press, 2016. | Series: The North's Civil War | Includes bibliographical references and index. | Description based on print version record and CIP data provided by publisher; resource not viewed.
Identifiers: LCCN 2015042313 (print) | LCCN 2015042061 (ebook) | ISBN 9780823271832 (ePub) | ISBN 9780823271818 (cloth : alk. paper) | ISBN 9780823271825 (pbk. : alk. paper)
Subjects: LCSH: United States—History—Civil War, 1861–1865—Social aspects—New England. | College students—New England—History—19th century. | New England—Intellectual life—19th century. | New England—Civilization—19th century. | New England—History—19th century. | Character.
Classification: LCC F9 (print) | LCC F9 .W88 2016 (ebook) | DDC 973.7/1—dc23
LC record available at http://lccn.loc.gov/2015042313

Printed in the United States of America

18 17 16   5 4 3 2 1

First edition

For my parents, who taught me leadership,
and Kathryn, who taught me character

Contents

        Introduction | 1

1   "A Stage with Curtains Drawn": New England College Students and Their World | 19

2   "The Great People of the Future": American Civilization and National Character | 35

3   To Act Like Men: Building Character in the New Brahmins | 61

4   "To Put Those Theories into Practice": Secession and the Crisis of Character | 86

5   Marching into "Rebeldom": The Failure of Southern Character | 112

6   The Character to Command | 137

7   Character Triumphant: Reconstruction, Reform, and Reconciliation | 163

        Epilogue | 189

Acknowledgments	*193*
Notes	*197*
Bibliography	*239*
Index	*255*

Northern Character

Introduction

Edward Waldo Emerson, in commemorating Harvard graduate Charles Russell Lowell, killed at the Battle of Cedar Creek in 1864, explained, "He fought because the war was of a character which left no choice to a man of his condition." The young men who answered President Lincoln's call, Emerson maintained, did not volunteer for "mere adventure or glory-seeking." Rather, they rose to defend "the free institutions" of the republic "from wreck."[1] In Elizabeth A. Dwight's introduction to the letters of her son Wilder, she praised his "*character*," claiming that it "developed early" and included his "love of right and aversion to wrong." Dwight, like Lowell, graduated from Harvard and also died in the war, although death found him at Antietam in 1862. Discussing her son's generation, Dwight declared that these "true patriots and soldiers" responded when "their country's life was in danger," giving "themselves body and soul to her service, thus 'doing,' as has been justly said, 'the highest duty man can do,' and alas! too early 'dying,' some of them, 'the best death man can die.'"[2] A cynical reader might find the words of these editors and grieving relatives hyperbolic and disingenuous. But these commemorations accurately reflect how many young men of privilege expressed their intentions when they volunteered in the war. Because of the cultural forces at work in American society at the time, and especially among the circle of professional-class individuals, these young men felt compelled to respond to the dictates of proper behavior as honorable northerners living in a world that desperately needed their leadership.

An intellectual and social history of college-educated northerners who came of age in the 1850s and fought in the American Civil War reveals a world animated by gentlemanly codes of conduct and visions of an ever-expanding, free labor–based republic. In this world, the word "character" implied a whole of host of traits, which served to motivate men to fight but also held the seeds for gentlemanly reconciliation. It was a world where class, education, and a person's bearing meant a great deal. The elite young men who inhabited this world—the New Brahmins—developed their leadership-class identity based on the term "character," which they understood as an *idealized internal standard of behavior consisting most importantly of educated, independent thought and selfless action.*

Oliver Wendell Holmes, Sr., initially coined the term "Brahmin caste of New England" in his 1861 novel *Elsie Venner*. He described these "races of scholars" as "the harmless, inoffensive, untitled aristocracy." Literary critic Edmund Wilson, writing about Holmes and the class he characterized, elaborates: "The distinguishing mark of the Brahmin is that, from generation to generation, he maintains a high tradition of scholarship: the Brahmins are all preachers, lawyers, doctors, professors and men of letters." The definition, Wilson himself admits, rarely allows for any "rough ambitious young boy . . . from the New England countryside" to join the ranks of the Brahmins. Expanding on Holmes's original idea—hence the term "*New* Brahmin"—allows scholars of nineteenth-century America to isolate and examine an understudied and influential group of young men who became wartime and postwar leaders.[3]

Character should be regarded as a northern variant of the better-known code of southern honor. The actions and writings of this influential group of individuals who became social leaders in the latter half of the nineteenth century reveals the prominence of this northern honor culture, rarely examined by historians. A focused inquiry aimed at a group of individuals to whom honorable conduct motivated and influenced their behavior offers a glimpse into the northern world of honor. Scholars have been dissuaded from pursuing a close investigation of this northern honor because the region's diverse society limits any generalizations one can make about the entire population. Additionally, the North lacked a key element essential to the development of southern honor: slavery did not constitute the backbone of the region's economy.[4] But just because the North lacked an essential component that historians have identified as part of southern honor does not mean that no comparable social system existed in the Union's most populous region prior to the Civil War. Scholars must locate new environments to observe northern honor in action.

Young men's socialization on college campuses in the antebellum period and continuing through their wartime and postwar experiences reveals the formation and application of northern honor. The concepts of personal conduct that northern gentlemen learned in college motivated them throughout their lives. Through their college writings, these young men formulated idealized traits of "character" that they attempted but ultimately often failed to achieve. Additionally, college students applied the concept of individual character to their nation as a whole, articulating their vision for a perfect American republic led by well-educated, independent-minded, and selfless individuals such as themselves. It should come as no surprise that their version of American nationalism stemmed from regional ideas about the importance of free labor, an ideology that championed "equal opportunity for social mobility and economic independence." Thus they offered a New England–centric thesis of American perfection.[5] They viewed industry, the spread of technology, and signs of urbanization and culture as proper civilization. Such an idea clashed with the vision espoused by proslavery advocates who wished to extend their form of labor into the American West. Young college men trying to establish themselves as northern gentlemen also hoped to see the United States free of slavery, an institution that had no part in these men's projections of the future. However, as a result of their own conservative worldviews, these young professionals condemned radicals who would upend social harmony for either pro- or antislavery causes. These men championed national leaders they hoped would pursue moderate courses for the nation. When the secession crisis arose, they rallied around the Union banner because their sense of honor included a strong commitment to duty but also because secession threatened the nation's future. The war simultaneously presented a challenge and an opportunity. Through their service and sacrifice, these men had a chance to cleanse the Union of slavery and put the nation back on its intended course, lighting a path of freedom for the rest of the world. In the process, they could prove their character, enact their vision of nationalism, and secure their position as societal leaders.

As the New Brahmins entered the armed forces and traveled through the South, they evaluated the region, its development, and its inhabitants by comparing it to their model of a free labor society. When compared to the New England states, the South seemed to lack the essential elements of civilization. New Brahmins viewed this as a failure of the region's leadership class. Sojourns in the South also forced the young men to ruminate on the future role of African Americans. Because their perfect vision of the United States did not include a role for minorities, the New Brahmins revealed their own prejudices, prevalent among white Americans at the time. These men demonstrated their class and ethnic biases even in dealing with the men wearing Union blue. The war offered them an opportunity to preach the importance of their class-based value system and to instill character-forming traits in their men. In handling immigrant or African American troops, New Brahmins made the case that rigid discipline and obedience to orders bred good behavior and honorable conduct, echoing the lessons that had marked their own college courses. As far as they were concerned, immigrants and blacks could only become good citizens by adopting some of the character traits that white northerners already possessed. To become a full man of character, however, required a level of education that matched that of the New Brahmins. In essence, they equated *character* with civilized behavior and argued that to succeed, the Union needed more men such as themselves.

As arrogant and self-righteous as these individuals appear, their commitment to the Union cause as well as their dedication to behaving as honorable gentlemen compelled them to join the armed forces, even though their class positions would have shielded them from service. They served because they wished to do so. These men exposed themselves to devastating enemy fire, and among their ranks the Union counted some of its best commanders. After the war, those who returned lauded the triumph of northern character and expected the moral republic that they had envisioned to come about at last. Disappointed that the postwar era did not witness a blossoming of independent and selfless national leaders and finding their own efforts to build a just society impeded by corruption, these elites retreated behind old class barriers, embracing their old foes, members of the South's aristocracy. Character, in the end, proved elastic enough to encompass even the acts prompted by the South's own code of honor.

This book tells the New Brahmins' story from the campus to the battlefield and, for the fortunate ones, home again. But why would the elite young men of northern society sacrifice their lives for the Union when they could have remained on the home front and furnished a substitute for the war effort? Why did they feel compelled to volunteer and lead others into combat? A recent scholar who studied Harvard-educated volunteers noticed that the men expressed a "desire to survive . . . as 'gentlemen.'"[6] But how was a "gentleman" supposed to behave, and where had these men learned to place such value on the concept? For answers, historians must address two interconnected questions: what roles did these men see themselves playing in society, and why did they think the war effort required the participation of the gentleman class? In truth, the war also offered these men an opportunity to demonstrate their character in a direct manner, thus allowing them to display their leadership abilities in a very public way.

When Civil War soldiers volunteered to serve their respective governments in the first confused hours of the four-year conflict, many of them claimed to have answered the call of "duty" to act on their sense of civic responsibility and honor. However, in discussing the differences between Union and Confederate troops, scholars have attributed the underlying trait of "honor" to southern soldiers without proposing a corresponding behavioral code for the men of the Union army.[7] Surely Yankees also possessed a code of values that prompted their enlistments. In order to study northern honor, it is useful to identify the traits of the better-known southern version. At its heart, southern honor required societal approval. Bertram Wyatt-Brown defines honor as "the cluster of ethical rules . . . by which judgments of behavior are ratified by community consensus." Honor is "both internal to the claimant, so that it motivates him toward behavior socially approved, and external to him, because only by the response of observers can he ordinarily understand himself." Honor, Wyatt-Brown concludes, "serves as ethical motivator between the individual and the community by which he is assessed and in which he also must locate himself in relation to others." In short, southern honor depended on one's public reputation. Kenneth S. Greenberg reinforced this interpretation, advancing that "southern men of honor were 'superficial,'" concerned with "the surface of things—with the world of appearances." Historians agree that honor, as a cultural code, pervaded southern society.[8]

Although no major works fully engage the topic, some scholars have attempted to grapple with northern honor by discussing how it differed from the southern version. In brief, southern honor involved exterior displays while, in the North, honor culture had retreated into a more private setting: a person's inner self. Wyatt-Brown traces how punishment in the North became a private rather than public affair as penitentiaries, with their focus on individuals' internal reforms, replaced other means by which society imposed justice on offenders through public shaming. Northern observers identified one of honor's weaknesses: the crowd's mood overwhelmed and subsumed a person's individualism. Honor, Nathaniel Hawthorne declared, "was defective." One's identity fell victim to the honor-based society. Greenberg, meanwhile, reveals how northerners and southerners disagreed about how to regard internal and external characteristics. Whereas white southerners saw "the mark of the whip" as "a sign of the slave's bad character and 'vicious temper,'" northern abolitionists "disagreed, interpreting the scars on a slave as a sign of the bad character of the master or as an expression of the evils of enslavement." As Greenberg explains, "Abolitionists read for meaning beneath and beyond the surface," but southern men of honor "did not linger over the scene that gave rise to the scar; it was irrelevant. The scar, in a sense, spoke for itself—or rather spoke about the man whose body carried it—regardless of the process or the larger set of relations that brought it into existence."[9]

Honor, southern or northern, relates directly to the development of nineteenth-century masculine identity. The New Brahmins closely resemble the model of "restrained manhood" outlined by historian Amy S. Greenberg. According to her, "Restrained men were often successful in business (where they might employ aggressive tactics) and in other areas of life as well." Attracted especially to the "reform aspects of the Whig, Know-Nothing, and Republican parties," these individuals based their manhood on "being morally upright, reliable, and brave." Such an image contrasted with the "martial manhood" model, which emphasized physical strength and dominance.[10] As refined members of the professional class in the North, New Brahmins certainly placed more emphasis on self-restraint and economic success.

Edward L. Ayers focuses on the term *dignity*, defining it as "the conviction that each individual at birth possessed an intrinsic value at least theoretically equal to that of every other person." He also identifies the importance of self-restraint in "a culture of dignity" where "people were expected to remain deaf to the same insults that Southern men were expected to resent." Dignity, therefore, "might be likened to an internal skeleton, to a hard structure at the center of the self; honor, on the other hand, resembles a cumbersome and vulnerable suit of armor that, once pierced, leaves the self no protection and no alternative except to strike back in desperation." "Honor in the Southern United States," Ayers maintains, "cannot be understood without reference to dignity, its antithesis and adversary to the north." Rather than seeking retribution when wronged, northern men restrained themselves and kept their passions in check. Patrick Rael, meanwhile, argues that, for northerners, the term *respectability* "served as a master value, encompassing a host of traits—not all of them compatible—that came to define an ideal for human character in an expanding market society." More recently, Lorien Foote has demonstrated that Union soldiers used the language of southern honor in their social interactions. Pointing to the complex nature of northern society, she also suggests that Union men who employed southern ideas of honor "were often elites who had traveled or resided for a period of time" in the South or overseas.[11] While Foote's findings reveal elements of the southern honor system in northern men's interactions, New Brahmins also used a unique code of honor that differed from the southern version.

Dignity, respectability, and southern honor offer hints of what constitutes northern character. However, an investigation of college-era writings—student essays, letters, and diaries—fully reveals the northern code of conduct so important to the gentlemanly class. The world of northern honor or *character* revolved around concepts of individualism, civic responsibility, and societal leadership. An equally important avenue of investigation focuses on these young men's conceptions of American nationalism. Men who lived by the code of character expressed concern for the fate of the republican experiment as embodied by the United States. Their actions as society's leaders in a time of crisis, they believed, also revealed their nation's character. Simply stated, these privileged individuals fought for the Union because they believed it part of their responsibility as society's trained leaders to defend both the legacy and future of the nation and to demonstrate their "character" by facing danger and shepherding other men through the fires of war.

Although the topic of northern honor remains relatively unexplored, several scholars have examined the North's intellectual class during the conflict. All of them owe a debt to George M. Fredrickson's fifty-year-old classic *The Inner Civil War*. In it, Fredrickson describes how northern intellectuals responded to society's rejection of their authority and the downfall of their position as social leaders. In Jacksonian America, an age of greater democratic opportunities for white males, intellectuals could either admit to having "no special claim to prominence" or wage "an apparently hopeless battle against the new forces, attempting to shore up the collapsing institutions that formerly provided positions of prestige and authority." Fredrickson's intellectuals yearned for some national crisis that would force the unappreciative masses to call on their leadership again. The war offered young intellectuals "a hope for personal salvation." Citing the death of Robert Gould Shaw, commander of the famed 54th Massachusetts, the first African American regiment raised in the North, Fredrickson argues that intellectuals paid a heavy price but needed to demonstrate that "the American aristocracy had not been emasculated by luxury after all." The deaths of the young had "redeemed" the elite classes.[12]

Although *The Inner Civil War* has withstood the test of time and its conclusions are sound, Fredrickson suggests a similar antebellum experience for both older and younger intellectuals. An examination of younger men on their own terms, however, suggests that they did not aimlessly wander through the mid-nineteenth-century world waiting for a conflict to erupt. Rather these young men concerned themselves with codes of conduct that qualified them as members of the gentleman class, worried about their careers, and observed national affairs with interest. Fredrickson also focused his query on Boston's elites, missing the broader intellectual community of New England. Finally, *The Inner Civil War* weighs the contributions of writers and reformers of the era above other members of the professional classes such as attorneys and businessmen. Other scholars of antebellum America generally agree that a sense of cultural anxiety pervaded the era. Uncertain about how to follow in the footsteps of the founders, the children of the Revolutionary generation concluded that they had two tasks: to spread liberty and to protect the republic from tyranny and anarchy.[13] Studying the New Brahmins, thus broadening Fredrickson's original sample, provides a new perspective on northern intellectuals.

The New Brahmins at the heart of this study possessed both a positive, Whiggish—that is, progressive—view for the nation's future and an abiding fear that it had lost its moral bearings. In their nationalistic vision, they echoed the founding generation by tracing America's ideological roots to classical times. But they constantly feared that selfishness and radicalism would derail the American experiment. Fears of government corruption and a misuse of state power most influenced these young men's worldviews. They hoped to infuse virtue—the act of sacrificing one's own desires for the greater good—back into society. All of America's troubles, they believed, could be traced to two sources. First, poorly educated citizens failed to understand the importance of virtue and lacked independence in thought. Second, the political system of the day, dominated by self-serving politicians who maintained their positions through patronage, had corrupted American government.[14] Modern historians have identified such concerns with the concept of republicanism. Although such ideas appear outmoded given the changing nature of American society, these young men's classical education kept the concepts at the forefront of their thought. The fact that they continued to espouse these same concerns about society in the postwar period suggests the ongoing influence of their undergraduate educations.[15]

Northern intellectuals formed but one part of a larger community of gentlemen and professionals. The members of the professional class came from diverse backgrounds and engaged in many different occupations. College-educated men, the New Brahmins of this study, distinguished themselves from other young men of the period in several ways. Their preoccupation with class-based issues, both in and out of uniform, for example, set them apart. Colleges taught, and the men themselves believed, that they represented the ideals of the gentleman class. Confident in their opinions and dedicating themselves to societal leadership and service, the New Brahmins relied on the code of "character" to guide them in their actions. When the war began, these men served but demanded roles commensurate with their standing in antebellum society and thus became officers. More than most, these young men spent a considerable amount of effort worrying about their rank, their position, and how they were supposed to behave as gentlemen at war. Unfortunately for the New Brahmins, their war service did not mean that American society would accept their ideas or leadership in the postwar era.

There is little doubt that college-educated men should be considered elites. In 1800, colleges enrolled only 0.59 percent (1,151) of white males between the ages of fifteen and twenty. In 1840, that percentage had increased to 1.05 (8,028 students), and in the 1850s, the college population had only inched up to 1.18 percent of fifteen-to-twenty-year-old white males (16,521). Whatever measure one considers, college men made up a minuscule proportion of the antebellum population.[16]

Despite a distinction between urban colleges with long-standing traditions and enormous wealth such as Harvard and Yale and smaller, rural schools such as Amherst and Bowdoin, all served to qualify young men to professional standing. Whether he came from a wealthy merchant's home or a struggling farmer's field, a young man, once graduated, found himself elevated to the professional class. Of the men who graduated from Amherst College between 1850 and 1865, approximately 253 (34 percent) entered the clergy (missionaries included), 121 (16 percent) became attorneys, 121 entered the educational field (teachers, professors, principals), 139 (19 percent) went into business, and 60 (8 percent) pursued medicine-related professions.[17] At Bowdoin College, of the who men graduated in the classes between 1850 and 1865, approximately 81 (14 percent) went into the clergy, 181 (31 percent) practiced law, 99 (17 percent) became educators, 33 (6 percent) went into business, and 52 (9 percent) became physicians.[18] After 1800, a third to a half of each graduating class from Yale became lawyers.[19]

This book focuses only on New England colleges and the young men who emerged from their hallowed halls. The sample, however, is not limited to New England–born students. While most of the subjects came from New England, others such as Samuel C. Armstrong and James A. Garfield, both of whom attended Williams College in Williamstown, Massachusetts, grew up in other regions (the Hawaiian Islands and Ohio, respectively). Regardless of their home region, attending a New England college had a formative influence on young men. New England, as a region, represented northern distinctiveness for antebellum Americans. Thanks to its urbanization and industrialization, New England also offered the greatest contrast with the slaveholding South. Many southerners also sent their sons to northern schools, and the care with which they tried to inoculate the next generation of slaveholders from embracing any antislavery ideas they might pick up in the North suggests the influence these colleges had on young men's minds.[20]

By instilling character, colleges guaranteed the credibility of their graduates. The college men themselves then helped to identify and spoil the plans of dishonest individuals preying on society. In this period of industrialization and greater mobility, middle-class Americans became anxious about scammers and swindlers. They believed that youth, with their "soft wax" minds, were particularly susceptible to the spells and lures of crafty confidence men. Corruption of their youth, Americans feared, would lead to the collapse of republican virtue and society itself. Antebellum etiquette manual writers, educators, and other social thinkers believed that instilling a strong sense of character would help blunt the effects of rapid societal change. Only the strong character of the people could combat the hustlers and confidence men.[21] College-educated men, because their training had supposedly immunized them against trickery and morally suspect actions, could protect as well as lead the less fortunate and more gullible. A person's college degree served as a guarantee that the bearer was a man of character who would "subordinate personal ambition to higher purposes." In an age of distrust and fear, Americans could supposedly still turn to the best-educated members of society. College diplomas reassured potential employers and creditors that educated members of society deserved their trust because they could stand up for moral righteousness.[22]

At the start of the war, desperate military authorities, scrambling to find men to officer the newly forming units, turned to college-educated men, whom they believed had the discipline and leadership qualities to train soldiers and prepare them for combat. As historian John Pullen observed, colleges "constituted the Civil War equivalent of the R.O.T.C." Indeed, the young men themselves understood their military rank to reflect their potential usefulness to the Union cause. Harvard graduate Charles Russell Lowell told his mother in May 1861 that he was "confident" of being "right for a commission in the first batch of civilians," having noticed that since he applied for one, "none have been given except to the graduating class of West Point." With professional soldiers in short supply, college graduates believed themselves next on the list of young and qualified leaders.[23]

Union army commanders relied on college graduates precisely because of their extensive education compared to other Americans at the time. They could trust the elite young men to make tactical command decisions and keep undisciplined troops in check. When considered as a whole alongside the rank and file of the Union army, college men had received much more education. Historian Earl Hess notes that "most Yankees made a living with calloused hands and strong backs rather than with professional training and intellectual finesse."

Indeed, almost half "of all Federal soldiers were farmers, and about a tenth of them were common laborers. Most of the rest were skilled artisans." In the 154th New York, 73 percent of the men had been farmers and "only twenty-three men, 0.02 percent of those who gave their occupation, made their living by means other than manual labor." Hess also cited a study of over ten thousand federal soldiers, which found that "881 out of 1,000 had either a limited or good grammar school education" and "only 47 out of 1,000 had any education or professional training beyond grammar school." Both Union military authorities and the northern gentleman class themselves believed that such a rabble required the leadership of men certified as possessing superior character.[24]

A vast majority of the men in this sample identified with the Republicans. While character dictated that an individual think independently and not become a "party man," the nationalistic vision that these men articulated resembled what the Republican Party promised to establish. Political party affiliations helped antebellum Americans shape their responses to questions about the nation's future course. Of the forty-nine individuals at the core of this study, thirty identified as Republicans and four as Democrats. One voted for the Constitutional Union ticket in the election of 1860 but supported the Republicans after the war began. Fourteen men's political affiliations remain unclear although many of them likely supported Republican ideas. Some Democrats' political affiliations shifted to support Republican plans during and after the war. Although it is difficult to pinpoint the degree of their support for the abolitionist movement, at least ten of the men in this group supported abolition before or early on in the war. Most of the college men considered in this study traced their political ideology to the Whig Party, believing in national development, internal improvement, and support for American industries. Socially conservative, these young men rejected radicals in both sections. They favored gradual and conservative changes as opposed to the revolutionary ones that proslavery and abolitionist forces advocated; in essence, they agreed with the opinion held by older Whigs.[25] Their political lineage helps explain why, after the war, many of them became disillusioned with the Republican Party's shifting priorities. Some expressed interest in the Liberal Republican movement in 1872 and others switched support to their onetime political rivals, the Democrats.

Beyond looking at political beliefs, several historians have attempted to use the lens of class distinction as an analytical framework to study Civil War soldiers. One concluded that the Union side lacked a "defining class model" for its officers when compared to the Confederacy with its aristocratic families, a rather surprising statement given the number of prominent northern families whose young men served and sacrificed for the Union cause. A broader definition of social class reveals the North's counterparts to southern aristocrats. Some scholars have employed rank as a surrogate for class in studying the world of Union soldiers. Although a useful barometer of an individual's class ranking, a method that traces members of the North's professional classes from the antebellum period provides a more complete picture of the experiences of the class divides in the federal army. This book offers such an approach.[26]

Because these New Brahmins' conceptions of character included ideas of civic duty and patriotism, this northern honor is bound up with their antebellum understanding of American nationalism. When federal soldiers marched to war in the spring of 1861, many of them spoke of defending "the Union." But what did this amorphous entity represent to them? What was their conception of their nation, its boundaries and its history? Why did they believe that the American republic was worth fighting for and sustaining? Why did they consider themselves qualified to save the Union, and what would have been the consequences for their self-conception if their inaction led to the breakup of their inherited nation? Although Americans may not have tested their "loyalty to the nation" before the war, their attachment to the nation-state did not arise out of nowhere.[27] Most works examine the development of nationalistic beliefs only up to the breakout of the fighting or begin their examination of this topic after the start of the war. Such studies leave unexplained the question of how northern gentlemen reacted to what they witnessed in the southern states, and how they related that to their preconceived notions of the region and its place in a broad vision of American nationalism. Susan-Mary Grant has argued that "nationalist ideology was predicated on the northern image of the South in the antebellum period."[28] Although that observation is accurate, New Englanders of the younger generation had a more complicated relationship than simply defining their world in contrast to a dominant Southern vision. Rather, the young men who came of age in the 1850s accepted an intentional fostering of New England identity put in place by the preceding generation. As a result, the students of the 1840s and 1850s did not distinguish a northern and southern narrative but simply identified the triumphant New England–centric history as *the* American story. This vision of progress through industry meshed nicely with their forward-looking Whig—and later, Republican—political ideology.[29]

A true reassessment of character, nationalism, and the professional class must also take seriously the historical experiences of youthful individuals. Historian Peter Carmichael has used the generational lens to examine young Virginian elites born between 1831 and 1843. He concluded that these young men—the southern counterparts to the present sample—"craved bourgeois respectability, hungered for professional success, followed personal ambition, and desired the material trappings of a middle-class lifestyle." These Virginian youths had been "groomed to become the state's next generation of leaders" who believed "that a higher mission awaited them." As young men, they hoped to follow their ancestors' footsteps and enter the respected upper classes as they led their state into the future. These men eventually became the dedicated "second-echelon officers" in the Confederate army.[30] Unlike Carmichael's cohort, the New Brahmins did not appear too worried about their region's loss of prestige and political power. They continued to work toward maintaining or proving themselves worthy of their professional status without fearing any obstructions to their success. Taught to celebrate the New England characteristics of industry spreading into the West, and finding ample occupational opportunities themselves, young northern elites tended to envision a far more optimistic future—that is, as long as the Union, their inheritance, remained intact and slavery, that system of labor incompatible with their vision of a free republic, remained restricted and secluded.

A Note on Sources

Although this book draws on the words and experiences of dozens of men who attended colleges in New England and fought in the Civil War, forty-nine individuals lie at the heart of the study.[31] Out of this group of forty-nine, twenty-one attended Harvard, twelve went to Bowdoin, seven to Yale, four to Amherst, three to Dartmouth, and two to Williams. At least fifteen out of the forty-nine men left documents that spanned both the antebellum and wartime years. Sixteen out of the forty-nine were killed or died as a result of wounds sustained in the war. At least six others suffered serious wounds. Five of the men in this sample received the Congressional Medal of Honor for their valor during the conflict.

This project, like all historical studies, is not immune to a source selection bias. The search for the core group of individuals began by identifying men who fit the project criteria—Civil War soldiers educated at a New England college in the 1850s and early 1860s—and had left significant writings and observations. Additional names became part of the project as a search of their records in libraries and repositories identified them as qualified candidates for the study. While this group cannot be considered representative of all the college-educated Americans at the time, it does provide a glimpse into the world of these privileged and dedicated men and a sense of how they viewed their role in it.

As any historian who has attempted to write about a specific group's characteristics knows, not all individuals will conform to the overall sample's patterns or generalizations. I have chosen to forego any modifiers to account for individual nonconformity to the model as a whole. Students of history should always be aware of the imprecise nature of their craft and the varied beliefs and complex actions of human beings. Because of these, there are always outliers in even the most scientific of samples.

The core group of individuals in this study all served in the war. The focus on men who translated their college lessons into military service came about because an attempt to understand why they volunteered led back to the wealth of writings about character and nation that their college courses guided, prompted, and inspired. Many other college-educated New Englanders lived through the Civil War era without serving in the armed forces, but their experiences and motives require analysis that is beyond the scope of the present study. References to New Brahmins throughout this study, then, should be taken to describe only those men who served in the military during the American Civil War.

Some of the letters, diaries, student publications, and college essays that these New Brahmins left have been published, but others remain in manuscript collections, historical societies, and college and university archives in New England and the mid-Atlantic. Many alumni donated their college and wartime writings to their alma maters. Additionally, many nineteenth-century college librarians keenly preserved the contributions of their students and graduates. That said, the richness and usefulness of the sources here remain at the mercy of human interest and spatial constraints. Gaps in the student records sometimes appeared when schools changed archivists or librarians. One case in point is the collection of student commencement essays at Wesleyan University. While the university retains a wealth of material from the 1840s to the mid-1850s, such documents became scarce after that point.

Although many contemporary college compositions were formulaic in nature, they reveal important patterns about commonly accepted traits. Students had a greater opportunity to express their own voices when composing public speeches and presentations. By triangulating essays, letters, and diaries, a more complete and reliable picture of students' intellectual beliefs comes to the fore. Historians who have worked on American nationalism have relied on sources with wide distribution such as travel narratives, political speeches, and pamphlets. Print culture, after all, contributed to the creation of a national conscience. College orations also drew large crowds, and some essays lived on through print and distribution. Such public presentations, therefore, help historians establish what these individuals considered behavioral and nationalistic ideals. Private student writings including essays reveal the concepts and values that college men wrestled with as well as themes they had to consider as society's young leaders. Additionally, such sources allow historians another way to explore how nationalism and ideas of proper behavior were cultivated through avenues other than those of print and public ritual.[32]

The nature of the surviving records renders difficult an attempt to follow young men from their undergraduate days through the war. While documents may exist from a student's college courses, they may not be available for when he served in the war. In some instances, a useful essay or poignant composition from college is all that remains of an individual's writings. Conversely, some individuals' wartime writings have been preserved but none remain from their school days. In this book, only a few individuals' papers cover the entire expanse of their education and wartime service. As such solitary sources employ rhetoric and themes similar to the writings of the individuals who left more complete records, they make important contributions to the re-creation of these young men's intellectual environment. The same holds true for records in cases where the author's wartime service cannot be established or the author did not volunteer in the armed forces. Colleges exposed young men to lessons about personal bearing and national leadership and provided them with a stage to develop and test gentlemanly traits. Some individuals acted on those teachings, applying their college lessons to their wartime thoughts and actions.

Despite their education, college men still misspelled words and composed poorly written essays and letters. During the war, they sometimes did not have the opportunity to check their grammar or spelling, quickly scribbling missives to reassure loved ones of their safety after a bloody confrontation. I have corrected typos and added punctuation and capitalization where necessary. So as not to interrupt the flow of the narrative, I have opted to forgo the addition of "sic" after each mistake in the primary documents.

The following chapters are divided into two parts. The first three chapters focus on the antebellum period, while the remaining four follow the New Brahmins through the wartime and postwar years. Chapter 1 describes the social world that the New Brahmins experienced in mid-nineteenth-century colleges and the challenges that they faced. Chapter 2 explains these young men's vision for the United States and their beliefs about the national character. Believing the United States represented the culmination of human progress, the New Brahmins highlighted industry and love of liberty as American traits. They offered the vision of a blessed Union, destined to expand into the West and inspire democratic revolution around the world. Young northern men coming of age in the 1850s accepted a New England–centric vision of nationalism deliberately crafted by northeastern intellectuals to bolster their region's contributions to the national story. These young men professed a nationalist vision that excluded African Americans, whether enslaved or freed. As a result of this racial view, they also erased blacks from their region's past and dismissed southern narratives, which encouraged the expansion of slavery into the West. Slavery, because of its incompatibility with free labor ideas, threatened, in northern gentlemen's eyes, the national character for it undermined the industry of white men. This vision of America's future course helped inform college men of their own roles in society and also set up the ideological conflict between the New Brahmins and their southern counterparts.

Chapter 3 examines how the New Brahmins, preparing for societal leadership, understood the term "character." Colleges taught students to think independently, restrain their emotions, control their behavior, and act like gentlemen. A man of character maintained his individualism in the face of societal pressures and sacrificed himself for the public good. Although the idea of good character permeated to other segments of northern society, colleges amplified the lesson for their students. College men, viewing themselves as gentlemen, also took these roles much more seriously. In fact, gentlemen had the duty of living by high and idealized standards as examples for others to follow.

Chapter 4 witnesses the transition of word into deed as New Brahmins reasoned, in the wake of the secession crisis, that they needed to volunteer to save the Union and secure their place as society's leaders. The chapter discusses the generational conflict between eager sons and parents who did not believe that their children ought to fight in the war.

Chapter 5 follows the New Brahmins into the South and observes how they viewed the region through their New England–centric lenses. The New Brahmins developed a harsh indictment of southern leaders after they had observed the region's environment and society. As they marched into the Confederacy, these northern gentlemen entered into a world that few of them had seen before. Cloistered in New England towns or traveling only to the West and Europe, these youths brought with them biases about the South as well as notions about what constituted civilization. They saw the South as a beautiful land filled with plenty. But they contrasted this admiration for the physical properties of the region with the lack of developed resources. So much potential in both the land and the people sat idle and uncultivated. In addition, southern towns and southern people, specifically poor whites, appeared degraded and lacking in industry and energy. The New Brahmins pointed to slavery as the primary culprit. They criticized southern leaders for neglecting their responsibility to poor white southerners and for relying too much on the regressive institution of slavery. As for the enslaved themselves, these men viewed them with curiosity and pity. Some did not believe freedmen would survive in a world without anyone to care for them.

Chapter 6 explores how New Brahmins conducted themselves as leaders in the armed forces. College-educated men discovered that their rigid codes of good behavior, instilled in college, meshed well with military life. Good character, in fact, appeared easier to attain and evaluate in the armed forces. Most directly, New Brahmins could test their character by enduring the hardships of campaign life and surviving the ordeal of battle. They expressed considerable concern about their actions as gentlemen in arms and fretted about their rank, their chances for promotion, and their conduct under fire. Because they believed themselves the social superiors of their troops, New Brahmins brought to their tasks an unshakeable belief in discipline. Those men in charge of African American units believed that traits of character, especially self-discipline, would elevate formerly enslaved individuals to soldiers. Even as the men wrestled to bring discipline to their camps, they also faced their own fears of battle, the ultimate test of character.

Chapter 7 explains how the New Brahmins who survived the war believed that victory had affirmed the superiority of their character and set out to refashion the postwar world as society's leaders. New Brahmins prescribed a healthy dose of character to all elements of society in their attempts to shape national affairs. Many of them, however, faced disappointment. Instead of promoting the rise of honorable social leaders, the Union's victory paved the way for a new generation of party politicians and profit-driven industrialists to dominate American society. New Brahmins sympathized with but did not always support the liberal reform movement of the period. Many of them called for greater morality in political life, a character-based education system, and a reunion with the South's "natural leaders," their counterparts and onetime adversaries. The story of the New Brahmins, therefore, comes full circle as they found themselves turning to their fellow elites once spurned by what they considered a wayward society.

Young men who graduated in the 1850s and 1860s believed that they had the knowledge and character to tackle the nation's most pressing problems. But before they took the helm of society, they needed to focus on their professional development. They watched, therefore, the folly of their parents' generation, all the while attempting to behave like proper gentlemen worthy of future societal stewardship. They declared themselves ready for leadership roles by their idealism and the moral certainty of their convictions. Charles Russell Lowell, the future Civil War hero, declared as much in his well-received and much publicized commencement oration at Harvard in 1854. "No nation," Lowell began, "can view its young men with indifference . . . so each nation sees in its young men the means of fulfilling its wishes." Sounding an optimistic tone for the future, he declared that young men had "always been sought . . . and never more than at present," because they were "a power on the earth, because they bring zeal and vigor which the world is eager to use." Youths offered more than their labor and strength. The young also brought "their fresher and purer ideals." The Harvard graduate warned that "the old men, the men of the last generation, *cannot* teach us of the present what should be, for we know as well as they, or better; they should not tell us what *can* be, such knowledge in the world's march is only impedimenta." Lowell heralded the coming of a new generation. Before they could rise to prominence, however, the Civil War forced them to act to change the nature of society, not just by their ideals but also by their sacrifices. The war tested the limits of their ideals and the strength of their character.[33]

1

"A Stage with Curtains Drawn"

New England College Students and Their World

In May 1864, as U. S. Grant's armies advanced into the Confederacy on multiple fronts, Harvard students took a break from their studies to listen to orations by the senior class. For his presentation, William H. Appleton waxed eloquent about the importance of colleges in war and peace. A college education, he declared, benefited both the individual and "the country at large." He considered colleges the "educators of the community," because their graduates, in turn, spread knowledge to others beyond their campuses. The most important task of a college, however, was that it fitted "men to be rulers" and "the best legislators, & the best rulers are the men of the best education." The men with the highest educations thus helped "raise the standard which the people require in their rulers." The best political leaders—the college-trained ones—had "enlarged views of government," studied their nation's history, and "followed the life of a nation from its small beginnings."[1]

Turning to the present state of wartime America, Appleton praised the sons of Harvard who were bleeding and dying for the Union. "Amid all the sacrifice . . . between loyalty & rebellion," colleges had "sent forth from ancient halls of learning their sons as did the Spartan mothers of old with the parting injunction [to] return with their shields or on them." Colleges, therefore, had also instilled nationalism and patriotism, teaching young men about the honor and necessity of sacrificing for their nation. Although many Americans viewed college students as the spoiled sons of wealthy merchants, Appleton challenged that belief. He portrayed college men as loyal citizens who served their communities and nation in times of both peace and war. College graduates in Civil War America lived a life of service, whether by their battlefield sacrifices or their home-front exploits.[2]

This chapter examines the intellectual and social world of antebellum colleges, notes their emphasis on a broad and classical education, and describes the challenges that sons from working-class families faced. If they wanted a higher education, many young men who did not have the financial resources of wealthy parents needed to work hard to pay their way through college. Whether from elite or nonelite families, young men learned that by attending college, they fulfilled one of the founders' dreams: that of an educated and selfless public.

The founders of the American republic viewed education as the bulwark of liberty. Educated and elite themselves, the framers of the nation maintained that republicanism required a vigilant and educated populace. Fearing both monarchies and uncontrolled mobs, the founding generation hoped that their descendants would choose their leaders wisely and guard their institutions fiercely. In the mid-nineteenth century, education reformer Horace Mann declared elementary and high school education "a great equalizer of the conditions of men,—the balance wheel of the social machinery," for it gave "each man the independence and the means by which he can resist the selfishness of other men." Education had the power to "obliterate factitious distinctions in society."[3] A dedicated young man could exceed the common schooling available to most youths and seek a college degree, the highest level of education a young American could attain in the antebellum republic. Attending college signaled a profound commitment not merely to one's future but also to the public's as well. The burden of leading the nation would fall on the shoulders of the best-educated individuals.

Americans set out to fulfill the founders' dreams of an educated populace early in their history. In the 1790s, children of impoverished families could attend newly established Sunday schools. By the first several decades of the nineteenth century, these had developed into schools for middle-class children. Advocates of early education, historian Steven Mintz writes, hoped to "promote opportunity, prevent a hardening of class lines, shape children's character, create a unified civic culture, and instill the values and skills necessary in a rapidly changing society: basic literacy, punctuality, obedience, and self-discipline." Educators aimed to teach civic lessons while textbook publishers hoped to teach young readers about sacrificing for the community. Formal schooling even became linked to political culture. Educated citizens protected and perpetuated the republican system by engaging in public affairs and partaking in the processes of representative government.[4]

Although the spread of education benefited all classes of society by creating citizens to participate in the democratic process, the founding fathers appeared most interested in perpetuating the social hierarchy in which the elites remained on top. They saw the future generations of educated elites as the ones to take the national helm and steer young America through her trials. And America was indeed a nation of the young. In the late eighteenth and early nineteenth centuries, youths between the ages of fifteen and twenty-nine made up nearly 30 percent of the population. As the population increased, traditional familial controls and social barriers fell. Colleges and churches stepped into the role of policing and directing the nation's young. To combat the almost universal disciplinary problems instigated by troublemaking youths, college and university administrators came up with a number of solutions, including the establishment of literary societies and a system of meritocracy, which helped channel adolescent vigor into productive, academic paths.[5]

Usually viewed as the bastions of the elite and wealthy in colonial and early republic society, by the turn of the nineteenth century colleges began to spread to more rural areas and accept the sons of laboring-class families. The antebellum period saw remarkable growth in the number of New England colleges and their graduates. Compared to the decade between 1751 and 1760 when New England schools graduated 544 individuals, between 1851 and 1860 five thousand youngsters emerged with their degrees from such institutions. This growth paralleled the expansion of the New England population, which increased from 1.2 to 3.1 million residents between 1800 and 1860.[6] Despite this expansion of higher education, only a small portion of society sought an undergraduate degree.[7] By and large, college students took advantage of the demand for professionals—lawyers, doctors, and ministers—in the growing nation. Another reason for going to college was the decline of farming and the swiftly disappearing parcels of land handed down to sons. College graduates set their sights on other professions to cope with the changing face of the republic.[8]

Although colleges in North America had been established under religious auspices, they trained young men for both theological and secular purposes. Even in the seventeenth century only slightly more than half of the men who graduated from Harvard became ministers. The young nation, which boasted a variety of religious groups, also saw the establishment of large numbers of schools affiliated with these different denominations. Scotch Presbyterians, Dutch Reformed, and Baptists, respectively, established Princeton, Rutgers, and Brown. After the American Revolution, religious revivals spurred Congregationalist New Englanders and Presbyterians from the mid-Atlantic states of New Jersey and Pennsylvania to action. By 1800 they had founded Williams, Bowdoin, and Middlebury. Presbyterians and Reformed churches had collaborated and established Union College in New York. Whatever the denominational background of the colleges, as the nineteenth century progressed, religious orthodoxy declined. Additionally, these colleges all based their curricula on a classical education, requiring that undergraduates demonstrate a knowledge of both Latin and Greek. This stemmed from the founders' beliefs that the children of the new republic know something about the civilizations on which they based the United States.[9]

The changing nature of American society may have offered increased opportunities for the establishment of new colleges, but it also challenged the very idea of higher education. Following on the heels of the Jacksonian revolution, colleges faced a backlash from critics who claimed that their exclusive nature made them incompatible with republican values. To a certain extent, critics had a point. In the South, young sons of wealthy planters and merchants went to colleges, perpetuating the system that had made them social leaders in the first place. According to one scholar, colleges "occupied the position of greatest strategy in the making of Southern leadership."[10]

Of all the colleges in New England (and the United States), Harvard held a preeminent position. By the middle of the nineteenth century, the college had established itself as the school for Boston's upper-class community. Few families outside of this class could afford the annual fee of approximately $400. Around 70 percent of those enrolled at Harvard often had paid $2,000 for their four-year education and more if they had attended preparatory school before that. Some believed the investment worthwhile and considered a Harvard education essential for becoming a member of elite society. As Henry Adams, himself a graduate in the class of 1858, noted, parents began "sending their children to Harvard College for the sake of its social advantages." By the antebellum period, "a Harvard diploma was like a passport, a declaration of a man's residence in Boston's 'upper stratum.'" Harvard boasted resources that dwarfed those of its fellow colleges, including Yale. In general, Harvard students hailed from the wealthier classes that resided in and around Boston. Most practiced Unitarianism and represented the progeny of the merchants who had invested in the finance and manufacturing industries.[11]

Harvard's students also expressed a recognition of their class difference, using their pursuit of a college degree to distinguish themselves from the masses. William Richards, a Harvard student, acknowledged the fact that "universities educate but a few and a favored class at that," but he claimed that "human nature" stood in the way of a larger college population. Richards explained that the want of "natural ability and a disinclination to higher pursuits" would "have a constant tendency to keep the number small," because most youths seemed "satisfied with a common school education" and were more "eager to rush forth into the varied and exciting scenes of active life; to gain notoriety in the world as skillful artisans, enterprising merchants or keen politicians." Without recognizing that financial circumstances prevented less fortunate young men from attending colleges, Richards offered the elitist argument that higher education did not suit the majority of society. It "would be fairer ... to say," he concluded, "not that they educate few, but that there are few for them to educate." He dismissed the idea that colleges bred aristocratic tendencies, explaining that, in monarchies, universities were "especially favorable for aristocracy" but "plant them on republican soil, and their true essence gleams forth in beauty and purity, untarnished by contact with incongruous forces." In open societies, institutions of higher learning were "founded on true democratic principles" that determined "rank not by the criterion of blood but of mind, by the wealth and the nobility of genius." Colleges and universities, he claimed, could not "become more democratic anywhere than in our own free land."[12] Perhaps Richards seriously believed that American colleges did not breed aristocrats, or perhaps he simply remained oblivious to his own elitist rhetoric. He was, however, correct on one other claim.

American colleges in the early nineteenth century did, in fact, move toward becoming more democratic and accessible institutions. "They are the people's colleges," Amherst College's president declared in 1856: "Scarcely anything in America is more distinctively American than the relation between the colleges and the common people." By the middle of the nineteenth century many more Americans could actually afford a college education. Historians who have disregarded antebellum colleges as "retrogressive" and "dated" ignore these institutions' key contribution: they provided poorer, rural students with a pathway into the middle and professional classes. Colleges in this period did not demonstrate their importance by producing major innovations in the field of education. Their existence, however, remained crucial for ambitious young men.[13]

Smaller, rural colleges catered to the needs of Americans who could not afford to go to Harvard or Yale. On the whole, students who attended the smaller colleges came from poorer backgrounds and needed to both work and ask for charity to support their ambitions of graduating and entering the world of the middle-class professional. Additionally, these students represented an older set of Americans. According to one researcher's tally, between 1830 and 1860, men over the age of twenty-five represented approximately one-fourth of all New England college graduates. In the newer, rural colleges, the proportion was higher: one-third. Obligations to families or the need to earn tuition money may explain their late arrival in college. In order to accommodate and attract working-class students, rural colleges designed their calendars around work and harvest seasons. Young men also took winter breaks as an opportunity to teach in local schools, an activity that helped them develop their leadership skills. Cheap tuition and inexpensive lodging fees all catered to the needs of poor, rural young men. These new schools may have represented the last hope for parents who could not provide land to their children but wished to set them up for a successful life in nineteenth-century society. Regardless of the lowered tuition at some schools, colleges remained out of reach for many. Dartmouth student Eri D. Woodbury estimated that "the whole cost of my education has been, reckoning up to the end of this term, $1,086.13." "I have given all these figures," he explained, "because perhaps you may be interested in knowing just what it has cost me to get a collegiate education. If to this my actual expense, we add what my time would have been worth at work, the amount becomes far greater." Although he did not know "how much in dollars & cents such an education is worth . . . I believe that it at least is as well for me as it would have been to have had a legacy of ten thousand dollars without the education." Ambitious young men knew that attaining a college education demanded enormous sacrifice and determination.[14]

Whatever the college or its reputation, all served as finishing schools for the nation's young leaders. One historian notes that young men in the antebellum period "went to college . . . to gain respectability and honor." Classrooms throughout the nation served as "miniature theaters" where young Americans could practice their citizenship skills. Colleges also taught these privileged youngsters to develop leadership abilities for their future roles in society. Classes during the senior year focused specifically on how a young man ought to conduct himself. The required capstone "moral philosophy" course incorporated various issues ranging from political science to history and from legal philosophy to economics. Viewed as "society's moral navigators," moral philosophers, as one scholar explained, sought to "bring all knowledge into a proper moral focus, instilling in the nation's educated class an enlightened respect for basic Christian beliefs and virtues and shaping the character of her future leaders." In order to ensure the stability of society, the moral philosophy courses also instructed young men to police themselves and uphold the highest standards of personal character. In 1842 the president of Brown put it succinctly: "The most important end to be secured in the education of the young is moral character." After he had mastered his own emotions, the moral man could lead society by example.[15]

Antebellum colleges imparted a conservative lesson by teaching their undergraduates that only educated and morally righteous citizens had a duty and right to lead their communities. According to James A. Berlin, schools taught their graduates who entered authoritative positions in the professions of law, politics, and the ministry to speak on "behalf of the *status quo*." College graduates had a duty to defend "truth," which was "fixed and certain in the nature of things" and "accessible only to those who had learned to use the faculties correctly."[16] On the one hand, this philosophy taught the most educated men in society to have confidence in their knowledge and position but, on the other, it smacked of righteousness and elitism for it gave college graduates license to disregard the criticisms of less-educated individuals.

Rather than prepare their students for a specific profession—those who wished to pursue medical, legal, or theological careers often required additional training—antebellum colleges offered a broad education, allowing graduates to converse in many different fields. In 1859 Joshua L. Chamberlain, a product of and professor at Bowdoin College, described his "ideal" curricula. "My idea of a College course," he wrote, "is that it should afford a liberal education—not a special or professional one, not in any way one-sided." Chamberlain's ideal system would not "be a finished education" but rather "a general outline of a symmetrical development, involving such acquaintance with all the departments of knowledge and culture—proportionate to their several values—as shall give some insight into the principles and powers by which thought passes into life—together with such practice and exercise in each of the great fields of study that the student may experience himself a little in all."[17]

In response to critics who argued that a classical curriculum did not serve many practical purposes, colleges linked their curricula to the founding principles of the nation and slowly integrated modern languages and modern history classes as electives over the course of the nineteenth century. In the late 1820s the Connecticut State Legislature asked Yale to stop requiring Greek and Latin language competency for admissions. The institution responded with the Yale Report of 1828. In it, the authors noted that their course of study did not "teach ... any one of the professions," but had been designed, instead, to "lay the foundation" for the "expansion and balance of the mental powers." Yale president Jeremiah Day argued that the "models of ancient literature" could "hardly fail to imbue" the minds of students "with the principles of liberty, to inspire the liveliest patriotism, and to excite [young men] to noble and generous action, and are therefore peculiarly adapted to the American youth." Even a school created to "impart professional and technical skills" such as the United States Military Academy at West Point could not escape the antebellum colleges' broad and character-based educational influences. West Point also exposed cadets to moral philosophy courses and a broad education, putting it in line with other institutions of higher learning nationwide.[18]

Students at antebellum colleges themselves recognized that their broad education merely laid the groundwork for their future and prepared them for the unknown challenges of adult life. Wilder Dwight, a student at Harvard, defined a "well educated man" not as "one who is the most capacious reservoir of facts" but rather one "whose mind is healthy, active, and ready both to acquire and use knowledge." By concentrating too much on developing one aspect of knowledge, he argued, an individual risked becoming "utterly unfit for the duties of life and" would be "no more educated than if he were entirely uncultivated." In his opinion, "a complete education should qualify one for the discharge of all his duties and should strengthen and develop all the faculties to their utmost capacity so as to give vigor, comprehensiveness and liberality of mind." Dartmouth student Edward Savage, meanwhile, maintained that the "distinguishing characteristic of a truly educated man is thought." Anyone could memorize facts and dates but only the scholar could put knowledge in perspective and develop the right course of action.[19]

Many students viewed colleges as a "staging ground" for what they would face in their adult lives. Their college education, therefore, consisted of more than just book learning. Students also learned about decision making, how to apply their knowledge, and social interaction skills. Harvard student Lucius Buckingham admitted that "the more literary influences of a college are, in every respect, of secondary importance." The college campus served as a "miniature" model of the world where young men could evaluate their own nature in relation to others and correct their faults before facing the real world. Fellow Harvard student William Colburn compared college life "to a stage with curtains drawn, and prompter and critic at their posts, upon which we rehearse the part we are afterwards to play." If the college students succeeded in this rehearsal, "we go forward with confidence when the curtain rises and the *probability* is that we shall also succeed in the representation." Colburn cautioned, however, that a man's "future instructors will be even less indulgent to mistakes and imperfect preparation than professors and tutors," while the "temptations to mental and moral dissipation will be different and perhaps greater." In the outside world, the student's "course will not be so definitely mapped out as here; to a certain extent it will be over an unknown sea; fortunate will he be if some unexpected dangers do not arise."[20] Because of the challenges that a graduate faced in the outside world, he needed to pay close attention to his behavior and actions while in school.

Choosing to go to college, especially for men who did not come from wealthy families, required deep reflection, sustained commitment, and sacrifice. Once he began his course at Bowdoin, John Deering, Jr., recognized the commitment required of him. "Whatever others may think of it," he wrote, "*I* think that going to College is quite an era in a young man's life. I begin to feel that it is so now, and I become more and more sensible daily of how great is the responsibility which I have taken upon myself." "You give up a great deal for me, dear mother," Yale student William Wheeler wrote upon learning that his mother had rented out their Brooklyn home and moved to New Haven. He promised that he would "strive to repay you by my heart's affection, and by becoming worthy of such a sacrifice." Luther C. Howell thanked his sister for awaking in him "some longings for a better & a nobler manhood within my soul." Without her he would not have "*dared* to brave the face of poverty & the wagging head of the business world to cultivate my intellect." He professed that he owed her "a debt that I can never pay."[21]

College students, especially those who sacrificed the most to attend their chosen institutions, resolved to do their best to succeed. Upon entering Williams, an ambitious James A. Garfield vowed that he would "stand at least among the first in that class" and admitted that the "bare thought of being far behind makes my flesh crawl on my bones." When students did succeed, they reveled in their accomplishments. Samuel C. Armstrong, writing to his mother, happily reported that his class standing was "39.816–40 is perfection." He bragged that only four others ranked above him and "they are all valedictorians from the finest preparatory schools in Massachusetts," whereas he, the son of missionaries, had come from the Sandwich Islands.[22]

The prohibitive cost of tuition presented the most basic obstacle to college attendance. Students who had to save up funds generally could not enroll until they were older. In some instances, financial aid for these men was tenuous and unpredictable. Committed to their education, however, they went to great lengths to save and borrow money to support their schooling. James C. Rice came from a farming family and had to work as a clerk and teacher before saving and borrowing enough money to attend Yale. Before attending Brown, Sullivan Ballou worked as a clerk in a dry goods store until securing the financial support of relatives to go to preparatory school. When he finally arrived at Brown, Ballou did not wish to be a heavy burden on his benefactors. In order to earn money and cut down expenses, he taught school and gave music lessons. He also lived at home and walked four miles to Brown every day.[23]

While some men worked during breaks to help with tuition, others turned to their parents for financial aid requests, whether large or small. George L. Hayes, writing to his father from Bowdoin, claimed that circumstances had "rendered it so that I am obliged to write earlier than I thought" for more money. Although he "dislike[d]" and "grieve[d]" to "press so hard upon your patience, & good will, & love, & *purse*," he could "do no better." Getting straight to the point, he wrote, "So if it should be convenient & pleasing to you—I must say in a Yankee way, I am in want of 5 dollars."[24] Not everyone's parents, however, could cover their expenses.

Rigorous and demanding entrance examinations also presented a challenge, especially for poorer men who could not afford to attend preparatory school beforehand. Oliver O. Howard and Joshua L. Chamberlain both studied very hard, dedicating months to preparation for the entrance exam at Bowdoin College, which required knowledge of Greek and Latin. At Brown in 1848, entrance examiners asked Sullivan Ballou to "translate English into Latin and Greek, construe and parse any assigned portion of Caesar's *Commentaries*, Virgil, or Cicero's select orations, and prove a knowledge of quadratic equations in algebra." In order to gain entrance to Yale in 1855, Joseph H. Twichell needed to prove a knowledge of "Cicero's *Select Orations*; *The Bucolics, Georgics*, and the first six books of the *Aeneid* of Virgil; Sallust, Andrews and Stoddard's *Latin Grammar*; Jacobs' *Greek Reader*; Xenophon's *Anabasis*, first three books; Professor Sophocles' *Greek Grammar*; Thorman's *Higher Arithmetic*, and Day's *Algebra*, to quadratic equations."[25]

Although outsiders had the impression that college students, living the life of the mind, lounged in comfort by cozy fireplaces, undergraduates faced many challenges throughout their four years. John Deering, Jr., a student at Bowdoin, became homesick, surrounded by people "related to us only by the ties of a common ancestor; no one seems to care particularly for us, and we think of home with more of sadness than of joy." He also discovered his "entirely erroneous" expectations of college life. Deering thought "that college was some mysterious place, shut out from the rest of the world, full of the order of sanctity and learning, within whose venerable walls nothing of commonness and vulgarity ever entered," but found out "that students, yea even Professors—are like every body else, and I can't discern much difference between them and the outside barbarians—otherwise called 'Yaggers'—only the former sometimes wear glasses and look wise." In some cases, their very living conditions caused major problems. "The thermometer stands at 7 below zero this morning," Benjamin W. Crowninshield wrote in his journal. All his thoughts, he scribbled, "were occupied with trying to keep my room warm, warm! no inhabitable rather!" To combat the New England cold, he "stuffed two lamp wicks in the key hole, and succeeded in keeping out a hurricane." Unable to employ the same method with his windows, he ingeniously used the cold air to his benefit and filled the cracks with water, which "immediately froze solid [so] I could make my windows airtight."[26]

If they survived the harshness of the New England winters, college students then had to cope with their rigorous schedules. Donald G. Mitchell, a student at Yale in the early 1840s, remembered waking up at 5:30, sitting for prayers at 6:00 in "the old chapel . . . lighted only by whale-oil lamps, flickering in the frosty atmosphere," and going to breakfast at 7:30. Oliver O. Howard, beginning his four-year tenure at Bowdoin College, described the daily routine to his mother:

> In the morning at 5 o'clock or ½ past we are waked up by the ringing bell, requesting us to arise & make ready for prayers, which have to be attended in about ½ an hour after, at the tolling of the bell, and as soon as prayers are over we attend recitation, which generally lasts about an hour & then we have our breakfast . . . after our morning meal, . . . Prof. Upham hears us in Latin, & Prof. Packard in Greek, Prof. Smyth in the afternoon in Algebra.[27]

College curricula across the nation in this period drew on the same classical tradition, which taught Latin and Greek for the first two years of study. In the junior and senior years, however, schools varied the course work to include philosophy, composition, literary criticism, mathematics (arithmetic and geometry), and sciences such as chemistry, botany, and astronomy. Benjamin W. Crowninshield at Harvard recorded in his journal that his course load included Latin, chemistry, French, Greek, and physics.[28]

Students had their favorite courses. Oliver O. Howard was excited to commence a course on logic because it focused "on the mind, its reasoning *powers* & faculties, which especially ought to interest any one or every one who wishes . . . to investigate intricate truths & principles." He thought it a student's "duty to study so as to understand as fully as possible the mind its powers & abilities, in order to direct it in the . . . right channel for moral & intellectual advancement." In addition, logic skills "assist in reasoning & investigating so as to have clear ideas on any subject, that we may judge for our selves not dependent on the skill or seeming superiority of others." Benjamin W. Crowninshield, however, referred to logic as "that cursed nonsense," preferring other topics of study. He thought a lecture "about the Sanskrit Epic poems and Homer's works" was "very interesting" and found a lecture by famed biologist Louis Agassiz on the topic of Floridian reefs "extremely interesting." Frazer A. Stearns was surprised to discover an affinity for chemistry. He had thought he would become a minister but, he wrote, "knew I wasn't good enough, and I knew, too, if I waited until I was, I should never be one." He prayed that God would set him straight and allow the study of chemistry to be his "duty." Stearns declared that he loved chemistry "with no boyish enthusiasm; but for its own sake,—for *itself.*" Caleb P. Wickersham at Wesleyan wondered whether "a science which affords so many advantages for disciplining the mind, that creates a love of truth and morality, that inspires the soul with a reverence and love for the Deity," deserved "the strongest claim on the attention of every friend of education?" He complained that Wesleyan had limited facilities, libraries, and specimen cabinets and could not support a more serious science program.[29]

The formative years of a young elite did not purely revolve around book learning. Three cultural forces in particular influenced college students' worldviews. First, the spread of religious revivals around the country converted students on many campuses. Second, America's expanding borders and debates about expansion sparked conversations about the nation's role and course. And, finally, politics of the era mobilized and engaged opinionated young men.

Associated with the Second Great Awakening, religious fires burned brightly on antebellum college campuses. Although morning prayers, sermons, and other religious activities dotted the college student's schedule, some young men embraced religious awakenings in even larger areas of their lives. A religious revival swept the Amherst College campus during the winter of 1857 and the spring of 1858. Caught up in the euphoria, Frazer A. Stearns hoped to spread his religious convictions to others. "I have great hopes for Amherst College," Stearns wrote, praying that "God grant we may have a powerful revival!" Many college men, in his opinion, needed recommitment to faith. College was "a hard place, at best, to keep straight in," but in an environment where Christians "get 'fast,' what can you expect the rest will do?" The same wave of religious revivalism also affected Bowdoin College, where Charles H. Howard reported to his brother that "there has been some religious interest in College of late." While attending Yale, James C. Rice wrote, "I know of nothing which has so entirely accorded with my own feelings as the exhortation made at the last communion, that we should each of us make a personal effort to win souls to Christ." He regretted that Christians did not do more to "win souls to Christ, Redeemer," and declared that religious men who had been "raised from the lowest poverty, through the misery of Christ, to become the rich heirs of his grace, would consider no sacrifice too great, no labor too onerous, so that we might win one soul to Christ."[30] This sense of religious certainty actually corresponded with the social philosophy that colleges imparted to their undergraduates. After all, these religious certainties further strengthened young men's righteous beliefs that they knew better than did their fellow citizens. The evangelical zeal of rescuing souls by converting people to Christianity also matched with the belief that they could spread both their religion and their ideals to the rest of the nation and ultimately the world.

The language of religious revivals also fed into the topic of national expansion. Americans embraced the idea of "Manifest Destiny" as they looked westward in the 1840s. The nature of that expansion, however, remained a source of contention. Expansionists argued that a benevolent deity had entrusted the United States with the task of spreading its influence and civilization over the entire North American continent. New England intellectuals, although supportive of expanding American dominion, remained ambivalent about using military force to do so. Their confused responses revealed their indecision on the issue.[31]

Like their parents' generation, the New Brahmins expressed ambivalence about how the United States expanded its borders. Their real concern lay in the consequences of expansion, fearing that any new territory might rupture the peaceful balance between slave and free states. In the name of maintaining sectional peace, New England students preferred that America spread her influence by example. In 1853 Isaac Parker, a student at Dartmouth, rejected the idea of welcoming an independent Canada into the Union, citing sectional concerns. To increase the "political influence of either the North or South by farther additions," Parker argued, "would kindle flames of discord and create a tempest of party strife, such as no lover of the Union could contemplate without the deepest concern." In 1854 Wesleyan student C. B. Ford condemned those who advocated the conquest of Cuba, Mexico, Canada, and South America. Expansion in this manner reminded him of nations "whose downfall can be traced to national pride and love of conquest."[32]

Questions about U.S. foreign policies naturally flowed into political debates of the era. College students paid close attention to national political campaigns; indeed, part of campus life revolved around political rituals, pageants, and activities they themselves organized. During the tense months of 1850 when debates over the admittance of western states made the threat of civil war seem all too possible, students at Dartmouth's student lyceum debated whether "the

Northern states should secede from the Southern" and concluded that the free states ought to leave the Union behind. During the 1852 presidential campaign, Edwin Thomas at Dartmouth told his parents that "there is little thought of or talked about except politics. [Franklin] Pierce and [Winfield] Scott furnish almost the entire subject of conversation." He also reported that the young Whigs and Democrats engaged in debates and pranks. Thomas observed that most of the students supported the Whigs. As a way to ask his parents for "any speeches sent you last winter relating to . . . any . . . part of the Democratic platform," he reported that a Democrat "finds a hard time unless he is posted up and can show the documents to maintain his principles." He resolved to "look into political matters some until election as I do not care to be run over by the Whigs."[33]

Bowdoin College also witnessed frenzied political activities throughout the 1850s. In 1852 the Democratic Party had nominated a Bowdoin graduate, Franklin Pierce from the class of 1824, as their presidential nominee. On campus, the pro-Democratic "Granite Club" championed Pierce's candidacy while the pro-Whig "Scott & Graham Club" supported the Whig nominee, Gen. Winfield Scott. The secretary of the Granite Club, Joseph Emerson Smith, told his father, "Politics never runs higher here than they do this campaign; every student in college thinks it his duty to *rave* about some of the great principles of party," adding that the Whigs "find it rather hard to do so, they having no principles." Smith claimed that Democratic meetings, despite drawing fewer students, were "characterized by much more unanimity, and much better speeches. The Whigs have about 3 to our 2 but two of their men aren't worth one of ours." In the pivotal election of 1860, Samuel Fessenden, a student at Bowdoin and son of U.S. Sen. William Pitt Fessenden, told his father that the "contents of newspapers are devoured with avidity." "Bell and Everett have only one supporter here in college, and he is a Republican in case of your nomination," Fessenden reported. When Republicans nominated Abraham Lincoln, Sam promised that the college Republicans would "try to do something towards the cause" and requested "any good campaign speeches" that his father could spare. "I am a little behindhand as to politics, and want to be posted up," he explained.[34]

As products of their time, the New Brahmins got swept up by the various beliefs and movements prevalent in society. Nearly all of them accepted the idea of American exceptionalism and engaged in the political culture of the period. Yet, despite the fact that these individuals may have taken their cultural cues from others, their class position as well as their college education meant that they could claim to stand above the fray and serve as watchful guardians over the nation's well-being. The popular belief in American exceptionalism merely served to strengthen the New Brahmins' commitment to defending against any threats to the nation's progress. Their political engagement, meanwhile, worked toward increasing the deep political polarization of the period since they increasingly viewed their political opponents with suspicion. As the following chapters will demonstrate, New Brahmins constantly called for men of character to stand up for "right" principles in order to maintain both the Union and American progress.

Amid their hectic schedules, college men did find time for some relaxation as well. Some reveled in the activities of secret societies (fraternities). "I look forward with much pleasure to the time when I shall be gobbling poor Freshmen for the Brothers," Yale student William Wheeler eagerly declared. And, indeed, much of secret society bonding took advantage of junior members. Benjamin W. Crowninshield at Harvard remembered that after initiating Robert Gould Shaw, the members "proceeded into town to Parkers where we took a pleasant supper at the neophyte's expense." Not all campus activities revolved around secret societies, however. Crowninshield also read popular novels such as *Ten Thousand a Year*, *David Copperfield*, *History of Samuel Titmarsh and the Great Hoggarty Diamond*, and *Diary of a Late Physician*. In addition, he practiced his cello, played billiards, skated, attended the ballet, and even participated in an amateur opera arranged by Theodore Lyman. When not taking advantage of Boston's bookstores and cultural offerings, he participated in the competitive sport of rowing. Crowninshield raced in the *Harvard* with teammates that included W. H. F. "Rooney" Lee, the son of Robert E. Lee. Such team activities marked the beginning of institutional competitions and helped rally the school's spirit. Before one important rowing contest, Crowninshield noted that professor of theology John Ware added to his sermon "curious hymns" with rowing imagery. "Everybody," he wrote in his journal, "smiled in chapel."[35] These social events in college life as well as the students' individual friendships helped form a bond that lasted after the young men graduated and entered the working world.

Students came to develop enormous pride in their colleges. In June 1850 Wilder Dwight wrote about a rousing address that President Jared Sparks gave after prayers one morning. The president urged Harvard men to attend a ceremony marking the anniversary of the Battle of Bunker Hill. Sparks "made us an enthusiastic patriotic speech and told us that he hoped to see such numbers as should make him proud of the name of *Harvard*." The president's final comment had come "well near resulting in a desecration of the college chapel . . . by a universal class." "You must know," Dwight explained, "that if there is any one word or appeal to which a Cambridge student is susceptible that word is 'Harvard.'" The very name brought "more enthusiasm than any other word." It was, he explained to his brother, "the watchword in a fight," "the open sesame to the pocket," and "a perfect talisman for all emergencies." Dwight himself had witnessed the raw power of his school's name. He mentioned an event in which police officers and students scuffled. When the officers struck the students, someone yelled the name of the college and soon "the police were vanquished almost before the first sound of the war cry had died away."[36] Students from other colleges also felt pride in their alma maters and love of one's school also helped solidify a respect for men of a similar educational standing. Graduates, therefore, also viewed another man's college education as a marker of that individual's character.

Many students faced tough challenges as they left the fraternity of boys and entered the world of men. Some expressed their anxiety as they prepared to begin behaving as adults. William G. Hammond noted in his diary that he had "assumed a new frock coat" and had taken his "first step toward the habiliments of manhood, though it is one usually assumed long before my present age." He was "very loath to take" on this new role, wanting to "remain a boy as long as possible, for a boy can do and say a thousand things that would be undignified or impolite in a *young man*." Two days later, Amherst College held its commencement exercises. The class of 1847, Hammond noted, "were dismissed from their Alma Mater to the arms of that most ill-tempered step-mother, *the world*."[37] Ready or not, young college men left their safe haven to test their character in nineteenth-century society. The curtain had been drawn. The show had commenced.

The experience of college, while fun and enlightening for some, torturous and boring for others, ultimately served an important function in the lives of young men in antebellum America. Rather than becoming innovators of educational techniques, these schools became clearinghouses for training the nation's young professionals. The schools taught them how to behave, imparted to them classical knowledge, gave them a venue to meet and interact with fellow elites, and opened the doors to new professions that would, under normal circumstances, be denied poor students from rural New England. Trained as leaders for the new generation, these young men also cultivated a sense of nationalism and became particularly concerned with their social bearing. The following chapters will address their national ideology and beliefs about character.

2

"The Great People of the Future"

American Civilization and National Character

"History," Harvard student Wilder Dwight explained, "is . . . but the description of a nation's character." For the United States, "history has hardly commenced, and we have but just taken our place among the nations of the earth." At the time of the essay's conception in November 1851, however, Dwight thought he could "already judge accurately of the present character of our people, and this judgment will furnish us with a key to their future history."[1] The Harvard student looked west to find evidence of American character in action. A new society had sprung up with "few of the salutary and healthy influences at work," such as literature, religion, and "female society." This barren land, however, would "furnish improving lessons to an observing man": industrious laborers toiling to erect a new civilization in the wilderness. He thought California seemed like a microcosm of the polyglot United States. "There never was," Dwight wrote, "a community formed of such various elements." From the "money-loving, industrious Yankee" who "carried there the habits of a New England life," to the "Southern, the Mexican, the Chinese, the Sandwich Islander," these various groups went to a land "without law or order" but "in a few short months" had "provided for themselves a government, formed a constitution, and became a state."[2]

Born in 1833 and educated at Phillips Exeter Academy before joining the Harvard class of 1853, Wilder Dwight fully represented the traits of the New Brahmins. Conscious of the importance of maintaining good character, he became an attorney at the law firm of Caleb Cushing (President Franklin Pierce's attorney general), Ebenezer R. Hoar, and Horace Gray, Jr. By all measures, he was on his way to a successful and profitable career, having taken his place as an elite member of America's professional class.[3] Wilder Dwight's description of the American character reveals much about what the New Brahmins considered the key traits of their fellow citizens and their civilization.

When the Civil War began, the New Brahmins thought the Union worth preserving because of all it represented. In articulating their defense of the Union, they recalled their college days when they internalized lessons about America's place in human history. They espoused a "metaphysical Manifest Destiny" whereby the Americans laid claim to the progress of Western civilization and, as they expanded across space, also broadcast their ideas to faraway lands, inspiring other peoples to seek political liberties and adopt the American example. Having embraced the language of northern honor to become professional gentlemen, the New Brahmins sought to explain their nation's character through the same prism. They believed they could tell a lot about America's character by studying its citizens. Ultimately, they infused Americans with the traits they thought best exemplified their nation: the love of liberty and industriousness, which, the men claimed, had emerged from New England.

By the 1850s, college-educated New Englanders had drawn on the Whig concept of history to establish a national narrative that was forward-looking. The New Brahmins believed that the founding fathers had lit a revolutionary light that would guide all of humanity toward democratic reform. Americans, they believed, had proven their distinctiveness and worth by fighting for political freedom and taming the vast expanses of their continent. This imagining of America's place in human history came amid a revival of New England identity. These young men, therefore, rooted their ideas of American nationalism in New England's unique past. The northern narrative expurgated the South's contributions (and crimes) from a sanitized version of American history. Industriousness, in this rendering, developed in the North and spread to the West and South. Free laborers epitomized northern industry by relying on their own skill and enterprise to succeed. Slaveholders stood against this self-made success since they benefited from the toil of others. This did not mean, however, that the New Brahmins sympathized with the enslaved, whom they viewed as racially inferior. Only when the rest of the nation embraced free labor ideas could the United States achieve its full promise. Free labor, New Brahmins believed, best represented the nation's character and the system that must triumph in the West.

The New Brahmins' vision of American nationalism included both spatial and temporal elements. Rather than simply limiting their arguments to repeating the popular notion of "Manifest Destiny" to justify the America's physical expansion over the entire continent, these writers suggested an even greater sense of American influence as its success inspired democracies all around the world. Their calls for expansion, however, did not resemble the armed conquest of land advocated by more aggressive expansionists. Rather, New Brahmins appear to fit historian Amy S. Greenberg's model of "restrained manhood," which espoused spreading American influence through peaceful and economic means.⁴ Having justified America's "destiny" to civilize the continent, student writers argued that their lofty metaphysical version of Manifest Destiny should be the basis for putting the world in order as well. The New Brahmins articulated this broad nationalist vision as a way to unify American society, not realizing perhaps that their ideas conflicted with the desires of other groups. New Brahmins believed that they articulated not a partisan view but, rather, the "right" one that all "good men" like themselves could agree on. They had an aversion, in fact, to the more radical elements in American society that they viewed as a threat to the nation's peace and prosperity. Because they infused so much meaning into the Union, they later came fiercely to its defense in the nation's time of crisis. In their conception of the United States, the republic represented not merely the culmination of Western civilization but also the salvation of the world. Furthermore, the New Brahmins realized that if the nation failed, their prospects for societal leadership ended, too. Their own fate and the fate of human progress hinged on the preservation of the Union.

Lacking their own history, language, religion, "ethnic homogeneity," and powerful neighbors jockeying for influence, American nation builders of the early and mid-nineteenth century compensated by drawing on their Revolutionary record and unique geographical position to establish an ideology that promoted both political freedom and economic opportunity. Without a strong central government to base themselves around, however, Americans had only the symbolic elements of their past heritage to bind them to their nation. Some scholars have addressed this problem by emphasizing the importance of familial and local relationships as a substitute for loyalty to the federal government.⁵

Furthermore, historians have presented northern-based nationalism as a reaction to the more prominent slave-based southern nationalism, which ultimately culminated in the Confederacy. On a variety of issues, including the nature of labor and the organizing of orderly societies, scholars have emphasized the northern *reaction* to southern *action*.⁶ Why would a society based on the economic exploitation and racial oppression of enslaved laborers command greater attention in the formation of a national identity? Might historians, in a post-emancipation era, be reading history backward in claiming slavery as the aberrant form of labor? Should they not rather view the free labor and slavery visions of the United States as companions rather than adversaries?

New England college students in the 1850s had internalized a New England–centric vision of American history deliberately crafted by the preceding generation. Northern intellectuals, worried about their region's loss of political clout in the 1820s, influenced this version of American nationalism as an effort to establish their dominance in culture. By emphasizing their region's contribution to the American story, New England authors whitewashed both the South and slavery from the narrative. When the New Brahmin generation heard the story of their nation, their parents had already edited the South out of the picture. Thus, when they confronted the topic of southern slavery, they viewed it as an aberration.[7] They saw the New England–centric vision as *the* narrative of American history and viewed the South as an anomaly. During the Jacksonian era, New Englanders also embarked on a mission to revise the history of their region. Beginning around 1820, in response to expanding factories and manufacturing cities, New Englanders projected an image of the "white village" to showcase a regional uniformity and mask local dissent. By uniting their region's heritage with the ideals of the Union, New Englanders presented a vision of nationalism that they thought was the one and only version. These stories also held sway because the earliest writers and historians of American national identity came from the North.[8]

By the 1850s, beliefs about free labor representing the "correct" vision of American history had spread beyond New England. Adopted by William Lloyd Garrison, abolitionists, and members of the short-lived Liberty Party, the idea eventually permeated into the rhetoric of even moderate antislavery politicians. Abraham Lincoln, for example, adopted the idea that the founders sought to limit and ultimately get rid of slavery. Campaigning for Republican candidates, the Illinois lawyer helped spread the concept among the public. No matter how much the idea of free labor representing the original intent of the founders infused American culture, it still rested on a "selective reading" of the historical record. Lincoln, as one of his more recent biographers observes, "in effect erased proslavery Americans from the nation's founding."[9] No wonder, then, that so many New Brahmins supported the Republicans. They shared a similar vision of America's founding.

Although northern nationalism might, in its conception, have been established to distinguish the North from the South, by the time the New Brahmin generation came of age, that northern-based narrative had become the standard one. New Brahmins viewed any southern-based narrative history with slavery at its core as alien and illegitimate. They also saw the South as an anachronistic and mutant variant of the "true" and heroic American story. When they responded to political debates of the time, therefore, they opposed the spread of slavery. That institution simply had no place in their vision for America's future.

Land of Liberty

New Brahmins believed that Americans stood at the midpoint in a historical process of progress. They thought that the founding of the United States marked a new epoch in human events, dividing history itself between an age of oppression and one of freedom. America had led the way. But it was New England, these young men advanced, that had led America along the road to freedom. The older generation of New England's leaders could not have asked for anything more. After the collapse of the Federalist Party, faced with the prospect of dwindling power and clout, the region's political and social elders attempted to counter their loss of influence by emphasizing cultural developments. They played down the Pilgrims' and Puritans' religious zealousness, emphasizing, instead, the themes of freedom and economic success. The New Brahmins who came of age in the 1840s and 1850s grew up learning about their region's greatness. They accepted the narrative as truth and incorporated it into their vision of the United States.[10]

For the New Brahmins who believed in the progress of civilization, humankind's search for freedom had culminated in the founding of the United States. Recently, at least one scholar has considered "how a diverse array of American historical thinkers imagined America as an empire extending through time rather than across space." This is the mold that the New Brahmins followed when considering their national identity. Their ideas crossed temporal barriers, connecting American civilization with a lengthy past and linking it to a vast and unknown future as well.[11]

New Brahmins shared their belief in American exceptionalism with other contemporary intellectuals. No less a figure than George Bancroft, the period's preeminent historian of the United States, believed that historical events all followed God's plan for humankind. According to Bancroft, the Almighty had placed the United States at the vanguard of human progress. One scholar has characterized Bancroft's *History of the United States* as an "epic of the development from colony to nation, demonstrating through that development God's unfolding design for the New World, culminating in 1776 in the revolution to end revolutions." Although not a Whig himself, Bancroft echoed one of the central tenets of the Whig interpretation of human progress.[12]

New Brahmins embraced the belief in constant human progress. Tracing the long history of civilization in his commencement address, Wesleyan University student Daniel Whedon concluded that since "the earliest ages of the world, progress has been the watchword of society." Robert Paine of the Harvard class of 1855 explained that no one could deny a "*fixed law* of *progress*" after eighteen centuries of Christianity. In 1851 Dartmouth student Joshua Hall identified the sixteenth century as "the commencement of modern civilization" because of the rise of royal dynasties. With the emergence of the monarchies of Europe also came the realization that "the mass of mankind were mere retainers upon titled greatness and loiterers for the crumbs of aristocratic favor disdainfully bestowed." From this spark emerged the concept of representative democracy, which he credited Pilgrims and Puritans for spreading to North America.[13]

In the story of their Pilgrim and Puritan ancestors, the New Brahmins discovered a usable history that tapped into deep historical roots and fit well with what they considered the American tradition of liberty. As historian Anders Stephanson has observed, "The Exodus narrative revolved around a powerful theology of chosenness that was to be decisive for the course of colonization as well as for the later American self-concept." This religious imagery drew on "the Jewish notion of chosenness, migration, and redemption, the idea of a mission of spatial separation."[14] New Brahmin authors either overlooked or justified the rigid religious code of conduct that the Puritans practiced, emphasizing instead the desire for religious freedom. Harvard student John D. Long of the class of 1857 lamented the image of Puritans as "men of narrow views and intolerant disposition and with scarce any other active virtue." Instead, he described them as "earnest busy men" who jealously guarded "every encroachment of their rulers" and "men of wisdom and worldly judgment; men who would have been an honor to any age or station." The Puritans, he continued, based their laws on a "high, liberal tone, of legal ability, of practical common sense and of a wise knowledge of legislation to be bound in the same volume with Magna Carta and the Bill of Rights." In 1850 Harvard student Hermann Warner traced American traditions to "our Puritan fathers" who "sowed those seeds of political equality, and watered them with their tears, from which our civil liberty sprang—that liberty which could thrive through oppression and mature through outrage and civil war."[15]

College writers transformed the Puritan settler into the industrious and freedom-loving New England trailblazer who lit the spark of the American Revolution. In 1848 Benjamin S. Savage, a Bowdoin student, elevated New Englanders above all other colonists in the Americas. He described the Dutch as "remarkable for stupidity and slothfulness" and the Spanish as "pompous" and "grave" in their demeanor. The "New Englanders who boast of Anglo Saxon origin," however, were inquisitive, inventive, and filled with "Energy of character." The New Englander was "determined to excel . . . and nothing will prevent him from pursuing the onward road to distinction." When faced with difficulty, he would "place his own shoulder to the wheel, and with his own genius alone . . . will overcome all opposing barriers." New Englanders cherished liberty and abhorred anything "that partakes of the nature of servitude" such as slavery. "Suppose," Savage noted, "a body of New Englanders were placed upon a Southern plantation." Unlike the "African slaves," they would not "remain there and cower beneath the lash."[16] Criticizing slave labor, the student writers also conveniently forgot or failed to include any mention of the founding of Jamestown and the southern colonies in their essays. According to them, Americans' love of liberty had grown up on New England's shores.

Industriousness represented one of the keys to the New Englander's character. College writers commended early settlers for turning barren forests into commercial centers. In 1854 Dartmouth student John Allard applauded New England's development and suggested that "what has been done is most valuable as a foreshadowing of *future* achievements." Allard hailed the "hardy sons" for what they had accomplished and celebrated that the features of the region had spread beyond its hills. Furthermore, he thought New England could see "her own image so often reflected, and reproduced in the West." Settlers from the region had moved westward and taken their admirable traits with them. Thus he argued that New England ought to be considered "the very cornerstone of the Republic."[17]

American industry and love of liberty, nurtured in New England, made the nation distinct from others. Acknowledging that the idea of freedom stemmed from English traditions, New Brahmin writers reasoned that the English had betrayed their own ideals.[18] Wesleyan student Edwin Rushmore observed that "Civil Liberty," from its beginnings in "the British Magna Charta to the present day has . . . been gradually rising in the estimation of the world and in its influence upon the character and destiny of nations." The only system of government justifiably "better than all others" in its ability to "give effect to its laws, and secure their obedience," was one which proceeded "from the people." Americans had, in effect, upheld and expanded on English freedoms when the English themselves faltered. The Revolution defined the United States, as the colonies broke with the past and took the lead in furthering human civilization. Now, in "the vanguard of the restless Caucasian family," Americans could become "the pioneers of progress." Having overthrown a tyrannical king, Americans distinguished themselves from others by their commitment to liberty. Rushmore argued that "only in the lofty & independent mind of the son of Liberty . . .

[could] the true principles of honor and magnanimity . . . take root." The man who "obeys only the beck of a master" could not stand guard over civil liberties. Instead, place a "man in a situation to make use of his reason, and treat him as a rational being," teaching him "that moral evil is to be avoided as the bane of civil society," and, Rushmore promised, "more will be affected than by the cruelty and the inflexibility and vigilance of the most despotic of Tyrants."[19]

Liberty became the watchword for the young nation, and its blessings united a diverse population. In 1855 Silas Hardy, a Dartmouth student, observed that American colonists, people "of opposite habits, tastes and religious faith," had successfully "colonized beside each other." "For awhile," he explained, "the dissonances of nations and creeds prevented entire harmony; but from the circumstances of their settlement, their proximity to each other,—the perils and hardships endured,—the freedom enjoyed,—the influence of intermigration,—their dependence upon the same power and distance from the civilized world, arose a feeling of mutual dependence and common interest." The "unyielding adherence to their common inheritance—*the rights of Englishmen*" united the colonists. They rebelled against King George III's government, Hardy explained, when the power that the colonists "were wont to love . . . turned with iron grasp upon them . . . it roused the fiercest indignation of the Colonies whose hearts were already thrilled by the eloquent denunciations of [James] *Otis*, and the patriotic response of [Patrick] *Henry*." Chastened "by a relentless Parliament on one side, and threatened by hostile French, Spaniards and Indians on the other," the colonists banded together. "'Give me Liberty or Give me Death' was the spirit of all and was echoed by many of the most popular songs of the American Revolution," Dartmouth student Leander Collamore declared. "The spirit of unobtrusive self-sacrifice," Harvard student Francis Balch wrote in 1858, "pervaded the whole country, the women gave up their tea, and left party and gossip to work for those who fought, the boys did the work of their absent fathers and wished that they were men, the men obtained a nobler victory over discomforts and vexations and delay than over the enemy."[20]

Victory in the Revolutionary War gave Americans new building blocks with which to construct their national myths. Highlighting battle narratives, college writers used inspirational tales of sacrifice to build pride, inspire, and mask social conflicts that had lingered well into the nineteenth century. Writing about and visiting historic sites provided another concrete way to erect and shape national myths. In 1857 Dartmouth student David Noyes urged Americans to "cherish in lasting memory the birthday of our nation's independence and *above all* the birthday of *him* who achieved for us our nation's glory—*our immortal Washington.*" Bowdoin student John Marshall Brown argued that historical connections enhanced the rich landscape of North America. The "whole nation," Brown wrote, "makes its pilgrimage to that venerated spot," Mt. Vernon, George Washington's stately mansion. Feeling connected to the father of their country, observers' wails of sorrow went "up to Heaven as they stand before the gated portals of his tomb." Because of its connection with Washington, every "pebble of the graveled walks" and "even the leaves of the trees seem hallowed and are treasured with religious veneration." In the same vein, Bunker Hill appeared "ever beautiful in our patriotic eyes" as did the "green fields of Lexington appear bluer & greener as we think of its terrible baptism in blood."[21] When William E. Potter first arrived in Cambridge to attend law school, he found himself outside the home of Henry W. Longfellow and marveled that George Washington had also resided at the location. "Every spot in Cambridge seems hallowed ground," Potter mused. Many sites awaited the eager patriotic tourist: "The old chapel still standing, in which the Legislature of Mass. met during the stormy period of the Revolution; the old Elm under whose protecting shade the Commander in Chief first took command of his troops; the ancient residence of the same beloved general, made still more attractive as being the present home of a gifted poet; the road down which the 'minute men' of Cambridge hastened on that eventful day when blood was shed on Lexington Green."[22]

The United States Constitution also represented a key legacy of the Revolutionary era and served an equally unifying purpose. In 1854 Charles Connor, a student in the Harvard class of 1854, maintained that the Constitution was "as perfect as human skill, the deference due to conflicting interests could make it." In 1858 Willard Heath from Dartmouth declared it a "hallowed monument of human reason." Edwin C. Hand, a student at Amherst College urged his fellow citizens to "rally around the constitution" when "the dark clouds shall surround our political horizon." By turning to the founding document of the republic, they would "remember that the blessings & liberty which it secures to them were bought & cemented by kindred blood." Once transported back to the "dim shadows of the then past," Americans would "call to mind the bloody battlefields of the revolutions, the hardships & sufferings" and be united again in their zeal to "love[,] cherish & defend the constitution as the world's last best hope."[23]

Americans could rejoice that they had created a model government for the world to follow. This was the republic's ultimate contribution to human civilization. According to Robert Paine, a Harvard student, democracy ensured freedom and represented "the surest cause of progress." Americans had created a "higher & more potent" power, and "this power alone," he predicted, "armed in the cause of liberty & justice" would defeat the forces of despotism. Fellow Harvard student Thomas B. Fox, Jr., explained that in the age of growing awareness of human rights, "a republican form of government is not only desirable, but essential to the best condition of the governed." Another student called America's form of government "a new phase in political history" and "the grand realization of the dream of by-gone ages—the perfect rule of the people."[24]

Coming of age in the mid-nineteenth century, the New Brahmins witnessed firsthand how America's shining light of liberty attracted oppressed citizens from other nations. Harvard student Charles Mitchell of the class of 1851 told his audience to appreciate "the blessings we enjoy in our country," especially when considering "the tyrannies in some of the European governments which have driven to our shores some of their noblest and truest patriots." In 1855 Wesleyan student J. T. Graham declared freedom of thought and action "essential to man's full development[,] civil liberty to his development as a social being," and "religious liberty to his development as a moral, accountable being." All three elements flourished in the United States. One might thus expect Americans to witness the perfection of man. As Harvard student James Chase declared in 1850, "Here on our own soil is growing up the great people of the future."[25] The leaders of those "great people" who protected their future and their freedoms needed education. College men, as social leaders, therefore, made America's perfection possible.

New Brahmins professed confidence that the success of the American republic would lead to a blossoming of democratic governments around the world. The American Revolution, wrote Harvard student David Kimball in 1856, "taught monarchs that there was a limit beyond which even the mightiest despots may not pass, that weakness becomes strength when its cause is just." The Americans had given "the oppressed of the world an example by which they can obtain a release from their sufferings" and had taught man "to think, to speak, to act for himself." "Every struggle of the persecuted against the persecutor," he continued, "every privilege, social, political, or religious that has been wrested from tyrants and from oligarchy, every step forward in human progress was heralded by the American Revolution." Oppress a people, Frederick Dodge, a student at Dartmouth, warned, and "Boston Harbor is black with unexpected tea; the oldest thrones in Europe are toppled down; kings surrender their dearest prerogatives to the people." He concluded with the declaration that *"every government must be Democratic."*[26]

In crafting their history, the new Brahmins reached back to pre–Revolutionary War periods and wrote a story that unified Americans around New England's founding story. They ignored references to slavery, whether in the South or in their own region, viewing the institution as incompatible with American ideals. Picking up from their parents' generation, they articulated a self-serving and regionally biased vision of American history. New England leaders in the 1820s and 1830s had crafted this regional nationalism, and by the 1850s it had taken hold for college men to promote as fact. Indeed, they invited Americans from all regions to join them in this national identity under the broad ideological umbrella of progress, industry, and freedom.

National Character

"National character" is a topic familiar to scholars of the early national period. After all, a new nation had to establish its unique defining characteristics. By the mid-nineteenth century, Americans still wrestled with their national identity. As young intellectuals, the New Brahmins offered their views, which they reached by conflating personal conduct with national ideals. They evaluated a state by the character of its people. As a result, the morality and actions of individual citizens spoke to the virtues and merits of the whole nation. In the same vein, New Brahmins pledged to influence their fellow citizens to behave nobly in an attempt to cultivate the nation's best traits.[27]

Just as character revealed the man, "national character" defined the nation.[28] Harvard student Charles A. Gregory told an Exhibition Day audience, "Whether this republic is to stand or fall—whether it is to remain as a light to the world, or to go down in the blackness of eternal night, depends on one thing—the character of the people." Indeed, when compared with character, "No property—no extent of territory or wealth of resources can compensate for want of virtue." According to Wesleyan student F. D. Hodgson, "Individual & national characteristics present a striking similarity" in that one needed a balance between "the ideal" and "the practical."[29]

Industry and a love of freedom, New Brahmins insisted, lay at the heart of American character. In 1858 Dartmouth graduate Franklin A. Haskell concluded that "the great leading, generic trait of American character and that which most controls action, and tinges most deeply the American civilization, is the love of personal freedom and personal enterprise." Haskell explained that "all the inhabitants of a great section subject to similar laws and institutions, springing from the same race, influenced by similar manners, customs, religion, acquire a certain likeness to each other, a certain uniformity of character, a national character." In their short history, Americans had demonstrated their practicality in thought. The "best American mind," Haskell observed, "has not been given to the dreams of philosophy, in the flowery fields of poetry," but has been focused on "devising good laws, in framing new states, and their constitutions, in inventing cotton-gins, steamboats, and magnetic telegraphs . . . and to this trait the whole commerce and internal industry of the country, are but the fitting monuments." Furthermore, the American "is always active, thinking, planning, scheming something." "Who ever knew of a lazy American?" Haskell asked.[30]

In the same manner that calamitous times helped to develop an individual's characteristics, threats to national peace aided in the formation of a "national character." Harvard student Leonard C. Alden, writing in the Union's anxious summer of 1861, tried to present a positive picture as he spoke to an audience a few days before the First Battle of Bull Run. No nation, Alden said, "attains the summit of moral greatness unless it has received some training in the severe school of adversity." After periods of rampant prosperity, people became "incapable of vigorous effort" but, more important, they lost their sense of duty, "close[d] their ears to the calls of benevolence," and failed to make "sacrifices for their neighbors in distress" or their country. Completely oblivious to others' needs and "wholly absorbed in his own mercenary interests," such a man lost "any noble aspiration." Alden suggested that "some great calamity, such as a distressful but yet a necessary war," might help a "nation whose energies have been enfeebled, and whose virtue has been paralyzed by a long experience of unmixed prosperity." Such a challenge would swiftly revitalize both "its spirit and character." An understanding of the challenges and dangers of the hour would awaken the people and give birth to "a spirit of energy, of generosity, of patriotism." Adversity bred harmony. National calamity allowed "the whole people . . . to think with a single brain, and to act with a single impulse." Thus a once-selfish nation could become "a nation of patriots and heroes."[31] In the same fashion that challenging times allowed a man to rise to the occasion and prove his masculinity, a national crisis tested the whole American population.

But who could call themselves an American? Although American nationality supposedly offered an alternative to the ethnic-based nationalities of European nations by implying that "an American was someone who chose to be an American," the New Brahmins preferred a more conservative interpretation. In theory, Americans rejected "ethnic nationalism," which classified people by their heritage and ethnic background, and embraced a "civic nationalism," which was more concerned with an individual's active participation in a democratic society. New Brahmins rejected the idea that one could simply declare oneself an American. Racially and ethnically conscious college students evaluated a person on both their "ethnic" and their "civic" nationalism.[32] They developed their idea of American characteristics from their beliefs about Anglo-Saxon traits. Other ethnic groups, they thought, held different traits incompatible with American national identity. Unfortunately for these young men who would have preferred a more homogenous society, they could not escape the fact that many other ethnicities shared the continent and nation with them: Native Americans, Mexicans, Asians, and African Americans. Ideas about race permeated the culture as Americans themselves tried to define their national identity.

Secure in their heritage as the true heirs of English—now American—liberty, young men expressed confidence that their race would dominate all others in the competition for land and resources. In fact, *only* Anglo-Saxon rule could bring civilization to uncultivated lands. In 1853 Dartmouth student John H. Morse speculated that even if they had to compete with other races in the West, Americans would ultimately prevail. "We feel confident," he wrote, "that these newly settled regions can receive among their citizens, those crowding to their shores from the half famished Chinese, without submitting to oriental manners, and customs, as the inferior will be compelled to yield to the superior, and take the form of their character from them." Commerce and mining in the Pacific would yield great profit "so long as the Anglo-Saxon enterprise controls it," Morse continued. California and Australia were already "doing much to promote general civilization" and were "destined to exert a still mightier influence." These regions, "integral parts of two powerful nations," had "favorable" situations, and counted among the inhabitants "celestials coming from China, by those bidding adieu to Albion's coast, by the noble sons of New England, trained and educated by Christian parents."[33] College students' confidence in the superiority of American civilization assured them of its triumph over all others in regions on the outskirts the United States.

New Brahmin writers offered immigrants a chance to become part of American culture as long as they professed their love of liberty and cultivated industrious traits. Dartmouth student Burrill Porter explained that in the United States, "this *mixing* of races goes on as never before," and "American character" was formed by "a concrete of many primitive elements." Broken down to their many parts, Americans contained "something of German comprehensiveness; something of Spanish pride; something of Celtic fire; and much of Northern seriousness." Once "these discordant elements now unequally distributed and grotesquely blended" had been "moulded into harmony," Porter predicted that

"American character may blossom in all the luxuriance of native impulse." The American race, therefore, took the best traits of different groups and blended them to create a more perfect people.[34]

Not all races, however, could rise to the level of American civilization. Blacks and Native Americans, New Brahmins believed, would benefit by associating with whites but could not be incorporated into their definition of American nationalism. Burrill Porter thought the "dark races" appeared to "travel under a cloud of divine displeasure which casts down upon them a blighting shadow." "In all the range of Negro life," he claimed, "not a single spontaneous civilization adorns a gloomy past." "Mingle all the Negro varieties, as we might," Porter concluded, "probably no education, no philanthropy, no missionary societies could raise them to a respectable rank among the nations." In an essay in which he praised English and American scientific developments such as the railroad and telegraph, Harvard student Daniel Preston declared that such advancements would also uplift lesser races such as those of African descent. "The steam-whistle which startles the crocodiles of the Zambezi," Preston wrote, "announces to the Negro that the first step in his regeneration is taken; that the day will come—long hence perhaps, but it will come—when even he shall be known as a respected member of the human family."[35]

Echoing another common nineteenth-century belief, college men pointed to the lack of industry among Native Americans as evidence of their inferiority. Henry Prentiss of the Harvard class of 1854 argued that Native Americans' own lifestyles handicapped them because they "subsisted upon the precarious supplies of the chase" and "perpetually engaged in war." The laws of civilization, he argued, demanded that less civilized nations adopt their superiors' habits. Sadly, the Native American had "remained unchanged in nature and disposition by his long acquaintance with the whites." Because they were "unwilling to be taught by" whites they had "acquired . . . only the evils of civilization, with none of its blessings." Given all these negative developments along with a declining population, "their final extermination may be regarded as inevitable." Prentiss reminded his audience that "we need not, on the whole, regret that it must be so." They ought "rather rejoice that the barbarism is to give place to an enlightened people."[36]

Racial and ethnic ideas dominated New Brahmins' thinking about the nature of the nation. In this, they shared similar prejudices to contemporary white Americans who could not envision a multiracial society on their shores. But neither the New Brahmins nor their fellow northerners could ignore the issue of race, especially after the war linked the cause of Union to emancipation.

The Blessed Dominion

Feeling landlocked in old New England, college men looked to the West as the next frontier for expanding their vision of American civilization. They hoped that western settlers would incorporate the traits they identified with New England's superiority and success. The West also symbolized the continuing American experiment. Its cultivation and successful growth under a democratic government would prove to the world yet again the superiority of the American model. New Brahmin writers speculated about the fate of the West and expressed their fears that slavery would spread to that region, thereby corrupting and ruining its potential.

The physical expanse and beauty of the United States gave student writers a canvass on which to paint their vision of the future. Biased in favor of their home region, they believed that New England stood above all others thanks to its natural resources and the industrious habits of its inhabitants. In 1854 John Allard, a Dartmouth student, claimed that the "genius of American liberty has been cradled on the hills of New England." "Where can be found a valley more fruitful, or, beautiful in scenery counting the painter's pencil, than of yonder river, our own Connecticut?" he asked. Allard could also point to the "timbered wealth of the Androscoggin and Penobscot" and "flourishing villages" on the Kennebec. New England was "pierced by many noble streams, affording abundant facilities for free intercourse and national defense." Furthermore, the White Mountains encapsulated "the wonder and glory of New England" with the "giant peaks," which were akin to "Gothic towers with walls and buttresses scaling the heavens."[37]

Behind college students' eloquent tributes to the grandeur of North America's beauty lay an implicit attempt to shape the rest of the continent in the New England model. By promoting industry, a trait these young men considered uniquely New England, they staked a claim for free labor in the West. In 1858 Dartmouth student Alexander Ingram noted that the West was "unsurpassed in richness of soil and variety of production." He speculated that the fields would "become gardens" and "its towns and villages would become cities full of life and business." Once opened up for settlers, "refinement and harmony will flow out from the old States until all are on a level." "Let us now," he enjoined his audience, "cross the desert and the Rocky Mountains and . . . reach that portion of our country, whose great mineral wealth has made its settlement an anomaly in the settlement of countries, comprising all elements, all sorts, and possessing all the resources a world could want." Franklin A. Haskell painted a romanticized view of the founding of the United States. Here, he wrote, "is in fact a new world, but a few years ago unknown to Christian men, now become the seat of a mighty republic, teeming with legislation, commerce, industry, the arena of new institutions, the field of a new civilization." "It is as if," Haskell continued, "the sun had gone down at night upon a boundless wilderness of worthless life, upon a whole hemisphere of savage desolation, and had arisen in the morning to look down in the same place with glad surprise upon a continent thickly dotted with cities and towns, all astir with millions of happy human beings, basking in its light, and the light of civilization." "This planet," he declared, "can never witness the like again."[38]

Some writers thought they could already see signs of a successful civilization forming in the West. Harvard student Charles Gregory, studying the results of the 1850 census, marveled at the fact that in "the period of the last half century, the United States have attained to a population of over twenty-three millions, having more than quadrupled their numbers in fifty years." Although a young nation, the United States had "nearly overtaken of population a kingdom which measures its age by centuries." Gregory could claim America's superiority in other ways as well. In the United States, he pointed out, accommodations for "religious worship far exceed those of England" while "asylums for the destitute, the unfortunate, or the vicious are of such marked excellence as to serve as models for other nations to imitate" and the "system of public schools has attracted the admiring gaze of the civilized world."[39] The character of American laborers had begun to transform the West and shape people in that region. America's destiny to civilize the West had become manifest.

Of all the Western territories, California held the greatest promise and young writers viewed it as a shining example of American success. The discovery of gold, wrote Harvard student Henry Pickering, started "an immigration to which the world's history affords no parallel." "From the yellow sands of the Sacramento" and "the silent shores of the Pacific, sounded a call, which drew forth a response from every nation of the Globe." Old shipyards sprung to action and, "on those waters once parted only occasionally by the keel of an occasional whaler," new vessels "now spread their white canvass, and our giant steamships furrow the once trackless sea with long lines of seething foam." Atop the "still smouldering embers of the Indian campfire, arose the dwellings of civilized man," while "on one of the busiest natural harbors of our coast, the foundation has been laid of a city which is destined to rank among the noblest of the New World." "Thus the waste places of the Earth are reclaimed," he concluded, suggesting that Native American "barbarism" had given way to civilization. Rather than "savages we have social communities, in place of ignorance a widely diffused education," and "law and order assert their rightful supremacy."[40]

The New Brahmins who grew up believing in the triumph of Yankee civilization watched developments in California with excitement. They hoped to witness the same swift growth, which would showcase American industry and ingenuity. "The imagination shirks," Dartmouth student H. R. Tarbell declared in 1852, "from picturing what the long extent of Pacific coast may one day become." There, one could find the "elements of a new order of things" that "only need development, to produce a civilization more striking than has yet been seen." Since the discovery of gold, "we have seen many men severing all the ties that bind them to home" to take "departure for those shores where" riches and treasures rolled "down the Sacramento from the golden heights laden with the rich grains of glittering sand." George Hobbs of the Harvard class of 1850 noted that where once California "was scarcely known save its name," now "cities and towns have sprung up along its shores as if by magic; its few hundreds, like outcasts from society, increased to busy, active thousands & the banners of every nation can be seen floating in the breezes."[41]

The West offered many prospects for ambitious young men who wanted to rise swiftly in the professional world and felt stagnated in their communities on the East Coast. Moving to less developed regions for their careers offered educated men an immediate shot at leadership positions. William D. Sedgwick of the Harvard class of 1851 thought that going to St. Louis might serve to advance his career. "I have been talking about going out West to settle," he explained, "for the reason that I believe from all I can gather that a young man can get on faster, make money rather more rapidly & attain sooner to an advanced standing in his profession there than in Boston." "I have heard," he continued, "that young men are allowed to come forward as fast, in proportion to their capabilities as old ones—Men retire earlier from professional life & age has no *intrinsic* advantage over youth. Energy, industry, & capacity give better title to a high & profitable standing than years." The "hope of attaining in a shorter time than I could in Boston, to the *dignities* of the law," his chosen profession, Sedgwick concluded, "would encourage & stimulate me amazingly, by giving me a natural, instead of a forced interest in my studies and pursuits."[42]

New Brahmins advocated swiftly spreading the mark of civilization—the railroad—to the West, in part to guarantee that the region remained firmly in the Union. Harvard student William Burrage argued in 1856 that a railroad linking California to the rest of the United States would assure the state's loyalty. Once connected to the East by rail, Alexander Ingram from Dartmouth

College declared, California would "be the diamond in the crown of jewels that would represent the United States, which will shed its luster to beautify the whole, while the crown remains entire the diamond's worth will not be its own, but will lend all to enhance the value of the crown, in which it is a single jewel." By constructing the transcontinental railroad, Americans would also have another opportunity to demonstrate their national character. In tunneling through mountains, bridging rivers, and stretching bands of iron across the continent, Americans would showcase their industry, tenacity, and ingenuity. Ingram described how "on the route mountains have to be crossed, rivers and ravines to be bridged, and other obstacles to be met." These challenges were "sufficient perhaps to awe into inactivity the timid," but "real men" would be spurred "to greater exertion." He praised the "energy of a free and earnest people, buoyed up by hope and urged on by ambition," saying that they would "assail the imposing front of hostile nature, and conquer her last stronghold of opposition to American grandeur."[43]

All these visions for the West revolved around a free soil and antislavery interpretation of the course of American progress. Slavery and the southern way of life had no place in young New Englanders' narratives. Slavery relied on the coerced labor of others and had no place in the free soil vision of American character that these young men articulated. Whereas free soil pioneers demonstrated their industry, slaveholders only reminded people of the cruel and coercive system that New Englanders had tried to banish from their version of history. In the summer of 1861, when the conflict between slavery and free labor had erupted into open warfare, Harvard student Stephen G. Emerson condemned slaveholders—whose hands were "free from the contamination of labor"—for believing "that work is dishonorable." There was "little nobility," Emerson commented, in the "opinion that labor is degrading," particularly "in a world where there are so many hard tasks to be done . . . and where man has been placed to earn his bread by the sweat of his brow."[44]

While slavery conflicted with the tenets of industry, free labor, with its emphasis on hardy individualism and enterprise, matched the image of the American character young writers described. According to Bowdoin student Joseph Wingate, a man's work needed adequate compensation and "just reward." In instances where the laborer worked "for others' good, not his own; the wealth which he produces is not for himself" and the worker saw "the fruit of his toil bestowed upon the idle." Wingate demanded that governments support their workers, guarantee them good wages, protect their hard work, and end the degrading practice of slavery. "The time is approaching," he noted, "when the world shall acknowledge the social equality of man; when labor, no longer degraded by slavery, shall be a blessing rather than a curse." Slavery, no matter where it existed, endangered free labor and prevented equality.[45]

The New Brahmins, whose postwar economic philosophies would encourage free trade, early on adopted nascent ideas about the civilizing and peaceful benefits of business and trade. They envisioned the United States as not only a nation of free laborers, producing goods for the world's markets, but also a center for trade and prosperity. Commerce spread as not only a pillar of civilization but also a guardian of peace. Again, this matches the beliefs of restrained men who argued that American influence could best spread through peaceful and commercial means. Harvard student Thomas Emerson of the class of 1856 explained that "a natural antagonism" existed between warfare and "the interests of industry." "The relations of modern Industry are so complicated, the amount of capital invested in industrial pursuits is so vast," he claimed, "that the effect of a war at the present time is felt in every part of the civilized world." Thus commerce and war could "never thrive together." A hypothetical war between the United States and Great Britain would result in the *"suspension* of Industrial operations." The "magnitude of this alone," he offered, was "enough to make us doubt whether even the most belligerent administrations can again involve these two countries in war." War, like barbarism, receded in the face of commerce and civilization.[46] In their idealistic dreams, New Brahmins believed that the United States might also contribute to world peace.

Balancing their political opposition to expansionist wars with their desire to see the spread of American influence, New Brahmins hoped that the power of the republic's ideas and example would inspire other nations to follow suit. This extension of the concept of "manifest destiny," however, went beyond geographical boundaries into the realm of the metaphysical. In the words of Dartmouth student Theodore French, Americans "would not like the followers of Mahomet with the sword compel the nations to be free even as we are free." Rather, the nation's "moral force" could be "found in the example of a great and growing nation: free in religion without infidelity; and free in the state without anarchy." "We," French told his audience, "present to the nations the strange spectacle of a stable government founded on the intelligence and education of the people." Harvard student William Burrage argued that the United States "as the first representative of true republican principles" might "serve as a nucleus around which other republics on this continent will cluster as they may be successively formed."[47]

New Brahmins expressed hope that other British colonies would follow America's lead and break their ties with the empire. Dartmouth student Isaac

Parker argued that the "history and condition of the British Colonies in North America" rendered it "probable that they will, at some time, follow the example of the Old Thirteen and sever the ties that bind them to the mother country." Canada, for the past fifty years, had been "steadily progressing towards independence" and, seeing the example of American "freedom and prosperity," would not allow "English nobles to occupy among them the stations of the highest honor" for long. Canadians, he predicted, would soon "demand independence and a government based on equal rights." Dartmouth student Thomas W. Ritchie expressed high hopes that Canada would boast "an enriching commerce with both . . . looking back to rich memories in the past & forward to bright prospects for the future." "Who can say," Ritchie challenged his audience, "that British America, equally removed from tyranny and anarchy—uncursed by slavery or by a liberty too nearly bordering on license, will not present almost the only example of a free & moderate government?"[48] Harvard's Herbert Sleeper thought that Australia might become "one of the richest colonies of Great Britain" if it was "rightly governed by its Mother country." If the British, however, ruled with an "oppressive and selfish policy . . . it will find that people following the glorious example of America, throwing off the yoke of oppression, and establishing another prosperous, happy republic."[49]

From its ideological headwaters in Enlightenment-era Europe, the American republic stretched to a potentially prosperous future. Many writers expressed optimism about America's future and continued advancement. "What will be the condition of this country in power and territory two or three centuries hence," wrote William Burrage, "is a question which we often ask of our imagination." He envisioned "a mighty republic extending over the whole North American, if not over the whole Western, continent, and holding moral sway over the whole world." America had the potential to be an "almost universal empire."[50] Therefore, when they went to war for the Union, New Brahmins sought to protect a sacred legacy but also what they envisioned as the nation's global destiny.

Threats to the Union

New Brahmins understood that although the Union's future appeared bright, many dangers threatened its continued progress. They identified the greatest threats as coming from within American society itself. Criticizing radical agitators in both sections for threatening sectional peace and national progress, New Brahmins appealed for a tempered approach to national affairs. Although opposing radical abolitionists' actions—since they saw no place for African Americans in their society—the New Brahmins maintained that a free soil approach best represented America's future, viewing slavery's continued existence and spread as the greatest danger to American success.

Advocating moderate courses and conservative policies, the New Brahmins feared that radical and revolutionary principles threatened the nation's future. Indeed, their prescription for national affairs paralleled their own ideas about self-control. If, on an individual level, a man needed to control himself, why shouldn't a nation also act with restraint? Wesleyan student Zebina Dean predicted that America's principles would "live and spread" because, "once enthroned in the hearts of an intelligent people, no power on earth can overthrow them." He only feared that "the bloody trajectory of the French Revolution" might be enacted "anew in the land of the Pilgrims" and that "the tie which unites us" could be snapped "asunder by the violence of faction, and the Constitution should be crushed by the iron tread of Civil War."[51] Internal revolution represented the greatest danger to the republic.

Taught to embrace a conservative worldview, New Brahmins rebuked radical reformers of all sorts, accusing them of attempting swift social changes, which would destabilize a peaceful society. While some young men went along with such programs, most, even those from well-known reform families, had other, more personal concerns. Their parents could engage in reform, but these men had not yet proven themselves and some worried that ongoing agitation would hinder their own prospects for success. Robert Gould Shaw, for example, came from a prominent abolitionist family but declared, "I don't want to become [a] reformer, Apostle, or anything of that kind." One of his biographers maintains that Shaw "was never quite an abolitionist."[52]

Gradual and moderate reform rather than constant agitation for radical change, these men believed, benefited society and their own futures. Of course, personal prejudices also mattered. Wilder Dwight accused reformers of finding inspiration in "an acrid and bitter philanthropy, which, despairing perhaps of improving itself, consecrates its untiring energies to the improvement of everything about it." "It is manifestly absurd," he wrote, making the common nineteenth-century case against women's rights, "that man should ever equal woman in gentleness, refinement, affection or curiosity, or that woman should equal man in strength, wisdom, manliness or sternness." Far from having no power, woman had "gentleness, refinement, and affection," which bound her to man and influenced "him more powerfully than could any other qualities." "Woman," he concluded "is not to improve her condition by changing her sphere, but to employ all the aids which can support her as a wife, sister and mother; for here her influence is unbounded enough to satisfy the highest ambition." Giving women new rights and roles, Dwight implied, would remove them from their proper sphere and cause social confusion.[53]

Slavery, however, represented the greatest threat to social harmony. Charles A. Gregory, a Harvard student, calculated that by the turn of the twentieth century, the United States would boast a population of three hundred million. However, the world might not see "the splendid spectacle of a hundred millions of free people united into a democratic republic." He warned of the existence of "one cause of alarm; one institution . . . which renders us obnoxious to keen reproach and the charge of inconsistency": slavery. The Harvard student hoped that "the moral conflict which has commenced, and the gentle but powerful influence of Christianity will render the institutions . . . obsolete before the opening of the twentieth century."[54]

The problem of slavery weighed heavily on New Brahmins' minds. William E. Potter, a student at Harvard's Law School, referred to slavery as "a blot upon the escutcheon of some of our states." Although he thought the institution's continued existence stained America's reputation as a beacon of freedom, he acknowledged that it existed by "the force of circumstances in the associated states . . . before our union as a Nation." Potter feared that slavery would continue to "distract our nation" until someone devised a solution. "I am opposed to the extension of slavery," he wrote in his diary, "because I do not wish to see another foot of soil, cursed by an institution, which now cripples the national progress of so many states." However, "because I revere the Constitution," he explained, "I would protect it, by every available means, where by the Providence of God it at present exists." Although he accepted slavery where it existed, he hoped "that we can constitutionally prevent its extension." Understanding that any political solution would take time and lead to increased sectional tensions, he also prayed, "God grant that this great mystery of Slavery, with all its dangers shadowy & real, with all its wrongs to the humanity of our present age, and all the burdens, which it will bring upon a future posterity, may be, in his good Providence safely removed, without interference from the North." Only "when no slave shall breathe the air of our free land," Potter concluded, "then shall we truly live a happy, free and united people."[55]

Slavery's spread, assuring continuation, however, worried some students who saw the institution's growing strength as incompatible with their free soil vision of American nationalism. In an 1856 address, Theodore Winthrop argued that the young nation's "composite people" might yet "attain to the most varied splendor of success in all pursuits that can make its future rich, refined, noble, and happy." "But," he warned, "let us not forget that our march must be sustained by a hearty devotion to the true principles of freedom." Failing in either "public or private duty" by cleaving "to any national wrong" would result in the failure of "this great experiment of mankind." To rid the nation of slavery, lawmakers needed to prevent it from spreading into the West.[56]

As conservatives, college-educated men urged gradual changes in society, even to the system of slavery. They feared that radical reformers threatened social harmony and sectional peace. In 1851 George Clary, a student from Dartmouth, described reformers as "impulsive in their nature" and "impatient of the slow moving wheels of society." Such individuals were "strangers to that cautious, conservative spirit which renders men loath to relinquish the old & well trodden paths" and instead ventured "upon the doubtful fields of experiment." Clary pointed to the "whole armies of independent reformers" that had come into existence in the past few centuries, "with religious toleration, right of suffrage, trial by Jury, Emancipation, chartism, socialism, congress of nations emblazoned on their shields." Although nineteenth-century citizens were "in large measure indebted" to some reformers "for whatever we are now accustomed to value as most contributing to our happiness & prosperity," Clary warned that "the zeal of these reformers" sometimes led "to effect no result but revolution & counter revolution threatening to leave society at last dissolved into its natural & barbaric elements." A year later, fellow Dartmouth student Osgood Johnson condemned "reformers of the present day." "Time," he declared, "is requisite to alter the whole tone of Society." Therefore, the "roaring of fanatics & crazy women has not relieved the condition of the slave." Revolutions could not "advance farther than the intelligence of the people," and the reformers appealed to "the worst passions of the multitude—not their sober & better feelings."[57] Abolitionists' demands for an immediate end to slavery directly challenged what college students had learned about self-control and moderation. Viewing abolitionists as uneducated and unqualified judges of society's best interests, they looked to educated men for moderate guidance on the reforms that the nation needed. They believed, after all, that one needed education as a prerequisite to making sound judgments.

Some student writers specifically condemned race reformers and warned against elevating blacks to an equal footing with whites. Here again, college men argued that race reformers simply did not understand the necessary steps for a race's elevation. Viewing blacks as lacking any cultivation, they claimed that only years or decades of training would even bring blacks up to the level of whites. Such beliefs foreshadowed New Brahmins' postwar opposition to granting freed people too many rights even though they had witnessed African Americans' brave performance during the war. These young men's racial prejudice, however, could not be easily overcome. According to Osgood Johnson, nature did not "work mighty changes in a day" nor did the child reach "full development in an hour." The cultivation of a person's inner capabilities required time. "If today every slave at [the] South," he wrote, "were set free, there would be undeniably no more real liberty than before." Though the "external form of Society would be changed," the "mass of slaves would be the same in internal character as now" because it would "take years to effect those changes necessary to advance them [the enslaved] in liberty." Johnson accused philanthropists and reformers of trying "to accomplish at once what cannot be done in a generation."[58]

William E. Potter had an equally low opinion of race and gender reformers. Potter regretted that firebrand abolitionist Wendell Phillips's "splendid talents are used only to revile his country, to overturn and trample under foot the religion of the gospel, and to destroy the present well ordered relation of woman to man." Potter pronounced Phillips a "dangerous man, dangerous because brilliant, captivating and bold." The abolitionist had used his immense talent to inflame the public rather than advocate for moderate reform. Potter pronounced the radical abolitionist William Lloyd Garrison a dangerous agitator as well. Attending a women's rights convention at which Garrison spoke, Potter heard the abolitionist declare, "I hate this accursed Union." The crowd "hardly hissed," surprising Potter. The convention itself drew up a resolution, which "denounced the Constitution as a compact with the devil, and an agent with hell." "Gracious Heaven," Potter wrote, expressing his disbelief, "can it be that men born in America, and fostered under the influence of our own institutions, can hold such sentiments as these?" He feared that if abolitionists achieved their demands, "the horrors of the French Revolution would be re-enacted on our own firesides, and around our own family altars." Where, Potter wondered, "does this sentiment have its rise? Is it the full development of a New England education, has it been imbibed from the writings of French philosophers, or is it like the origin of Evil, involved in an obscurity which cannot be fathomed?" Potter feared "that around our modern Athens, there are advocates of . . . a religion of hate, of a government which would be worse than anarchy itself, and of a society, which would be destitute of everything which renders society dear."[59]

In part, New Brahmins' fears about social agitators reveals their deep distrust of the American public. Convinced that only the most educated men such as themselves had the best interests of the community at heart, they questioned the motives of men who threatened the peace and inflamed sectional passions. The people, meanwhile, appeared in these elites' eyes as fickle and easily swayed individuals who fell victim to the influences of negative forces in society. This distrust of the people and concern with social order revealed much about New Brahmins' mind-set. They laid claim to the idea that they, and only men like themselves, had society's best interests at heart. While they spoke of spreading democracy, they harbored classist views about who should govern society, advocating the leadership of the elite over all others. They distrusted the uneducated and questioned their ability to recognize right from wrong.

Secession, however, as an overt act, always remained the greatest threat to the Union. The theme of disunion dominated Dartmouth student David Quigg's 1855 commencement address. He began by thanking the founders for handing down to their children "this precious inheritance—a free country." It was, therefore, "equally illustrious and praiseworthy to maintain & guard" the Union "as it was bequeathed to us, but most base & shameful if we prove incapable to discharge the duties necessary to fulfill this trust." Speaking to his audience of contemporary issues—perhaps the violence in the Kansas territory—Quigg noted that "in these times of our country, there must inevitably spring up in every American soul a thousand emotions—mingled of joy, hope & fear." "Anarchy & civil war, that destroyed the ancient republics & which is the destruction of all nations without God & conscience," he said, might yet reach American shores. "Indeed," he continued, "there has been going for the past few years in this land so boastful of peace & happiness, a civil warfare, more odious & more deprecated than any other history has yet recorded." This state of affairs threatened "to destroy, the fairest structure of government, that human prudence & human foresight ever reared." "The consequences of disunion," he concluded, "we will not attempt to describe" for "no human pen could enumerate them."[60]

By 1860 all the talk of a unifying nationalism expanding through space and time had actually become part of the problem. Threatened slaveholders and southerners did not believe that they had a vested interest in the Union as conceived by northern writers and thinkers. Even as New Brahmins promoted their own national identity, they advocated a vision of the Union that insulted southerners. Despite the fact that the New England version of American history avoided comparing the North to the South and drew on historical traditions reaching back into antiquity, southerners reacted with disdain to the claim that America's origins lay with the Puritans. Slaveholders did not appreciate the implication that their region's system of labor conflicted with human progress. The Civil War, therefore, although a conflict over the future of the nation, also resulted from conflicting historical narratives.

New England college students used their essays and addresses to build a unifying nationalism during the antebellum period. As products of a regional upbringing and adherents to the ideology of free labor and free soil, they proposed new origin stories that attempted to avoid controversial subjects and appeal to all regions. College writers emphasized liberty and industry as the national themes. Even these seemingly uncontroversial traits, however, carried an implicit criticism of slavery since they aligned with free soil and antislavery ideas. The Union for which New Brahmins risked their lives, therefore, represented liberty and industry but, more important, linked the American experiment to the spread of Western civilization and democratic ideals around the world.

Given the blessings that providence had bestowed on the United States, Harvard student Samuel C. Davis argued that it "should be the jealous care of all of us to see that they are not destroyed." He hoped that, despite their differences, Americans could, "when the national welfare is at stake, come up together and heartily cooperate for one object." Written and delivered in the middle of the Civil War, Davis's oration reminded his audience of the great potential of the United States and urged them to fight for the survival of that ideal vision of a nation in space and time.[61]

But what systems of beliefs might have compelled elite and professional men to risk life and limb for the nation, no matter how grand? Colleges taught not merely a nationalist narrative of American history but also emphasized the responsibilities of the nation's best-educated men. The New Brahmins knew this as the code of character.

3

To Act Like Men

Building Character in the New Brahmins

Even as a young man, Oliver O. Howard took matters very seriously. He valued education and hoped that the college classroom would fill his mind with the wisdom of the ages. One year before graduating from Bowdoin College, he wrote, "I wish to learn all I can. The *college course* will be but a beginning. If I had money nothing would hinder me from studying three or four years after I leave this place, before I commence a profession or the study of it." But the ambitious young man also saw his college years as a time to establish self-discipline. "I think I have accomplished a reformation in myself," he proudly wrote to his mother in 1848, explaining, "I have not only left off using tobacco, but over come the desire for it." He credited both his own resolve and college influence for this success. "I happened to be thinking one day that smoking was doing me no good," he later elaborated, "and also thought that I would put my self-denial to the test." Although he did have an urge to smoke particularly when he had free time, whenever he felt "any inclination 'there to' I immediately resort to reading or studying. It is very easy to keep from forming a bad habit but exceedingly difficult breaking it up."[1]

The internal qualities that Howard highlighted would be harder to achieve were he associated with individuals who possessed negative traits. Their bad behavior might influence his own. Early in his college career, Howard complained of "a certain class here" who "greet with a blander smile and meet, with perhaps a more flattering welcome, those who dress costly and eat the most luxuriously." He did not care for these individuals, reasoning, "What is the value of friendship founded on the external appearance, the mere outward show?" He preferred "love or friendship founded on real internal worth." The man "who by intellectual exertions has made himself celebrated, whether it be in oratory, or with the pen" most impressed him.[2]

Like a good older sibling, Oliver O. Howard imparted much of what he had learned to his younger brother Rowland, warning him not to become too close to "the pleasantest" and most welcoming men. The quiet men who seemed formal and cold, he suggested, might have the potential to "make a[n] everlasting & beneficial friend." Later, he cautioned Rowland "that in acquiring an education that which costs the greatest labor is of the greatest value." If only his brother would "labor against nature and study language and abstract science for one year steadily," Oliver wrote, "I would not fear with respect to your firmness or energy." "Strive to be a man," he urged. In that process of becoming a man, Rowland would not only acquire knowledge but also establish a foundation for good character.[3]

Oliver O. Howard pointed to his desire for knowledge, self-discipline, and ability to shun the company of shallow men as signs of his own gentlemanly character. These traits of which Howard, the good student, proudly boasted were also the characteristics that colleges hoped to impart to all their undergraduates. The educated northern gentleman would serve as a disciplined moral compass for a superficial American society.

Character encompassed many different traits and behaviors. A broad summary of its tenets allows for the following definition: an *idealized internal standard of behavior consisting most importantly of educated, independent thought, and selfless action*. Despite its focus on consistency with an internal code of conduct, others could still evaluate a man's character. But a man's character remained unblemished as long as he behaved consistently with what he believed was right and his course was grounded in knowledge and selfless sacrifice. For the New Brahmins, the path to attaining character included learning to control one's passions, ridding oneself of negative traits, bolstering one's broad knowledge of the world, gaining confidence in one's individualism, and accepting a gentleman's self-sacrificing role in society.

Peering into antebellum college classrooms allows modern scholars to examine how the New Brahmins conceived of character and its associated traits. Although the northern education system as well as a plethora of nineteenth-century self-improvement manuals taught schoolchildren the benefits of character, the individuals that most needed to demonstrate these traits resided in the middle and upper classes.[4] A classist belief, based on the attainment of higher education barred less-fortunate members from claiming the refined form of character, available only to those who viewed their actions through the prism of their superior education and knowledge.

The New Brahmins coming of age in their college years fused the good character traits they were attempting to cultivate with their developing masculine identities. Emerging into adulthood in the middle of the nineteenth century, they pondered what kind of men they wanted to become. The concept of manhood encompassed a wide variety of traits including courage, chivalry, selflessness, integrity, and virtue—along with more militaristic traits. For the most part these men's future roles in domestic life and a business-oriented world shaped their masculine ideals. Rather than the rugged male laborer and fighter so often associated with the term, however, these men's masculinity "derived from being upright, reliable, and brave." Victorian-era Americans viewed ideas about proper masculine (and feminine) habits as a way to control growing social problems of swiftly industrializing nations. The educated classes had to embrace, practice, and transmit ideal gender roles to others.[5]

In order to establish themselves as northern gentlemen of honor, the New Brahmins first had to establish their own individuality. This key trait of having good character seemed more important than ever, given the changing nature of antebellum northern society. Fiercely determined to maintain their independent judgment despite the powerful popular social currents, men of character prided themselves on the idea that they could not be easily swayed and that they—because of their education and ability not only to self-reflect but also to control their behavior—had the true moral compass to see the way clear in a confusing and deceptive world.

College courses reinforced the necessity of developing and maintaining good character worthy of the students' gentleman status. They taught their students to calibrate their inner qualities, which they could call upon in real-world situations. As historian Joseph Kett has noted, the inner quality of character served as "an internal gyroscope" that was "self-regulating."[6] In many ways, colleges served as finishing schools where young men, about to enter into professional lives, could interact with like-minded individuals on the ascendant in antebellum society. These networks served the young men well, but the colleges also certified the quality of their graduates to potential employers. Nineteenth-century colleges, in short, guaranteed the "character and trustworthiness and, hence, credit-worthiness and employability" of their graduates.[7]

Northern honor distinguished itself from its southern variant in several important ways. The most important difference lay in the form of audience. Historian Bertram Wyatt-Brown concluded that, at its most basic, honor was "the evaluation of the public" or "reputation."[8] Kenneth S. Greenberg, meanwhile, has observed that "southern men of honor were 'superficial'" and concerned with "the surface of things—with the world of appearances."[9] More recently, Lorri Glover has attempted to shift focus from the lens of honor to manhood. "To be a man" in southern society, she writes, "was to be male, white, and elite *and* to embody the proper gender attributes. A male lacking any of these qualities was not fully a man in the eyes of the region's ruling class." "Becoming recognized as men," she continues, "required gentry boys to put away their personal predispositions and put on the comportment and character of an ideal gentleman—to become what their society deemed manly." Note that even in this definition, a southern man's worth still required the consent of the public.[10] Northern men of character, however, supposedly did not cater to public opinion as long as they believed themselves in the right. Other scholars of the South have identified a term known as *mastery*, which is more akin to northern character. In contrast to honor, mastery was "less scripted and more of consequence to a man's self-identity." Referring to "patriarchy" and "paternalism," these scholars have pointed out that, in contrast to honor, mastery "depended more on personal conduct than public acknowledgment."[11] But any discussion of southern mastery must take into account the racial hierarchy of the slave labor system, something that the free states did not need to address. Northern honor, therefore, rooted itself much more heavily in an individual's subconscious.

Although southern and northern honor developed different and distinct emphases, individuals from both sections could sometimes recognize the traits of honor in each other. In the antebellum period, for example, scholars have noticed that even proslavery men could praise the courage of the radical abolitionist John Brown though they disagreed with his position and actions. According to one of Brown's modern biographers, "Brown was not *right*. He had certain admirable *qualities*: toughness, honor, daring, and humaneness. He was, in short, what the South had long said a gentleman should be." If only, one proslavery northerner lamented, he had fought "in a good cause." While they disagreed with his position, southerners respected John Brown's commitment to his beliefs. Kenneth S. Greenberg also observed that several important southern men, seeped in the culture of honor, "admired the abolitionist" because Brown had "faced death without fear." "At a deep level," Greenberg postulated, "they may have sensed that their hated enemy was also their comrade."[12] As the writings of college-educated New Englanders demonstrate, the New Brahmins also recognized key traits of character in their southern counterparts.

Nineteenth-century Americans encountered multiple publications discussing the topic of character. Among the many works concerning character, college-going northerners likely would have been most familiar with those of Ralph Waldo Emerson. The New England author and poet described character as "a reserved force, which acts directly by presence and without means. It is conceived of as a certain undemonstrable force, a Familiar or Genius, by whose impulses the man is guided but whose counsels he cannot impart." Even though an individual's fortunes might rise or fall, his character could remain "of a stellar and undiminishable greatness." The man of character was both trustworthy and confident in his abilities, possessed strong self-confidence and unshakeable principles, and could not be intimidated. Emerson considered men of character "the conscience of the society to which they belong," believing that they stood "united with the Just and the True, as the magnet arranges itself with the pole." Contemporaries who discussed character often employed the imagery and symbolism of the compass to illustrate how men of character could resist shifting circumstances and stand by their principles.[13] Another contemporary work, John Foster's *Essay on Decision of Character*, also emphasized the importance of decisive and confident action. A human being without this ability, Foster argued, was "a pitiable atom, the sport of . . . casual impulses." A man needed "complete confidence in his own judgment" and courage to execute the right course of action. Attacks of "contempt and ridicule" could not sway men of character.[14] Contemporary writers who wrote extensively on the topic, therefore, considered knowledge, self-discipline, and the courage of convictions as the essential components of character.

In discussing character, college students echoed many contemporary themes. Dartmouth student Ozias Pitkin defined "character" as "the result of all the artificial & accidental circumstances of life." Character "comprehends all the habits, tendencies, principles, everything connected with our present state of existence & our powers for attaining to a better state in the future." Wesleyan University student Robert Pitman told a commencement crowd that character was "above success." All knew, he said, "that it is of more consequence what a man *is* than what he *has*."[15]

Being oneself and having a strong sense of individualism constituted the most important aspect of character. A man of honor needed to display firmness and self-confidence. How could anyone rely on a man whose positions changed with each situation? How could society trust leaders whose morals were not fixed and who could be swayed by the emotions of the mob? Unswerving confidence in one's capacity to lead depended on a man of character knowing and trusting himself.

Be Yourself

New Brahmins thought of themselves as men of character, and a man of character possessed confidence in the moral righteousness of his own opinions.

Independent thought and judgment marked his actions. "We propose," Charles Russell Lowell said in an Exhibition Day oration, "to divide the world into the men who are themselves and the men who are not themselves." He warned that those who courted applause and had "a love of distinction" demonstrated a lack of individualism. According to Dartmouth student Charles Cutler, a person's position was "built upon a foundation of solid granite" if rooted in moral principles. This confidence in one's positions affirmed that one acted "in unison with all that is pure and noble."[16] The process of developing one's self-confidence, however, could prove challenging in a world filled with lures and temptations.

Threats to a man's self-confidence lay in the most innocuous places. Dartmouth student Levi Little observed that "very few men of the right sort" existed, pointing to the "prevalent idolatry of Fashion, that most *fickle* goddess" to prove his claim. "What one *is*," he wrote, "matters less than what he *wears*." Little complained that the "cut of a coat, the style of a hat, or pin or a ribbon, seem more essential to manhood than a sound judgment or an honest heart." "The world," he declared, "wants men of character: men whose minds are their own—who think for themselves & call no man master." In contrast to these men of character, "common men receive their opinions at second hand; derive their theology & politics from the commentary & newspaper under whose (too often baleful) influence they happen to have been born." Little called for "sensible, upright men of individual character" who would "stand when others fall or cringe; men who will honestly seek, and earnestly defend the truth, though all else prove traitors: men who love the truth better than themselves, and for the *truth* will fight with mind and muscle."[17] In order to maintain one's individuality, a man of character needed to view with skepticism anything that the general public openly endorsed. Wesleyan student Edwin Griswold thought public opinion "oppressive and perhaps still more degrading" than physical servitude. As a result, few men "possessed the courage to proclaim a very disagreeable truth in the face of an opposing and disbelieving antagonist." "We seek in vain," Griswold lamented, "to find men whose minds are not governed by [public opinion's] stern commands."[18] Young men concerned with the survival of republicanism feared that their fellow citizens lacked individuality, one of the keys to virtuous behavior.

The existence of college secret societies struck some undergraduates as inconsistent with the dictates of character. Although some young men believed that fraternities brought them close to "some of the best scholars and finest fellows in the class," they could hardly deny their exclusive nature. Some students, concerned with reconciling the dictates of character and individualism with unquestioned loyalty to a secret brotherhood, rejected such organizations. Oliver O. Howard, courted by several societies at Bowdoin, declared that he would "not annex myself to any society until I know the principles and motives of that society, and until I am more thoroughly acquainted with its members."[19] Samuel C. Armstrong did not belong to any of Williams's secret societies. When one became a member, he observed, "all in it are his sworn friends, right or wrong—this is childish."[20]

As they revealed in their postcollege careers, the New Brahmins pledged their loyalty to principles rather than to parties. They chose the "best" individuals rather than a particular individual's affiliation. Thinking about the nature of secret societies in college perhaps taught them that lesson. Williams student G. C. Smith contended that secrecy in any organization implied "a certain surrender of a man's judgment" because it limited "the appropriate exercise of his free will" and was "opposed to a proper spirit of self-reliance." "The renunciation of one's own judgment," Smith wrote, "which is implied by a willingness to give, while the aims of the Society are yet unknown, a pledge to reveal nothing is a humiliation no man should submit to." "A Secret Society man," he argued, "will almost invariably vote for a member of his Fraternity rather than for an independent candidate, although the latter may be incomparably superior."[21]

Establishing one's independence represented only the first step in a lifelong struggle to maintain that perspective. The independent-minded man of character, observed Harvard student Henry Spaulding, needed to constantly swim against the tide of "social inertia," "compliance and routine," and "thinking by rule and feeling by pattern." The "natural love of ease, our longing for position, our admiration of the glitter of popular praise," Spaulding cautioned, "all lead us to forsake our early visions, to yield our individuality, to become mere imitators, or, at best, only clever manufacturers."[22] J. S. Griffing, a student at Wesleyan University, warned against the "molding process," which could "mold, curb and fetter the expanding energies of our internal being into whatever form, custom, law or public judgment may prescribe as correct that would ennoble the mind into the opinions of the crowd." These traits, once implanted, "would cause a man to sacrifice his individuality [to] serve his country by acts which in the light of his consciousness are not only self-debasing but justly heart provoking." The "molding process," in short, threatened to take away man's "inborn freedom or individuality."[23]

Admitting that their actions would not always succeed nor their principles always prevail, college writers underscored that committed effort trumped outcomes. As long as a man had committed himself to acting in line with his conscience, success or failure was irrelevant. Harvard student Addison Brown defined the traditional "great man" as "one who in consequence of great achievements attaches to himself a numerous and powerful party, is sustained by them to the last, and by degrees rises to the highest honors which it is in their power to bestow." However, this was a "deceptive" standard when applied "as a test of the merits of the great men of history, or as a measure of the value of their services to humanity." Brown reasoned that some of the "most illustrious men whose names have come down to us," such as Demosthenes, Socrates, Bacon, and Hannibal, had "utterly failed in the chief object of their ambition." For example he pointed to men who "lacked that popular support which is the basis of the common notion of success." Why, Brown asked, "should we honor him less that fall . . . in the assault, than him who first rears the victorious banner upon the walls?" Those who failed to attain their loftiest goals, if they had fought fiercely for their beliefs, Brown argued, ought to rank with men viewed as traditional heroes.[24]

From their college attempts to explain character and all its dimensions, New Brahmins acknowledged that success or failure in a cause was inconsequential as long as one's belief in the righteousness of one's actions remained resolute. The risk of failure did not sway the man of character.

You Must Learn Control

A young man determined to form a good character needed to begin cultivating positive traits from an early age. At this stage, a young person's character was "malleable" and could be influenced in either a positive or a negative direction.[25] "Early studies," Ozias Pitkin said, "give direction to the future pursuits." It was in the "period of youth" that the "individual generally acquires that particular bias & those distinguishing features which characterize him in after life as a man of observation or reflection, a sage or a poet, as an enthusiast or an imposter," for it was at a young age that "the powers are unfolding." "Men of genius," Pitkin continued, "often refer to their early reading as giving tone & character to their subsequent lives." College men also dispensed advice about good character traits to their siblings. Bowdoin College student Arthur McArthur, Jr., advised his brother, who had just started his boarding school education, to "apply your self strictly to your studies so as to recite the best lessons for you don't know what influence you may have by being the best in your class." Urging his brother to strive for success and to practice writing, McArthur continued, "If you . . . become the best scholar your classmates will adore you and respect you. . . . And moreover maintain your dignity yet be kind to every one; do not appear timid but brave & noble. Be not too familiar with any one." Finally, he added, "Let your character be spotless."[26]

Burdened at a young age to think about their future course, some young men expressed their determination to succeed in their college lives and future careers. Writing in his journal, Harvard law student William E. Potter concluded, "One great secret of success in study, or in active life, is to have a fixed and absolute resolve to succeed at all events." "I am resolved," he continued, "that either success for me lies in the future, or my fortieth year, should I live so long, will see but the image of a man worn down before his time, with active duty and with application." Potter intended to overcome adversity at all costs: "If love for the law, if persistent application and attention to business, and a firm resolve will enable me to succeed, with the help of Heaven, my future is safe. Wherever I may be, I will not long be content with a subordinate condition. I will struggle for the mastery with every energy." On his twentieth birthday, Potter wrote of his eagerness to embark on a new period of life, which "seems to me the most interesting, and . . . probably the most important as regards its influence upon my destiny" because "Habits are forming, Resolves being made, the mental and physical qualities of the future man, are being molded, strengthened, and prepared for future success or future ruin. From the age of twenty to that of twenty five, is probably the turning point in the life of a young man." "I am resolved," he vowed, "with the help of Heaven, to succeed. To succeed in my profession, and as a citizen, and a man."[27]

Going to college gave students an opportunity to shed their bad habits and adopt a disciplined lifestyle. Some young men took this matter very seriously. Joshua L. Chamberlain wrote that in his first days at Bowdoin College it was "necessary for me to take a decided stand at the very commencement and resist the first temptation" to break college rules. His college mates soon accepted that "if there is to be a class cut a training or spree" they all knew, "O! No! Chamberlain won't go into it." This self-conditioning had not come without "many trials," but such challenges "brighten the Christian's hope, and temptations resisted strengthen his faith."[28] Another Bowdoin student, meanwhile, observed in his journal that he had been too distracted by gloomy winter weather to work. "I am influenced too much by outward circumstances," John Deering, Jr., admitted to himself. Having observed his personal failings, he resolved to "spend more time in study and less in idling and scribbling."[29] Aware that college life meant conditioning their behavior as much as learning, young students tried desperately in these years to attain self-discipline. Many young men maintained their desire to become upstanding gentlemen by resolving to stay out of trouble. "You may be assured," a very serious Oliver O. Howard told his mother, that "the bad habits & practices of college are disgusting & disagreeable to me." William Wheeler, after telling his mother about an incident in which several students attempted to cement the college bell, assured her that she "need not fear that I will embroil myself in any of these scrapes." Some young men even criticized their fellow students who behaved, in their opinion, shamefully. John Deering, Jr., regretted that, at a college ceremony, "some of our number were drunk. It is an evil to be deplored and remedied if possible." "How strange," he disappointingly commented, "it is that young men old enough to come to College and having sense enough of its advantages cannot refrain from such vicious and eternally ruinous indulgences. But it is a very prevalent evil in College."[30]

Concerned elders warned their children that associating with individuals with questionable habits also threatened their character development. Writing to Charles McArthur's parents, Bowdoin president Leonard Woods reported that their son had "not been doing his duty as a Student." "The trouble," Woods explained, "has probably been owing to his being too much associated with those whose company has been no benefit to him." Upon receiving the report, Arthur McArthur, Sr., forwarded the president's message to his son at college and demanded that Charles "read this letter over and over & ponder upon it and consider that your case is very perilous but not past redemption." How often, he then asked, had he reminded his son that a boy's "character, genius & taste are formed by his associates and Oh! how important that your more intimate acquaintances in College should be steady, the orderly, and the studious."[31]

College men themselves absorbed these warnings about bad associates and passed along the advice to their siblings. While at Harvard, Wilder Dwight wrote to his brother Howard, who had just begun boarding school. The older sibling recalled his own fortune for having "boarded in the house with several very pleasant, industrious, and excellent fellows so that I escaped being surrounded by bad influences." It was up to Howard to "choose good associates and companions," for "on your choice of friends depends in a great measure both your success as a student and a boy." Picking the right associates was a task of "the highest importance" because "[you] take the habits, thoughts, and motions in a great measure from those about you." Wilder recommended that Howard "select those only" who had the "best habits." Dwight warned his brother against fraternizing with men who used profanity because "from constantly hearing it you will be liable to fall into it." Profanity, he continued "clings to one long after he has learned to dispose it and . . . will always deform your conversation."[32]

In some instances, parents warned children about associates in order to keep them away from their social inferiors. This was particularly true of members of Boston's wealthiest families. While attending a preparatory boarding school in Northfield, Massachusetts, future Harvard man Caspar Crowninshield asked his parents for permission to attend a local dance party. Alarmed by this seemingly innocent request, Crowninshield's mother urged him to concentrate on his studies, promising that "once in college . . . it will be different." Attending such a party in the local community, she feared, would bring him "into the company of an ordinary set of women." She then pleaded with him to "please not ask to do anything to worry Father, for he is very feeble. . . . I have & so has he much confidence in your good sense. You only need to take time for reflection, & I dare say even now before you get my answer, you have concluded it were better not to go." The elite Crowninshields viewed a simple request to attend a local dance party as a threat to their son's character and social class.[33]

An Educated Elite

Colleges expected their graduates to behave like refined gentlemen and demonstrate their educational superiority. Colleges provided safe environments for young men to rid themselves of bad behaviors and cultivate good character traits. Faculty members as well as parents also used the language of character to encourage and evaluate students. Bowdoin College professor Alpheus Spring Packard, Sr., told a student that his "character" was "rapidly becoming fixed, for such is the law of our intellectual & moral being—& I would desire for you, as the best thing I could ask for a young man, a character in every respect such as will win the respect & confidence of men—a short time may determine for you what you are to be." Packard praised the young man for having "powers, which if properly cultivated, will command for you influence & respectability in all calling." Henry I. Bowditch, the famous abolitionist, thought that his son Nathaniel, while at Harvard's Scientific School, would "*take hold* [of his studies] with *energy*." "As you make your character as a student," he predicted, "so will it be as a man."[34]

Aside from providing a safe place where young men could cultivate their character, colleges also had the task of offering a broad education. Knowledge of the world allowed a man of character to determine whether his actions were in line with a righteous course. In his final weeks as a student at Harvard, Wilder Dwight posed a philosophical question: ought a man's "conscientious scruples" outweigh his loyalty to national laws? Given the national and state-level debates about the enforcement of the strengthened Fugitive Slave Act, the question had real-world implications. He concluded that only men who acted based on informed decisions could, if they conscientiously objected, disobey laws. A man's conscience, Dwight reasoned, developed only as he elevated "his moral and intellectual culture," and someone who claimed to be acting in line with his internal beliefs might yet "lack wisdom, or foresight or prudence or charity, or some other virtue or capacity, which will prevent him from seeing the right course." Only educated and knowledgeable people could act with confidence in the righteousness of their course. He reserved the right of disobedience for the most educated members of society. Only *they* had the sufficient knowledge to be sure that their actions were morally sound and thus consistent with good character.[35]

As Dwight argued, a man of character based his actions on his broad knowledge. New Brahmins, therefore, justified their leadership of society by arguing that only they had the educational basis necessary to inform their decisions. Amherst student William G. Hammond wrote in his diary that a "professional life" contributed more to happiness than an agricultural one because the former "developed the intellectual faculties more, and thus brought man nearer to a state of perfection." Dartmouth student Ozias Pitkin observed that studying was "peculiarly formative" to character development because it "enlarges the powers of the mind." Conversely, inaction in the mind was "fatal to the principles of true wisdom." Since man was an "active being, he must either advance in virtue & improvement or retrograde." Reading and studying, noted Harvard student Henry Spaulding, brought students "into contact with active, vigorous intellects" such as those of the "*priests of knowledge* at whose altars the scholar" worshipped in order that "he may catch the glow and fervor of their burning thoughts." James C. Carter, ruminating on the role he and his classmates would play after graduation, pointed to previous Harvard men who were "adorning every thing they touch, elevating the character of the merchant; giving to the councils of the nation an enlightened and comprehensive spirit; building a pure and vigorous literature; diffusing the benefits and extending the boundaries of knowledge, and gracing the Christian profession." Dartmouth's John G. Baker argued that "a nation of scholars is the only one that can safely be constituted a democracy." Inside the "educated masses," he claimed, lay "every nation's hopes for permanent freedom." "A nation of scholars!" he exclaimed, "what a sound it has for the ears! what a spectacle it must present to the eyes!" "Here," he finished, "rests the hope of the world." Harvard student Edwin Grover bluntly stated that although "freedom of thought should be encouraged among men of all classes," the educated men of society "should be best qualified to mould the popular opinion of their day." The "wisdom" that the men bore from their studies was "the result of experience in all times and in places widely remote, and hence fits them to guide those of narrower experience and less accurate thought."[36]

Possessing a college degree distinguished the New Brahmins from the rest of American society. Criticized as elites, out of touch with the masses, the educated young men argued instead that the burden they bore with their education was great indeed. With their superior schooling, they could see clearly, lead others properly, and make the best decisions for all. Education, they argued, was no luxury but rather a noble calling that allowed them to serve society.

The Selfless Leader

As part of their civic duty dictated by the code of character, northern gentlemen had to stand up for truth and morally righteous causes even when doing so courted ridicule and danger. Speaking one's mind even to a hostile public demonstrated courage, commitment to truth, and true character. Knowing full well that the public would not always need or accept their counsel, these men professed a willingness to speak their opinions, no matter the consequences. They acted selflessly on a conviction because it was right and not because they might reap rewards of acclaim in the distant future. "No man," Wilder Dwight declared, "can court applause and deserve it at the same time; for only generous and self-sacrificing efforts can meet with real and lasting approbation." He condemned the act of seeking public approval as "inconsistent with true manliness of character, with purity of motives, and with disinterestedness."[37] Educated men accepted the burden of continually serving an ungrateful public, warning against dangers, and always pointing their moral compasses to the true and righteous North.

The New Brahmins accepted that their elevated societal roles came with expectations of public service. Moral philosophy classes, required at the end of these students' college experiences, taught that a man of character gave back to his community by serving it. Students internalized these lessons. One Wesleyan student maintained that "each member of society is more or less responsible for the common good." Eli Bruce, another Wesleyan student, praised the man who "opens his ears to the cries of the perishing, casts his eyes pitifully upon the scenes of the distressed and opens his treasures, and resources to minister to their necessities, and elevates them to comfort, and happiness." "Every man,"

William E. Potter wrote in his journal, "is created to serve some particular purpose, the full development of which lies in his own hands. It should be the earnest endeavor then, of every man so to conduct himself that when in time he is called upon to cross the 'Stygian river,' he may have the proud consciousness of knowing that the 'World is better because *he* has lived in it.'" Potter concluded, "Such be my destiny."[38]

The educated class served society by maintaining their independent thoughts and offering the "right" course for the nation during all periods, whether in peace or war. In doing so, they saw themselves as guardians of the Union. The fate of a republic rested on the vigilance of its societal leaders who deliberately thought through all actions rather than rushing headlong into something at the whim of fashion, the expediency of politics, or the prodding of a mob. Looking out into nineteenth-century society, college men saw righteous causes and necessary debates—such as the one concerning abolition—silenced in the name of social harmony. Such censorship struck these men as a betrayal of truth, a behavior inconsistent with good character. "The Christian minister," Wesleyan student Edwin Griswold observed, "fears lest by a certain course he shall not please his people and in consequence hides his light and guards against every expression which might be considered as opposed to the general will." Griswold complained that "the ministers of Christ will not cry out against war, intemperance and slavery, with any earnestness and will in some instances strive to support these tottering remnants of barbarism."[39] Francis Balch, a student at Harvard, accused churches of seeking only "safe" men to become ministers, meaning those who did not discuss politics or try to apply "the Constitution to present affairs." If this continued, he feared, "you might see many leave their pews and step into the aisle, but no longer as defenders of their country, rather as protestants against the right of free speech."[40]

College writers knew that a skeptical public would not always accept their leadership. Regardless, speaking one's mind no matter how unpopular the position, standing by one's principles no matter the danger, and demonstrating a willingness to sacrifice oneself, marked one as a man of character, a great man. James Latimer, a senior at Wesleyan, observed that great men "burst upon the astonished world like meteors" and often passed away before society recognized their achievements. During their lifetimes, these men who sometimes presented "truths which are inappropriate" faced opponents who called them "fanatics" and "the multitude" who regarded them "no better than madmen." "Often," Latimer continued, "does the great man conflict with his age, by refusing to pander to the depravity of his fellows or endorse the frivolities of his time."

Having articulated unpopular views and faced hostile crowds "alone and without Sympathy," great men solidified their standing by remaining wedded to their righteous principles. C. F. Gerry and Daniel Martindale, also Wesleyan men, concurred. Gerry observed that original thinkers had always met with opposition "because they are in advance of the times." As he saw it, nearly "every mighty revolution can be traced to the miserable lodgings of some palefaced student, who shut up from the noisy world delighted . . . in his own bright realm of thought and fancy." Martindale praised great men for having "borne hatred and disgrace" and giving "up friends and cheerful hopes and human joys" in order to accomplish their goals. Another Wesleyan student commended men such as Copernicus, Newton, Galileo, and Luther for weathering "violent and fierce . . . storm[s] of opposition, which arose against them." The *"spirit,* which *burned* in their bosoms," however, *"could not* be *extinguished."*[41]

College men looked to history for examples of good and bad characters to emulate or reject. George Washington ranked the highest when it came to positive character traits. Harvard student George Whittemore argued that the Virginian planter turned soldier and statesman might "never have led this country through the gloomy and difficult paths of the Revolution had he paid any regard to the clamors which denounced him as a rebel, the slanders of his private enemies, or even the doubts and murmurs of the patriotic." "Through hope and fear," Whittemore continued, Washington "held firmly to the only course which was for him the way of honor and duty, and when the struggle was ended and the nation greeted him as a deliverer, he received its applause and veneration not as the reward to which he had aspired and the hope of which has sustained his efforts, but with the consciousness of a good and great work performed for its own sake." Washington's willingness to risk death for his beliefs made him even more heroic. Whittemore concluded "that those who would accomplish any good and great work cannot be impelled by the desire of applause or even of permanent fame." A man of character always accepted the risks of standing by his principles.[42] Dartmouth student William Weeks referred to Washington as "equally distinguished as a great general, a wise statesman, and an incorruptible patriot." "The name of Washington," wrote Solomon Lincoln from Harvard, "has become a household word to signify the most glorious combination of virtues, that ever fell to the lot of man." Time had not robbed the name of its "lustre." Washington's was "a character in which no virtue was lacking."[43]

New Brahmins, investigating historical figures to study examples of character, latched on the traits of service and sacrifice. They also condemned self-serving men in their past. F. A. Loomis, a Wesleyan student, criticized Aaron

Burr for using his "power and influence for self aggrandizement rather than for the well-being of mankind." Burr had been "goaded on by disappointed ambition" in his attempt to set up a new nation in the Louisiana territory after his political career ended. Wilder Dwight criticized Benjamin Franklin for encouraging people to act out of self-interest rather than purity of purpose. Franklin's character "was not of the noblest kind." In Dwight's estimation, "Franklin hardly ever appeals to our love of goodness simply as such, but ever holds out the present rewards which it will secure to us." Never in his writings did he offer "consolation in adversity and trial, or give us strength to go cheerfully on in the right path regardless of worldly interest." This opportunistic and hypocritical nature gave Franklin's character "an essentially low tone." If only Franklin's writings were "animated with a stronger and loftier feeling." Harvard's Addison Brown declared that "no statesman since the days of Washington" had ever "been actuated by a loftier and purer patriotism than Mr. [Henry] Clay." No one but Clay had presented such a "striking contrast to those artful interested politicians, which are the peculiar curse of republics." Ignoring Clay's national ambitions, Brown wrote that the Kentuckian had not been inspired by "the lust of power" but rather "the love of justice, and ennobled by the . . . concern for the honor of the country and its common welfare." "In the fearful struggle upon the Missouri question," Brown wrote, "when a . . . madness seemed to have seized upon the minds of men, & the elements of any political union were ready to melt and dissolve in the fervid heat, when . . . the quivering, lurid lightning of partisan fury was about to rend in a moment the little bark which our fathers had hardly launched upon the seas of time," Henry Clay took on the leadership role and managed to "assuage the fury & the elements, & bid the angry waves be still." His ability to find common ground and place the country's unity above politics saved the Union.[44]

Henry Clay's national reputation stemmed from his service in times of crisis. Stressful and dangerous periods, therefore, offered opportunities for men to demonstrate their character. New Brahmins claimed to cherish such periods, recognizing that trying times provided greater opportunities for a man to prove himself. Wesleyan student J. T. Dickinson, writing about Daniel Webster, pointed out that "great occasions alone could arouse his intellect, and set in rapid motion the grand machinery of his mind." Dartmouth's William Thompson declared that men "learnt many of the noblest lessons of Earth" during "times of adversity." Such periods brought "into activity man's noblest and best powers." During the early months of the Civil War, Harvard's Leonard C. Alden argued that "trials and affliction constitute one of the most important methods of moral discipline and one of the most efficacious means of purifying, strengthening, and elevating the moral character." In an essay he wrote in October 1852, Wilder Dwight argued that "living at periods commonly considered calamitous" was advantageous because such times afforded "favorable opportunities for the formation of character," demanding "great sacrifices, noble acts of heroism, and afford[ing] opportunities for a more active and intense exercise of virtue than more peaceful periods."[45] Times of trial could test and reveal a man's character.

College men discovered that professing the ideals of character was a much easier task than practicing its tenets. Although they tried, these young gentlemen-in-training could not always shed their negative traits and live as men of character. Harvard-educated William D. Sedgwick privately admitted the difficulty of attaining ideal character qualities. Having lectured "on duty—on all kind's of duties" to schoolchildren, he told his sister, "If I were only to practice one half [of what] I preach I should be in the very centre of the strait and narrow road." A year before graduating from Williams College, Samuel C. Armstrong told his brother, "While in college I wish to be dressed as well as the best. I find it pleasanter to be received as an equal than to be looked upon as out of my place when I meet with the well-dressed of New York and even of Williamstown." Perhaps attempting to compensate for his upbringing in the Sandwich Islands, Armstrong found himself trying to fit in with his more fashionable classmates. "When a man's history isn't known," he explained, "dress has a great deal to do with his position; when he is once thoroughly known, dress is a small matter." And although "with two thirds of the fellows in college, style in dress is nothing, and as for them I could dress anyhow," the remainder cared "much about fashion and are yet smart, fine and polished fellows."[46] Although he thought most Williams students did not judge a man by how he dressed, Armstrong did not want to lose face with the trendy sorts either. A man who fully accepted the tenets of character as inherently internal would not have fretted about appearances. A man who held inner qualities to be paramount would not have been so concerned with appearance.

Armstrong's dilemma illustrates the difficulty of living by the strict standards of character. During the developmental age when young men tried to establish themselves as respectable individuals, they still faced insecurities about fitting in. As college men graduated and entered the working world, they continued to wrestle with the enormous responsibility they bore. How could they serve as the paragons of moral rectitude in a world so full of temptation?

How could they live up to the standards that had been instilled in them? The search for character was an ongoing one.

Politics by Proxy

In republican societies such as the United States, the process of advocating political positions might appear similar to pandering to the public. Critics accused politicians of harboring selfish motives rather than seeking to better society and serve the greater good. The "selfish love of applause," Wilder Dwight claimed, was a "great obstacle to political purity." Not enough leaders were "willing to brave popular censure in the cause of justice and truth." Politicians appealed to "low motives and unworthy sentiments" in order to stay in office. For this, they were "open to flattery and easily influenced by an appeal to their interest, or by an artful excitement of their prejudices." Wesleyan student Robert McGonegal observed that some men "make a great mistake in thinking that to be quickly great is to bend most obsequiously to the caprices of the popular mind." By doing this, they "effectually compromise all that is truly valuable in their Manhood."[47]

College writers believed that public figures ought to possess the highest moral standards. McGonegal hoped public men, "servants of their peers for a season," could be trusted to be "exemplars of all that is nobly virtuous and generally just." "In them," he continued, "we might rightfully expect no compromise of a principle, which has ever been regarded by the good as infinitely essential to the stability of elevated Individuals & national character." McGonegal expected public servants to possess a "moral sense which has respect to the inner sanctuary of the heart, developes right principles and modes of thought." In the "holy temple" of the public man's "spirit, dedicated to God & his country, self-promotion & party interests must ever be regarded as secondary to the moral good & highest prosperity of . . . a free people." "To such men," McGonegal concluded, "can the helm of State be entrusted when the storm is abroad, & the tempest casts its chains of fire, corruption corrodes not their integrity, danger foils not their skill, & traitorism palsies not their steel-armored arm."[48]

College men presented a nostalgic vision of history, investing politicians of a previous generation with the noble qualities of character and selflessness. Harvard student Hermann Warner thought the "pathway of Political life" was "slippery and toilsome" and that "its duties and trials far outweigh its honors." "From Patrick Henry, who heard the voice of Omnipotence speaking in the roar of cannon," he wrote, harking back to the Revolutionary era, "to the stern patriot whose household God has been the guardian of his country's welfare, they speak to us in 'words that burn.'" Writing amid the debates over the fate of conquered Mexican lands in the summer of 1850, Warner reasoned that if "the Political life of the future take pattern by that of the past—to emulate its purity and rival its glory, the lessons of experience may serve to teach us how to weather the storm which seems to be gathering about us."[49]

Comparing nineteenth-century political leaders to those of an earlier era, college men found their generation of politicians sorely lacking in the necessary leadership characteristics. They condemned the spoils system—where a victorious political party rewarded its supporters with government offices—and lamented the unqualified men who rose to power as a result. Andrew Jackson's political revolution had exiled intellectuals in American life (exemplified by aristocratic New Englander John Quincy Adams) and ushered in the culture of political patronage. Taught to revere the rule of the learned, college men melded their political bias against the dominant Democrats with the elitist belief that only men of a certain education, such as themselves, ought to lead society.

The spoils system represented everything that young men had been taught to oppose: loyalty to a group rather than the greater good, and the elevation of unqualified men to positions of leadership. Harvard's Albert Hale declared that the spoils system had become "the source of great and permanent harm to the politics, the government and the general interests of the country." Indeed, government offices had become "the rewards, not for honesty and ability, but for partizan zeal and successful wool-pulling." Government bureaucracies were now "filled . . . with incompetent men who have neglected the interests of the country at home and dishonored its name abroad" while the system had made treason "to party . . . a greater offense than treason to the country." "In the appointments which are now made," said Hale, "individual capacity is of the least importance, and sometimes it would seem almost a positive objection." The spoils system had ushered in what college men considered the worst outcome: sycophantic men seeking personal glorification and profit controlled the levers of political power and neglected the greater good. Unlike during "the days of the first president," when questions about a potential appointee's honesty and capability rose to the fore, present political leaders only asked "how many votes did he get for us in the election?"[50] Such characteristics symbolized the dominance of corrupt rather than honorable men.

By the late 1850s, the rising New Brahmins blamed unscrupulous political operatives for steering the nation toward sectional conflict. They hoped that men of character would step forward and save the nation. In 1859 Frazar A.

Stearns encouraged his father, the president of Amherst College, to "write articles for the most patriotic papers, and to the most judicious men of the country." He hoped that "the extreme or the party men," would be cast aside while "the right men" were "sent to Congress, who would take up the slavery question honestly and kindly, and propose that the government and the nation should offer to bear a reasonable part of the expense of emancipation." The New Brahmins viewed the increasing sectional rhetoric as the result of "party men" rather than an actual disagreement between North and South. They hoped, therefore, that men of good character from both sections might step forward to arrange a compromise and, at the same time, correct the long-corrupt political system.[51] Rejecting what they considered the rather messy nature of popular machine politics, college men championed more refined and constrained leadership. Appalled at the ascendance of people they considered unqualified to make rational judgments, such as immigrants and rural voters, the gentleman class preferred conservative and moderate political leaders. This tendency to distrust the masses reveals their deep discomfort with democracy, which they considered tarnished and flawed by political parties and bosses. Longing for mythological days when "statesmen" rather than pandering politicians helmed national affairs, these young elites hinted as to their future position on the issue of a growing democratic system.

In portraying most public figures as corrupt and untrustworthy, the New Brahmins called for the rule of elites: men such as themselves and their parents. After all, as they had learned, only the most educated members of society had both the knowledge and the training to select the "right" course for the nation. Some openly spoke of curbing "the rash tendencies of popular liberty." According to Dartmouth student Charles Cutler, liberty, which was "so fondly cherished, at least in name, by our government and institutions, when guided and controlled by moral principle," was "a source of civilization and social progress." When it became "excessive," however, it also became "a compound of ambition, envy and self-will, subversive of order, and destructive to the best interests of man."[52] Harvard student Edwin Grover placed his trust in the conservatism of college men to weigh the conflicting forces in society. "Men of science and Learning," he said, "restrain the popular opinions of their very day from extremes." Grover praised them for checking "radicalism and ... reformation or even change in any direction." "If on the one hand," he explained, "radicalism is to be feared, lest in its too violent operation it defeat the end of reform, conservatism, on the other, tends to the same result by checking popular activity."[53]

Despite their elitism and arrogance, college writers earnestly believed that scholars and educated men had society's best interests at heart. According to Wesleyan student Daniel Pond, from their "high vantage ground, the scholar should scan well the wants of the age in which he lives and with a noble soul meet its urgent demands." Let the scholar, Pond argued, "as he stands upon the watchtowers of earth when he catches the first gleams of truth[']s rising sun send along the gloom shrouded valleys the joyous welcome bidding the fainting ones look up and be strong." Before the rise of the Republican Party, these men identified with the Whig's personal and ideological beliefs. Just as Whigs attempted to master themselves and their personal behavior (as a corresponding outcome of their need to demonstrate and exercise their control over society), these young college men, heirs to a Whig-influenced educational system, also prioritized self-control. They valued those who thought clearly in a world swirling with emotion and passion.[54]

In the election of 1860, most of the men at the heart of this study supported the Republican Party. Believing in the subservience of the states to federal authority, they also supported commerce, the development of the West, and internal improvements. By 1860 the Republicans had become the heirs to these governing principles. Although they backed the Republicans, these men remained committed to moderate ideas, rejecting the abolitionists on the radical fringes of the party. However, some men, particularly those who came from Democratic families, remained firmly attached to the Democratic Party.

As Whigs and, later, Republicans, young men were keenly aware that their region had not been in political power since John Quincy Adams's single presidential term. When they criticized the character of their politicians, their elitist undertones suggested their frustration with the supremacy of the Democratic Party, which primarily answered to its more dominant southern wing. College students, like their parents, found appalling the dominance of, in their mind, unqualified political appointees swept into office by the same tide that elevated Andrew Jackson to the presidency. Jackson himself, however, induced a more complicated response from college men who, on the one hand, admired his decisiveness but also disapproved of his unrefined nature. Additionally, Jackson represented the rise of popular democracy in the United States. Elites largely viewed this expansion of the franchise dismissively. Educated men preferred the leadership and decision making of their own kind. Thus, embedded in the language of selfless character lay an implicit criticism of societal leaders who did not share these young men's political views.

The New Brahmins understood that blind allegiance to a political party betrayed the foundation of their belief in independent thought. Parties also had tyrannical tendencies. As a result, men of character tried to distance themselves from party orthodoxy. "The party in the ascendancy," Wesleyan student Edwin Griswold observed, "no matter by how lean a majority and no matter which that party may be, thinks it right to accord to the minority scarcely more than the privilege to live and vote." Politicians might "do notorious wrong," but members of the same party did not speak against one another.[55] Men of character aimed to shun these negative aspects of party politics. College students who criticized fraternal organizations could condemn adherence to political parties for the same reasons: they elevated associations over independent thought and principles.

Regardless of their claims, these men held strong political perspectives but substituted the language of character for their true partisan nature. College men turned to American history to justify their own political positions. When writing about the Revolutionary period, New England college men praised the Federalists, believing that a more powerful federal government might have averted sectional tension during the Nullification Crisis and in the 1850s. They praised Federalist politicians for having the foresight to see problems arising from too much state power and also applauded them for having the character and leadership to advocate their positions in the face of opposition. The young men, in their reasoning, conflated historical precepts and ideologies that they agreed with for the traits of good character. In a sense, they cloaked political principle in behavioral garb, and "good character" translated to "agreeable political agendas."

College students infused their discussions about Revolutionary-era figures with a tinge of political posturing. Although supposedly nonpartisan, George Washington's support of many Federalist policies advocated by his energetic treasury secretary, Alexander Hamilton, made him a national hero for young nineteenth-century men who also supported a more rigorous federal government. College essayists largely discussed George Washington as a model of character and did not directly refer to his policies as president. In praising Federalists, these men preferred to heap their praises on Hamilton. Harvard student Charles Connor commended the authors of the *Federalist Papers* and Hamilton in particular, arguing that he had successfully "demonstrated the Utility of the Union, the inefficiency of the confederation, the necessity of some government equally energetic with . . . the true principles of republican government." Although the Constitution forced opponents who feared that they would be surrendering "state rights to build up a national government whose full development, they said, would eventually bring upon them all the horrors of a rigid despotism," Hamilton's "candid exposition . . . attracted attention & commanded respect."[56]

The New Brahmins, living in the era of sectional tension, identified the seeds of sectionalism in the Revolutionary era and condemned the philosophy of state rights advocates such as Thomas Jefferson. Amherst student George Warrington compared and contrasted Hamilton and Jefferson. He praised the former as a man who was "naturally brilliant" and through "industry and hard study" had risen to command the respect of Washington himself. Warrington emphasized Hamilton's "statesman-like qualities" and noted that the consummate Federalist had not always succeeded because he lacked "the tricky arts of the politician, the wire-pulling abilities of office-seekers." In an overly charitable portrait, Warrington declared Hamilton "too generous, too open, too frank[,] too decent to anything which had an air of secrecy and craft about it." In the Amherst student's estimation, Jefferson, "if not a statesman, was pre-eminently a politician," meaning that he "knew how to appeal to the people so as to gain adherents." Calling Jefferson "wily and cautious," Warrington argued that the third president's policies "would have produced a State equally powerless to protect itself, or the people." Where Hamilton appealed to "nobler feelings and aspirations of the heart," Jefferson "by his appeal to the party-spirit and the passions of the people" and conciliating "wickedness and ignorance," successfully coaxed Americans down a path that had "produced our nullification and secession schemes."[57]

The New Brahmins traced the origins of the secession crisis to Jefferson's appeal to sectionalism in his political philosophy. Some even argued that the weak central government, which lay at the heart of Jeffersonian ideology, inspired the rebels of 1861. James A. Garfield concluded in the summer of 1861 that "Jeffersonianism was now fully tested and had proved a failure. The Kentucky and Virginia Resolutions contained the germ of nullification and secession, and we are today reaping the fruits." At the same time, Hamilton's "main propositions" had been correct. "Hereafter," Garfield claimed, Hamilton and Jefferson would "change places in the popular estimation, at least in the estimation of statesmen and thinkers."[58] During the Fort Sumter crisis, William E. Potter also voiced his opinion that Hamilton's ideas about the government had been vindicated.[59]

By early 1861, compromise with the seceded states looked impossible. Gone were the days of statesmen like Washington and Clay. Now were the days when a new generation of Americans faced the consequences of Jefferson's ideals and Jackson's corruption. Politicians with selfish motives had led the nation to the precipice because such men lacked the character of the leadership class. Only honorable northern men could rescue the Union now.

Cloaked in the New Brahmins' discussions about the importance of individualism was a self-serving argument. In many respects, the "individual" that college men wanted people to listen to the most was someone like themselves. And why shouldn't they have expected that? Weren't their opinions more informed because they were the most educated members of society? "Individualism" and "independent thought" became clever ways of legitimizing their leadership. Believing in individualism justified their actions but also consoled them when they did not get their way. In the face of failure, they could easily blame the undisciplined and uninformed rabble for shunning the opinions of the educated and enlightened class.

As Commencement Day approached, graduating seniors prepared themselves for the challenges ahead. Their schools had trained them but, like good men of character, these individuals accepted that their success or failure depended on their own abilities and actions. Harvard student Robert Paine acknowledged that a college could only provide young men "with intellects trained & cultivated," but "the success of each one *then* depends upon himself; depends upon the spirit in wh[ich] he commences & continues the pursuit he selects." Without a "fixed purpose" or a "high resolve," he warned, a man's life "will be a failure." If a person lived "day to day merely for pleasure" or was "guided by circumstances as chance presents them," then "all the mental power that nature, all the training that alma mater may have given him, will avail him little." Only the "man of purpose" succeeded in life. "If a man thinks life is a farce," Paine explained, "too certainly will he be its laughing stock & clown," but let that man think of life as a "noble drama, & he will be its hero." Heroes, according to James Jackson Lowell, one of Harvard's Civil War martyrs and a descendent of two powerful Bay State families, were not those who "recite best here, or who know the most, but those whose knowledge best clears their perceptions" to do what was right for society. To clear-sightedness must be added "firmness and perseverance, true grit . . . and then we have the man who is needed now, the man who is loyal to the highest principles."[60]

During his Class Day oration in 1850, Harvard student James C. Carter implored his classmates to uphold virtue and behave like good citizens. Whatever "else we may be," he said, "let us at least be men." No one could expect any more from them, while "less than this we should scorn to attempt." He urged his fellow graduates to develop a "character that will secure respect" and bear themselves "as not to dishonor the cause of learning and the place in which we have been bred."[61] As the young men prepared to embark on their careers backed by Harvard's prestigious reputation, they must have mixed excitement with anxiety at the road ahead. They might have wondered if they had truly attained the character of gentlemen. Although the call to become "men" and cultivate a "character" worthy of respect may have seemed simple and direct, these words implied a whole slew of meanings for the young and educated antebellum man.

Recognizing the traits of character in themselves, New Brahmins used the same standards to evaluate others in American society. They regretted that so many nineteenth-century individuals lacked the character they thought so vital. New Brahmins, thus, justified their own leadership positions. Since these elites often judged an individual's character by the level of education they had attained, they advocated for "the rule of the learned," a conservative idea harking back to the founding generation. Only by reforming America's leadership class, these men suggested, could the United States also demonstrate its "national character" as the promoter of republican government the world over. The nation's character, meanwhile, faced its severest test in the winter of 1860–61 as the secession crisis began. The New Brahmins watched events and pondered their next move. Now they certainly seemed to be living in tumultuous times. How was a man of character supposed to act?

4

"To Put Those Theories into Practice"

Secession and the Crisis of Character

Joshua L. Chamberlain fully comprehended and embraced the dictates of character. As the Civil War dragged into its second year, the Bowdoin College professor could no longer resist his compulsion to physically do something for the Union cause. Prodded by his own conscience, Chamberlain may have also felt shame for not volunteering when so many of his students had already marched into President Lincoln's armies. One student, Walter S. Poor, had reported to Chamberlain from the front, "When I see what kind of men get positions and what influences are effectual, I have but little hope of success." "If you could see the soldiers drill, hear the confused murmur of voices in the ranks drowning the commands of the officers and distracting the attention of the men, could see the beardless boys, and see the lifeless, and characterless men who command them," Poor continued, "you would not be surprised at the panic at Bull Run or other reverses elsewhere. The only wonder is that they do not run sooner than they do." In order to produce victories, the army needed "cool, self reliant, self *controlling* officers, and disciplined *silent obedient* men." He noticed that "nearly all the Southern officers are gentlemen, accustomed to command, and enforce obedience, and the men accustomed to obey, or at least to respect their superiors." Additionally, "southern youths have made up as large a proportion as possible of the Cadets at West Point and rarely resigned," whereas "northern men have kept their sons out of the army and even after they have graduated persuaded them to resign."[1]

Chamberlain, who had wished to volunteer in 1861 but met with opposition from his family as well as college officials, finally ignored all objections and wrote to the governor of Maine to offer his services to the state. In his letter to Gov. Washburn, he expressed his fear that "this war, so costly of blood and treasure, will not cease until the men of the North are willing to leave good positions, and sacrifice the dearest personal interests, to rescue our Country from Desolation, and defend the National Existence against treachery at home and jeopardy abroad." The war "must be ended, with a swift and strong hand" and every man "ought to come forward and ask to be placed at his proper post." In short, the crisis of the Union demanded that men of character do their duty. Chamberlain also leveraged his position as a societal leader, suggesting that others would follow him into the ranks. He noted that almost one hundred of his students had already donned Union blue and "there are many more all over our State, who, I believe, would respond with enthusiasm, if summoned by me, and who would bring forward men enough to fill up a Regiment at once."[2]

Bowdoin faculty attempted to sabotage his plans by telling the governor that Chamberlain was "but only a mild-mannered common student" rather than a fighter. "I find I have to encounter an unexpected degree of opposition in the Faculty of the College," Chamberlain admitted to the governor, and reiterated his determination to volunteer: "I trust that the representations that they propose to make to induce you to withhold my commission, will have no more weight with you than with me. I feel it to be my duty to serve my Country." Chamberlain's pleas prevailed and Gov. Washburn appointed the professor to second in command of the 20th Maine Volunteers.[3]

Many of the New Brahmins felt the same compulsion to volunteer and also faced opposition from their elders. Elite young men arrived at similar personal impasses even as their nation confronted the most serious crisis of its existence. The moment of secession represented a crisis on two levels. Rebellious states now threatened the bright future that young college men prescribed for the American experiment—the Union could not inspire democratic reform the world over if it could not even maintain its own integrity as a nation. Additionally, how the North responded would define its societal leaders and people. Was the North up to the challenge of maintaining the Union? In considering their course of action, the New Brahmins returned to the lessons of their college days. They demonstrated that the words they had spouted to endless debate groups and crowds about personal and national character had been engrained in their being. The moment of crisis, the opportunity to test one's character, had arrived.

The New Brahmins viewed secession as a test of both personal and national character. How they responded would affect their lives but would also determine the fate of the United States and its role as the bastion of republican liberty. The secession crisis challenged the New Brahmins to think about the most appropriate course of action in line with their societal standing and personal beliefs. As northern gentlemen, they felt compelled by conscience and duty to serve the country in any way that they could. Secession, then, challenged them, but it also presented an opportunity for them to put their beliefs to the test.

The New Brahmins, having internalized their beliefs about good character, applied them in the nation's hour of need. They initially viewed the crisis prompted by southern secession as a political one, which called for resolute national leaders to stand firm amid threats to the Union. They directed their ire at selfish politicians whose loyalty, they believed, lay with slavery rather than the good of the Union. The New Brahmins also hoped that their own leaders would have the character to stand up for their principles and not capitulate to secessionists' demands. Once the war commenced and continued without abatement, however, these young men knew that an expanding conflict required the serious commitment of men like themselves. The threat of a severed Union forced them to restate their beliefs about America's role in human affairs. The nationalism they had cultivated in college courses came to the fore, as did their lessons about how men of character should behave.

Unfortunately for the eager New Brahmins, they encountered opposition from an unexpected source: their parents and elders. The two generations of northern gentlemen disagreed on the appropriate course of action for the professional classes in northern society. Whereas many elder northerners urged their sons to remain on the home front and serve the Union through their everyday professions, the New Brahmins insisted that they take a direct role in the conflict by leading others into battle.

From the very beginning of the conflict, college-educated men saw the war as an opportunity to test their character. In explaining why they enlisted, they combined both their personal and national ideologies. They, as society's young leaders, had an obligation to protect the Union, which represented freedom, civilization, and the hopes of democratic governments the world over. They had, through their college years, cultivated strong beliefs about the role of society's most educated citizens and the significance of American civilization. The national emergency called these lessons to the fore. Their parents reasoned that their class positions entitled them to duties other than risking life and limb for the government, an argument that contradicted what the New Brahmins themselves believed. Staying on the home front, they vehemently argued, was inconsistent with the dictates of proper character in a time of national crisis.

Although good character might have been difficult to attain and maintain in the antebellum world—upholding one's composure, holding independent opinions and, generally, leading an exemplary life were not necessarily the most heroic actions—a national crisis that required the services of loyal men offered an opportunity to demonstrate one's inner qualities in a more public fashion. The war presented the New Brahmins with a new environment in which to test themselves and challenge others to be as true as they were to the principles of character. The crisis of secession demanded that members of society's leadership class come forward, display their best qualities, and do their duty.

The New Brahmins volunteered not just their bodies but also their leadership traits. As such, they insisted on military rank commensurate with their peacetime societal positions in the professional class. Initially, caught up in the excitement of the war and believing the conflict might end swiftly, some eager New Brahmins volunteered as privates. But when these short-term enlistments expired and they realized that the war would last longer than predicted, they sought officers' commissions. Indeed, as the war continued, they sought the highest rank possible, revealing their personal ambitions and, ultimately, flaws in their character.

The Winter of Secession

After Abraham Lincoln's victory in the election of 1860, Deep South states led by South Carolina began cutting their ties with the Union, a move that threatened the vision of an expanding democratic republic that the New Brahmins had articulated. They hoped, therefore, that their new national leaders would remain firm in the face of southern secession. More than ever, the nation needed unflappable men who would stand by their principles. According to the tenets of good character, a man held his ground and defended the righteous cause in the midst of a crisis. The New Brahmins waited to see if the man who would become their sixteenth president had the character of a northern gentleman. From Maine, Rowland B. Howard, writing to his brother Oliver, reported that the locals rejoiced "in the Election of Mr. Lincoln." But he himself remained unsure of the president-elect's character. If only he knew that Lincoln "had grace in his heart," he would "have no fears for the Spirit & tone of his Administration."[4]

The New Brahmins looked to Lincoln because they doubted President James Buchanan's ability to manage the crisis. After learning that federal installations had fallen to secessionists in Charleston "and that the Palmetto flag floats from the Post Office and Custom House," William E. Potter exclaimed, "Alas my country!" If only, he prayed, "that a *man* was in the Executive chair of thy Govnt, and not the weak, trembling Imbecile that now fills it." He hoped that God would "impart patriotism, discretion, and nerve, to the Prest of the United States, 'And all others in authority'" and wished the chief executive would have "the decision & patriotism of President Jackson." Charles Russell Lowell thought that a mob mentality had taken over the South "and *no man* can tell whither a mob may rush." Having no faith in President Buchanan, he predicted that "whatsoever course is most to be avoided, that Mr. Buchanan will select. If war is possible J. B. will make it a sure thing." Charles H. Howard disapproved of President Buchanan's "dallying policy." He expected that Lincoln, once inaugurated, would be "unquestionably a man of *energy*."[5]

Before the fighting commenced, New Brahmins continued to view the crisis as a political problem. In the anxious months between Lincoln's election and inauguration, they had time to ponder the course of events and imagine the consequences of successful secession. On the last day of 1860, with one state out of the Union and more preparing to follow, Oliver O. Howard decided that slavery alone had not brought about the nation's woes. "Good men," he said, had "shrunk from offices of public trust," and "infidelity licentiousness & all sorts of wickedness have prevailed amongst our public men." He also blamed the general public, for they had "allowed business & private interests to absorb them, & been sadly negligent of the public weal." William E. Potter discussed the importance of preserving the Union by reiterating America's position in world history. On the year 1860, which had just ended, he observed that China had been opened up "to civilization advanced and supported by the Christian Faith." In Europe, "Garibaldi, the Washington of Italy, has redeemed most of that fair land from tyranny. Napoleon, great man as he is, has just perfected and promulgated a plan to liberalize his own Government, and today is to inaugurate an act of the Russian government to liberate the millions of serfs in Russia." Potter countered these encouraging stories with negative domestic news: progress had stalled in "several states in our Republic." The blame for any bloodshed in the United States fell on the shoulders of those "who are striving to break down our government" and bring about "a civil contest without a parallel in history." "Those who support our government," however, would "struggle against the traitors who attack it, with Law, Justice, the principles of Liberty, and a true humanity as allies, and God help the right." A few days later, Potter prayed "that the Evil of Civil War whose dark shadow now stalks through our beloved land, may be mercifully averted," and hoped that the Almighty would "let not thy support given to the Fathers fail the children."[6]

New Brahmins hoped for firm national leadership amid the political crisis. Charles H. Howard resigned himself to the fact that "secession seems inevitable." He hoped, however, that "there'll be no sacrifice of principle." William H. Seward, once the most prominent and respected Republican, disappointed some of the New Brahmins when he signaled compromise measures in January 1861. Luther C. Howell viewed this move toward moderation negatively and wrote that he was "a little disappointed" in the New York senator. Charles Russell Lowell thought that Seward's proposal was "a stultification of his previous course, more worthy of a political dodger than a statesman." Although the sentiments in the speech "may save the Union," Lowell did not want to see the North capitulate in the face of southern threats. "We want higher thinking than that in times like the present," he declared. Concerning the president-elect's positions, Lowell hoped that Lincoln would "not consult too nicely what is *acceptable* even to the Border States, but will take his stand on the principles which the framers of the Constitution stood upon." Lowell continued to believe that secessionists merely wanted more northern concessions. This time, however, they had gone too far. Lowell thought the secessionists had "struck a blow at their Cotton King which he will never get well over. The mischief is already done.... Whether or not the agitators succeed in their political game or brag, it is certain they will repent hereafter the damage to their material interests in the Union or out of it."[7] The Union needed leaders who would stand firm and punish the brazen secessionists.

Even before the firing on Fort Sumter, the New Brahmins expressed outrage at the blatant violation of law and order. Rowland B. Howard, observing the seizure of federal forts and installations, admitted, "I want to be President terribly sometimes! . . . I would drive the thieves out and shoot if I couldn't hang them." "Gods Law," he argued, "has its penalties, so does common law and why not *National law*?" Without consequences or punishment, there would be "*no law*—all is liberty or *license*." It followed, therefore, that when "the laws of the land are violated," the "trespassers" should "feel that the penalty is as sure as the pain that follows putting the hand in the fire." If people disagreed with laws, he reasoned, "repeal them. If the Constitution unjust alter it, but if we are to leave our children anything but anarchy let us, for Heaven[']s sake, maintain the supremacy of law." "If traitors are not hung," he declared, "the Government will fall into contempt & New York will march with them as much as So. Carolina: Property, Life & real *liberty* will be jeopardized, if not ruined."[8] Secession threatened the credibility and stability of the federal government.

Secession tested national character, and the New Brahmins wondered whether their fellow Americans would rise to the occasion. "It seems impossible to imagine how a conflict can be avoided in the present state of affairs," wrote William Wheeler in early April 1861, "but, while I earnestly deprecate the beginning of civil war, I think that there are worse things than war, and that the dominant spirit of money-getting at the North is more corrupting and demoralizing." Wheeler thought that the North was "too much demoralized already: some through interest, some through fear, and a goodly number through a desire to obey law, even though it be weakly wielded."[9] Perhaps, however, a war for the Union might rekindle the American character.

Great hopes rested with the president-elect and his incoming administration. William E. Potter prayed that "this grave, earnest, thoughtful determined man [Lincoln], may prove, if need be, a second Washington, to our Country." He pronounced Lincoln's inaugural speech "eminently conciliatory, though firm in the tone and seems to be received with favor by men of all parties. . . . The address is characterized by great ability as well as conciseness. Its general effect cannot be anything but pacific." Potter seemed emboldened by the new chief executive. "If humanity is to be disgraced, civilization checked and Christianity overshadowed, by an internecine war upon this continent," he wrote, "it should be the prayer of the good in all lands, in light or darkness, on the battlefield or in the councils, that God will defend his unalterable *Right*. And who can doubt that such right lies upon the side of the Government?" "Lincoln," Charles Russell Lowell declared, "must *act* soon, or forfeit his claim to our regard." Robert Gould Shaw also hoped for firm policies from Lincoln, telling his sister, "If we gave them an inch, they would be sure to want thousands of ells, as is proved by their history and ours for the last 50 years." The slaveholding states would "not be content with anything less than a total change of public opinion throughout the North on the subject of slavery, and that, of course, they can't have."[10]

The Decision for War

After the firing on Fort Sumter marked the start of the war, a wave of anxiety and excitement washed over communities in both sections. Though the war brought peril, it also offered promise. Some men thought that the war, though horrible, would stir patriotism and strengthen American character through service. "Well, it has come at last," sighed William Wheeler. "War is fairly upon us, and April 12, 1861," he predicted, "will be marked as the day upon which began the fiercest civil war of modern times." Since hearing the news about Fort Sumter, he had been unable to think "of anything else, and I am almost sick with excitement and anxiety." He expressed concern that "the rebels may also take Washington by a *coup de main*, which would be the climax of our disgrace." The good news, Wheeler noted, was that "the North is now thoroughly roused" and there might "be a loud and speedy response to any call which the States may make for volunteers."[11]

Excitement and war fever swept college campuses where young men greeted the news from South Carolina with a combative spirit. From Amherst, Christopher Pennell reported that college business had effectively ceased. "Books," he told his father, "have been laid aside, amusements neglected; scarcely anything has been doing, except the discussion of the events of the day, in private rooms, at the dinner-table & in impassioned knobs at the news-office & upon the College campus." The college president led the students in prayers "for the success of the cause of the North." The audience responded with "deafening cheers." Pennell thought that Washington had been "surrounded by traitors" as one hundred thousand rebels rushed to counter Lincoln's call for seventy-five thousand militiamen. Meanwhile, "privateers are fitted out to harass our commerce. Our forts are shelled, our navy yards seized, & worse than all, our men have already fallen, while marching to defend the capital." "Until Massachusetts is sunk in the sea," he swore, "traitors shall not hold our capital." Many young men willingly interrupted their college careers for the sake of the Union. "If I enlist for three years I shall be obliged to give up forever all my long cherished plans," Luther C. Howell told his brother, adding, "I shall never return to College." He expressed his willingness to "sacrifice my prospects [and] my life to my country"; as he told his sister, "I had much rather live ignorant than to gain an education at the expense of a guilty conscience."[12] By the end of the contest, many college men had sacrificed more than their educations to serve their country's cause.

Not all students thought that serving in the war would necessitate sacrificing their education. Some viewed both schooling and service as their duty. For example, students from Norwich University (a military school) and neighboring Dartmouth College formed Company B of the 7th Squadron of Rhode Island Cavalry, known as the "College Cavaliers." Eighty-five students joined up in the spring of 1862, saw combat during Antietam Campaign, remained in the service even though their terms had expired, and then disbanded and returned to their schooling. Such individuals performed their military service and maintained their undergraduate standing, thereby affirming their character.[13]

New Brahmin abolitionists saw an additional opportunity and hoped that the war would lead to slavery's demise. "These are stirring times—the excitement is so intense here that it is almost oppressive," reported Luther C. Howell. Having enlisted in a company made up of college men, he explained his decision to his brother. "I ought to hold my life cheap in comparison with my country," he declared, "it will be well sold if I shall aid in purchasing freedom for shackled humanity or in saving my country." William Wheeler argued that he had no choice but to go to the war. "I could not in decency do anything else," he claimed, explaining, "I have been for years on the extreme Abolition edge of the Republican party, hoping for the practical assertion, in *some* way, of the rights and honor of the free North, and here is an opportunity to realize all those hopes,—to put those theories into practice." He dared not "be outdone in deeds by the very men whom" his words had condemned. He could not stand by while his political opponents, "the Democratic rag-tag and bob-tail," went to war and struck "good blows for the right." Republicans could not simply sit at home and say, "Oh, our lives are too precious to be risked in this conflict!" Theodore Winthrop, meanwhile, told his uncle bluntly that he was going to war to "put an end to slavery."[14]

For the most part, however, New Brahmins generally expressed more conservative reasons for fighting the war. The eleven states of the Confederacy had violated the Constitution and threatened representative democracy in America. Paul J. Revere declared that he needed to respond to the beckoning of "something higher" than the appeals of his loved ones. "The institutions of the country, indeed free institutions throughout the world, hang on this moment," he told his mother. By defending the physical Union, the men also fought for its symbolic meaning as well. Sullivan Ballou reminded one correspondent that "the world has never yet seen nobler institutions in peril than ours, and men were never yet called upon to die in a nobler cause."[15]

As they had done in their college essays, the men connected the fate of the United States with that of freedom all over the world. Writing to his father, Frazar A. Stearns declared that they were all living "on the eve of great events" and "we *shall* see what will astound the world." Stearns predicted that "a great nation, *free and independent*," would rise out of the fires of civil war and cause the world to "rejoice." Charles Russell Lowell, corresponding with a friend, doubted the "profitableness of a soldier's life, and would not think of trying it" himself "were it not for a muddled and twisted idea that somehow or other this fight was going to be one in which decent men ought to engage for the sake of *humanity*." When William D. Sedgwick's father-in-law tried to dissuade him from volunteering, the Harvard graduate responded, "The same reasons which should induce me to withdraw from the service of government would, if adopted by all those to whom they apply as well as to me, break up our armies and leave us at the mercy of Southern dictators." "For my part," he declared, "if my country is to perish, my hope is to perish with her. I could not wish to survive the downfall of what I regard as the world's hope." "Should America cease to be a first-class power, and be broken up in contemptible little fragments," he asked, "what would you think would become of England?" Sedgwick continued: "How long would it be before she would lie before the feet of France? What would become of the surplus population of Europe? What chance would be left to Germany and Italy in the struggle for eventual freedom after the failure of the grandest experiment of a free government that the world has known?" The Union's collapse would prompt "utter discouragement and dejection" to "fall upon the friends of freedom everywhere." The North, Sedgwick insisted, could not "yield to the entreaties of those who say, 'Do not persist in this war, for you will be only shedding blood to no purpose.'"[16]

Because they viewed the United States as a blessed nation, the New Brahmins could claim that they waged a holy war for the Union. They often conflated fighting for "civilization" with fighting in the name of a higher power. "Our cause is God's cause, & He will defend the right," Christopher Pennell wrote after Fort Sumter's capitulation; good men had "a sacred duty to fight now." In language tinged with allusions to civilization and barbarism, Pennell declared that yielding to southern demands would cause "the blackness of the dark ages" to "overspread the whole land." James Jackson Lowell compared the Union's cause to that of "the Greeks at Marathon and Salamis, Charles Martel and the Franks at Tours, and the Germans at the Danube, saved Europe from Asiatic barbarism." So, too, he thought, northern volunteers, "at places to be famous in future times, shall have saved America from a similar tide of barbarism; and we may hope to be purified and strengthened ourselves by the struggle." William Wheeler bid his mother farewell before he joined the army, attempting to calm her by saying, "You can have no objection to make this little contribution to the Great Cause." Wheeler could not "see how a life could be more worthily given up, unless it were for God's sake, though is not this God's cause?" Frazar A. Stearns professed his willingness to "fight, or even *die*, for my country." He declared that his trust was "not in Abraham Lincoln, not in General Scott, but in God, for the right *must* win."[17]

In their college essays, the New Brahmins had identified free labor and New England industry as the true source of civilization. Slavery, they thought, ought to stay in the South and eventually die. By adopting slavery as its foundation, the Confederacy had embraced a regressive and uncivilized system of labor. Furthermore, the Confederacy challenged these young men's own vision for the future of the United States. After reading Confederate Vice President Alexander Stephen's "Cornerstone Speech," William E. Potter summarized the meaning: "Under the new Government Slavery is recognized as the fundamental basis of the Government." To this point, Potter drew a sharp contrast. "The Government of the United States," he wrote, "is founded upon the eternal basis of the Freedom, the revolutionary Government has for its base and cornerstone the principle that human bondage is the only true condition of a perfect Government." The concept of the slave-based nation ran counter to historical progress, Potter argued, concluding that "two Governments are before the world, one based upon freedom, the other on Slavery. Can there be any doubt concerning their future history?"[18]

The New Brahmins professed their loyalty to the Union and all it represented. Sullivan Ballou, who had volunteered to fight, admitted that he missed his family but felt compelled to protect the republic. "If it is necessary that I should fall on the battlefield for my country, I am ready," he told his wife, explaining that he had "no misgivings about, or lack of confidence in the cause in which I am engaged, and my courage does not halt or falter." The fate of "American Civilization," he continued, "now leans on the triumph of the Government and how great a debt we owe to those who went before us through the blood and sufferings of the Revolution." In order to preserve that legacy, he was "willing—perfectly willing—to lay down all my joys in this life, to help maintain this Government and to pay that debt." Charles Francis Adams, Jr., meanwhile, told his brother Henry, "Against the rebels I could fight with a will and in earnest. They are traitors, they war for a lie, they are the enemies of morals, of government, and of man. In them we fight against a great wrong." The New Brahmins who had spoken eloquently on the subject in peacetime made the connection between the founders' republic and the future United States. By saving one, they preserved the other. In Connecticut, George Clary told his brother on the day after he volunteered his services as a surgeon that the time had come "for fighting over again the battles of liberty. The spirit of '76 has well nigh returned to Hartford." For others, the war presented an opportunity to end lingering national problems. William O. Stevens, a Harvard graduate, told his friends, "If I don't go now, my boy must."[19]

The burden of history weighed heavily on some New Brahmins given their relation to past heroes of the republic. Many New England families had played a pivotal role in the Revolution, and their grandchildren and great grandchildren felt pressure to protect their national inheritance and family honor. "Isn't a century's work for my ancestors worth a struggle to preserve?" Charles Francis Adams, Jr., asked his brother Henry. Great grandson of the second president and Revolutionary War patriot, Adams believed that secession had put his family's legacy at risk. Additionally, he did not think that he could avoid military service in a conflict over slavery because of his family's long opposition to the institution. "For years," he reasoned, "our family has talked of slavery and of the South, and been most prominent in the contest of words, and now that it has come to blows, does it become us to stand aloof from the conflict?" "I do not think it right that our family, so prominent in this matter while it is a contest of words, should be wholly unrepresented when it has grown to be a conflict of blows," he later explained. It felt right, he continued "to fight to maintain that which my ancestors passed their whole lives in establishing." Paul J. Revere, grandson of the silversmith turned Revolutionary War patriot, likewise told his mother that he could "carry other men with me" as he set out to "struggle for freedom & the principles that have built up this country."[20]

For some men, service became a matter of sibling rivalry and self-esteem. John B. Hubbard felt ashamed to stay out of the fight when "boys ... mere half-grown boys—of every grade of life cheerfully [were] coming forward." He could not, he told his father, "stagnate in all my energies, when the times offer activity to active men." Thomas H. Hubbard admired his brother John for entering the army and admitted that he himself had "thought of this subject not a little" and felt "something much akin to disgust and contempt at my own position." Henry Adams, serving as his father's assistant in London, felt that he ought to return to the United States and enlist. His brother Charles, however, dissuaded him from doing so.[21]

The New Brahmins distinguished themselves from others by claiming that they had the ability to explain the purpose of the war to regular civilians and thus inspire men to exert themselves and perform their duty. Frazar A. Stearns called on "everybody, particularly the best portion of our community, to enlist and come down here." He thought that this was a war that needed to be fought "not only with arms, but to be *waged with words*." Only the most educated northerners could "reassure the South" and demonstrate "the utter absurdity of their fears." He suggested that his father, Amherst president William Stearns, also join the Union cause, reasoning, "If all the *colleges* would organize themselves in a brigade, and their *presidents* go as *chaplains*, and their *professors* as *officers* or *privates*, the effect throughout the South would be *electrical*. Thousands would spring up to welcome them, and some to *pray* with them on Southern soil." Stearns argued that the sight of the country's "educated men going to fight the battles of the Lord" would "rouse the country quicker to a sense of its danger." Christopher Pennell predicted that once the early rush of volunteers subsided there would "be a need of men who shall fight treason from principle, & not from desire for spoils, of educated soldiers who understand what they are fighting for." Since "Tom Dick & Harry will not be so ready to enlist then," the North's most educated men had to fight the war from principle.[22]

Whatever their primary motives for volunteering, New Brahmins argued that their education and social position made their service essential. Charles Francis Adams, Jr., feared that, having justified and articulated reasons to combat slavery, his family's absence from the rosters would mar the Adams name. Words needed to match actions. On the other hand, men like Frazar A. Stearns and Christopher Pennell thought that elites needed to volunteer in order to explain to the men in the ranks why they needed to sacrifice for the country. Words needed to inspire and justify actions. However they approached the subject of volunteering, the young men's education and their societal position almost always influenced their decision.

The crisis of secession threatened northerners' sense of masculinity. Gentlemen, as Lorien Foote has argued, defined their own group as "men who had attained social prominence and a set of attributes that usually included superior education, travel, and civil leadership." The war represented a special test for those who viewed themselves as the perfection of northern manhood. Their service would prove their masculinity as individuals but also that of their region. Charles P. Bowditch complained that the North "seems in a torpor from which nothing can wake them except some terrible disaster ten times as severe as that which we have received [at Bull Run]." He thought that "every gentleman and gentleman's son ought to go into the field," for such a "proceeding would exercise a good influence on everybody. If a company or a regiment of gentlemen should be raised, those in the lower classes would be brought to understand that they too should be willing to sacrifice their lives for the good of the country." A year later, Bowditch argued that if cultured and educated men joined up, they would demonstrate the need for all members of society to enlist. "The example of gentlemen volunteering," he explained, "would be extremely advantageous. The common people, so far from the war as they are here, cannot perhaps understand the necessities of the occasion simply from newspaper addresses and enthusiastic speeches. But if they saw that the time is so threatening as to require gentlemen to enlist, they would have an example before their eyes, which their own senses would lead them to follow."[23]

A strong sense of duty as gentlemen and social elites compelled the New Brahmins to volunteer. Thomas H. Hubbard explained to his father, "I have followed, as well as I could, my most deliberate and sincere convictions of duty" and as far as he was concerned, "it seems no hardship to die, if need be, in maintaining these, but to live renouncing them." "I shall try," he promised, "to do my duty in a manner not discreditable to you." Henry L. Abbott, admitting that he was "constitutionally timid" and his tastes were "not warlike" when compared to his brothers, nevertheless felt duty bound to volunteer. William Wheeler, meanwhile, explained to his mother, "I have felt all along that it was my duty to go, and that it would be disgraceful if I did not." "What is a person worth at such a time, if he do[es] not strain every nerve to uphold the stars & stripes," asked Christopher Pennell. The war for the Union required the North's best men. He reported that many Amherst students planned to volunteer and that "men of the most talent, the soundest minds, *the men*, in short, of College are signing." As Robert Gould Shaw succinctly put it, he would "not be satisfied to stay at home idle when such a war is going on."[24]

New Brahmins thought that their example would encourage others to enlist, particularly when they sensed social apathy or observed others taking the serious business of war too lightly. Bowdoin graduate William Lewis Haskell quit his job at a Quaker school in Maine, "sick with *army fever*." He complained that the Quakers "studiously avoid every allusion to the actual state of things, and indulge in harmless platitudes about the beauties of peace; and in their common talk they do nothing but keep a continual cold watering of every just and noble sentiment." The nation's crisis demanded action. William Wheeler criticized those who took war matters lightly. "A large number of the men, especially the younger ones," he observed, "seem to look upon the whole affair as a gigantic spree, and to form no true conception of the serious character of the undertaking." In the spring of 1861, Theodore Winthrop described the Union armed forces as "regiments, and not an army as yet." To win the war, however, "we must move in an impregnable body, to reclaim the country." Winthrop worried that "the men best informed about the South" underestimated the task before them and did not "anticipate much severe fighting."[25]

The war offered a chance for New Brahmins to demonstrate their character in the cause of the Union. The act of volunteering in the armed forces proved both personal and national character. Additionally, it meant that these men could demonstrate their character in a very dramatic manner before a public audience. William T. Lusk wrote to his cousin on the day that he enlisted, "You must feel with me in my happiness! At length I am judged worthy to expose my life for my country's sake." He was "going to see real danger, real privation, real work—not as a mere Carpet-Knight, talking valorously to girls, but going forth in all humility to help to conquer in the name of God and my Country."[26]

Understanding that their education gave them special skills, college men offered to serve in any position that would best benefit the war effort even if they had to forego personal military glory. James A. Garfield offered his services to the governor of Ohio and noted his willingness to serve "in any capacity he may see fit to appoint me. He may not require me to enter the army now, he may not at all." After deciding to volunteer, Joshua L. Chamberlain explained to the governor of Maine, "I only want to be where I can best serve you." In a previous letter, he had written, "Your Excellency presides over the Educational as well as the military affairs of our State, and, I am well aware, appreciates the importance of sustaining our Institutions of Learning. You will therefore be able to decide where my influence is more needed." Chamberlain placed his fate in the governor's hands. He would fight as a soldier or remain at his college post to do his duty.[27]

Hopes of a swift victory after one dashing battle came to a crushing end in July 1861. The realization encouraged more New Brahmins to enlist and declare their belief that the conflict needed serious leaders to see it to the end. In the aftermath of the Union defeat at the First Battle of Bull Run, Thomas H. Hubbard demanded an even more rigorous effort. He defiantly stated, "We should never think of compromise or peace until the South is soundly whipped. Even if it takes a thirty years war to accomplish that desirable result." At the very least, the North "ought never to retire under a defeat." Early in the war, Frazar A. Stearns observed that troops enlisted "faster than they can be supplied, or officered, or sent off." He maintained that he would "*not hesitate to go* at a moment's warning" if needed. After Bull Run, Stearns told his father, "We have been beaten, and now there is a call for Frazar Stearns."[28]

The motives that initially inspired New Brahmins to volunteer intensified after the rush of enlistments in spring 1861 ended. In the fall of 1861 James A. Garfield explained his decision to volunteer by noting that with "men of military experience" all serving, "still more [men] were needed for the new regiments." In the summer of 1862, Samuel E. Nichols, responding to Union defeats on the battlefield, argued, "It was our imperative duty to take the places of our fallen soldiers, to meet the expectations of those whom we have bidden Godspeed, and who now are in extreme peril, and also to increase the original strength of the army." Where would reinforcements come from, he asked, "unless such men as you and I signify our willingness to go?" Theodore Lyman, whose European travels kept him from volunteering early on, found the war still raging when he returned to the United States. Securing a staff position and a commission, he prepared to leave for the front in the fall of 1863. "Tomorrow I leave for the Army," he wrote in his diary, "may I do my full duty; without that there is nothing worthy." William H. Fessenden, whose physical disability prevented his earlier enlistment, attempted to get a commission in September 1864. "You cannot imagine what I had had to hear on account of my being the only one of the family not in the service," he told his father, referring to the service of his three brothers. Indeed, Fessenden admitted that he had "not the face" to participate in the political campaign because he had not served in the war. With a new call for troops, however, he hoped to "benefit the city by raising her quota and . . . set my own mind at ease and put me on good terms with myself."[29]

Late in the war, the ideological motives that pressed the New Brahmins into army service persisted as the men, now veterans, renewed their commitments to the Union cause. The ideological and patriotic commitments of the conflict's early months might have ebbed, but those same sentiments survived well into the war. In August 1863 William Wheeler wrote his mother that he held his life no dearer than any other's as long as the Union won. The war, he explained, had "become the religion of very many of our lives, and those of us who think, and who did not enter the service for gain or military distinction, have come more and more to identify this cause for which we are fighting, with all of good and religion in our previous lives, and so it must be if we are to win the victory." Before the opening of the 1864 Overland Campaign, James C. Rice told his mother that he trusted "that God may again spare my life, as he has in the past," but reminded her that, "one cannot fall too early, if, loving Christ, he dies for his country." In April 1864 Oliver Wendell Holmes, Jr., still referred to the war as "the Christian Crusade of the 19th century." "If one didn't believe that this was such a crusade, in the cause of the whole civilized world," he continued, "it would be hard indeed to keep the hand to the sword."[30]

Debating Duty

Although the New Brahmins believed volunteering consistent with their duty, their parents had a different opinion. This disagreement led to a generational debate about the responsibilities of the leadership class in a time of war. Older professionals argued that college-educated men should aid the Union war effort on the home front. The New Brahmins, however, believed that they could best serve their country on the battlefield, literally leading other northerners into the fray. The older and younger members of the leadership class, therefore, had different conceptions of service. Parents who objected to their sons serving did not wish to see their children returned in caskets. They also embraced the classist viewpoint whereby the nation's laborers risked their lives while the professionals performed essential duties more suited to their elevated status. The older professional class certainly believed that they needed to sacrifice for the war effort, but their notion of service did not include sacrificing their sons on the field of battle. New Brahmins' sense of character and masculine ideals, however, pushed them into the armed forces. Parental protestations may have prevented some from volunteering, but the ongoing conflict made remaining on the home front increasingly uncomfortable. Many young men who had been taught to listen to their consciences disregarded their parents' wishes and demonstrated their character by volunteering despite opposition.

New Brahmins did not believe that their societal position should prevent them from serving their country. On the contrary, they pointed out that their education and civilian training had actually prepared them to become officers. They, as civilian leaders, could transfer their leadership qualities to a military environment. A good officer, according to Frazar A. Stearns, possessed "besides courage, intelligence, energy, good breeding, and a certain knack and power in commanding men." Despite pleas by family members and friends, these men had no intention of hiding behind their education and class position. They maintained their independent beliefs when resisting their loved ones' objections. Indeed, many thought that their positions, rather than exempting them from service, made their participation even more vital. "The only ground on which I could have stood aside two years ago," Thomas H. Hubbard remembered in 1865, "was the very Egotistical reason that I, a mere lawyer's clerk, was more useful in civil life than the many good and brave men who were soldiers."[31]

In some instances, strong objections by parents temporarily prevented New Brahmins from volunteering. Benjamin W. Crowninshield, who would eventually enter the army, had to turn down Paul J. Revere's offer of a captaincy in his regiment, explaining, "My own wishes about active military life and those of my family do not agree. All my efforts to get away have proved vain." "So long as I am not *needed*," he continued, "I suppose I must consider that I am doing my duty by remaining at home." Some parents urged patience, believing that their sons would soon think twice about joining the army. Immediately after hearing of the Union defeat at the First Battle of Bull Run, Charles P. Bowditch scribbled a rushed note to his father, pleading for his permission to enlist. "We have been defeated most abominably, and must retrieve our fortune," he explained. "The feeling which induces you to go to the war is natural and proper," his father responded, continuing, "and if I thought your services were required by your country I would not hesitate. Under the bitter accounts received of the battle of Bull's Run, I don't wonder at your excitement." He did not, however, "perceive any necessity" at the present time and promised that when "the time comes for your fighting, and come it may, I will cheerfully give my consent." Jonathan I. Bowditch instead urged his son to pay attention to his studies, "so if you should be called into service you may be able to take the position your knowledge may entitle you to." If Charles entered the Union army, his father wanted to assure him an officers' commission commensurate with his college education.[32]

Bowditch deferred to his father's wishes and stayed in school in 1861 but remained determined to enlist a year later. "I think no one will deny that it is the duty of every one, who is not held back by duties or ties which he cannot break, to volunteer and set an example for others to follow," he wrote his father in August 1862, continuing, "Now here I am, of no earthly use in my present position, and having completed with the exception of one year, my whole college course." He viewed volunteering as a man's duty and wondered "why is it not mine as much as other people's? I have nobody to depend upon me and am not in a position to bring misery on any one by going. What can be more clearly my duty than to go?" "If you are not willing to send your sons," he asked, "why should others be willing to send theirs?"[33]

One day later, Bowditch cited President Lincoln's call for three hundred thousand men and argued that he might have a chance at a commission if he volunteered. When his father told him that he was too frail for campaign life, Bowditch retorted, "Look at the number of young men who have gone much younger in years and without half the strength of constitution that I have, and see how they have borne the fatigues and exposures." He cited the example of Oliver Wendell Holmes, Jr., who, Bowditch claimed, "has not half the stamina that I have and he has been sick but once, and then got over it in a short time." He ended this letter on a similar note: "You seem to think that it is a very great sacrifice to let both your sons go off, and so it may be; but think how much greater sacrifice it is for those parents who send an only child to the wars. You have all the children to stay with you and why should you not be willing to send those who can be of so much use elsewhere?"[34] In response to the argument that the draft exempted students, Bowditch replied, "How much more proper is it that I should volunteer then, instead of retreating behind the fact of my being exempt! It seems to me a pitiful way of acting." The letters between Bowditch and his parents became even more contentious after this exchange. There was no use in continuing to discuss the topic of enlistment, he wrote his mother, "as you and Father have fully made up your minds to keep me at home, so I will only say as I have said heretofore that I think you both show a lack of patriotism."[35] The eager Bowditch eventually prevailed and served in the war.

Other New Brahmins experienced similar exasperation in trying to procure their parents' consent. Charles Francis Adams, Jr., told his father that he felt ashamed "at home when so many of my friends have already gone, and gone in such a war." When he sailed for London to take up his post as the new ambassador to the Court of St. James, Charles Francis Adams, Sr., left the family's affairs in young Charles's hands. The elder Adams had "an earnest wish" that his sons would "keep out" of the military contest. "I confess," he wrote, "my aversion to see any of my blood either a victor or a victim in this fratricidal strife." But the embarrassment of staying on the sidelines and the urge to serve in the war eventually got the better of Charles, Jr. How could he sit idly by in a national crisis when his father, grandfather, and great-grandfather before him had all served the country in trying times? Despite his father's objections, Adams eventually joined the 1st Massachusetts Cavalry Regiment. In July 1861 Henry L. Abbott wrote to his mother explaining his decision to volunteer after he had accepted a commission in the 20th Massachusetts Regiment, nicknamed the "Harvard Regiment" for all the college men who served in it. "I came to the conclusion," he explained, "that it was the thing I ought to do, that nothing could possibly be so good for me in the way of experience of going in the army." Elaborating on his justifications, he told her, "Every day I had to go through things that you don't know of. . . . I felt that I had never done any thing or amounted to any thing in the whole course of my existence." He had become "disgusted with being nothing & doing nothing" and thus volunteered. Abbott then appealed to his mother's own sense of character, saying that he knew she "wouldn't, like a great many weak women without character, feel any useless regrets about it."[36]

Debates about service led to prolonged conversations about the proper duty of educated professionals in wartime. Upon learning that his son, John, Jr., was thinking about volunteering, former Maine governor John Hubbard wrote to dissuade the Bowdoin graduate. He warned that joining the army would "not prove an advantageous step for your future prospects in life." Although the contest was "now a question of life or death to our institutions of government, or no government, of order or anarchy," he had misgivings about allowing his flesh and blood to serve. Eventually, however, he consented to John's service. Thomas, John's brother, expressed interest in volunteering after his brother enlisted. Faced with losing both his sons, John, Sr., tried to dissuade Thomas. He made the case that "there are other ways than that of bearing arms, other means than going to the field of battle and of slaughtering and death, in which a man may quite as efficiently and usefully render his aid in discharge of his whole duty." He drew on the Revolutionary War as an example, pointing out that the "Franklins and Jeffersons, and Wythes" provided "aid and council in her . . . struggles," while the "Madisons and Jays" laid "the foundations of our constitution." All these men served as civilians and contributed to the cause. Every man, he continued was "fitted for usefulness in his proper sphere of action," and "in my judgment, you have capabilities and qualifications, which, in the ordinary course of Providence, will, with such efforts as you will make, insure to you a *high* position of usefulness and distinction in civil life." He did not think that Tom's "tastes" would "incline" him to military service.[37]

New Brahmins pushed back against parents whom they accused of viewing the conflict as a "rich man's war but a poor man's fight." Instead of seeing their service in the war as a risk to their morals, they took it as an opportunity to elevate other men by their example. When his father argued that the Union could call on plenty of lesser men to fight its battles, Christopher Pennell rejected the notion that volunteers "can be had in plenty from among a class which will not be missed, whose lives are not worth so much as yours or mine." Even the "poor boys" of the 6th Massachusetts, who had been "murdered at Baltimore" as they marched to the relief of Washington, D.C., in April 1861, he argued, "left families. Do not say they are not missed." "When our soldiers, be they Irish, Dutch or Yankee, shall be mown before the enemies' cannon in ranks, even though they come from the very humblest classes," he asked, "shall not the wail of the widow the orphan & the *childless* go up for them as piteously as for the dead of the proud & petted Seventh Regiment?" "Do not say they will not be missed, that their lives are worth nothing," he insisted.[38]

Not all parents prevented their sons from enlisting in the war. Abolitionists enthusiastically supported their children, hoping that they would have a hand in purging the nation of slavery. The Shaw family, for example, committed itself to the war effort and expressed particular satisfaction when Robert took command of the first black regiment raised in the North. Olivia Bowditch reminded her son Nathaniel in 1862, "*Be brave* my boy; *bear all with courage, and consider that the greater the suffering you have to bear, either mental or physical*, the more your native country will be proud of you as one of her true sons." Olivia expressed her pride at her son's labors by noting her desire "to cheer you on and encourage you in your noble calling & trust that the people of the North, who are not personally engaged in the war, will so fully appreciate the sacrifices that so many thousands of their fellow countrymen are making that they will ponder long before they yield one iota or make a shadow of a compromise." Later, she encouraged him to "keep up a good heart" and to "come home when all is over & peace is proclaimed or Victory shouted feeling proud that you have been able to add your might to the great cause." A time of trial, she reminded him, was "good for us, it elevates & ennobles our character." Nathaniel's father, Henry, also supported his son's service, writing, "I can not tell you what a pride I have in your corps." "I felt proud of your having offered yourself to your country and also your willingness to submit to trial . . . for the sacred cause," he wrote. Henry urged his son to think of "the essential nobleness of this struggle for freedom" and remember "to act well and . . . cheerily . . . in behalf of your country."[39]

The debates about an educated man's duty in a time of war reveal a generational conflict. Older professionals knew that a college education guaranteed their children entrance into the middle and upper classes. Their sons, therefore, ought not to have to risk their lives in the war like common laborers. However, the young men who had been taught about proper character took their social responsibilities very seriously and rejected their parents' interpretation. In times of peace, professional young men did not object to separating themselves from laborers and their mundane tasks. In wartime, however, they believed that they had a duty as society's leaders to guide their fellow citizens. The sons had learned the lessons of character too well and, in time of crisis, stepped forward to perform their duty despite their parents' objections.

To Serve as Gentlemen

The New Brahmins volunteered more than their physical bodies for the Union cause. They offered, they believed, their superior character, education, and leadership abilities. These gentlemen volunteers, therefore, did not intend to merely be used as cannon fodder. For their services in whipping the masses into shape through superior example and discipline, they demanded military rank commensurate with their civilian class status. Most educated individuals entered the military as commissioned officers, allowing them to transfer their peacetime social positions to the armed forces.

Both the Brahmins and their parents demanded that state and military authorities honor their middle- and upper-class status with military commissions.[40] When John Hubbard, Sr., finally allowed his son Thomas to volunteer, he despaired that his child would enlist and serve as a private, "subject to the order of any *upstart* officer, set up as a mark to be shot at, and to die unheeded, unknown without the chance even of distinction." Hubbard preferred to have his son "go into this war, in some position suited to his capacity and merits, from which should he survive the contest, there would be a probability of his reaping some advantages in his future course of life," adding that "the idea of his going into the crowd to be mixed up with rabble, without identification[,] is to me absolutely intolerable." Writing to John, Jr., who had already joined the army, John, Sr., noted, "If you are to continue in it I want you both [John, Jr., and Thomas] at least to be in such positions as shall enable you to bring into requisition all the capacities you have arising from natural talent, education, and energy." He wished his sons would have rank so that their "efforts may stand a chance of being useful to the country beyond that of being merely one of the crowd to fill a space for a mark to aim at."[41]

For the most part, New Brahmins made obtaining a commission a condition of their service. Thomas H. Hubbard, working as an attorney in New York City when the war began, declared that he did not have "the remotest design of enlisting as a private." Such a step, he commented, "is asking too much of patriotism." He reiterated this sentiment a few months later, writing, "I intend to play 'sojer' by the fall if possible, though I shall not in any event *volunteer* in the ranks." Having observed that "many of my juniors and inferiors have commissions," he saw "no reason why I should give up everything for nothing." New Brahmins maintained that gentlemen had no place marching in the ranks. "I do think a man must be very patriotic or a very great fool to enlist in the army," John C. Gray wrote. Those who served as privates, he surmised, probably led "a dog's life at home." After several failures to gain a commission, George Whittemore wrote, "I have come to the conclusion that a man of ability and education is not only under no obligation to go into the ranks as a private, but that he ought not to. He thereby puts it out of his power to use his advantages. He has no opportunity to do any good proportioned to his ability."[42]

Ambitious New Brahmins viewed wartime as an opportunity to elevate their social position, in both a military and a civilian sense. Whereas a young man might take years to build his reputation in peacetime, the war offered a chance for them to gain fame swiftly. Military rank served as an indicator of a man's success. While imprisoned in Richmond, George Kenniston, a Bowdoin graduate, learned that many of his friends had moved quickly up the ranks. "All my friends are getting promotions and honors and I am caged up here wholly inactive and useless week after week both to myself and to others," he wrote in his diary. "It is too bad. Damnation." He was, he admitted, "never ... more wrought up by news in my life." William T. Lusk complained that he had "been in the service so long, and so long in the same place," that he was "fairly ashamed to visit old friends, all of whom hold comparatively high rank." Later, Lusk acknowledged his shame when he saw his colleagues promoted ahead of him. "I could not bear the thought of their recognizing me less honored than themselves," he told his mother. John B. Noyes, who enlisted as a private early in the war, lamented his position after noticing that his Harvard class was "rapidly enlisting" with "one Lieut. Col., one Major, besides other officers," in the service. He urged his brother to "make a dash, and see if you can't get me a commission in one of the new regiments" being formed in Massachusetts. The fact that "about twenty of my classmates are at the seat of war, but all as officers," may have influenced Noyes's urgent plea. Frustrated, Noyes complained to his father: "It seems hard that those who first volunteered in the service of the flag in an humble position should be debarred from rising higher while [those] who come after them reap easily the honors which open to them had they been more careful of their own interest." Exasperated, he insisted that "rather than not fight at all," he was "ready to finish as I began a year ago last May, indeed last March, an humble private in our splendid army & if I am to die out here by sickness, or the bullet, I am content to have it said that I fell doing the duty I was ordered to do in the hope that my country might once more become a united nation."[43] Noyes would eventually receive the promotions he desired, rising rapidly in the latter half of the war to the rank of colonel.

For all their patriotic rhetoric and proclamations of duty, New Brahmins also looked toward their own future. Some combined nobler ideas with thoughts about postwar benefits. They accumulated rank in a conscious effort to better their reputations as society's leaders. In the same way that they substituted social class for rank, military laurels and promotions could enhance a person's social position. They understood that a war record would add to their stature and authority in the postwar world. Before he volunteered, Thomas H. Hubbard explained to his mother that "the men who shall have helped against this controversy in armor, will justly have the preference in Counsel, when they reassume the toga: that they who have done the work, will claim the rewards." Although he admitted that "certain men may do their duty as good citizens and patriots, peacefully even in war," these were "men of ripe age and influence." He himself saw a contrast between "what I might do as a 'Sojer,' and what I am doing now. For in the former capacity I could give at least physical labor, and direct assistance; but in my present condition [as a civilian], absolutely nothing." After he volunteered and served with distinction in the war, Bowdoin graduate Thomas W. Hyde's ambition grew. After the Battle of Antietam, he boasted that if only the war would last two more years, "I am coming back to you a Brig. Gen."[44] In the end, he kept his promise.

Once in the service of the armed forces, most New Brahmins expressed their determination to see the job through. A combination of duty, camaraderie, and personal ambition motivated them to stay at their posts. "I shall not, unless I change my mind, go home, until the unhappy cause that alone called me out here has been removed," Charles P. Chandler declared. "This war, and the duties of the field are not my normal state I am sure," wrote Franklin A. Haskell, "but I never shall leave it until the war is over." Theodore J. Holmes, who served as a chaplain, noted that he might resign at any time, but "the reason would have to be such as would satisfy others as well as myself, or it would be impossible to secure an honorable release." Without a "sufficient excuse," he declared, "I should never wish to leave." Oliver Wendell Holmes, Jr., took offense when his father misinterpreted a letter and his intentions about his army career. Denying that he had any plans to leave the service "before the campaign was over," the younger Holmes wrote, "I must say I dislike such a misunderstanding, so discreditable to my feeling of soldierly honor, when I don't believe there was a necessity for it." Sen. William Pitt Fessenden urged his son James to resign his commission a few months after he had lost his youngest child, Samuel, on the field of Second Bull Run. James responded, "I am always sorry when I cannot follow your advice and wishes, but I cannot think of resigning." He reasoned that "thousands of men whose wives and children are dependent upon their daily wages for their bread, have gone into the ranks where there is no resigning." In addition, Fessenden did not believe "that my family imperatively needs me at home and," perhaps more important, "I do not wish to resign for personal advantages." These "personal advantages" included his "experience of the last two years," which had "rendered my services valuable." Resigning now, he implied, would jeopardize his chances at future promotions.[45]

Joshua L. Chamberlain also hoped for military promotion, rejecting prompts from his family to resign his commission and return to civilian life. In February 1865, he told his father that he could accept a position as collector of customs in Maine. Although he described it as "a very good position," he did not "at present encourage the idea, preferring, if possible, to continue my duties in the Field, where my services were never more needed, or more valuable than now." Instead of leaving the army, he considered resigning from his professorship at Bowdoin College. Chamberlain hoped to "either remain in the military service (as is most congenial to my temperament) or strike into some other enterprise of a more bold + stirring character than a College chair affords." His attitude epitomized that of a man who had been energized by the military lifestyle. The life of a college professor appeared dull in comparison to active duty and military adventure. In a follow-up letter to his parents, Chamberlain defended his decision to turn down the civilian position. There was "no promise of life in peace, + no decree of death in war," he reasoned, explaining that he owed "the Country three years service" at "a time when every man should stand by his guns." Chamberlain also noted that his "prospects in the Army were never better." He stood "among the senior officers of my rank" and, after all he had endured, was "not willing to back out just at the decisive moment, + leave the rewards + honors of my toil + sufferings to others." "I would rather see another man in the Custom House," he concluded, "than see another next commander of the 1st Division."[46]

Although discussions about rank seeking may make the New Brahmins appear callous and opportunistic, they did continue to serve with distinction. By rejecting plans to return home after their terms expired, they continued to demonstrate independent thought, choosing the path of risk over that of ease. They maintained their character by remaining selflessly attached to their duty. Again, their reasoning combined elements of nationalism with ideas about proper gentlemanly conduct and personal ambition. A man of character, after all, stood by his convictions until the end. The New Brahmins had volunteered because they wanted to see the Union preserved and victorious. They would not return until that goal had been achieved. Luther C. Howell found the "ceremonies and Regulations" of the army more "distasteful" with every passing day but remained in service because of a "strong sense of duty." Joshua L. Chamberlain admitted to his wife that he sacrificed a great deal by remaining in the army, but he did not wish to go back home, explaining, "I feel that I am where duty called me." Joseph H. Twichell admitted that he thought about his home more than usual but did not know what could "induce me to leave here now." "I wish," he told his father, "to witness the 'great day' which will blow the trumpet of Freedom for the oppressed, and proclaim to the world that the Republic is not a failure." George Clary declared that he had "no desire to get out of the service, however, till the war ends if my health is spared." Samuel E. Nichols remained motivated by "the same sense of duty which prompted me to enlist." Even sustained military setbacks could not shake the resolve of determined New Brahmins who echoed their college lessons and maintained that times of adversity tested a man's character. "Anything immediately comfortable in our affairs I don't see, but comfortable times are not the ones that make a people great," Charles Russell Lowell wrote.[47] Northern honor motivated young gentlemen to remain at their posts, where they continued to fight for the cause of the Union.

* * *

Declaring one a man of character was certainly easier than proving it, especially since character referred to an internal quality. The New Brahmins whose college educations had certified them as honorable men with the requisite traits of societal leadership longed (perhaps anxiously) for the opportunity to prove themselves worthy of their claims. The war gave them the opportunity to test just that. Having professed to cherish the Union and all it stood for, having proclaimed themselves willing servants who would stand up for righteous causes as dictated by their superior education, the New Brahmins felt compelled to demonstrate their sincerity and the depth of their character when President Lincoln summoned the nation to arms.

But the New Brahmins also had other options. As members of the professional class they did not need to volunteer in the war, as many of their parents reminded them. But what they had repeated and professed in college came bubbling up in their consciences, propelling them toward the battlefields. Even as they donned the blue uniform and prepared to risk their lives for the cause of the Union, however, they wished to maintain their societal positions, refusing to relinquish their class status. As such, they offered their education and certified character to the Union army in return for commissions. Now, clad with officers' bars, they led the men under their command into the South with their character guiding the way.

5

Marching into "Rebeldom"

The Failure of Southern Character

Samuel C. Armstrong announced his arrival on "the 'sacred soil' of South Carolina" to his mother. With 1,300 soldiers aboard the *United States*, Armstrong had sailed down "the dreaded Cape Hatteras" to "lay at anchor in the magnificent harbor at Hilton Head." Sitting in his tent, he heard a "strangely pleasant sound ... for the first time in more than three years. It is the long, unwearied moan of the sad sea." Armstrong had come a long way since he last listened to the waves. Having crossed the Pacific and the North American continent to reach Williams College in western Massachusetts, he had spent the early years of the war in the Eastern Theater, fighting at Harpers Ferry and Gettysburg. In March 1864, however, he found himself in South Carolina, once again mesmerized by the siren song of the sea. He elaborated: "I cannot tell you how it affects me—how welcome it is—how it binds me again to home, revives sacred recollections of home and brings to my memory those long evenings of unearthly sweetness which we used to spend on the front verandah, listening to the very sound I now hear after so long."[1]

Describing his camp near Port Royal, Armstrong declared the spot "beautiful!" A few days earlier, the location had been "a rough, dirty place" but, as he wrote, "it is covered with spotless white tents which open upon wide, well-graded and smooth streets; and between the tents are young pines transplanted, and along the officers' street are rows of pine boughs planted and there are a few trees besides throwing a grateful shade over the tents." The African American soldiers under his command had transformed "a dirty, rough place" into "a paradise of order and neatness." "I am happy tonight, almost perfectly happy," he reported, and his soldiers, too, seemed pleased, "singing a beautiful, rich negro melody to the words 'Jehovah has triumphed, His people are free.'" Here, African Americans in Union uniforms sat "on soil which for generations has been cursed with slavery—the richest, cotton-growing land in the South." Nearby, he noted that the "stately mansions" in Beaufort served as "hospitals for the very slaves whose masters not long since fled in terror from the same doors into which these sufferers have been carried."[2]

All around him, Armstrong saw efforts to set up a free labor system and remake southern society. Northerners had come to this secured area to teach freedmen and invest in the conquered South. He lamented, however, that "the poor freedmen of these Islands have been much abused by Northern speculators and have found that Liberty is no dream—many of them are no better off than before." Armstrong promised to combat these abuses: "I am doing my best to throw light upon the evil deeds and speculators and to help the people. I am in a position to do so."[3]

For Samuel C. Armstrong, the Civil War was a dramatic and surreal experience. Swept up by historic events upon his graduation from college, he found himself at the head of a black unit and witnessing firsthand the enormous changes to African Americans' lives. Implying that slaveholding secessionists had been justly driven from their homes, he also discovered some gentlemanly and honorable rebel officers in his southern travels. As he weighed the relationship between white and black southerners, this educated son of a missionary also pondered the prospects and problems of the future. As an abolitionist and commander of African American troops, he sympathized with the plight of freedmen, recognizing that they faced an unwelcoming postwar world. As a man who believed in white racial superiority, he nevertheless tried to find the best way to accommodate southerners of both races in a new society with sensitive racial boundaries. Armstrong, would, after the guns of war fell silent, be in a position to "help the people" in his own way again.

Marching into the South, New Brahmins encountered what they considered a rich land dotted with undersized towns and inhabited by ignorant people. They diagnosed the South as suffering from slavery's effects but, perhaps more important, they chastised southern gentlemen for failing to develop the region and setting good examples for other southerners to emulate. In a sense, they evaluated their southern counterparts through the lens of character and concluded that the degradation of the region as well as the war resulted from the failure of the South's leadership class. Selfish slaveholding men had denied education and developmental opportunities to their fellow whites, taking the South on a course inconsistent with the triumphal vision of American nationalism that northern gentlemen had articulated. The southern leaders' lack of character adversely affected the region's growth, preventing it from fully developing its potential.

Traveling through the South—for many, their first visit—New Brahmins treated southerners with pity. They viewed both black and white southerners as victims of slavery. Because southern leaders focused on upholding slavery, they denied a proper education to southern whites, suppressed industry, and instigated a rebellion against the federal government. New Brahmins considered everyday southerners as the victims of lies, and reasoned that they could not be fully committed to the Confederate cause. When it came to enslaved African Americans, however, they expressed racist sentiments, not uncommon among whites at the time. They worried about what role the freed people would play in the postwar South and doubted their capacity to assimilate into American society.

Union soldiers distinguished between the southerners that they encountered and their true enemies, the "secessionists." One young soldier blamed "the educated class of the South" for "all this trouble." "The poor unlettered masses" had merely served as "dupes and instruments" who could not "understand they are in reality fighting for the negro and not for themselves."[4] New Brahmins also made a distinction between southern men they faced on the battlefield and the unseen southern slaveholders whom they blamed for the conflict. Because southern men of honor met them on the battlefield, northern officers admired their courage and resolve. Although northern and southern honor may have prompted them to fight for different causes in different ways—southern honor through public shaming and northern character through one's conscience regardless of public/parental opposition—the demonstration of bravery united professional-class men. New Brahmins interpreted their southern counterparts' actions as a reflection of the code of conduct that motivated northerners without realizing the differences in southern and northern honor. Regardless of underlying motives, they saw southern men lining up to bravely and dramatically fight for what they believed. Instead of seeing the underlying fear attached to southern honor, they saw only the courage of their counterparts' convictions.

Both Civil War veterans and historians have disseminated the experiences of the almost two million Union soldiers who marched through the South during the conflict. As one early scholar has pointed out, northern soldiers' writings shed "valuable light both on the observers and the observed."[5] Despite their New England–centric interpretation of history, New Brahmins did not view the South as a foreign land alien to American culture because it included historical sites critical to the nation's founding. By incorporating former battlefields or the homes of historical figures as part of the nation's past, they asserted their national vision and claimed historic sites in the South as *American* ones. Such

The Failure of Southern Character

beliefs also explain their rejection of Confederate independence. The northern narrative of America, emanating from the pines of New England, swept through the southern colonies. In part, their insistence that historic sites in the South belonged to the United States affirmed the righteousness of their course. The Confederates, in this interpretation, purported an aberrant and illegitimate national vision.

While traveling through and writing about the South, northern soldiers also envisioned the region's future. According to one scholar, they believed "in the superiority of Northern civilization" and "thought that Southerners and the culture that had produced them were inferior." The Union soldier pointed to "signs of sloth—decaying houses, ill-tended fields, poverty," and subjugation of southerners, white and black, by the slaveholding aristocracy. Northern soldiers believed they were battling "an enemy that was un-American, somehow foreign—a savage enemy." Meanwhile, they viewed southern blacks as "exotic beings" who were "dirty, ignorant, superstitious, and lazy."[6] While New Brahmins agreed that they came from a superior part of the country, they did not view southerners as "un-American." Rather, they considered them victims of a corrupting power and poor leadership. New Brahmins believed that the wayward South could transform to match the North's success with the aid of Yankee industry and free soil ideas. These men's observations and views later influenced their actions during Reconstruction. Pitying poor southern whites who had been corrupted by slavery and misled by dishonorable leaders, and questioning African Americans' ability to live as independent farmers, they exhibited their paternalist attitude toward freed blacks and set the stage for postwar reconciliation with whites.

Although intriguing and rich in detail, northern soldiers' observations of southern society need to be considered in view of the writers' preconceived notions. For most individuals, such a comparison is not possible given the lack of sources. New Brahmin men who had articulated a free labor vision before the war and would serve as leaders in the postwar Union offer scholars an excellent opportunity to place observations of the South in proper historical context. These men's previous notions of civilization helped them analyze what they witnessed and also informed their thoughts on how best to reincorporate the South into the reunited Union.

The Land of Rebeldom

"What names they have here in the land of Rebeldom!" Joshua L. Chamberlain wrote to his wife from Snicker's Gap, Virginia.[7] A few months after arriving on

Confederate soil, Chamberlain continued to express fascination with the region that was attempting to break free of its Union bonds. As New Brahmins attempted to describe the South to their correspondents, they marveled at its beauty while also criticizing southerners for not better exploiting their region's natural resources. They concluded that the South needed a dose of northern industry in order to become a fully developed part of the nation.

Like other northern visitors, New Brahmins appeared captivated by the South's natural scenery. From the valleys of Virginia to the rivers and bayous of Mississippi, the South enchanted the northern visitors who sought to capture the grandeur and preserve their memories in words shared with loved ones. "We are encamped on a place which for natural beauties is one of the finest I have ever seen," Paul J. Revere wrote home from the York–James Peninsula. From the Mississippi River, George Clary described the "magnificent" scene, especially "the luxuriant foliage, magnolia trees in full bloom, orange groves, pride of the Indias." "The Creator," he declared, "has lavished the people with wealth. Earth rains its treasures into the laps of these feudal provinces most bountifully." John Marshall Brown wrote his sister about "the most charming valley you ever saw between the Blue Ridge & the Ketocktan hills" south of Harpers Ferry. William T. Lusk described Hilton Head, South Carolina, as "beautiful with palmetto leaves, cotton fields, magnolia and orange groves, and plantations of sugar cane." Theodore J. Holmes wrote of a "glorious sunrise" as his unit camped on the "outskirts of Staunton [Virginia] a very pretty little city nestled cozily among the hills." Thomas H. Hubbard wrote his mother from Martinsburg, Virginia, calling the countryside "superb, more pleasing to me than any I have yet seen." William Wheeler commented on "the fresh, young, bride-like earth, dressed in the robe of this loveliest of seasons." He sometimes found it difficult to realize "that anything is awry or at war here in this beautiful valley where all is so green and fair and bright." Campaigning in "a superb region," Wheeler noted, "beautiful deep valleys, full of orchards, and farmhouses, and fields of grain; and on the higher slopes are countless blackberry pastures, just like those in which my soul used to delight among the Catskills."[8]

Despite the richness of their region's soil and the bounty of its forests and rivers, southerners had not fully made use of their resources. In fact, natural resources alone, without industry and development, signaled negative qualities about the inhabitants of a land. New Brahmins criticized southerners for failing to cultivate their resources in the same way that they censured Native Americans. Charles P. Chandler blamed slavery, arguing that enslaved laborers had no incentive to make full use of the land. "You have no idea of this country, and the people and the 'darkies,'" he wrote in December 1861. "I hate the very *idea* of the system of Slavery. It is degrading, wicked, contemptible. Thank Heaven I was educated in happy New England, where ignorance is *not* bliss." Although they had favorable climate and land, the "ignorant, stupid, lazy, contemptibly mean" residents had not made the most of their circumstances. "Fifty good Yankees with farms here," he predicted, "would frighten the citizens." Charles Francis Adams, Jr., found that Virginia possessed "in natural attributes more that would belong to an earthly Eden than any region I ever set foot in." "The climate," he wrote, "is wonderfully fine, the soil naturally fertile, the rivers are beautiful to a degree, the mountains fine and the valleys almost perfection." Once the war had "effectually destroyed a pernicious system of labor," he predicted, a Yankee model of free labor would take over. Virginia might even some day "be as prosperous as New England, and, if it ever is, it will be a land of milk and honey." William Wheeler thought that Yankee industry and ingenuity might help the residents of northern Alabama. He sarcastically recorded that "under the hand of Southern enterprise" the town of Bridgeport had "grown to a place of *four* houses" despite being "at the junction of two great railroads, on a most noble river, the centre of a region rich in coal, and iron, and saltpetre, and marble, and corn-lands."[9]

New Brahmins criticized the sophistication and habits of southerners in several ways. One common tactic involved describing the poor upkeep of southern structures with the implicit criticism that northerners better maintained their buildings. Stephen M. Weld, campaigning in Virginia, described a house, "one of the best in this town, being built of brick and being two and a half stories in height," which served as the headquarters for Gen. Fitz-John Porter. Despite its stately appearance, the house possessed "the true Southern look about it, viz., the air of neglect, of something wanting to complete the estate, as if the owner had begun with the idea of making a fine place and had been stopped short for want of funds." Furthermore, the southern owners had employed "the most common" material "such as we see in our pastures" to construct the fences. Nathaniel Bowditch visited a "very large and fine" plantation house on Edisto Island but noted that it was "rather dilapidated and dirty as nobody has been in it with the exceptions of negroes for some time." The house had "two immense piazzas . . . both covered, and very handsome rooms inside." Like other southern homes, however, the rooms "all look very slovenly and all around the house looks in the same manner."[10]

Aside from their shoddy appearances, the feudal look of some southern homes demonstrated to New Brahmins that slavery had indeed corrupted southern culture. Observing plantations along the Mississippi River, George Clary noticed the "little village of negro huts, many of them neatly painted," clustered around "the large sugar houses." The "mansion of the manor" stood "fronting the river, with its broad acres of sugar cane extending for a mile or two in the rear." Such scenes "told of a race of proud princes—the Feudal System of the Rebellion." At a nearby plantation he saw the "mansion of the Nabob fronting close upon the river" surrounded by blooming magnolias and "vast fields of sugar cane." The scene, he wrote, remained "unsurpassed for its luxuriance by anything that I have seen." "No wonder the lords of the manor fancied themselves the lords of creation," Clary quipped. "But how are the mighty fallen!" "I love to hear them wail over their departed blacks," he wrote on another occasion, admitting that he felt "a satisfaction, after so many years of enduring their haughty overbearing manner, in seeing them at length obliged to own up to their weakness and to be compelled to ask favor from Yankees."[11]

Accustomed to larger and more advanced urban areas, New Brahmins criticized inferior southern towns. William T. Lusk witnessed soldiers ransacking homes in Germantown, Virginia, and commented that it was such "a poor place" that "$200 would probably cover any damage done to it." John B. Noyes described Williamsport, Maryland, as "this decayed village of 3 hotels." Stephen M. Weld reported that one such town he came across had its courthouse—"an old-fashioned brick building with a portico in front"—situated on the main turnpike. This collection of buildings, Weld remarked, would be called "a small village in Massachusetts, but here it is quite a city in the estimation of the F.F.V.'s [First Families of Virginia]." Theodore J. Holmes remarked that the "chief vestige of civilization" in a Virginia town that he was visiting was "a tailor's shop." A few months later Holmes wrote that he had "just passed through the town of Smithfield, an old dilapidated place like most of the southern villages we have seen." He called the system of public roads, something taken for granted in the northern states, the "one prominent mark of civilization in Virginia."[12] Criticisms of southern towns implicitly indicted the South's leadership class but also affirmed northerners' beliefs in their superior civilization.

Despite their northern biases, these men could not deny that the South had contributed to America's past. Campaigning near historic sites reminded them that the South remained inseparable from the rest of the nation. By their celebration of historic locations, these men rejected the notion that they fought in a foreign land and reinforced their commitment to preserve the entire Union. Landing on the "vile and 'Sacred soil'" of Virginia, Charles P. Chandler declared it "a heaven forsaken place." Soon afterward, however, he found himself outside

Yorktown during the Peninsula Campaign. He immediately pointed to a local building where the British had surrendered to George Washington during the Revolutionary War. "Strange," Chandler mused, "that we of this generation must attack the same place that Washington did. Could he but see us now! Heaven grant that we may gain a similar result!—and may it end the war, as it then did!" Later, he noted the historic importance of Williamsburg, where his unit camped. There, Washington had served as "a member of the House of Delegates" and "Patrick Henry made those speeches that stirred up the Revolution." As he reflected on the historic sites he had seen, Chandler had to admit, "It seemed a sacred place even in this country. Such soil of Virginia is indeed 'sacred soil.'" Uriah N. Parmelee, also campaigning in Virginia, camped opposite from "the old antiquated brick church in which Washington was married." Describing the sunset from this historic location, Parmelee mused, "Perhaps Washington once took a stroll out here when he was 'young and patriotic' and saw the same old sun set. Perhaps sat down by this brook near which I write." Camped near Charleston, Tennessee, Charles H. Howard recorded that the area "was until 1838 the land of the Cherokees." He claimed that John Ross, the principal chief of the Cherokee Nation, "once lived . . . at the house we first occupied there," while Gen. Winfield Scott, former general-in-chief of the army, "had his Head quarters . . . upon the very spot where stands this house in which I am writing."[13]

Even events in recent history stirred young men's imagination. Because it was the site of John Brown's dramatic raid, the New Brahmins expressed great interest in the town of Harpers Ferry. Some of the officers in Charles F. Morse's unit, while sifting through the papers of a Confederate official, a man "employed by the Government in the John Brown case," discovered "some very interesting documents; such as a letter from Governor Wise to Mr. Hunter before the trial came on, saying that he had made up his mind not to pardon John Brown or any of his accomplices, but that every one should suffer death." About sixty men in William Wheeler's unit "took up their abode in the Court-house where 'Old John Brown' was tried and condemned." Recognizing the significance of the room, the men "immediately constituted a court, and proceeded to reenact the scenes of November, 1859." "Whether we shall see the ghost of John Brown I cannot say," Charles P. Mattocks commented in his journal as the 17th Maine crossed the Potomac near Harpers Ferry during the Gettysburg Campaign. A few weeks later, Mattocks's company camped near "where John Brown frightened the good people out of their wits some time since." John B. Noyes, crossing into Harpers Ferry in 1863, thought that John Brown's famous arsenal "aptly typifies the structure of American Slavery." "At the close of the war," he mused, "the miserable gun barrels will be removed, so also the still remaining husks of slavery, and the slave power."[14]

The war itself created new sites of interest. Joshua L. Chamberlain thought the Antietam battlefield so peaceful he wished that his wife could be by his side. The two of them might "mount to the summit of one of those blue hills, whence you can see forty miles into Virginia—see the long lines of rebel fires fifteen or twenty miles away & villages & streams & bright patches of cultivated fields—& on our own side the great battle field of Antietam—the hills trodden bare & the fields all reined with the tracks of artillery trains, or movements of army corps."[15] The armies, while fighting the war, created new sites of nationalism for the embattled republic.

The People of Rebeldom

New Brahmins encountered many groups of southerners—upper class, poor whites, rebel soldiers, and free and enslaved African Americans—as they marched into the Confederacy. Each encounter confirmed their beliefs that exploitive slaveholding politicians had drawn impoverished, ignorant southerners into a war that they could neither understand nor afford. New Brahmins also blamed their southern counterparts for failing to elevate fellow southerners. Even as they condemned the haughty southern gentlemen, however, these young men wondered how individuals so similar to them in many ways could become so deluded and corrupted. Slavery and a misunderstanding of American history, they reasoned, must have perverted southern gentlemen's beliefs. The enemy, since they were men of the New Brahmins' own social class, never seemed too foreign.

New Brahmins made a distinction between different groups of southerners. They blamed politicians and aristocrats for leading the region down the path of ruin. Additionally, they viewed the men most resembling them in age and status—the young southern professionals that some of them had met and befriended in college—as foolishly following southern leaders and misunderstanding the true nature of America's free labor mission. They accepted that their southern counterparts earnestly believed in the cause of Confederate independence. Those *real* gentlemen of the South fought because they believed it was their duty to do so. Even though they fought for an unjust cause, they had noble motives. Southern professionals, therefore, never seemed like the actual enemy. "It is one of the painful facts of the rebellion," James A. Garfield wrote his wife from Kentucky, "that nearly all the most cultivated and enlightened people in this country, at least, are on the side of the rebellion." He surmised that anti-Union sentiment grew "out of the fact that leaders of the rebellion were the aristocrats of the South, and they have led off that element with them."[16] As he saw it, the "most cultivated and enlightened" members of southern society had failed to see the foolishness of their ways. Instead of using their cultivation and enlightenment to promote Unionist sentiments and criticize secession, they had failed the test of individualism and marched to a war instigated by corrupt politicians.

The New Brahmins accused haughty aristocratic slaveholders of bringing on the war. Furthermore, they resented decades of criticism from upper-class southerners. When they marched into the South, these men thought they might have an opportunity to humble the arrogant aristocrats. Landing at Hilton Head in South Carolina, William T. Lusk declared that "we vile Yankee hordes are overrunning the pleasant islands about Beaufort, rioting upon sweet potatoes and Southern sunshine." "Here," he continued, "lived the Pinckneys, the Draytons, and other high-blooded Hidalgos, whose effervescing exuberance of gentlemanly spirit have done so much to cause our present troubles." In a mocking tone, he declared, "Yankee hordes, ruthless invaders—the vile Hessians—infest their splendid plantations." Caspar Crowninshield declared the ruin of wealthy southerners' homes a "just retribution for their insolent pride and arrogant spirit."[17]

Despite their disgust at wealthy southerners, New Brahmins found the process of intruding on the private property belonging to their own professional counterparts an unpleasant and surreal experience. It made them ponder where southern professionals, so similar to themselves, had gone wrong. Exploring Beaufort, South Carolina, together, Charles Francis Adams, Jr., and Caspar Crowninshield came upon "a new house on a beautiful island . . . surrounded with magnificent cotton fields, built evidently by a gentleman of refinement." Inside Adams found "broken furniture, scraps of books and letters, and all the little tokens of a refined family." He "wandered round and looked out at the view and wondered why this people had brought all this upon themselves; and yet I couldn't but pity them." The house reminded him of his family's own and he thought about how he would "feel to see such sights at Quincy." Crowninshield "felt a greater pity for the misguided gentlemen of the South than I should care to acknowledge." Upon entering the home of a local secessionist, Crowninshield reported being unable to "shake off a feeling of sympathy for the poor seceshers, as I look round and see their fine houses, and old family furniture, clocks, glasses, & everything else destroyed." He imagined the owner as "a fine fellow, with a pleasant family of, girls, lovely, and well educated, boys manly, frank, and hospitable." "What the devil am I doing here in their house?" he asked. "What am I fighting for? Is it in order that dirty illiterate New York politicians may rule the country, or Massachusetts abolitionists?" Feeling lost and upset by the scene, Crowninshield lashed out at the politicians who had brought on the conflict. He wished that "the *gentlemen* of the North & the *gentlemen* of the South" might "unite to take the government of the country into their own hands."[18] The nation's troubles had come about, he reasoned, because the most refined and selfless individuals had not managed affairs. Even as they waged war in the South, New Brahmins like Crowninshield cursed the men who had started the conflict and longed for a time when gentlemen might again lead society.

New Brahmins also blamed the South's leaders for the poor conditions under which southern whites lived. Instead of elevating their fellow southerners, the southern leaders had neglected and exploited them. As a result, poor white southerners displayed a lack of initiative and industry. Young southern men, Charles P. Chandler reported, "are not . . . energetic and able like northern men; they do not depend upon themselves; they are overbearing and supercilious." What, William Wheeler asked, "has the dominant class done for the poor white in their midst?" The powerful men of the South had "closed the doors of industry upon him, their own brother, thus keeping him poor; they have refused him education, thus keeping him ignorant; and they have encouraged him in all the vices that spring from idleness, thus ruining body, mind, and soul." This intentional neglect, Wheeler explained, had kept poor white southerners as tools for slaveholders' "political and, now, for their military purposes."[19]

Living in what northerners considered an underdeveloped region and lacking educational opportunities as well as ways to better themselves, poor whites seemed to have suffered the most from the southern leaders' neglect. Seemingly lacking in culture, manners, morale, and class, these men and women also demonstrated how slavery degraded whites as well as blacks. By writing about how association with enslaved blacks harmed white southerners, the New Brahmins revealed again their racial prejudices against African Americans. Charles P. Chandler observed, "Association with the negroes from early age has given to many of the people a sort of darkey accent to their language," which "is marked in the young men. Most all of them use certain words, and drop out certain sounds as the colored folk do." John Read described the "poor white" who lived along the Mississippi River as the "most despicable creature in these parts." These individuals, he recorded, lived "in these huts, you may say in a *wild state*— with no principle—slovenly, dirty, & disgusting. Away from all civilization in their dirty huts, they spend their lives in ignorance—emulous of no higher standard." Read observed, "One cannot but be struck with this difference between the N. & South viz.: the lack of energy manifested in the latter, as compared with the former." He concluded that the southern people's "narrow mindedness & general ignorance" could be attributed to "the degrading,— demoralizing influence of Human Slavery." Although "not a radical Abolitionist," Read thought the northern people, "with their Enlightenment," could not allow such "a Curse (as a Curse it is) as Slavery to exist in a country the laws of which they sanction." Read described the residents he encountered as *"semi-barbarians"* and "uneducated—dirty beings" who bore "no *comparison* to our northern working men." These individuals, he noted, had "vague ideas of *citizens rights* & talk of the *Constitution*, giving interpretations of many parts, which I fear would open the eyes of the *framers*," and "their *chief* topic is 'State Rights,' giving each state power to act as she chooses—secede if so desired, without consultation of the government." "It is *aggravating* indeed," Read admitted, "to hear these fellows in *this State*, for the most part of foreign descent—French, Germans & Irish talking of overthrowing American Institutions & despising the flag *that has fed them!*" These ignorant citizens, who preferred a "*'crowned head'* by far to the tyranny of Lincoln, whom they believe to be a *negro*," believed "the most *extravagant stories of Northern destitution!*"[20] Poor southerners' ignorance about the North and its intentions added weight to New Brahmins' criticism of poor regional leadership.

Believing that selfish politicians had brought on secession, New Brahmins viewed any southern dissatisfaction as a sign that common folk lacked a true commitment to the Confederate cause. They hoped that evidence of desertion signaled a southern rejection of their leadership. Such beliefs also delegitimized the rebel cause. John C. Gray, posted along the Virginia–Maryland border, observed Virginians crossing the Potomac in order to avoid conscription. From Union Mills, Virginia, Charles H. Howard observed that "many, many people are coming in for protection." One man, Howard recorded, "came in saying his family got no rest last night. He had a gold watch stolen from him & many other things. He was glad to take the Oath. . . . He cried like a child." James C. Rice wrote down his observations from near Yorktown, Virginia: "Aged men and women with tears streaming down their wrinkled cheeks looked upon the old Union flag again and thanked God." Old women displayed their affection for the Union men by clasping "our soldiers' hands in theirs with gladness, as tenderly as if we had been their children."[21]

In very rural areas, the lewd behavior of the civilians mirrored the poverty of the setting. William Wheeler, describing southern civilians he encountered daily, told his mother, "I am sure that you never saw such creatures in your life, so ragged, dirty, and woe-begone,—such spiritless faces, and drooping, slouching figures." These poor whites "are hardly worthy of being classed as Caucasians, but more nearly realize the idea of some intensely inferior race, the Papuans, or Australian Indians, or the Diggers." This was, he assured her, not the result of the war but "the normal condition of the 'poor white trash.'" "Nothing that I have ever heard or seen of the injustice and injury done by slavery to the blacks," Wheeler declared, "ever made my blood boil so with indignation, as this spectacle of white men, the same flesh and blood as ourselves, offshoots, perhaps, of the same families that dispense such elegant hospitality in Virginia and South Carolina." He expressed outrage at seeing whites "brought lower than the slave" and considered both groups victims of a system that denied "them the power of acquiring worldly prosperity, and at the same time, causing mind and body to rust in miserable inaction." Under such conditions, the enslaved black "who works, thus becomes the physical and mental superior of the white who does not, and the slave-holders have little or nothing to fear from their degraded white brethren."[22] Such scenes proved to New Brahmins that both slavery and neglect stunted the potential of white southerners.

Even as they observed and diagnosed the South's problems, New Brahmins also prescribed solutions to set the region back on the right path. What the South needed most was a good education system. Writing from the Maryland–Virginia border in October 1861, William D. Sedgwick observed, "The number of people about here . . . who can't read, is really astounding." One man told him that "they never had a chance to 'get learning,'—that there were no free schools, and they could not afford to send their children to any others." This "sacred soil," he concluded, had been "desecrated by the barbarous influences of this damnable institution." William Wheeler, while stationed in Lookout Valley, near Chattanooga, Tennessee, admitted that he "felt the deepest pity for the miserable condition of the poor whites of the South." He thought that "in the aggregate, the condition of the negro has been improved, and his moral and intellectual faculties developed, by his connection with the white man." But slavery may have left a more damaging mark on poor whites. Northern education, he hoped, would help the South's unfortunate citizens. In spring 1864, Charles H. Howard reported on how army-built schools helped to educate the people of Lookout Valley. He helped teach in a Sabbath school "held at the Chapel tent of the Christian Commission" and had "a class of little girls from 8 to 12 years old." All the children were illiterate: "They do not even know the letters. . . . They are totally ignorant of God and all the instructions of the Bible."[23]

New Brahmins did not find all their duties quite as rewarding. They discovered that some military tasks challenged their self-conception as gentlemen. Conflicted by orders to invade private property, New Brahmins had no choice but to perform their duty. William Wheeler could not help but feel "that we were invaders, laying waste a fair and blooming country, and that our opponents were men fighting to save their firesides and their homesteads." "It is by no means agreeable," he admitted, "to deprive farmers of their grain and hay, and to carry off favorite horses amid the tears and supplications of the women folk; and you can yourself imagine how hard it was when we came back from Cross Keys, to see in Harrisonburg and New Market the women dressed in black and weeping as if their hearts would break." He could not help "mentally transferring the whole trouble to the Northern country, and thinking" about how he would feel "if the 'Louisiana Tigers,' or some such notorious corps, should have a chance to march through Connecticut." He had to remind himself that the war's successful termination and the Union's ultimate victory would "bring for us 'a more exceeding weight of glory,' in a preserved Constitution and established laws." "Our duties are those of scouts, and a more wicked duty as practiced by large bodies can hardly be imagined," a disgusted Charles P. Chandler wrote to his mother, admitting that "thinning, stealing, hooking, and taking what is not ours seems to be our ruling motive with the men." He asked his mother to imagine "seven hundred hungry, tired men entering a little mean village, one fifth the size of your own Foxcroft [Maine], with the idea that all the inhabitants are enemies and you easily understand the fear the people must be in even if the officers do their best." Chandler ultimately could not bear the guilt and quit the assignment after telling his colonel, "I was not brought up a villain."[24]

Not all men could easily quit assignments given to them by their superiors. New Brahmins might have soon realized after joining the military that they needed to check their individualism. And most willingly did so, thinking of the greater cause for which they labored. While they liked that military discipline allowed them to give orders to subordinates (a subject explained in the next chapter), they did not always agree with orders that came down to them from men of higher rank. Some traits of character, therefore, could not survive in the military environment.

Under certain circumstances, however, New Brahmins could not conceal their pleasure at punishing secessionists by confiscating their goods. They distinguished between secessionist supporters, whom they did not respect, and other southern civilians, whom they did not wish to harm. Charles P. Chandler, who detested invading southern homes, made exceptions for secessionists. In one incident, he reported that a company of Union troops had taken over a young lawyer's "nicely furnished home, and now occupy the carpeted rooms. The parlor is used by the officers." The actions seemed "the legitimate result of this war" because "a fierce secessionist" owned the property. Chandler noted that the men were still "as careful as possible over his property—our men must be sheltered from the rain, and must be fed. We take beef and hay stacks for use, giving receipts which will be good with the government at Washington." In February 1865, Thomas H. Hubbard commanded a detachment to collect firewood from Millwood, Virginia, "a notoriously secesh little town." He made his way to "the most stylish private Edifice of the place and while Engaging in pleasant conversation with its surly and suspicious proprietor, ordered the men to load his fence on the trains." "The gentleman," he remembered, "gave a look of mingled anguish and disgust as he saw his chief gate, followed by the palings, travel towards our mules, and went into his house without a remonstrance. The trepidation of the populace was manifest." By the end of the mission, Hubbard sarcastically noted that the citizens "didn't ask us to come again" and he did not "care to, alone and recognized, unless to lay a sacrifice upon the Country's altar." "How unreasonable these people are!" he exclaimed.[25]

The Character of Confederate Soldiers

New Brahmins judged rebel soldiers in the same way that they evaluated southern civilians. Most rebels, they maintained, fought bravely and sincerely in an unjust war instigated by unnamed politicians. As early as April 1861, Charles H. Howard thought southerners "honest but mistaken & fanatic for the most part though I could hardly say this of the leaders."[26] Although the New Brahmins viewed the southern fighting man as courageous, they still saw rebel foot soldiers as ignorant individuals, fooled into serving a cause that they did not fully understand. Young rebel officers—men who held similar rank and positions in southern society—meanwhile, impressed the New Brahmins. Not only did they fight for a cause their consciences declared righteous, rebel officers also demonstrated their commitment through their bravery on the battlefield. Recognizing honor in their opponents and faulting only the cause for which they fought, New Brahmins lamented the conflict and hoped to clasp the hands of their worthy foes in peacetime.

The bearing and behavior of southern officers made an impression on the New Brahmins. Joseph H. Twichell, for example, expressed positive views of the rebel soldiers he encountered. "They are a quite respectable lot of men, or rather boys, for some of them ought never to have left their Ma's," he told his father, continuing, "They are intelligent and [have] shown a disposition to cultivate acquaintance." Working with wounded Confederates, Twichell declared them "as a class . . . very intelligent and many are gentlemen of education." In one other instance, treating the wounded from Gettysburg, he noticed that many of the captured rebels "are gentlemen, evidently of good birth and education, and there are not a few pious men among them." Samuel C. Armstrong, taken prisoner by Stonewall Jackson's troops during the Antietam Campaign, felt compelled to counter the negative image that his mother had of rebel soldiers. He described them as "very civil and intelligent, though most miserably dressed." They fought "nobly" and several among them were "noble-hearted." Samuel E. Nichols noted that the United States might have had "the best engineers and artillery" but admired the Confederates because "they fight. The Rebels fight." During the Chancellorsville Campaign, Charles P. Mattocks came across "a company of the 'Rebs' which our forces had captured." "They were," he wrote, "captain and all—a fine-looking set of chaps." While being treated by Confederate physicians, Francis C. Barlow met several rebel officers on the field of Gettysburg. He described them as "pleasant fellows" and "more heroic, more modest + more in earnest than we are. Their whole tone is much finer than ours." Assessing the Confederate soldiers at Gettysburg, Franklin A. Haskell admitted that they "showed a determination and valor worthy of a better cause;—their conduct in this battle even makes me proud of them as Americans."[27]

Other New Brahmins echoed Franklin A. Haskell's wish that the valiant rebel soldiers serve in "a better cause." New Brahmins admired the courage and discipline of Confederate troops. "Many and many a time," Joseph H. Twichell wrote, "have the Confederate ranks been marched right up in the face of our grape and canister, when every discharge mowed a wide gap through their lines, yet without halting or breaking." Thus, positions "supposed impregnable have been carried, with dreadful loss to the enemy it is true and with little to us, but *carried*." "This character of their fighting," Twichell continued, "accounts for their enormous losses." "The ungodly ambition of which the rebellion is a hideous outgrowth," he argued, "is recklessly lavish of what it cares little about—the deluded rank and file of the Confederate army." The rebel leaders did not care if "every one of them perished" as long as the top echelon survived. In the Union army, by contrast, "every head that bows in battle is that of a citizen of a free Republic" and "each man fights for what is dear to *him* personally and he in turn is dear to the nation as a son to whom his equal share of the universal inheritance is due."[28] Twichell delegitimized the rebel cause by claiming that only Union soldiers knew the righteousness of their cause and Confederates were too ignorant to understand the folly of their rebellion.

Confederate foot soldiers, New Brahmins maintained, had fallen victim to slaveholding secessionists who misinformed them about their cause, the Union's intentions, and then kept them in the ranks under pain of death. As a result, rebel soldiers lacked a real understanding of the conflict. Such a belief served only to strengthen New Brahmins' belief that many rebels fought because of coercion and ignorance. Confederate prisoners told Henry L. Abbott that they had been "forced into it, fighting for the rich man, when they didn't own no niggers themselves." After speaking with a group of rebel prisoners, Charles F. Morse wrote, "You have no idea what innocent, inoffensive men most of them seem to be; a great many are mere boys; there are some old men, too, with humped backs." Few of these rebels had "any idea of what they are fighting for, and they were almost all forced into the army." One deserter told William Wheeler, "If our whole Brigade only knew that you would neither imprison us, nor conscript us into your army, they could not be held together a week." Wheeler learned that rebel soldiers subsisted on "a half a pint of corn-meal per day, and nothing else, not even fresh meat,—and a thin cotton jacket and pants, without overcoat or blanket to keep off the cold of these frosty nights!" "Human nature cannot endure these things," he declared, "unless sustained by the conviction of performing a sacred duty, or being actuated by noble principles." Wheeler, however, believed that "it is the dread of being shot or hung that is the cohesive power of the Southern army." Eri D. Woodbury noted in his diary that five rebel soldiers deserted and told him that "many would do so, did they not fear being pressed into our army." One month later, three more "quite intelligent" deserters arrived with tales of Confederate mistreatment: "Said their shoes (government) were charged to them at $10.00." "Never saw men more thankful than they at being once more under the protection of the 'Dear Old Flag,'" Woodbury wrote. Theodore J. Holmes met a conscript who had served two months, and then "deserted & hid in the woods near his home where his wife and other friends brought him food by night. He says the mountains in that vicinity are full of men who would gladly get into our lines if possible."[29] Such stories confirmed the belief that many rebels did not support the war.

New Brahmins sought to combat misinformation about the Union cause by treating prisoners of war with kindness. As a provost marshal Charles P. Chandler had the task of calling "on wounded officers of our own side and especially to show attention to rebel officers of rank." The Union officer hoped to "show them that we are more cultivated than they." Rebel soldiers in Union hospitals expressed the "greatest astonishment . . . that even our private soldiers are well educated and civil, all well dressed and gentlemanly. They cannot help liking us though they try to hate us." Chandler impressed and surprised southerners with his attention to burial details. "They really believe us half civilized I do not doubt and any attention or kindness surprises them," he wrote, continuing, "They hardly think us capable of any decency!" Chandler found the situation humorous because he considered southerners "not our equals by any means," and yet they acted "at first and until they knew us, as if we were not of so good a race as they." During the Atlanta Campaign, Charles F. Morse noted that "hundreds of deserters" came into Union lines during the Confederate army's constant retreats. These rebel troops "all say that half the army would do the same if it dared, but they are told fearful stories of our treatment of prisoners and are also closely watched, and, when caught, shot without mercy." "Without a single exception," Morse reported, "I have seen these men always kindly and hospitably received by our soldiers; it is always, 'How are you, Johnny? We're glad to see you; sit down and have some coffee, and tell us the news.'"[30]

Shared suffering on the battlefield and mutual demonstrations of kindness helped the fighting men form a bond. New Brahmins, who always maintained that the majority of southerners had been fooled into secession and war, affirmed that they fought for the cause rather than against the deluded men in the rebel ranks. Wounded federal soldiers told William Wheeler that they "had been very kindly treated by most of the enemy among whom they fell." Although a few rebels acted "barbarously," most displayed "tender and delicate humanity." This information made Wheeler "feel more kindly to our erring brothers than before" and wished that, since they all seemed like decent people, they "could join hands and be friends once more."[31] "When we fight," Charles F. Morse wrote, "we fight to crush the rebellion and break the power of the rebel armies, not against these men as individuals; there is no enmity felt, yet no one can complain of a want of earnestness or desire on our part for victory."[32] Once secession had been defeated and slavery, its cause, destroyed, the New Brahmins could see a clear path to working with their "erring brothers" whose bravery marked them as honorable foes.

The Curse of Slavery

Regardless of whether they were abolitionists, New Brahmins understood that the conflict had been caused by southerners who had an interest in slavery's perpetuation. For many of these men who had never been to the South, their first encounter with slavery reinforced perceptions of cruelty. Although they might have been appalled by the treatment of the enslaved people, such sentiments did not translate to sympathy for blacks themselves. The New Brahmins continued to believe negative stereotypes about blacks and expressed doubts that the two races could peacefully coexist on an equal footing. Even abolitionists and men who admired the valor of African American troops did not think that freed people could survive without enormous help from northerners in the postwar world.

New Brahmins who saw slavery firsthand found scenes that they encountered horrifying. "I have been about the plantations, at the houses, have seen the people, the gentlemen and ladies, and their slaves," Charles P. Chandler reported from Maryland, and concluded, "I do not change my opinion at all of Slavery. It is a mean and contemptible institution. It is debasing & barbarous." Some New Brahmins saw the effects of slavery on the bodies of runaways. "Day before yesterday," George Clary wrote from New Orleans, "a boy came in with an iron collar fastened round his neck, strong and heavy—it was difficult to get it off." In another instance, "a girl came in . . . from over the river with her arm cut badly. She said her master threw her on the floor against some crockery." Their revulsion at the cruelty of slavery, however, did not lead to sympathy for the enslaved themselves. "So far as slavery is concerned," Joseph H. Twichell wrote, "nothing could deepen my hatred of it. All that I have personally seen and heard has only confirmed what had before been told." His "abhorrence of the system," however, went beyond his "commiseration of its negro victims." Indeed, he would have preferred "the present generation of *slaves* be exterminated than that the Curse of another generation of *Slavery* rest upon the shoulders of the nation."[33] Twichell, at least, seemed more concerned about what slavery did to the white nation.

New Brahmins expressed the greatest distress and surprise when they encountered enslaved mixed-race individuals. Long believing in the superiority of Anglo-Saxon civilization, meeting mulattos and quadroons challenged their racial hierarchy, especially when they could not immediately tell a person's race. Some enslaved laborers had such pronounced white features that New Brahmins expressed their shock and revulsion. Nathaniel Bowditch encountered a runaway whom he described as being "a very pretty girl who was very near white. She had none of the negro features but all white." Robert Gould Shaw had a similar experience. In March 1862 he encountered a man that he mistook for white before being informed otherwise. "There he stood there in front of us," he reported, "& talked for two hours, as eloquently as any educated man I know. The simplicity of his language made it all the more impressive. He said he had nine children all whiter than the two boys with him." The enslaved man explained that "his Master was his Father & that it had often been a bitter pill to swallow when he had been badly treated by him to think that it was so." After seeing slavery in action, Luther C. Howell admitted, "I don't think my hatred of the system of slavery is abating in the slightest degree now that I am brought in close contact with it." He witnessed "a quadroon mother with an infant child as white as" someone he knew.[34] The enslavement of a seemingly white person and the threat to clear racial hierarchies underscored the fact that slavery corrupted both races.

Having little experience with African Americans in general, New Brahmins often wrote about them as curiosities. John C. Gray described blacks in Maryland as "a dirty, lazy, docile, laughing set who vex and amuse us alternatively." "We have the negro race in full perfection," he later wrote from Suffolk, Virginia, "unaffected by free institutions or Gideonites, and very interesting to look upon they are, especially the women with their turbans and their baskets on their heads." In another instance, he recorded, "the negroes are funny enough particularly the little ones with whom each cabin is filled to overflowing."[35]

Most interactions with African Americans took place in camp, where many runaways served as officers' personal attendants. In this setting, many New Brahmins observed their behavior. Joseph H. Twichell described his "colored servant Joseph" as "ignorant, reading and writing being not in the list of his accomplishments." Joseph, he told his father, "talks the real Uncle Toms Cabin negro dialect to perfection, and has many negro ways which I have read of but never saw before." He did, however, give the young chaplain "great satisfaction" and knew "how to take care of himself and his master." Although a freeman, Twichell complained that Joseph "betrays his association with slaves by rather servile manners." Aside from these negative characteristics, Joseph was "rather good looking—cooks admirably and is a scientific forager—having a peculiar faculty of moving the sympathies of neighboring farmers in the interest of our mess." John B. Noyes reported that his "contraband" became "an object of considerable attention" because many "of the officers would like to get negroes, but find it difficult to do so." Some men simply did not trust black servants. When William F. Bartlett lost his "little leather-covered pocket flask," although he had no proof, he accused, "Some nigger picked it up after we had gone, probably."[36]

Even abolitionists expressed racist sentiments, writing deeply demeaning statements about blacks they encountered. William T. Lusk told his cousin that he had never seen "the article called 'nigger'" until he came "to 'Ole Virginny.'" His unit, he explained, "own an African of the Pogo species, a sort of half idiotic monkey-man, partially possessing the gift of speech, and totally possessing the gift of doing nothing." "I consider it a curious study," Lusk continued, "to see how, when he is ordered to perform any service, he manages most ingeniously not to do it at all." Writing to his mother, Lusk made similar remarks: "Our darkeys give us some amusement and much more trouble. Ours, we have dubbed the 'Pongo,' who knows how not to do it, in a manner to excite our unbounded admiration." "In the evening," Lusk described, "these Africans have a way of getting around the fire and singing real 'nigger melodies,' which are somewhat monotonous as regards the music, and totally idiotic as regards the words." After quoting a few lines from a favorite song, Lusk commented, "This will sometimes be repeated for a couple of hours by the indefatigable nigger—indefatigable in this alone."[37]

New Brahmins raised on the ideas of free labor believed that enslaved people lived in a state of natural laziness. They feared that no one could teach or motivate freed people to take responsibility for their own affairs. William T. Lusk described blacks who had congregated near Union lines in South Carolina as being "happy in the thought of freedom, dancing, singing, void of care, and vainly dreaming that all toil is in future to be spared, and that henceforth they are to lead that life of lazy idleness which forms the Nigger's Paradise." John B. Noyes referred to a campaign to educate freed people at Port Royal as "a wild goose expedition." He thought teachers ought to focus their efforts on helping poor southern whites. "Are darkies better than white men?" he asked. Why, he wondered, should "these cultivated scholars . . . waste their talents on such barren soil?" He had "seen enough of Southern darkies, free slave, and contraband to say *no* to any such journey."[38] No amount of education, he thought, could elevate freed blacks.

Revealing the depth of their disrespect of African Americans, many New Brahmins adopted roles similar to their southern counterparts in dealing with servants. They took advantage of their laborers and used them in ways that resembled slavery. Writing from New Orleans, George Clary described his servant as "a bright mulatto boy of some 19 years who succeeded after 3 attempts in making his escape. The last time he broke the lock which held him in the stocks by one blow with a piece of brick which he managed to reach." Believing himself a fair employer, Clary did not feel obliged to pay for more than "his clothing and what I choose to give him." In South Carolina, Charles Francis Adams, Jr., found himself "driving a gang of niggers." As he described the scene to his brother, "My horse was tied to a tree and my pistols and coat lay near him, while I, in heavy boots and spurs and my shirt sleeves, handled a spade by the side of my sable brethren in the midst of a combination of rice-field and cotton swamp, while my sergeant, axe in hand, headed another gang in clearing away underbrush."[39] The image of Adams, scion of one of New England's most prominent and powerful political families, directing a black work crew represents many of these men's views of their relationship to black laborers.

Racist beliefs and stereotypes about African Americans influenced what New Brahmins thought of freedmen's capabilities. Enslaved laborers who had never worked on their own before, New Brahmins worried, might fear freedom and all it entailed. The prevalence of such ideas suggests their acceptance of southern propaganda. Charles Francis Adams, Jr., believed that blacks' prospects were "not . . . encouraging." Their freedom, he predicted, "will be the freedom of antiquated and unprofitable machines, the freedom of the hoes they use which will be swept aside to make way for better implements." Emancipation would, therefore, "be a terrible calamity to the blacks as a race" because "rapid emancipation as the result of an economic revolution" would destroy "their value as agricultural machines." Discussing Gen. David Hunter's emancipation order in the Department of the South in 1862 and believing slavery "virtually over in the United States," Caspar Crowninshield observed, "I have not perceived any wild demonstrations of joy on the part of the Negroes and am not surprised that there should be none." The enslaved "do not know as yet what freedom means, and dread the idea of having to look out for themselves." Although he acknowledged that there were "some great exceptions to this, in the persons of some few negroes, who are already working on their own account, and are making money quite fast," many others, "especially those who have kind masters, long for the return of their masters & the old state of affairs." "If the Nigs are free," Crowninshield asked, "what becomes of the masters?"[40]

Pondering the future of the South, New Brahmins wondered what fate awaited the freed people. They foresaw only hardships for the blacks in the postwar South. John C. Gray thought that freed people would "have a much harder time now than they ever had in their lives before." Economic competition and the introduction of free labor, Charles Francis Adams, Jr., believed, would revitalize the South. Unfortunately, it would also push black labor out of the picture. Adams applauded northern men "with Northern ideas of economy, agriculture and improvement" who were "swarming down onto the South." These entrepreneurs, seeing "how much behind the times the country" was, would also grasp the potential for investment. "If fair competition in the growth of cotton be once established," Adams predicted, "a new system of economy and agriculture must inevitably be introduced here in which the slave and his hoe will make room for the free laborer and the plough." Slavery, and consequently blacks, would have "small chance."[41]

In thinking about how to restructure southern society, New Brahmins turned to the panacea of education. They believed that only schooling and close supervision would ensure African Americans' readiness to assume the responsibilities of freedmen. Early in the war, Charles P. Chandler declared slavery "an infernal sin" that "sooner or later must cease" but thought "it would not do to liberate all these ignorant people at once. They are in their present depressed state, better off." "They could not take care of themselves," he reasoned, "after so many years of oppression. The law relating to their education and marriage must first be changed. This will ensure their liberty for they could then gain it themselves." Charles Francis Adams, Jr., observing African American soldiers, thought that they lacked "the pride, spirit and intellectual energy of the whites, partly from education and yet more by organization." They were "sensitive to praise or blame, and yet more so to ridicule . . . diffident and eager to learn . . . docile and naturally polite." Despite his hopes, Adams retained his pessimistic view and his impressions were "not encouraging either for my success individually or for theirs as a race." He still had "little hope for them in their eternal contact with a race like ours."[42]

Belief that black men could wear Union blue did not translate to viewing them as ready citizens. Charles F. Morse expressed his satisfaction after reviewing black troops on dress parade. The men "had not been in camp quite a month and had not yet been drilled on account of the heavy amount of picket duty, so we went prepared to excuse a great deal." He was, however, "very agreeably surprised by the whole appearance of the regiment; the men had a soldierly bearing, marched well, and stood in line better than nine-tenths of the white regiments I have seen." After visiting black troops on the picket line, Morse's superiors attested to the fact that "they never saw sentinels do their duty better." Despite positive reviews, Morse still described the men as "nearly all of the blackest description, and very ignorant."[43]

New Brahmins' doubts about African Americans' abilities may have had more to do with their rigid beliefs in the superiority of Anglo-Saxons. In September 1863 Theodore Lyman expressed complete satisfaction with the black troops he had seen in Washington, D.C. "Here," he wrote, "were men who have performed feats in marching and in fighting, on a par with the best armies of the world; but each man looked just as before he was a soldier, only browner and more trained." A few months later, he seemed to have changed his opinion, writing that "the Negro cannot change his nature; thus hath God made him. As a rule he cannot fight against the White. This is leaning on a broken reed." He declared that there simply was "no general historical precedent for their being efficient troops." Coming upon a division of black troops in the 9th Army Corps during the 1864 Overland Campaign, he wrote, "It made me sad to see them.— Can we not fight our own battles?"[44] Lyman, like members of his cohort, had a noble concept of American character and a negative view of African Americans. Seeing blacks as successful fighters threatened to challenge these men's rooted ideas about race relations. Unwilling to alter their core beliefs, these rigid purveyors of racial attitudes tried to convince themselves that any instances of black bravery and success were exceptions rather than the rule. Sojourns in the South confirmed white northern superiority rather than challenging it.

In the same way that they sought to control other members in society, New Brahmins thought they knew what was best for African Americans. When blacks rejected advice, however, white supporters ascribed their disobedience to ingratitude and lack of character. Elites maintained that only the most educated in society, such as themselves, could act on their independent beliefs. James A. Garfield, for example, met a black man named Jim in May 1862. After observing him for a few weeks, Garfield described Jim as "very intelligent and thoroughly honest and faithful. . . . He is greatly attached to me and I believe he would die for me cheerfully if it were necessary." Jim was bettering himself by "learning to read and has much more than ordinary Negro talent." Garfield felt so impressed that he offered to help the runaway after the war. One year later, however, his opinion of Jim had soured considerably. "I am disgusted with Jim," he wrote to his wife, explaining, "I don't want anything to do with that stubborn kind of laziness and wrong-headedness which he has manifested." Garfield did not clarify the exact reasons for his disappointment but implied that Jim had rejected his advice and, in Garfield's opinion, was no longer "willing to help himself."[45]

New Brahmins believed that blacks needed to master the tenets of good character—gain an education, develop a work ethic, and adopt free soil ideas— in order to survive in the postwar society. Charles Francis Adams, Jr., stated his support for "a semi-military system" which made education compulsory. Any "thieving and violence" would be swiftly punished and the schooling would emphasize "the first great lesson, that they must work to live." "If," he continued, "they choose to live in their own huts and cultivate their own land and so support themselves I see no objection, if the young went to school; but the first lesson must be work or starve." Regardless, Adams doubted that blacks could survive if more white immigrants came to the South. "The inferior will disappear," he declared, "before the more vigorous race." The war had started a new era of freedom but "the African has little to hope." Although they suggested ways to educate freedmen and bring them into the American republic, New Brahmins, with their belief in white racial superiority, would have preferred not to build a biracial society. "Niggers," Caspar Crowninshield wrote in disgust, "were made to bother white men, & ruin nations."[46] Crowninshield's expression spoke to the barrier that remained even as many men accepted emancipation as a legitimate war policy. It also hinted at problems that blacks would face if the North's future leaders could not even acknowledge them as capable human beings.

Physically being in the South led New Brahmins to think about their adversaries, the cause of the war, and the thousands of blacks they encountered. Their understanding of character—both personal and national—framed their responses to everything they witnessed. Northern gentlemen criticized southern gentlemen for failing to uplift their fellow citizens and improve the land. Poor southern whites suffered as a result of this neglect and lacked the traits New Brahmins expected to find in white Americans. The poor whites they encountered lacked industry and ambition, traits that the New Brahmins viewed as universal to all American citizens. At the same time, they assessed African Americans on their character and found them wanting. The rich land of the South, meanwhile, remained uncultivated and underdeveloped. By the standards of character, the region and its people had failed. The South's residents, because they lacked the character of northerners, were a blight on America's national character.

New Brahmins discovered that the fighting men of the Confederacy—and especially the officers most similar to themselves—demonstrated their character on the battlefield. This admiration for the rebels' commitment opened the door to eventual reconciliation. New Brahmins reasoned that slavery had misled and corrupted their southern counterparts. They laid the blame for the war not with the South's gentlemen class but with greedy, slaveholding political leaders and secessionists. They desperately wanted to believe that most southern gentlemen were, like themselves, bound by duty to serve. Northern men of character, therefore, learned to respect southern men of honor. With slavery dead and secession defeated, they could reconnect with the South's leadership class and rebuild the nation. This pathway to reconciliation did not bode well for the freedmen, whom New Brahmins never learned to accept as equals.

6

The Character to Command

The weary veterans of the 7th Maine Volunteers, Maj. Thomas W. Hyde commanding, arrived on the field of Antietam around noon, September 17, 1862. The fighting had raged for hours but more bloodshed remained on this, the single bloodiest day in American history. Checked by enemy fire near the center of the line, Hyde's men took cover and rested as the battle's momentum shifted to the southern part of the battlefield.

The 7th Maine's contribution to that bloodiest day had yet to begin. Between four and five in the afternoon, Col. William Irvin, the brigade commander, rode up and ordered the regiment to advance on a Confederate sharpshooters' position near the Piper Farm. The heavily defended location seemed impregnable. Hyde protested the order and Irvin responded, "Are you afraid to go, sir?" His character questioned and unable to refuse a direct order from his superior, Hyde assembled the regiment. He and the 7th would perform their duty. As they marched toward the Confederate position, the Mainers withstood a murderous fire. Confederate bullets hit the major's horse and, as he landed on the ground, he saw "how the twigs and branches of the apple-trees were being cut off by musket balls, and were dropping in a shower."

The regiment had no choice but to retreat. Several men rallied long enough to rescue Hyde from would-be rebel captors. Returning to Union lines, the Mainers counted their casualties and wept. "I have the reputation here of leading the most daring charge ever made in our military history," Hyde bragged to his mother a few days later. "Sixty brave and mutilated fellows told me that night that they would follow me again, even to the gates of hell," he wrote, concluding, "That is what we need in this war—some one to lead and the men never refuse." Bravery alone was not enough, and Hyde attempted to distinguish himself by pointing out his calmness under fire. "I never was so cool or thought so quick as in the battle, and idea of personal danger did not enter my head," Hyde remarked. He had passed the test of true leadership. After the war, with years to reflect on his actions, Hyde criticized one aspect of his action. He learned that the attack on the Piper Farm had not originated at army headquarters but rather from the brigade commander. If only he had known this at the time, he wrote in his memoirs, he might have saved many of his men's lives. "I wished," he lamented, "I had been old enough, or distinguished enough, to have dared to disobey orders."[1] Hyde had been willing to lead his men forward against his better judgment because the Union cause required sacrifice but, when he realized that his actions had not served the greater good, he felt saddened by what seemed a wasteful loss of his brave men.

Demonstrating character in wartime required modifications to the usual peacetime model. As part of the chain of command, New Brahmin officers had no choice but to obey the orders of their superiors, sometimes contradicting their own personal judgments. At the same time, the men demanded absolute adherence to their own commands and maintained that rigid discipline bred victories. Thomas W. Hyde's fight at the Piper Farm demonstrated the complications of wartime character and showed how the ambitious New Brahmins both cared for their men and used them to demonstrate personal leadership skills.

The Civil War allowed New Brahmins to put their antebellum character to the test in a profoundly different way than during peacetime. The war presented them with an opportunity to step forward, volunteer their services, and take a leading role in rescuing the Union. Rather than maintaining self-control and composure in silence while waiting for society to call them to action, the men could demonstrate their character in the face of battle. Their supposedly internal character was now on external display, observed, and evaluated by fellow officers and men. For this reason, battles proved to be particularly anxious. Combat provided New Brahmins with the opportunity to test their inner qualities, all the while offering an external model of behavior for their men.

As officers with reputations on the line, New Brahmins used camp time to instill harsh discipline into their units. In essence, they transferred lessons from their undergraduate days to army life. The issue of self-control and discipline, so important to developing the character of a gentleman in college life, became ever more important to men marching into battle. These men conveyed the value of discipline to their soldiers, viewing the unit as an extension of themselves. How a unit performed also demonstrated a New Brahmin's success as its leader.

New Brahmins adapted ideas about character in their peacetime lives to wartime circumstances. The term "character," as usual, encompassed a wide variety of traits and habits. Although the men did not always use the term directly, they implied elements of this overarching standard. The most important elements of a gentleman's character included discipline, individualism or independent thought, and selflessness. Recognizing that the army command structure left little room for independent action, New Brahmins accepted orders from others but also demanded strict obedience to their own commands. Although these good traits could be difficult to maintain in the antebellum world, the war changed how and who evaluated a person's character. Suddenly, personal behavior under fire and the performance of the men under one's command revealed the extent of one's character. By combining individualism, discipline, and self-sacrifice, New Brahmins could demonstrate character on two levels: by maintaining their own composure under fire as the ultimate test of the individual will, and by exercising control over the troops under their command. They also demonstrated character by not buckling in the face of challenges from their men and by withstanding the hardships of campaign life.

Historians who have studied Civil War soldiers have tended to focus on the experiences of "common soldiers." Since a diverse variety of individuals made up Civil War armies, especially Union ones, however, searching only occupations, nationalities, and circumstances for the typical soldier may ignore the unique experiences of different groups of men.[2] The search for "common" traits has caused scholars to shift their focus away from individual groups' motives and experiences. Conflating the experience of junior officers and enlisted men also masks differences in their experiences. Generalized studies by their nature cannot take into account the unique circumstances that led specific groups to participate in the war. Although historians have related and analyzed the combat experiences and painstakingly described camp and campaign life during the war, relatively few works have examined the social world created by the men and their officers. Lorien Foote's work on the interaction between the gentleman class and the "roughs" who made up a good proportion of the Union army suggests the fruitfulness of such an examination. Armies, after all, represent contemporary society in a concentrated and hypermasculine form. For the purposes of this study, the camping ground allows for a consideration of how New Brahmins interacted with people they considered their social inferiors. Such explorations reveal the qualities of character northern gentlemen considered most important for the masses and the war effort.[3]

The study of combat experiences has also yielded important findings about motivation and behavior. Gerald F. Linderman combined the key terms manliness, godliness, duty, honor, and knightliness under the rubric of "courage," which relied on a man's internal strengths. "The primacy of courage," Linderman wrote, "promised the soldier that no matter how immense the war, how distant and fumbling the directing generals, or how powerful the enemy forces seeking his destruction, his fate would continue to rest on his inner qualities." Earl J. Hess, in his study of Union men in combat, distinguished between moral and physical courage. While the "man of physical courage responded only to the nervous stimulus of combat; his bravery was the unthinking action of one who foolishly ignored danger and indulged in the rush of sensation," the man of moral courage rose above his fears to perform his duty.[4] Linderman's emphasis on courage and Hess's description of moral courage highlight the importance of conquering one's apprehensions in combat, a feat that lies at the heart of how New Brahmins defined character under fire. They recognized the importance of standing firm and blended their understanding of the sacrifices they were making with the noble instincts of patriotism and nationalism. The dangers that they faced were worth the risk only because they fought in a just cause.

A soldier's position and experiences in antebellum society informed his motives, actions, and interactions. This was especially true for soldiers from the gentleman class. Scholars have observed, for example, that units with large contingents of Harvard graduates among the officers—the 2nd and 20th Massachusetts Regiments, for example—appeared most concerned about class issues and social boundaries. Such ideas also influenced the organization of and discipline in the units. As Lorien Foote has noted, class "informed their leadership style in the army," and the Harvard-educated officers applied "ideals of courage, self-discipline, and duty to other officers." They also employed the organizational and institutional skills they had acquired to help manage the men in their unit. Men with degrees from other colleges also emphasized similar qualities in their troops, suggesting that they valued professional and gentleman class distinctions as well. New Brahmins believed that they knew how best to make their units combat-ready by instilling rigorous discipline and a firm understanding of the noble cause for which they fought. New Brahmins throughout the North offered their undergraduate diplomas as proof of their qualifications for leadership, believing in their superiority over the men who usually staffed the army and viewing regular soldiers as social outcasts who lacked the morals and the ideological drive of volunteers in general and educated men in particular. New Brahmins believed that they had a true understanding of the causes of the conflict and thought they had the responsibility to explain to less fortunate members of society why they needed to fight and win the war. "The Union Army in the Civil War," as Lorien Foote has written, "was northern society in miniature, reflecting its culture and values and imbued with its strengths and weaknesses."[5] In fact, the Union army, with its hierarchy enforced by discipline, allowed men of the New Brahmin class to set up not a reflection of actual peacetime society but an *ideal* one in which everyday individuals obeyed orders from their social superiors.

Despite their eloquent proclamations about nobly serving and uplifting the American masses, New Brahmins brought their class biases with them into the armed forces. This manifested itself in the men's exclusiveness. They wished to interact only with men of their own social class and generally detested serving in units made up of immigrant or foreign-born soldiers. They also shunned the company of officers who came from different backgrounds, preferring to fraternize with men of their own rank and social status.[6] Henry L. Abbott hoped for a position in Col. George H. Gordon's 2nd Massachusetts Volunteers, "officered by gentlemen, a great many of whom I know, & by sober respectable fellows who more do suit a staid graduate like myself than harum scarum young fellows." When they chose their associates, the men preferred those with college backgrounds. William F. Bartlett chose two Harvard classmates, George N. Macy and Henry L. Abbott, when recruiting officers for the 20th Massachusetts Volunteers. Later, when he organized the 49th Massachusetts, he picked a Williams man as his lieutenant colonel and another Harvard man as an adjutant. Stephen M. Weld—who had not formed any "intimate friendships" with his fellow officers for they had "no interests in common with me, except, of course, the ordinary civilities of everyday life"—made an exception for an officer named Johnson, "a graduate of Yale in '60, and . . . a first-rate fellow."[7] Charles Francis Adams, Jr., found it "pleasant and refreshing to meet a man like [Francis C.] Barlow among the crowds of mediocrity which make up the mass of an army."[8]

New Brahmins hoped to avoid serving with certain groups of soldiers, particularly foreigners. Early in the war Thomas H. Hubbard feared being drafted into a regiment of Irishmen. "However ready I feel to do my share in this crisis it would be disagreeable, to say the least, to look out from the ranks, from Irish and verminiferus surroundings," he told his father. William Wheeler, serving in a unit with many German recruits, complained that he had to "live with these men, to eat their onions and drink their lager, and very rarely to hear a word of musical English from American lips, as I am almost the sole specimen of a Yankee in the Company." A soldier's life was hard enough, Wheeler said, "without adding the mental agony of continual uncongeniality and disagreement of modes and habits of life." John B. Noyes asked for a transfer to a new regiment in part because his regiment boasted officers "not of my social standing, and for the most part uneducated Irishmen raised from the ranks." In command of a brigade of mostly German troops during the Battle of Chancellorsville, Francis C. Barlow openly criticized the men, declaring his "indignation + disgust at the miserable behavior." "You know," he told his mother, "how I have always been down on the 'Dutch' + I do not abate my contempt now." Promoted to division command after Chancellorsville, Barlow found the men "in a most disgusting condition as to discipline and morale." At the Battle of Gettysburg, his men broke and ran after a sharp engagement. Critically wounded during the battle, he later poured out his anger in a letter. "This is the last of my connection with the Division," he declared, saying that he would rather "take a *Brigade* in preference to such a Division." Theodore Lyman, visiting Oliver O. Howard's headquarters, remarked that the general had "been placed in an unfortunate position, being given the 11th Corps, a body of very inferior material, and full of insubordinate Germans &c."[9]

Despite their deeply held prejudices of individuals not from the gentlemen class and their fear of leading foreign-born troops, many New Brahmins thought positively of commanding a unit of the United States Colored Troops (USCT). Charles H. Howard, for example, explained, "I never could consent to go into the Regular Army as it used to be, so aimless and unproductive of moral results." However, he saw the chance to lead African American soldiers as a "worthy moral endeavor very attractive to me." Leading black men "opened a great field for usefulness to such as have humane & Christian hearts and a purpose to do something for humanity & the Kingdom of Christ without special regard to ends distinctively selfish." The organization of African American units attracted many of the sons of prominent abolitionist and antislavery advocates, for example, Robert Gould Shaw and Charles Francis Adams, Jr. But USCT units did not limit their officer pool to those with abolitionist sympathies. Those who had the duty to recruit USCT officers "wanted only intelligent white men with high morals." Recruits required letters of recommendation, attesting to the applicant's moral characteristics, as well as other exams. As Col. Reuben D. Mussey, a member of the Dartmouth class of 1854 and an officer recruiter, explained, "My idea is that a few questions on important subjects will determine a man's character as a military student, and show his fitness or unfitness for the position he seeks." All these requirements, according to one scholar, tested the candidate's "knowledge and character to command others in combat." College-educated men, with their stellar recommendations, veteran experience, and strong belief in personal character, became important leaders in the USCT regiments.[10]

New Brahmins constantly wondered how they, as unit leaders, ought to comport themselves. They wrestled with how to apply antebellum ideas about character to a wartime setting. How should gentlemen behave in the army? Understanding that their men looked to officers for guidance and leadership, New Brahmins realized that, more than ever, they needed to exemplify good character. Throughout the war, with pressure to test themselves on an individual level and behave like officers in front of the troops, New Brahmins constantly monitored and evaluated their performance. Wartime offered a very public stage for the demonstration of one's character.

Character in Command

New Brahmins believed that they contributed to the Union cause in many ways. First, they sacrificed their peacetime affairs to serve in the war. Second, they took on the responsibility of leading other men. But they also thought that their class position, undergraduate training, and gentlemanly character made them natural leaders. They volunteered not merely themselves but their education and special abilities as well. Joshua L. Chamberlain thought he could "be of service in the field, where my natural tastes & early education lead me & for which they in some small degree qualify me." Thomas H. Hubbard heartily endorsed his brother John's choice to volunteer for military service. The nation, he acknowledged, "needs her best men, not a rabble, to fight her battles." Accepting a command position also served the interests of young men in need of testing their character and gave them an opportunity to become a role model for other soldiers. Charles H. Howard served as one of his brother's staff officers until late in the war. When offered command of an African American unit, he leapt at the chance, explaining, "I have been so situated as to cultivate self reliance too little and I often think one of the principal defects of my character is a want of independence. It amounts too often to a lack of moral courage and following this a strict and firm adherence to principle." As the commander of men, however, he thought, "I am somewhat in the relation of a father as well as governor" and "this new position may not only be wholesome & beneficial to my character but result in mutual good to officers & men, to our country and the Kingdom of our Lord."[11]

Other New Brahmins also used the language of patriarchy to describe their responsibilities. Such a role entailed not just caring for the troops but also positioning and commanding them. Here, New Brahmins could see their societal roles on a small scale and they relished their positions as leaders of men.

Samuel C. Armstrong explained that a captain "is practically the father of ninety children. Men in camp, sensible men, lose all their good judgment and almost their good sense; they become puerile, and come to the Captain on a multitude of silly, childish matters." "A Captain," he concluded, "does not only his own but all the thinking of the company." Thomas W. Hyde pointed out that officers suffered "nearly the same privations, added to a terrible responsibility." "A private," he reasoned, "has no care, nothing to think about but himself, but often the fate of many others depend upon the officer to whom many people at home think the brass buttons and miserably inadequate salary are ample reward."[12]

New Brahmins saw the war as an opportunity to uplift the men under their command. Joseph H. Twichell volunteered as a chaplain in a regiment comprising mostly of Irish Catholics, hoping that his own Protestant theology and good character would influence them. He explained that he had chosen to volunteer in this regiment "composed as it is of rough, wicked men," because he saw "the companies of the better class of citizens were all attended by Chaplains, but nothing was said about these." He told his father that he had always thought of himself "fitted by nature to influence this class of men" and "hoped to make some good impressions, by treating with kindness a class of men who are little used to it." Merely associating with men of education and skill might just improve the character and quality of soldiers in the ranks. John B. Noyes, lobbying for his promotion to a new command, argued that volunteers would benefit by "association with officers of social standing at home and of liberal education and refinement" such as himself.[13]

New Brahmins called on their ability to learn in order to master the skills needed to thrive in military life. Despite believing themselves superior to career military men in terms of personal traits, many attempted to emulate the habits of professional soldiers and learn as much as they could about military affairs. When first assigned to the 1st Massachusetts Cavalry Regiment as an adjutant, Nathaniel Bowditch "felt very blue," fearing he could not "perform the duties of the office." When James C. Rice became the lieutenant colonel of the 45th New York, some officers signed a petition criticizing his lack of experience. Rice, who recognized this deficiency, secured the help of a sergeant, a Crimean War veteran, to help him practice military drills. Other men took similar measures. From camp, Thomas W. Hyde told his mother that he was "'making up' the West Point course" and expressed his determination "to be second to none" in his military knowledge. Theodore Winthrop noted that both he and his brother "intend to apply for commissions, from Captain down," and whatever they did not know "of the mere machinery of the trade" they would "quickly learn." Joshua L. Chamberlain admitted, "It is no small labor to master the evolutions of a Battalion & Brigade," but he was "bound to understand *every thing*." He asked his wife to send him "*'Jomini, Art of War*' in a package" because his West Point–trained colonel, Adelbert Ames, had promised to review the material with him.[14]

Despite some personal doubts early on, New Brahmins' belief in their superiority asserted itself after they thought they had mastered the requirements of military life. John B. Noyes offered his "liberal education," his yearlong experience as a private, and "sobriety and gentlemanly traits" as evidence of his qualifications to lead others. He claimed to be "far more qualified to sustain the position of an officer than many who are now in the service." Some men had complete faith that their character would shine through and influence their soldiers. Upon his transfer to command of the 1st U.S. Sharp Shooters, Charles P. Mattocks told his mother that he faced "an undisciplined and poorly drilled command of 300 men, and am expected to bring order out of *chaos*." He warned his mother not to think of his new men as *"roughs."* Rather, he explained that the "rank and file have no superiors in regard to character and intelligence," implying that his arrival would enhance their discipline and behavior. Some New Brahmins argued that their volunteer soldier status immunized them from the temptations of power that might corrupt professional military men, echoing a fear the founding fathers had constantly articulated. Theodore Winthrop worried that the expansion of the army might attract a "class of men" who would not "be of the best tone." He wanted men of good character who would "oppose any scheme of any one to constitute a military government." Winthrop hoped for men who would "imitate Washington," relinquish power after the conflict, and exemplify good behavior for the rank and file.[15]

The belief that the professional classes alone could save the army and the nation stemmed from their poor estimation of regular soldiers. William D. Sedgwick feared for the outcome of the war when he observed regulars in action. It was, he admitted to his mother, hard to "hold on inflexibly to your faith in the designs of Providence when you see what wretched instruments it has in so many of the men by whom if by any one, those designs must be carried out." Whereas he first thought "it was only necessary, in order that we might have a respectable Country, to Exterminate about 4/5 of the population of the South," Sedgwick now believed "the Extermination of 3/5 of the North would have to be added, in order to rid the whole Country of its damned fools and cursed thieves & hypocrites." The situation made "an honest patriot's heart ache." Oliver O. Howard was "very much disappointed" upon learning that his brigade would be assigned to Gen. Philip Kearny's division. According to his brother, Howard "would have rather had any other General over him," explaining that Kearny, a regular soldier, "is a man reported to be without principle, morally."[16]

Although New Brahmins hoped that their superior character alone would inspire others, they understood that, practically speaking, they needed to rely on discipline to mold their men into combat readiness. As professional men, many of them having barely completed their college educations, graduates found the discipline of the army beneficial for their character as well as for the task of asserting authority over their troops. Caspar Crowninshield confessed in his diary, upon preparing to drill his troops for the first time, "an anxious moment it was for me when, as I buckled on my sword, I saw the men drawn up in the company street, and of course prepared to criticize the new captain." He suspected that "the men saw that I was a little green, and I could have sworn that the Sergeant smiled as he made the men present arms & said 'Captain the Company is formed.'" "For a short time," he noted, "a feeling came over me which was very similar to the one which I remember having experienced when first called upon in College to recite before the class." After a few days, however, he "found that giving commands came quite naturally" and he had even sent a few men to the guardhouse. He hoped that such actions demonstrated that he would not "stand a great amount of nonsense." Crowninshield had resorted to discipline to assert his authority. Thomas H. Hubbard observed, "I never had, and do not now have, such confidence in my ability to succeed in civil life as you, Father, seem to have." In the army, however, "honesty, courage, and fair soldierly ability tell quicker . . . and are sooner recognized, than similar qualities in civil life."[17]

The relish with which New Brahmins embraced military discipline suggests that they had additional reasons to enforce strict behavioral conduct. First, they needed to establish themselves as respected commanders, and they used their authority and rank to do so. Second, because they held such a low opinion of some men under their command, they treated such individuals as completely lacking in positive traits. Only strict discipline could prepare these lowly individuals for combat, the ultimate test of any military unit. Both of these reasons also stemmed from the New Brahmins' social status. As Lorien Foote has argued, the military's hierarchical system and emphasis on discipline "matched so closely the values of their own class."[18] Unlike in civilian life, however, these young officers could shape the men beneath them into soldiers with good conduct and character.

New Brahmins called on their own undergraduate training in promoting the importance of discipline. They repeated the lessons of their college courses, arguing that all elements of behavior required control, especially in the military. One could not master drill and stand firm in a fight if one could not control profanity and alcohol consumption. Here, New Brahmins believed that their example could influence their men. Charles Russell Lowell expressed concern with the "prevalence of profanity in the command." He admitted that he himself "had not set them a good example in this respect. I don't swear very much or very deep,—but I do swear, more often at officers than men, and there is a great deal of swearing in the regiment which I wish to check." He promised to "stop it . . . entirely" and attempt to check it in the regiment. Nathaniel Bowditch admitted that he had, at times, sworn because "men are so stupid," but he did not "make a habit of it" and "in fact I try as hard as I can to over come it and am gradually doing it at any rate I pray for strength to do it and try with all my might to do it for your sake for I know that it is not gentlemanly."[19]

New Brahmins used strict discipline to maintain order, reasoning that it eliminated weakness and helped mold civilians into soldiers. Charles P. Mattocks complained that many soldiers dropped out of march because of feigned illnesses, but "in such cases" the troops were more concerned with "personal ease." "If one thinks he can go along more comfortable after a short rest he will take it," Mattocks observed, but then added, "not if he belongs to Co. A however." Strict discipline and intolerance for excuses, these young officers maintained, cured all personal weaknesses among the men. Upon his promotion, Mattocks took command of a regiment with lax discipline and recorded how he set out to correct the unit's deficiencies. He schooled the officers three times a week and, after a short while, detected "a great improvement in my lawless command." "I am bound to improve 'especially the appearance of evil' in these fellows," he continued, "and I think that by the time the appearance of evil is destroyed, the evil itself will be '*non est.*'" He said nothing to the privates but was "*hazing* the officers most unmercifully." Although few of the officers "fancy the operation," Mattocks consoled himself that "a few . . . see and approve the drift of all this." "I don't care a fig," he claimed, "(so long as I accomplish the end of which I am striving) viz: to make a good and well disciplined Regt. out of a mob of three hundred men."[20] Charles H. Howard told his mother that the soldiers of the 11th Corps had "begun with unwanted vigor to rob, steal, kill and devour everything convertible into food—worse, they are taking horses by the half dozen." Corps commander Oliver O. Howard was "taking severe measures to prevent it" but, as Charles explained, "more for the preservation of proper discipline in his own command than for any other reason." Theodore Lyman praised Francis C. Barlow for stringing up stragglers and thrashing them. Such actions, he wrote, would be "to the great benefit of the service!"[21]

Having observed the discipline of the Confederate forces, New Brahmins hoped to purge all civilian notions of democratic governance from the ranks. A frustrated Wilder Dwight wrote that American troops would "only become efficient in proportion as they abandon their national theories and give themselves up obediently to the *military laws* which have always governed the successful prosecution of war." He thought the army "crippled by the ideas of equality and independence which have colored the whole life of our people." Because the men had the ability to elect their own officers, they held too much sway and the officers, in turn, could not maintain proper discipline. "Obedience" was "permissive" rather than "compelled, and the radical basis is wrong." Union troops needed to "recognize authority and obey without knowing why,— obey from habit and instinct, not from any process of reasoning or presumed consent." Some New Brahmins suggested that the Union needed an army of automatons who would set aside their democratic ideals and unhesitatingly obey every order. Samuel E. Nichols argued that line officers and men "must content ourselves to be machines." "We need," Charles H. Howard maintained, "a single-hearted unanimous devotion to the Government in order to receive the blessing of God without which it is vain that we fight." "If there is one thing I detest in military matters," Charles P. Mattocks remarked, "it is a town-meeting system of managing affairs."[22] Although they proclaimed independent thought as an essential component of character in peacetime, New Brahmins expressed the need for unswerving allegiance during wartime. Their call for the obedience of common soldiers, however, was not entirely different from their criticisms of antebellum society, where they claimed that undisciplined mobs ruled by passion. Only the educated could hold independent thoughts. In the army, they deferred to those educated in the military arts and called again for the men in the ranks to obey without question.

New Brahmins continued to maintain that only good leaders would lead to effective discipline and deliver battlefield success. William Wheeler complimented the Confederates for managing to "pick out their best men, and have put them at the head of their army." He admired rebel leaders for their mastery of the art of battle. "With the prospect of victory when advancing and impunity when retreating," he observed, "the dirty, half naked, ill-fed white trash of the Southern army will march twenty miles a day, and fight days on empty stomachs." With inspirational leaders on the Union side, he thought, "our boys would do and suffer as much and more." He advanced "that officers who are willing to expose themselves, and lead their men on intelligently, will never lack support."[23] To succeed, the Union needed proper leadership at all levels of command.

As in peacetime, New Brahmins found it difficult to master all the qualities of good character. Whereas character dictated that one's inner qualities trumped societal acceptance, many insecure young officers still hoped for their men's approval. Joseph H. Twichell, perhaps conscious that his role as chaplain did not entitle him to the same level of respect that the men reserved for their combat officers, reported that a "strong bond of sympathy has grown up between" him and the men of his unit. Twichell claimed that the faithful in his camp would "come out in the absence of a better place under the open sky in a storm to help maintain the institution of Sunday religious exercises in camp, if I desired it," in the same manner that they would "follow a captain into a galling fire." Nathaniel Bowditch reported to his mother that he had "got on very well with the men and I think I am gradually getting their good will." Caspar Crowninshield declared himself "happy and satisfied" because he had "the best company, the best servant & the best horse on the field, and the Lt. Col. says that I am a very fine officer." He could claim all these laurels, he added cheekily, "without vanity for you know there is not a particle of that in me." John B. Noyes boasted to his brother, "I am liked by my Company, and no officer is probably more generally liked by the Regiment,—doubtless because I have exhibited pluck both in camp & field." Charles Francis Adams, Jr., observed that his men "seem to think that I am a devil of a fellow. They come to me to decide their bets and to settle questions in discussion; they wish to know before they re-enlist whether I am going to remain in the regiment; and finally they came to the conclusion that it would be safe to recruit if I promised not to go away until I saw them home for their furloughs." "To be egotistical," he added, "I think I see the old family traits cropping out in myself." Although he thought the men had "no affection" for him on a personal level—thinking that he was "cold, reserved and formal"—they had "faith in my power of accomplishing results and in my integrity." William McArthur told his mother that he had "the *respect* of the whole reg't and *have* the good opinion of the superior officers up to the Corps Commander."[24] Undoubtedly, many of these men could be proud of their achievements, but their laudatory claims of personal success served to inflate their opinions about themselves and suggested their own personal anxieties about being respected.

Whatever they thought about their fellow officers and how they received their commissions, New Brahmins believed that the greatest test lay on the battlefield and that combat would weed out those unsuited for their positions. New Brahmin officers who invested so much time in their men hoped for the best results. While training his new regiment in Baton Rouge, William F. Bartlett oversaw the men in drill and proudly observed, "Their fire by battalion was like one gun." He later hoped the men "would only do as well as that in real action, keep cool, and not fire until they were sure they had the word from me, no matter how near the enemy encroached." Paul J. Revere predicted that the "time is fast approaching when men in the army are to be measured by their capacity . . . for service and those found deficient will have to go to the wall." "It will prove to have been anything but fortunate," he noted, "for those who have been placed in positions of which they are not masters."²⁵ Battle would reveal the character of true men.

Leaders of Black Men

Before the Union army began accepting African Americans into its ranks, many New Brahmins—even abolitionists and those who would later command black troops—doubted that freedmen would make good soldiers. They based their reasoning on stereotypes of African Americans' capabilities and their concern that people who had been in bondage so long lacked self-discipline. When his father suggested that he seek a commission in a black unit being raised by Gen. David Hunter in 1861, Charles Francis Adams, Jr., scoffed. Such a command would amount to being "a 'nigger driver'" for his responsibilities, rather than leading men into battle, would be "seeing that they don't run away, or shirk work or fatigue duty." He argued that black men should be "organized and officered as soldiers," but, he continued, "they should have arms put in their hands and be drilled simply with a view to their moral elevation and the effect on their self-respect, and for the rest they should be *used* as fatigue parties and on all fatigue duty." It would take years before freedmen could "be made to stand before their old masters, unless . . . some leader of their own, some Toussaint rises, who is one of them and inspires them with confidence." Under white officers, black soldiers might become "equal to the native Hindoo regiments in about five years." Luther C. Howell cautioned his sister in August 1862 against being too impatient about arming blacks. Although they might be "strong enough to work" he did not believe them "brave enough to fight," reasoning that blacks had long been "taught to be coward[s]." "Every spark of courage is undeveloped," he explained. The army could not expect "good fighting" from African Americans, Howell concluded after being in charge of "180 contrabands." It would "take years of independence to make them soldiers who will not cower like a whipped spaniel at sight of a white man's eye."[26]

New Brahmins who agreed to command black troops, putting their character and lives on the line, felt an enormous amount of anxiety. Leading black men, they thought, required more effort than did training whites. They wondered whether they could impart sufficient discipline and maintain control over their men. More than in white regiments, success would depend on officers' leadership skills. When the 54th Massachusetts Volunteer Regiment under Robert Gould Shaw marched to war in 1863, his brother-in-law and close friend Charles Russell Lowell expressed great hopes for the unit's success. Lowell trusted Shaw's character and judgment. He thought that experimental black regiments ought to be "started soberly and not spoilt by too much fanaticism," and that "Bob Shaw is not a fanatic." In another letter, Lowell remarked that Shaw would "select the best white officers he can find, letting it be understood that black men *may* be commissioned as soon as any are found who are superior to white officers." Charles F. Morse, meanwhile, declared, "As a military measure, I entirely believe in" raising black troops, "and I hope it will be entirely successful." There was, he continued, "no reason in the world why black troops raised in this country shouldn't be as good as those used by the English and French." He had always believed "that any men who have understanding enough to obey orders implicitly, where they are led by brave officers, can make good soldiers."[27]

Only battlefield bravery could overcome whites' doubts about black troops. In July 1863, after months of training and serving in supporting roles as laborers and guards, the 54th Massachusetts Volunteers went into action at Fort Wagner, near Charleston, South Carolina. Confederate troops inflicted heavy damage on the assaulting columns and killed Col. Shaw. News of Shaw's death spread swiftly. Abolitionists cited this example of heroism, bravery, and sacrifice. When Charles P. Bowditch heard the news, he declared, "Col. Shaw died nobly. He was the first man on the parapet—the 54th leading the charge. . . . Hurrah for the negro troops." Charles Russell Lowell was devastated by the loss but tried to focus on the positive example that Shaw had set. "It was very noble of him ever to undertake the Fifty-Fourth," Lowell reflected, "but he had great satisfaction in it afterwards, both of himself and from his friends' satisfaction." "Will it not comfort his Mother a little," he asked rhetorically, "to feel that he was fighting for a cause greater than any National one?" To his fiancée (Shaw's sister), Lowell wrote, "It is a very great comfort to know that his life had such a perfect ending." "I see now," he claimed, "that the best Colonel of the best black regiment had to die, it was a sacrifice we owed,—and how could it have been paid more gloriously?" Shaw's sacrifice gave Lowell "a stronger *personal* desire to help make it clear that the black troops are *the* instrument which alone can end the rebellion." Shaw had "died to prove the fact that blacks will fight, and we owe it to him to show that that fact was worth proving." Indeed, it was "better worth proving at this moment than any other." "Since Shaw's death," he told a correspondent, "I have had a personal feeling in the matter to see black troops made a success; a success which would justify the use (or sacrifice) made of them at Wagner."[28]

African American soldiers proved themselves in battle, much to the relief of men who had risked their reputations to lead them and those who had championed their cause from the start of the war. From Port Hudson, Louisiana, George Clary declared that one "mooted question was settled definitely . . . *the niggers will fight*." Referring to a recent engagement, he wrote, "All accounts agree in the statement that the negroes with their white officers just rolled up their sleeves and went in with a rush. Their loss in killed and wounded was heavy." In May 1864, after an engagement, Charles P. Bowditch reported to his mother that "the colored troops fought very well . . . and gave the chivalry an idea of what the negroes can do, when they have freedom and Fort Pillow to nerve them." John B. Noyes reported that black troops from the 9th Corps came to relieve his men in front of Petersburg. "They are fine looking fellows," he recalled. Among his own men, "I don't hear any body say now we will not fight beside negroes. The only cry is for more." Noyes praised black troops as men "whose bravery is unquestioned." Noyes's men had seen evidence of African American heroism. "As we drew near Petersburg," he told his father, "we saw beside the road a dead negro sergeant and a dead rebel lying side by side. No other bodies were visible." Such a scene, he suggested, symbolized the overall struggle. As men who evaluated their own character through battlefield actions, New Brahmins judged African American troops using the same standard. Allowing black men to fight might just strengthen their claim to freedom. Reuben D. Mussey, a committed supporter of black troops, wrote in a will prior to a dangerous operation, "May my black friends be worthy [of] the independence and freedom they have helped to achieve."[29]

Yet deep prejudices remained even after black soldiers had proven themselves in combat. John C. Gray played down the 54th Massachusetts's performance, noting that "no one says they behaved remarkably well." Personally he thought "they did fairly, no better than the white troops and probably not so well for they came back two hundred muskets short of the number of men, while the other regiments had a surplus." "With long and careful discipline," Gray wrote, "I suppose a regiment of negroes might do as well as a poor white regiment, but negro troops disciplined no better than many of our white regiments are would be useless." Racist beliefs lingered despite displays of battlefield heroism. John C. Gray thought black troops "well worth using, worth their pay and feeding," but could not "be relied on as a substitute for white troops." Henry L. Abbott, meanwhile, outright refused to acknowledge the bravery of the 54th. "Poor Shaw," he remarked, "he was too good a fellow to be sacrificed for an experiment, & an experiment I think that has demonstrated niggers won't fight as they ought." Abbott claimed that the men "went back on their officers at the first shot. Their losses were so great because they couldn't [advance] in time."[30]

The success of African American units convinced some skeptical men to volunteer for service in black regiments. Charles Francis Adams, Jr., whose opinions about black troops changed constantly and who had earlier stated that he had no interest in African American units, became commander of the black 5th Massachusetts Cavalry, a unit he led until the end of the war. In July 1863 he declared that "the negro regiment question is our greatest victory of the war so far." Black regiments had become so successful that "they will soon be the fashion." Adams believed that he needed different methods to train African American troops. The "rugged discipline which improves whites is too much for them" he explained. Harsh discipline might just "crush them into slaves." He proposed appealing to their "affections" instead. "The negro," he later reasoned, "makes a good soldier, particularly in those branches of the service where a high order of intelligence is less required." He thought blacks serving as infantrymen, if "properly officered, would ... be as effective as any in the world," but "a negro is not the equal of the white man." A black soldier, Adams explained, "has not the mental vigor and energy, he cannot stand up against adversity. . . . He cannot fight for life like a white man." He thought that a "sick nigger" would simple give up, lie down, and "die, the personification of humanity reduced to a wet rag." From his own men, Adams noticed, "if you degrade a negro who has once tried to do well, you had better shoot him at once, for he gives right up and never attempts to redeem himself." Blacks' "animal tendencies" were "greater than those of the whites." Black troops "must and will sleep; no danger from the enemy and no fear of punishment will keep him awake."[31]

Northerners' beliefs about African Americans' brutal passions and uncontrollable nature—a clear difference from whites—led them to emphasize discipline in training black units. Fearing a race war sparked by encountering their former masters on the battlefield, educated officers remained vigilant in policing their men. Charles Francis Adams, Jr., recorded on the battlefield of Petersburg that black troops had "greatly distinguished themselves and the most skeptical on that score were forced to admit that on that occasion the darkies had fought and fought fiercely." Rebel soldiers, he claimed, "dread the darkies more than the white troops; for they know that if they will fight the rebels cannot expect quarter." Pointing to the spirit of revenge that he suspected animated these men, he noted, "Our black troops are not subject to any of the rules of civilized warfare. If they murder prisoners, as I hear they did, it is to be lamented and stopped, but they can hardly be blamed." In April 1865 Luther C. Howell observed that Confederate troops were "afraid of the negroes and it is a wholesome fear." In a recent engagement, black troops had "charged with the cry of 'Fort Pillow'" and "the Rebs turned white with fear and ran to give themselves up to the white troops." Howell admitted that the black troops "did kill a few after they had surrendered but were quickly stopped by their officers." He did not sympathize with the rebels, calling the animosity that blacks held for rebel troops "beer of their own brewing."[32]

Character under Fire

Combat tested a gentleman's character by forcing him to confront his own internal fears and maintain a courageous demeanor for the men under his command. It demonstrated whether an officer had successfully prepared his unit for its ultimate trial. Combat, therefore, represented an especially stressful time for the New Brahmins. Even as they focused on the performance of their soldiers, New Brahmin officers also recognized and accepted that, as line officers, they faced grave personal dangers as well. William Wheeler realized that he was in an "actual, bloody war" after "meeting officers one day in courteous society, and seeing them on the next, mutilated or dead." "This," he remarked, "is emphatically a war deadly to officers."[33]

Like most Civil War soldiers, New Brahmins wanted to prove themselves in action. "Courage," Lorien Foote reminds students of the war, "was intimately connected with honor, an ideal of manhood historians rarely credit to northern soldiers, and with self-control, one of the most powerful concepts in northern society." At least once, New Brahmins wanted to see just how well they performed in the face of mortal danger on the battlefield. "I am horribly afraid we shan't see any more service & that the fighting will all be done in the rear of the Southern Potomac army," wrote Henry L. Abbott. "I don't mean, of course, that

I love fighting for itself," he clarified, "but I do earnestly long to be in a grand battle." Charles Russell Lowell admitted, "Like every young soldier, I am anxious for one battle as an experience." After that, he would "be content to bide my time, working where I can do most service." The men maintained, however, that they would always be willing to risk their lives in the name of the cause. William Wheeler promised not to "expose my life except when duty demands it" but added, "If I fall in the performance of that duty, you will know that it so pleased the Director of all events, and will not sorrow unduly at my dying in the noblest way, and for the highest and best cause."[34]

New Brahmins filled their letters with descriptions of battlefield dangers. Such writings underscored the deadly nature of their task, emphasized their sacrifice, but also allowed them to proclaim their personal triumph over fear. After the "awful" Battle of Williamsburg in which his division "suffered dreadfully," Charles P. Chandler reported that he survived "a rain of shot and shell." On the field, he felt "as cool as at home" even though stuck in "a hot place." "You don't know how queerly the bullets sound whistling about your head," Robert Gould Shaw told his mother after several close calls. Such a barrage made it seem "as if you must surely be hit." Charles Francis Adams, Jr., admitted to feeling frightened as "shells went shrieking and hurtling just over our heads and sometimes broke close to us," but it was not the type of fear he expected. "I knew that my nerves were a little braced," he explained, "but my mind was never clearer or more easily made up on points of doubt, and altogether the machine worked with a vigor and power which, under the circumstances, I had never hoped it possessed." Eri D. Woodbury recounted "the most terrible fire of Canister that ever I saw" in a sharp engagement. During the fight, "the woods were constantly lighted up with the flashing of their cannon: and then that awful shrieking as the shell and canister came ploughing and tearing through the trees." In the midst of this, "I felt a blow and a numbing sensation across my breast" that knocked him down. "Getting up," he continued, "I found where I was wounded: my fingers were completely knocked out & hanging over the back side the hand by a little shred of skin." He dodged rebel bullets as he attempted to escape. "The balls," he remembered, "whistled unpleasantly near my ears, and one struck my horse in the head instantly killing him."[35] These anxious young men proved the strength of their character by withstanding the punishment of battle and overcoming their fears.

New Brahmins had to subsume their personal concerns to the demands of leadership. "Officers as a class," Harvard-educated Lt. Henry Ropes observed, "must be men to whom the slightest taint of cowardice or the exhibition of fear before an enemy would be perfect destruction and everlasting indignity." The best officers needed to possess "a Gentleman's sense of honor and regard for character." At the Battle of Ball's Bluff Oliver Wendell Holmes, Jr., feared for his personal reputation but, at the same time, needed to serve as a model of leadership for his men. In the midst of the fight Holmes remembered, "I felt and acted very cool and did my duty I am sure—I was out in front of our men encouraging 'em on when a spent shot knocked the wind out of me & I fell." Ordered to return to the rear Holmes disobeyed, explaining, "I felt that I couldn't without more excuse so up I got and rushed to the front where hearing the Col. cheering the men on I waved my sword and asked if none would follow me when down I went again by the Colonel's side." Lying in a hospital, convinced that he had but a short time to live, Holmes felt "very happy in the conviction I did my duty handsomely." Summoning a passing doctor to his side, Holmes "gave him my address and told him (or meant & tried to) if I died to write home & tell 'em I'd done my duty—I was very anxious they should know that."[36]

The efforts of these character-conscious officers had a positive, calming, and reassuring effect on the men in the heat of battle. At the Battle of Chancellorsville, Francis C. Barlow made his presence known to the men by walking calmly in front of the line as shells and bullets flew by. One soldier remembered that Barlow "although strict in camp is as cool as a South Sea Islander." "When the shells are flying," the soldier continued, "he [Barlow] walked up & down our lines & coolly said 'Lie down, lie down & take it easy' although he thought us to be surrounded & that we would have to make our way out on the point of a bayonet." Men who commanded untested units thought that they had an even greater task to inspire the troops. "You see, I have a green regiment," Franklin A. Haskell explained to a friend. Thus he could not "get behind the lines as I might do in the case of seasoned troops. I shall be obliged always to lead." As a result, he predicted, "Of course I shall be shot."[37]

New Brahmins took it upon themselves to bolster morale on the battlefield by any means necessary. "In the battle, we cheer when we are doing well, and when we need to keep our courage up," Charles P. Chandler explained, noting that he needed to keep his men from wavering. "Yesterday," he recalled, "just in front of the Enemy, when the firing was roughest, I got the men cheering for some cause that I *invented*. It keeps the men in good spirits and frightens the Enemy, who believe reinforcements are coming in for us." Some chose to call upon the men's patriotism and speak to the noble cause for which they fought. Before an assault on Petersburg, Joshua L. Chamberlain reminded his men that they had "great duty for our country to perform, and who knows but the way in which we acquit ourselves in this perilous undertaking may depend the ultimate success of the preservation of our grand republic." Although some would fall, he expressed his confidence that the troops would "go in manfully and make such a record as will make all our loyal American people forever grateful."[38]

New Brahmins had no time to think of their own fears in battle as they focused intently on their duty as leaders. Only afterward could they assess their performance. After his first experience under fire, Theodore Lyman recorded that he had "stood it better than expected." "There is," he explained, "a certain discipline and a sense of necessity that bear you up." "What surprised me greatly," William Wheeler wrote after the Second Battle of Bull Run, "was that so very faint an idea of danger was in my mind at the very hottest of the fight; I was so thoroughly occupied with working my pieces to the best advantage, that I hardly noticed the bullets whistling and shells exploding around, and even some of the most revolting sights of bloodshed and death seemed to me very natural under the peculiar circumstances." "Every man, however brave," Wheeler later explained, "must feel unpleasantly when the shells begin to fall into the Battery before it is unlimbered, but as soon as the guns are 'in battery,' and the work has begun, this unpleasant sensation passes away, although more or less excitement is still felt, chiefly physical." Thomas W. Hyde declared that he had never felt fear "simply because I have had too much to do and have been obliged to incite the men by example—for any soldiers will fight if their officers are brave men." After the Battle of Shiloh, Harvard graduate Samuel H. Eells wrote down his impressions: "I did not know but what I should get frightened in the first battle; but I believe I didn't. I was too busy; and, if I had been ever so much scared, I don't think I could have run off and left our wounded crying for help." After his first experience under fire, Sidney Willard, another Harvard man, wrote, "I don't think I either showed or felt the least fear." While Confederate shells rained down on his position, he had to maneuver his unit "back under the fire of our battery over our heads, and of the Rebels from a hill opposite directly into us." In the midst of executing this order, "a fragment of shell (so the men said, I thought it was dirt) struck the road, and bounced right over my cap, about two feet above my head; and shot and shell struck and whizzed about in all directions. The Lieutenant of the battery was killed, and an artilleryman had his arm torn to pieces, besides wounded men in other regiments than ours." Despite the carnage, Willard kept his cool, reporting, "I was reading your letter during the shelling, while my regiment was lying under cover, and when that bit of dirt or iron, I don't know which, bounced over my head."[39] Remaining calm amid carnage helped New Brahmins demonstrate character to both themselves and their men.

In their accounts of battle, New Brahmins described a heightened sense of focus as they faced dangers on the battlefield. At the climax of Pickett's Charge during the third day of the Battle of Gettysburg, Franklin A. Haskell watched in horror as "the larger portion of Webb's Brigade . . . was breaking from the cover of their works, and without orders or reason, with no hand lifted to check them . . . falling back a fear-stricken flock of confusion!" At this moment, he realized that the "fate of Gettysburg hung upon a spider's single thread!" and a "great magnificent passion came on me at the instant, not one that overpowers and confounds, but one that blanches the face, and sublimes every sense and faculty." He described his actions:

> All rules and proprieties were forgotten all considerations of person, and danger, and safety, despised; for as I met the tide of these rabbits, the damned red flags of the rebellion began to thicken and flaunt along the wall they had just deserted, and one was already wavering over one of the guns of the dead Cushing. I ordered these men to "*halt*," and "*face about*," and "*fire*," and they heard my voice, and gathered my meaning, and obeyed my commands. On some unpatriotic backs, of those not quick of comprehension, the flat of my saber fell, not lightly; and at its touch their love of country returned; and with a look at me as if I were the destroying angel, as I might have become theirs, they again faced the enemy."[40]

Haskell successfully demonstrated his command of the situation, took charge in the heat of a crisis, and forced men to stand by their duty. He had, in the most dramatic fashion, demonstrated his character and leadership abilities.

In the midst of battle, if an officer had trained his unit well, the bravery of the soldiers could reinforce the commitment of the commanders. Men and officers alike could support one another in withstanding assaults and perform their duty. "I have not been afraid of anything in battle," Franklin A. Haskell commented, explaining, "One does not mind the bullets and shells much, but only looks to the men and the enemy, that all is right." Henry L. Abbott discovered that he "wasn't frightened at all" in combat. "Indeed," he explained, "it would be hard to be frightened when men whom you are accustomed to think more ignoble than yourself are cool all round you."[41] A unit's success in battle proved the character of the officer and demonstrated his success as a model for and leader of men.

New Brahmins greatly regretted their absence from any battlefield, especially if their comrades or units under their command engaged the enemy or received fire. Oliver Wendell Holmes, Jr., agonized that he could not join his regiment for the Battle of Fredericksburg. Sick with dysentery and "growing weaker each day from illness and starvation," in the days leading up to the battle in December 1862 he watched from his hospital bed as the Army of the Potomac crossed the Rappahannock River toward the rebel lines. "I see for the first time the Regt going to battle while I remain behind," he wrote to his mother. It was "a feeling worse than the anxiety of danger, I assure you—Weak as I was I couldn't restrain my tears." On the day after Confederate forces repulsed the Union assaults, Holmes wrote again, "We couldn't see the men but we saw the battle—a terrible sight when your Regt is in it but you are safe—Oh what self reproaches have I gone through for what I could not help." Luther C. Howell fell ill before a campaign and could not participate. Disappointed, he explained to his sister that it was "not the grand desire of a soldier to keep out of danger," and although a soldier might "not love fighting[,] will never shun it."[42]

The exhilaration of battlefield success led to pride and self-promotion. Even before the wide publication of his exploits at Little Round Top in July 1863, Joshua L. Chamberlain claimed full glory and credit for himself and his men. During the second day of the Battle of Gettysburg, the 20th Maine "held the post of honor on the extreme left of the whole army where the fiercest attack was made." He praised the regiment's "magnificent conduct" and described the odds against them: "I was attacked by a whole Rebel Brigade & after two hours fighting during which we exhausted our ammunition & snatched the full cartridge boxes from the dead & dying friend & foe, & when that was gone & we were pressed two to one, & had lost one hundred & fifty from the field, we *charged* & utterly routed the whole Brigade—killed & wounded 150 & took 308 prisoners & 300 stand of arms."[43] In Chamberlain's description, he and his unit appeared as a single entity. He used the first person to describe the target of the rebel attack but then shifted to a collective narrative of the unit's heroics.

New Brahmins often attributed the success of a unit to its leadership and took credit for commanding well-disciplined troops. Frazar A. Stearns argued that his unit performed well in a recent battle for several reasons: "1st. Because every officer knew his duty and did it. 2d. Because the men were *well fed* and *care* taken of them. 3d. Because they had a Colonel who knew what he was about, and is a gentleman besides." The success of leadership under fire fully demonstrated a gentleman's ability to mold lesser men into a disciplined and successful fighting force. On the other hand, failure of one's unit marred a gentleman's reputation. After the rout of the 11th Corps at the Battle of Chancellorsville in May 1863, Charles H. Howard admitted, "We deeply feel the disgrace of our Corps." "Otis," he continued, referring to their brother and corps commander Oliver, "is trying to devise plans of reorganization of different Brigades so as to have good Brigade Commanders and try to redeem our character in case another chance is given us." Later, Charles admitted to his mother, "It was a terrible blow to Otis to have his Corps so signally fail."[44]

Combat also helped seal the relationship of trust between officers and men. For the former, a unit's successful performance under fire helped justify all their discipline and training. The simple act of suffering together through adversity also strengthened bonds. "One of the pleasantest things that has developed by our late action is the kindly feeling shown by the men to the officers," Charles F. Morse wrote. "They have learned their dependence on them, and have confidence now in their pluck and willingness to share every danger with them." After the Battle of Chancellorsville with his company, Charles P. Mattocks praised the men of the 17th Maine: "When two Regts. were panic-stricken," he wrote to his mother, "they [his command] stood by me like heroes." Given the hard-fought battle and the loyalty of the men, Mattocks asked how he could part with them. "Would I abandon men who showed themselves willing to give their own lives to save mine?" he asked.[45]

The horror of war took its toll on New Brahmins. Not even these realists who accepted that war required sacrifice could imagine the dead and wounded after a battle. Witnessing the carnage became part of these men's wartime experiences, and they tried to come to terms with such sights by fitting them into their frameworks of character. Joseph H. Twichell found that he was "getting, not hardened, but accustomed" to the sights of blood. Early in the war he "shrank from witnessing operations and more than once . . . was compelled to decline my aid, fearing that I should prove useless when the knife appeared." He had, however, "overcome all this and by a little care in observation, I have acquired a skill and handiness which enable me to act as an assistant in an amputation." After the Battle of Williamsburg, Charles P. Chandler reflected on the horrors of war. "When . . . all is passed, and a night has intervened and rest and quiet again rule, and you look over the field and reckon up the results," he wrote, "there horrid war stands out before you in all its wicked horror." The lesson, however, had "not been a disheartening one for me." Rather, it was "a *hardening process*," for he felt "able to look on most anything now." A couple more battles would "quite fit me to stand unmoved amidst any scene of filth, of suffering[,] of slaughter, of terrors and of wickedness, physically speaking." "*The battle*," he told his mother, "is but a small part of war." Burying the dead and caring for the wounded from both sides was also "*war* itself, and not the glory of war." After reporting that he had taken part in "the severest & grandest [battle] of the war" at Antietam, Charles H. Howard admitted, "I had never before seen such terrible sights—the heaps & rows of dead! You can discern where the Rebel lines were by the line of dead lying side by side."[46] Despite the suffering they witnessed following battle, these men remained committed to the task of preserving the Union. They did their duty, proved their character, and endured.

Driven by notions of proper character to physically lead less cultivated men into war, New Brahmins still demanded recognition of their social status in the armed forces. They would serve but only as men of the gentleman class. As many of them argued, their qualities as educated men could do more for the Union cause than simply catch a bullet. Their concern with their rank and class status in the armed forces set them apart from their fellow comrades in arms.

As young officers, New Brahmins emphasized the importance of discipline in line with both military codes of behavior and their own undergraduate training. They quickly adapted to the military regimen, bringing their studying skills to bear. Some even thought of themselves as better than regular troops and West Point graduates. These young social leaders, after all, viewed themselves as superior men who had both the best education in the country and the passion of their convictions. Class conscious throughout their time in service, these men shunned the company of foreign soldiers and revealed their antebellum biases. At the same time, their treatment of African American soldiers signaled their acceptance of common racist beliefs at the time.

Officers felt a great sense of anxiety when combat—the ultimate test of one's character and ability to train and lead others—approached. Even as they wondered if their internal character could withstand the ordeal, they also hoped that the discipline they had instilled would keep their men in line and fighting efficiently under fire. Men of the New Brahmin class hoped, more than ever, to demonstrate exemplary traits to others.

Ultimately, as junior officers, these New Brahmins' positions brought them into harm's way. To test their character they exposed themselves to the dangers of the battlefield. Many paid the ultimate price. Of the forty-nine men at the core of this study, sixteen (32.7 percent) died in the war—killed in action or as a result of wounds received in battle. Counting wounded men, the casualty list rises to twenty-three out of forty-nine (46.9 percent). This does not include all the minor injuries that the core group sustained. With great risk also came rewards. Five of the men discussed in these pages (Chamberlain, Oliver O. Howard, Hyde, Mattocks, and Woodbury) received Medals of Honor for their bravery in the war.

These men's leadership skills ultimately brought mixed results. For example, while some units such as the 2nd and 20th Massachusetts Volunteers turned out well, Francis C. Barlow's German troops in the 11th Corps did not appear to benefit from his discipline. On a personal level, however, most of these men expressed satisfaction and believed that they had proven their character during the war. They had, after all, volunteered, survived harsh conditions, interacted with and led common soldiers, and faced enemy fire. They demonstrated discipline, independent thought, and a willingness to sacrifice for their beliefs. If one could not easily demonstrate one's inner qualities in the antebellum world, wartime service helped clarify the situation, and the New Brahmins affirmed themselves as gentlemen of character.

7

Character Triumphant

Reconstruction, Reform, and Reconciliation

News of President Lincoln's death came as "a thunderclap" to New Brahmins everywhere. Oliver O. Howard remarked to his wife that the late president had "sealed his great work with his life." "The grief," he continued, "is almost unnatural and completely depressing amongst the officers." He wished that Lincoln had "lived to enjoy in this life the fruits of his faithful labor." Joshua L. Chamberlain lamented Lincoln's death by contrasting the joyful feeling that the men felt before they heard the sad news: "In this hour of exultation, in this day of power + joy + hope, when our starry flag floats amid the stars of Heaven, suddenly it falls to half-mast—'Darkness sweeps athwart the sky,' + the President of the United States, with his heart full of conciliation + charity + forgiveness is struck down by the assassin's hand. Words will not tell the feeling with which this Army receives this news." He wished that his wife, Fanny, could have been with him to see the funeral services held in camp with "the drooping flags—the dirges of the bands—the faces of the men." "Nothing of this Rebellion has so filled my heart with sorrow," Charles H. Howard remarked. "The loss seemed so irreparable, so unexpected and so terrible in the manner of its occurrence."[1]

Swept up by their emotions, some New Brahmins initially demanded swift vengeance and retribution. Thomas H. Hubbard told his sister that Lincoln's death had "made me a radical." He declared that any leniency "towards the rebels" would be "a crime" and proceeded to detail the charges against them: "It is not enough that they have brought a *causeless* war upon the country, have desolated their own section and made ours sad, that they have starved and murdered our soldiers, that they have returned generosity with cruelty, and insolence for kindness." Now, in defeat, "like cowards as they are, they adopt the congenial employment of assassins." Hubbard expressed anger that "the majority of the rebels will approve the act, and rejoice at it." After learning of "strong demonstrations of joy in Charlestown, on Saturday evening after the murder was known," he wanted the city destroyed. Additionally, he thought, "the whole South should be traversed and wasted until its people are as humble as they have been arrogant." Such outbursts lasted only a brief time. While Hubbard had let loose his emotions at least on paper, the New Brahmins restrained their physical actions in the tense atmosphere, mindful of their position. Additionally, they vigilantly watched for trouble, fearing that a loss of control among the troops might lead to reigniting hostilities. Joshua L. Chamberlain even asked a chaplain to speak to his men to urge them against seeking revenge on southerners.[2]

After the initial shock of the assassination, New Brahmins soberly reflected on the situation and pondered the reunited nation's future course. Looking forward, they believed that the government needed to secure the war's legacy: the salvation of the Union and the liberation of the enslaved. They supported the rebuilding of the South but remained ambivalent on the issue of freed people's civil rights. The war may have changed much but it did not shake their prejudices against blacks. Bias, coupled with these young men's new found respect for the character of their wartime enemies, led to their lukewarm support for Reconstruction and paved the way for reconciliation between the gentlemen class of the two sections.

New Brahmins believed that Union victory affirmed the strength of northern character and bolstered the triumphal narrative of the New England–centric nationalist story. The North, led by its gentleman class, had demonstrated the superiority of its ways and claimed a triumph for free labor and industry. The war tested the character—the inner strength—of the North and had found it not only sufficient but also abundant. Victory over the Confederacy confirmed the superiority of northern civilization. New Brahmins could rejoice that slavery—the system of labor incompatible with their understanding of American history—was no longer an incubus on the national conscience. And, perhaps equally important, these men had proven their character both to themselves and to society. Their leadership had seen the Union through its fiery trial.

Although they pursued various paths after the conflict, the New Brahmins during their postwar careers shared three major interests. First, although they fully believed that the South needed some supervision during Reconstruction, they vigilantly warned against the reemergence of radicalism for fear that it might lead to the eruption of another conflict. These concerns merged with their worries about corrupt government as Reconstruction seemed to drag on without measurable progress. Second, New Brahmins continued to value the traits of character above all else. They prescribed character-based education as necessary for both freed people and the next generation of young men entering college, and used it as an avenue to make peace with their former adversaries. Finally, as moderate men of character, they sought to reform and shape American society. Stymied and rejected by the political process, the New Brahmins turned to business, law, and education to try to craft their vision of a perfect republic. Through all this, the lessons of their college educations, tested and affirmed by the war, remained firmly in the back of their minds.

In waging the war, New Brahmins had recognized traits of northern character in their Confederate counterparts. This recognition that even their enemies—by their bravery and resoluteness in defending their cause—embraced elements of character, allowed for a reconciliationist movement based on professions of mutual admiration. Indeed, such a movement emerged in the decades after Appomattox. New Brahmins accepted southern gentlemen who had demonstrated traits esteemed by men of character as trustworthy and honorable. They could reconcile, live together again in peace, and shape the nation, now firmly guided by a triumphal, New England–centric vision of American nationalism. Even as they accepted the character of their former foes, New Brahmins never compromised on the fact that the Confederacy's cause had been a terrible one. As Reconstruction dragged on and the violence continued in the former rebellious states, news of government scandals also emerged, prompting New Brahmins to seek remedies for the nation's corrupt system of governance. And, in extricating themselves from what they deemed southern issues, they looked to the southern men who seemingly shared their traits of character to guide the South.

Whatever positive character traits New Brahmins recognized in their southern counterparts, they could not see such qualities in the freed people. New Brahmins feared that freed people, without proper industrial skills and education, could not survive in the postwar world of free labor. Only aggressive instruction and development of good character traits could rescue the freed people from a lifetime of dependence. Southern elites encouraged their northern counterparts' beliefs in the inferiority of freed people, securing another plank of northern and southern reconciliation: celebration of white bravery and the questioning of African Americans' contributions to the war.

The New Brahmin class, having affirmed themselves in the conflict, attempted to retain their leadership positions afterward. Hoping that they might improve other imperfections in American society and the political system, these men's ideals intersected with two key postwar groups: intellectuals and liberal reformers. Leslie Butler has examined how intellectuals "devoted their post–Civil War careers to the reformation of American democracy, to the elevation and broadening of its cultural life, and to a sharp critique of its late-century imperial adventures." The Civil War represented "the defining event of these men's lives" because it "remained . . . a moment of heady idealism when American slavery was abolished and American democracy vindicated on a world stage." These liberals, part of a larger Atlantic community of intellectuals and reformers, "took it upon themselves to elevate, nudge, challenge, and inspire their citizenries" by "keeping before the public a vision of how individuals and the larger nation might venture beyond the pursuit of material wealth toward higher civic and cultural ideals."[3]

The liberal reformers, meanwhile, emerged from the war with great hopes for the future. Influenced by a liberal interpretation of market forces and a republican vision of governance, these reformers soon lost faith that the era's politicians could solve the issues they thought needed the greatest attention: "'good government,' economic orthodoxy, and moral rejuvenation." Because of their particular concern that selfishness and the desire for personal gain had compromised the nation's lawmakers, the reformers, according to one scholar, "glorified the independent man in politics, the man who refused to permit the base spirit of party to corrupt his individual judgment." The liberal reformers thought government corruption had caused a decline in public morality and framed their proposed currency, trade, and civil service reforms as "efforts to end government-permitted stealing." Liberal reformers had the simple goal of freeing both the market and the government. Historian Nancy Cohen summed up their logic: "Laissez-faire deprived the state of effective power in the market; administrative governance insulated the policymaking institutions of the state from the influence of the people." Such plans to purify the government stemmed from long-standing efforts on behalf of reformers. Andrew L. Slap has pointed to an antebellum origin for the liberal reformers, arguing that "classical American republicanism was one of the primary prisms through which they saw and interpreted the world." Additionally, he concludes that their desire to deal with "issues they thought more threatening to the existence of republican government" forced them to compromise on the civil liberties of blacks in the South, in essence leading to the end of Reconstruction.[4]

In the years after Appomattox, New Brahmins sympathized with many of the causes espoused by the two groups mentioned in the preceding paragraphs. Yet they remained distinct because of their broad set of occupations and by their wartime service. Not all of the individuals involved in the liberal reform movement served in the Union army. Serving in the war proved a formative experience for the New Brahmins who, instead of fearing the consequences of wartime policy in enlarging the federal state, demanded greater power and effort to win the war at all costs. Their calls for an active government continued after the war as they supported a limited Reconstruction policy.

Instead of changing or challenging New Brahmins' worldviews, the war only confirmed their faith that moderate political and social leaders best served the needs of the public. These men remained convinced that radical politicians and agitators had brought on the war. Meanwhile, they feared that northern radicals might jeopardize the peaceful sectional relations by pressing for vengeance against southerners and calling for controversial measures such as the granting of civil rights to the freed people. The course of events and their desire to safeguard the war's legacy ultimately led most New Brahmins to support the postwar constitutional amendments. But Reconstruction alone did not preoccupy the New Brahmins who now took their positions as society's leaders. They also continued to target what they believed had caused the war: a corrupt political system and an uneducated populace. These men shared the liberal reformers' sentiments when it came to tackling inefficient government. They sought to fix the civil service, lower the tariff rates, and curtail what they considered unsound monetary practices. Having lost faith in the Republican Party as a reform-minded organization, some New Brahmins left to join the Liberal Republican movement, while others sought to reform the party from within. More important, these men continued to ponder how to behave in accordance with the principles of good character. In their estimation, good character had won the war and proven itself a model for success. In the postwar world, New Brahmins continued to use character as a guide and hoped to impart its lessons to future generations as well. Sound character, they believed, would strengthen the nation and prepare it to confront future crises.

Unfortunately, the societal leadership positions that these men sought did not always fulfill their desires. Indeed, they discovered that the next generation of Americans rejected the authority of their class. In political and education reform, New Brahmins viewed defeat as a rejection of their authority. No surprise, then, that in their elder years their minds returned to past battlefields where they had triumphed. The glory of days long passed comforted them in the cold light of a modernizing republic.

Reconstruction and Reform

New Brahmins believed that agitation by radicals had caused the war. They feared that the same forces would also threaten the peace. Charles Francis Adams, Jr., voiced his concerns about the influence of Radical Republicans on the postwar period as early as 1862 when he argued that the greatest menace to the nation's progress was "a spirit of blind, revengeful fanaticism in the North . . . which, utterly deficient in practical wisdom, will, if it can, force our country into any position-be it bankrupt, despotic, anarchical, or what not—in its blind effort to destroy slavery and the South." Adams warned that radicals "will always in troublous times obtain temporary supreme control, will bankrupt the nation, jeopard[ize] all liberty by immense standing armies, debauch the morality of the nation by war, and undermine all our republican foundations to effect the immediate destruction of the one institution of slavery." When the war ended, such fears of radicalism run amok remained. Upon hearing of Lincoln's assassination, John C. Gray immediately suspected that one of two groups orchestrated the murder: radical secessionists bitter at defeat or radical abolitionists upset by Lincoln's moderation on emancipation. Moderates such as themselves, New Brahmins believed, had helped end the war that radicals in both sections had ignited. Theodore Lyman praised moderates for saving the Union but criticized radical abolitionists, charging that "no extremist . . . *did* anything notable in the struggle."[5] After the sacrifices moderates already had made, how could they allow radicals to continue to agitate and threaten the hard-won peace?

New Brahmins believed that by laying waste to the South and destroying slavery, the war had exacted a just price for secession. With the Union secure, the boil of slavery lanced, and the poison of secession neutralized, they extended an olive branch to their southern counterparts and hoped for a speedy resumption of national affairs. John C. Gray feared that controversial issues such as granting civil rights to freedmen would prevent southerners from swiftly reembracing the Union. The loyalty of future generations "depends entirely on the treatment they receive," he told his mother, explaining that "if they are kept under military government or reduced to the state even that Ireland was in at the beginning of the century, I see no reason to suppose that the children will grow up with any less hatred of the North than their fathers have." He proposed instead to allow southern whites who had taken the loyalty oath to "choose their legislature, make the members of the legislature take the same oath, and let them work away without interference." Granting civil rights to freed people, he feared, "would embitter the white men as much as if all negroes were allowed to vote, while the number who could vote would be so few that it would not materially strengthen the loyal vote for the state." With pro-Union men in charge, he predicted, "personal liberty would be secured to the negroes and their families, and more it would not seem to me wise to demand for them."[6]

Many New Brahmins supported a lenient Reconstruction policy, which meant limiting freed people's gains. While this makes them appear lukewarm on Reconstruction, note that the trajectory of their beliefs matches ideas they had articulated since 1861: they fought the war to preserve the Union and did not view blacks as capable of assuming equal roles in American society. Joshua L. Chamberlain, eyeing the governor's mansion in Maine, supported Republican moderates when it came to Reconstruction but knew that the public wanted the South punished. He called for "guarantees good and sufficient against any future attempt to destroy this government whether in the exercise of a pretended right by open war, or by the more artful and insidious assaults against the principles on which this Nation is founded." He remained unconvinced on the topic of freedmen's suffrage. As far as he was concerned, the war had been waged to save the Union and emancipation had simply been a by-product. Changing the political composition of the southern states and adding blacks to the voter roles seemed like a step too far. Although he initially endorsed the Radical Republicans' plans for Reconstruction, Chamberlain remained opposed to blacks gaining the franchise.[7] Joshua L. Chamberlain dreamed of the old Union and could not envision a new, more complicated and diverse one.

Some New Brahmins participated directly in Reconstruction efforts and attempted to implant their northern vision of progress in the soil of the South. Men such as Oliver O. and Charles H. Howard and Samuel C. Armstrong became Freedmen's Bureau officers. Luther C. Howell, meanwhile, moved to the South to take advantage of economic opportunities. Relocating to Selma, Alabama, after the war, Howell rejected the "bosh" of Radical Republicans who spread stories of oppressed freed people in the South. In March 1866 Howell dismissed such reports, explaining that a freed person's "value as a laborer is his protection & it is proving to be a very sure one hereabouts. I don't take any stock in the idea that they are being oppressed[.] [E]very negro who desires to work can get plenty of it to do and their employer uses them well in order to keep them as there is nothing else to keep them from breaking the contracts." After spending over a year in the South, Howell admitted, "Politically I am more in sympathy with this people than I should be if I lived north for there are so many lies told about them that I get indignant at the northern papers." He promised not to become "a good southern Rebel" but declared, "In my opinion it is not a good thing to keep sticking pins into your enemy whom you have already knocked down with your club."[8]

At the same time that they sympathized with their southern counterparts, the New Brahmins uniformly feared freed people's dependence on government largesse. When he took command of the Freedmen's Bureau, Oliver O. Howard emphasized to his commissioners that "the negro should understand that he is really free but on no account, if able to work, should he harbor the thought that the Government will support him in idleness." Bureau officers took their cue from headquarters and viewed freed people's unwillingness to work as the greatest threat to their mission.[9] Having unshackled the South from slavery, they hoped not to attach the yoke of government aid to those in greatest need of building new lives. The idea of free labor championed by the New Brahmins had triumphed. They would not see it compromised for anyone. In reality, however, Reconstruction's fate rested in other arenas.

After initially promising to exact vengeance on the South, President Andrew Johnson soon embarked on a lenient Reconstruction program that not only prevented Congress from having any say but also allowed former rebel officials to resume their posts as representatives of their various districts. In the South, the new state governments established under Presidential Reconstruction set up strict measures to control the movement and rights of the freed people, leading to the accusation that their "Black Codes" appeared to preserve slavery in all but name. President Johnson also pardoned large numbers of rebels and returned their lands, which, under the federal government, had already been portioned off to freedmen and their families. Finally, the president removed Freedmen's Bureau agents who impeded his orders. When Congress reconvened in December 1865, even moderate lawmakers could not tolerate the presence of former rebels taking their seats and barred their admission. James A. Garfield, then a member of the House of Representatives, had helped the former Confederate vice president, Alexander Stephens, gain his freedom but fully opposed his and other former rebels' return to Congress. Attempts to work with President Johnson ended in failure; in an effort to ensure the legacy of the war and provide freed people with the tools to protect themselves, Congress contemplated granting them civil rights.[10] The drama of Reconstruction spun out of control at first at the highest levels of government rather than in the destitute freedmen's camps.

Having judged Presidential Reconstruction a failure, Congress stepped in to manage affairs. Led by Radical Republicans, the measures, especially those concerning blacks' civil rights, greatly alarmed conservatives. New Brahmins themselves tacitly supported Congressional Reconstruction given the circumstances but also remained ambivalent about the outcome. James A. Garfield received letters from southern residents opposing the elevation and integration of freed people. One woman who had taught African Americans protested "an attempt to compel blacks and whites to mingle more together." "I would not consent to our children's attending a mixed school," she declared, "for as the blacks are now, their society would be degrading." "They are a *strange* race," she explained, and "my experience among them . . . makes me fear that they are not reliable—and have little forethought, economy and perseverance." These, she argued, "are the virtues of a *free* people, and have not had time to take root."[11] Garfield sympathized with this assessment. And yet Congress somehow needed to secure the war's legacy, which had come at such a high cost.

Despite their initial misgivings about freedmen's rights, New Brahmins overcame their hesitancy on the issue. Unwilling to leave freed people in legal limbo, they reluctantly acknowledged the need for citizenship rights, including suffrage. But New Brahmins did not think that everyone had the qualifications to participate in a democratic government. Here then, they returned to their roots and prescribed education as the panacea for all they saw in the South. An education that emphasized teaching good character, they insisted, would cure the region's ills and provide freed people with the traits they needed to survive in the postwar world and participate in American democracy.

New Brahmins, therefore, focused their efforts on providing or supporting educational efforts in the South. Oliver O. Howard recalled that after the war, the "prevailing thought was: The slaves are becoming free; give them knowledge—teach them to read—teach the child!" In 1867 Howard acted on his commitment to freedmen's education by helping found the university that bears his name in Washington, D.C. Established especially for freedmen, Howard University differed from other freedmen's schools in one key respect: it placed no limits on the level of education students could receive. Some opponents told him "that *no* high schools or colleges were wanted for the freedmen." His own beliefs, however, led him to the conclusion that "you cannot keep up the lower grades unless you have the higher." Briefly taking the helm of the university, Howard "regarded that institution as of the first importance as an object lesson—a complete exhibit in its organization of the higher grade of school work."[12]

As Freedmen's Bureau commissioner, Howard helped fund the establishment of several other black schools. In this endeavor, he did not stand alone among New Brahmins. Samuel C. Armstrong began his long career in education while working for the Freedmen's Bureau. Despite his experience as the former commander of the 9th United States Colored Troops, Armstrong never overcame his paternalistic view of blacks. He fully supported the Bureau's hard line, maintaining that white agents knew how best to help blacks regardless of what the freedmen themselves believed. He prescribed the same lessons he had learned about the importance of character as the solution to freedmen's problems. Comparing African Americans to the Polynesian islanders among whom he spent his childhood, he declared, "Of both it is true that not mere ignorance, but deficiency of character is the chief difficulty, and that to build up character is the true objective point of education." Even though he committed himself to the cause of black education, helping to establish the Hampton Normal and Agricultural Institute in 1868, he continued to doubt blacks' abilities to advance, declaring them unfit for full political citizenship. Instead, Armstrong argued that blacks ought to focus on acquiring technical and agricultural skills. As he explained, "In all men education is conditioned not alone by an enlightened head and a changed heart, but very largely on a routine of industrious habit, which is to character what the foundation is to the pyramid." Armstrong taught a young Booker T. Washington at Hampton, and Washington, in turn, helped spread the philosophy of industrial education into the twentieth century.[13]

In building Hampton, Armstrong drew on his past experience with native Hawaiians. Hampton's students were not required to learn the classics but rather to focus on skills. Armstrong, therefore, developed a segregated curriculum, which designated certain topics as belonging solely to whites. Historian Jeremy Wells has argued that Armstrong had a colonialist mind-set. "By borrowing a vocabulary that hinted at colonialist supervision," Wells writes, "Armstrong was effectively denying black Southerners the identity of citizenship that had been afforded them with the passage of the Fourteenth Amendment in 1868. He was construing them instead as a barbaric, foreign population within the nation's borders." Hampton, Wells contends, cultivated a "colonized consciousness: a belief system that involved reverence toward the colonizer, self-loathing among the colonized, and a patient faith that, at some point in the distant future, the colonial protégé might become like his or her civilizing mentor." Armstrong's ideas, however, did not come from his childhood observations alone. New Brahmins, as a group, held similar beliefs about character-based education. As Armstrong told his investors, he hoped to "civilize" rather than prematurely press the issue of social equality. He likened Hampton to "a remarkable machine for the elevation of our colored brethren." "Put in a raw plantation darkey," he advertised, "and he comes out a gentleman of the nineteenth century." Armstrong's curriculum involved the development of character, which he thought blacks lacked. Only whites could determine when the freed people had attained the level of character that would allow them to exercise their full citizenship rights. Hampton's challenge, Armstrong said, was to figure out "how to skip three centuries in the line of development and to atone for the loss and injustice of the ages." On another occasion he joked that blacks would not reach the level of white character until the twenty-fifth century.[14]

New Brahmins hoped to practice what they preached. Even as they prescribed character training for freedmen, they attempted to demonstrate their own ideals by charting a moderate political course, a difficult proposition in the years of Presidential Reconstruction. They became increasingly concerned with the conflict between the executive and legislative branches. Vetoing legislation and demonizing congressional lawmakers, President Johnson also attempted to remove officials who disagreed with his stance. Appalled by the president's behavior, frustrated congressmen spearheaded impeachment proceedings. Although the New Brahmins had once begrudgingly supported the radical agenda when it came to southern Reconstruction, they considered actions like attempting to remove the president too extreme. While congressional Republicans succeeded in impeaching the president, they failed to convict and remove him from office. Joshua L. Chamberlain publicly broke with the radical faction of the party when he defended Maine Senator William Pitt Fessenden's vote to sustain President Andrew Johnson in office during the conviction trial in the Senate.[15]

Although New Brahmins had high hopes for the new Ulysses S. Grant administration, which took office in 1869, they quickly soured on the former general's leadership. With the ratification of the Fourteenth and Fifteenth Amendments, guaranteeing freed people citizenship and black men the right to vote, New Brahmins thought that the nation had done enough to help the freed people. When violence continued in the South and Grant sparingly used military force to maintain order, the New Brahmins balked at the treatment their southern counterparts faced. Additionally, Grant's lieutenants took advantage of their positions, and the scandals that emerged soon after marred the former general's reputation.

New Brahmins' criticized the Grant administration for using the army to pacify unruly southerners bent on curtailing the influence of blacks and their white allies. Their concerns about the corrupting influence of military power overrode all other considerations. Terrorist violence by groups such as the Ku Klux Klan had prompted Grant to use force. When the army failed to bring peace to the entire region—an impossible task given the army's reduced size and the scope of its missions, which included pacifying Native American tribes on the frontier—New Brahmins joined opponents of the military policy. Rep. James A. Garfield, who had reluctantly supported black suffrage early on, wrote, "It goes against the grain of my feelings to favor negro suffrage"; he "never could get in love with [the] creatures." After the Fifteenth Amendment's ratification,

Garfield thought that the government ought to leave southern blacks to their fate. He strongly disagreed with President Grant's use of force to bolster besieged Republican state governments.[16]

New Brahmins' own failure to understand the nature of white southern resistance also prevented them from offering appropriate solutions. Even Oliver O. Howard, a man who spent years trying to balance the demands of white and black southerners, misjudged the nature of opposition to federal control. Instead of realizing that violence resulted from the ousted social leaders seeking to regain political power, he, and others, blamed "the baser classes" in the South. Howard went as far as to exonerate the upper class from wrongdoing, writing that "the better portion of the communities had not been engaged in these acts, and there was no evidence that respectable Confederate soldiers were involved in these enterprises." Howard credited the army with helping to suppress Klan violence, but he also heaped praise on southerners. "By procuring the support of good citizens all over the South" alongside the use of force, he wrote, the freedmen's schools could continue their operations. The New Brahmins felt confident in criticizing interference in the former Confederate states because they also thought the federally supported Reconstruction governments had failed to usher in an age of free labor prosperity. News of waste and corruption also convinced New Brahmin observers that national Reconstruction efforts had lost their way. As a result, they, like liberal reformers of the period, looked to the old ruling class in the South, their own counterparts, to solve the region's problems.[17]

New Brahmins also hoped to quickly resolve the issue of southern Reconstruction because they wished to focus on reforming matters pertaining to the history of the war as well as northern society in general. Appalled by the vicious party politics and corruption, they attempted to remain true to their conscience and take principled stances. This sometimes resulted in detrimental effects but, of course, a man of character ought not to care for the consequences of acting righteously. Joshua L. Chamberlain, for example, acting out of a sense of loyalty and a desire for justice, attempted to set the record straight on a controversial wartime event. In the final offensive against the Petersburg–Richmond line in 1865, Gen. Philip H. Sheridan, one of Gen. Grant's favorite officers, relieved Chamberlain's corps commander, Gen. Gouverneur K. Warren, for failing to press the assault with vigor. Grant affirmed the decision. Chamberlain maintained that this action had been unwarranted and unjust. In 1869, speaking to the Society of the Army of the Potomac, a veterans organization, he took the opportunity to make a stand for Warren and directly criticize both Gen. Sheridan and President Grant. He hoped that "tardy justice . . . may be done to officers whose character and service in behalf of the Republic, deserve something better than its hasty and lasting rebuke." Although no evidence suggests that Grant held a grudge, one of Chamberlain's biographers notes that this critique had been "aimed squarely at those who . . . stood at the peak of political power" and that the president, as leader of the Republican Party, might have prevented Chamberlain's ascension into other party offices.[18] For Chamberlain, remaining true to character appeared more important than his own political prospects.

On the national level, New Brahmins identified many pressing issues: government corruption, unsound financial practices, threatening concentrations of economic power, and the debate over imperialism. Yet northern men of character had little faith in the nation's politicians to manage these affairs. One scholar of the period concluded that Americans everywhere feared that "ruthless men had usurped the government and were now wielding it for their private benefit." From his vantage point in the House of Representatives, James A. Garfield regretted that the war had "brought to the surface of National politics many men who are neither fitted in character, nor ability, to be leaders of public thought or representative of the true men of the country."[19]

Critics of the Republican Party in this period claimed that it had drifted away from the issues that had vaulted it to victory in 1860. Its fall mirrored the general collapse of social morality. Lincoln's party, according to one historian, "seemed to have degenerated into a patronage machine" and the "Grant administration had become a spoils system promoting graft and bribery rather than public virtue." Additionally, reformers saw no attempts to inoculate the civil service against office seekers or to lower the tariff, issues dear to them. Dissatisfaction with President Grant led Charles Francis Adams, Jr., to flirt with the Liberal Republican Party in 1872—that is, until the party nominated the newspaper editor Horace Greeley for president.[20] Divided and inconsistent, the Liberal Republican movement ended in defeat.

During Grant's second term, the federal government and northern society shifted even further away from both Radical Reconstruction and the war itself. Joshua L. Chamberlain discovered this change in public mood when he attempted to introduce military drill as part of an undergraduate's course of study. In his varied postwar career, Chamberlain took on the task of modernizing and leading his alma mater, Bowdoin College. In addition to raising funds and creating new departments that emphasized science and engineering, Chamberlain tried to prepare the next generation of Bowdoin students for the possibility of military service. Never again, he hoped, would the nation be unprepared in a time of crisis. Remembering the chaos of the early days of the Civil War, he believed that this drill program would better prepare college men for military service. Students who initially approved of the drill soon balked at the martial routine and refused to participate. This "drill rebellion" in 1874 directly challenged Chamberlain's authority, and he took the drastic step of expelling three-quarters of the student body. Forced to eventually back down, he watched as the college boards phased out the drill. The economic depression of the 1870s also sapped funds for his new programs. When he retired from the presidency, Chamberlain left a checkered legacy.[21] His attempt to introduce military drill to prepare young men for future conflicts did not take root in the postwar environment in which New England was no longer threatened by secession and slavery, and the aging war hero seemed too military-minded to young men aiming to conquer not hillsides but boardrooms.

Chamberlain's infatuation with military life notwithstanding, a decade after the war New Brahmins and Americans in general concluded that the conflict's issues had been settled and that military rule in the former rebel states had gone on long enough. Appalled at the lack of progress in the South, they argued that only a reunion of the educated classes could restore peace and prosperity to the region and that only a weakening of the Union's military stance could reduce the threat of corruption at the national level. New Brahmins couched their opposition to President Grant's Reconstruction policies in the language of character. At a celebration of the centennial anniversary of the Battle of Lexington in 1875, William F. Bartlett, whose dissatisfaction with President Grant had led him to support the Liberal Republicans, directly criticized the administration's policies in his speech. Grant himself, seated at the ceremony, listened to his former subordinate's plea. Bartlett declared, "I have a prejudice, which is shared by all soldiers, in favor of peace. . . . Between the *soldiers* of the two great sections of our country, fraternal relations were established long ago." He hated "the men who would, for the sake of self or party, stand in the way of reconciliation and a united country," and urged the president to "look to their heroes, their leaders,—their Gordons, their Lees, their Johnstons, Lamar, Ransom, and Ripley,—and tell me if you find in their utterances anything but renewed loyalty and devotion to a reunited country." "As an American," Bartlett continued, "I am as proud of the men who charged so bravely with Pickett's Division on our lines at Gettysburg, as I am of the men who so bravely met and repulsed them there." Men, he explained, could not always "choose the right cause; but when, having chosen that which conscience dictates, they are ready to die for it, if they justify not their cause, they at least ennoble themselves." Referring to the occasion and setting of his speech, Bartlett argued, "The men who, for conscience' sake, fought against their government at Gettysburg, ought easily to be forgiven by the sons of men who, for conscience' sake, fought against the government at Lexington and Bunker Hill." Because Confederates fully committed themselves to their course, they had proven their character on northern terms.[22]

Debates about Reconstruction and concerns about corruption came to a head in the contested election of 1876. Here, Francis C. Barlow, a loyal Republican, faced another test of character that ultimately spoiled his relationship with his party. Committed to pursuing the right course as they saw it, New Brahmins like Barlow found peacetime ways to demonstrate their character in the world of politics. Barlow respected many Democratic lawmakers, including that party's presidential nominee, Gov. Samuel J. Tilden. In the election, however, Barlow supported the candidacy of Republican Gov. Rutherford B. Hayes, explaining, "I believe there is too much good sense in the American people to turn this Gov't and its credit to those who 10 or 12 years ago were trying to destroy it." "Neither Mr. Tilden nor anyone else," he maintained, "can stem the rebel influence if he is elected." Barlow's concern illustrates the delicate balance that New Brahmins attempted to preserve. Accepting southerners back into the political fold did not mean allowing them to control the levers of national government. Barlow remained concerned with surviving rebel sentiments that he had fought to suppress a decade earlier. Charles Francis Adams, Jr., however, appalled by the Republicans, backed Tilden's candidacy. While he admitted that the Democratic candidate had "paddled in dirty water" and "belongs to a set which I thoroughly despise," Adams preferred the former New York governor to Hayes, "a man of the caliber of [Franklin] Pierce on a meaningless platform."[23]

Although Gov. Tilden won the popular vote, Republicans clung to and disputed the electoral vote results from three southern states: Louisiana, South Carolina, and Florida. With the electoral votes from these three states in the Republican column, the party could retain control of the executive branch. Sent to Florida by the outgoing President Grant as part of a committee to investigate voter tallies, Barlow suspected that fraud and corruption had marred the process. After his investigation, Barlow publicly reported his conclusions that Gov. Tilden had carried Florida. Party loyalists condemned and pilloried him for his actions. Years later, Barlow mourned the disappearance of men of character from public life. Trying to explain his inability to succeed in politics, Barlow wrote in a 1888 letter that "the one thing which impresses and influences me most, after many years of experience[,] is the unwillingness of most men ever to take any position hostile to themselves or their friends." As a man of character, he had been unwilling to sacrifice his independence in the name of party loyalty and, as such, found that he had no place in the political world.[24]

Some New Brahmins hoped that President Hayes would be more amenable to reforms than his predecessor. In April 1877, shortly after the new administration took office, Joshua L. Chamberlain wrote to Secretary of the Interior Carl Schurz, a well-known liberal reformer. He promised that he had remained "firm in adherence to the great principles of the Republican party" but "still believed in the purification of the civil service, a constant regard for local self-government, and the subordination of the military to the civil power in time of peace." In his letter, Chamberlain referred to the "best" elements in society several times. Here, he attempted to distinguish himself from one of his chief rivals, the powerful Maine politician James G. Blaine. Chamberlain asked Schurz to reassure President Hayes "of the hearty and unqualified support of the best minds in this section of the Country." Chamberlain pledged his "high respect" for Schurz and congratulated him on his "triumph and that of the principles for which many of the best men have been ostracized." A short while later, writing about President Hayes, Chamberlain declared, "I believe his policy, as I understand it, is all that is going to save the country or the party."[25]

Despite his electoral victory, the manner in which Hayes had captured the presidency marred his term in office. He also received criticism for his removal of federal troops from southern statehouses, thereby, ending the federal government's attempt at southern Reconstruction. Chamberlain, however, rushed to the president's defense. "We must do the best we can for the negroes," he proclaimed, but then wondered whether so many people had shed blood in the war so that "negroes might have no one to stop them in going to the polls." Making the case for state rights, Chamberlain opposed federal interference on behalf of African Americans' voting rights. He declared the United States a free country but foremost for "the men who made it so, then those who are cast upon it." "The voting business in the South will regulate itself," Chamberlain promised. On the issue of formerly high-ranking Confederate officials representing southern states, he reasoned, "You yourself took back the States which they represent, and besides they have sworn to support the Constitution and laws of the United States." Chamberlain had made up his mind and not even the earlier pleas of his former 20th Maine commander, Adelbert Ames, then the head of the embattled Republican government of Mississippi, could shake his resolve. The war, Chamberlain, believed, had ended with the preservation of the Union. The freed people would have to play the hand they had been dealt under southern Democratic rule.[26]

With the political process and the reputation of the Republican brand both tarnished at the end of the 1870s, one New Brahmin hoped to reform the party from within. James A. Garfield, the most prominent politician in this sample, entered Congress in the middle of the war, started Reconstruction as a radical, and shifted to a moderate position to become a party leader. Garfield seems to have chartered a muddled course in the field of reform. He certainly accepted the laissez-faire position that liberal reformers took when it came to the government's role in social affairs. When, in the midst of the 1870s financial downturn, President Grant proposed to fund public works programs, Garfield opposed the measure, saying that it was "not part of the functions of the national government to find employment for people—and if we were to appropriate a hundred millions for this purpose, we should be taxing forty millions of people to keep a few thousand employed."[27] On the issue of black education, he expressed sentiments consistent with other New Brahmins. When he visited Samuel C. Armstrong's Hampton Institute in 1881, he reiterated the New England–centric vision of American nationalism and character-based education. Without labor, Garfield maintained, "there can be no civilization." "The white race," he told the students, "has learned this truth. They came as pioneers, felled the forests and swept away all obstacles before them by labor." Blacks, Garfield continued, "have learned this text but you learned it under the lash. Slavery taught you that labor must be." The war, however, had established that labor "must be forever *free*." Garfield praised his fellow Williams graduate and encouraged the teaching of skills to build good habits of character.[28]

Critics claimed that Garfield picked and chose which reforms to back. He supported lowering the tariff, reforming the civil service, curtailing the wartime greenbacks, and regulating the railroads. He opposed the eight-hour-day movement and did not object to the use of federal troops as strikebreakers. However, he also used the levers of patronage to his benefit and supported a high tariff on pig iron because of the industry's importance to his congressional district. On the issues that he found most important—combating slavery, the protection of the Union, and hard money—he remained firm. In regard to currency, Garfield willingly staked his political future on his belief that the government needed to return to specie payments after the war. As the sole representative from a western state to oppose inflation, he contrasted himself with the "rabble of men who hasten to make weather cocks of themselves." Convinced of his righteousness, he declared as a good man of character that he would remain steadfast, no matter "the effects of such a doctrine upon me at home politically." No one will ever know what Garfield would have done on these issues as president since an assassin's bullet cut short his tenure. Whatever his actions, he liked and often quoted the British politician George Canning, who said, "My road must be through character to power."[29]

On the whole, New Brahmins who dabbled in politics met with limited success. Their stubbornness and unwillingness to compromise, which they viewed as individuality and a sign of good character, often led to their undoing. Although he began his tenure as governor of Maine with massive support, by his fourth one-year term Joshua L. Chamberlain's failure to work with members of his own party and his inability to address the state's myriad problems had eroded his popularity. Failing to march in lockstep with Maine's Republican leaders hindered his prospects for receiving the U.S. Senate seat he coveted. Despite his disappointment with party politics, Chamberlain remained loyal to the Republicans, refusing to consider the possibility of returning to the governor's office on a Democratic ticket. The Democrats and independents in his district sent Theodore Lyman to Congress for a single term in the early 1880s. Despite his backing by the Democrats, Lyman chartered an independent course and lost the party's support during the next election.[30] By the mid-1880s most New Brahmins had become disillusioned by party politics. When James G. Blaine, with a reputation for cronyism, became the Republican Party's nominee for president in 1884, many formerly loyal supporters of the party looked elsewhere. Joseph H. Twichell added his name to a newspaper article calling for Republicans to not support Blaine, and one of Francis C. Barlow's biographers surmises that he, too, likely backed the Democratic candidate in 1884.[31]

Frustrated and disappointed in the political process, New Brahmins looked for other avenues in which to reform American society. Unfortunately, their wartime service did not mean that they had learned to trust the public. In fact, New Brahmins shared the urban elite's suspicions about immigrants, blaming them for the rise of party bosses and corruption. When faced with fixing postwar problems, they prescribed the lessons they thought most effective in helping their own success and reiterated the importance of education. Reform-minded men diagnosed and offered solutions to many of the nation's problems, but they also hoped to shape the next generation's development. Character-based education, they believed, had both raised them and won the war. Thus they wanted young Americans to learn those same lessons and therefore sought to strengthen schools and colleges. The late nineteenth century witnessed the founding of many new boarding schools that had connections to the nation's best colleges and universities. Facing an increasingly corrupt and chaotic world, New Brahmins hoped these schools would fulfill the nation's growing need for steadfast and independent leaders who would not bend to the popular will of parties or mobs.³²

Meanwhile, Charles Francis Adams, Jr., chose to address social problems in ways that did not involve following in his family's political tradition. Professing an interest in railroads and their management, Adams became a member of the Massachusetts Board of Railroad Commissioners. Thomas McCraw has called Adams "the first modern regulator," who "sought nothing less than to rationalize the railroad system." After years of study, Adams continued to uphold liberal orthodoxy and generally argued that publicity and public opinion would correct the railroad industry's mistakes. His overarching concern, however, remained the issue of corruption, fearing that large corporations, in league with lawmakers, would threaten republican government. Years later progressive forces would rally behind his suggestion that the federal government might need to rein in and regulate large rail corporations.³³ Finding themselves unwelcome in the postwar era's political parties, some New Brahmins viewed reform efforts as a way to maintain their character and retreated to less-public roles to continue their fight against flagging moral standards in American society.

The New Brahmins who had pursued careers as attorneys, for example, had to decide whether to adapt to the changing demands of the profession or remain wedded to the dictates of good character. In 1908 a committee of the American Bar Association set out to draft new canons, which would govern whether lawyers had a duty to "concern themselves with the justice of their clients' cases." Some argued that lawyers ought not to worry about such matters and serve the interests of their clients as best they could. Others, however, contended that lawyers must advise and act in the most just manner. Thomas H. Hubbard succeeded as a corporate lawyer in the postwar world but affirmed his commitment to character. He taught a class on legal ethics at the Albany School of Law and maintained that a lawyer served the cause of justice above all else. Every lawyer, he suggested, "must decide what business he will accept as counselor, what cases he will bring into court for plaintiffs, what cases he will conduct in court for defendants." A man's consciousness, not the fee the client paid, still ought to dictate his actions. Hubbard wanted the canons to state that a lawyer's appearance in court on behalf of a client "should be deemed equivalent to an assertion, on his honor, that in his opinion his client is justly entitled to some measure of relief refused by his adversary."³⁴

The most famous jurist among these New Brahmin veterans is Oliver Wendell Holmes, Jr., whose worldview had been greatly shaped by the war of his youth. As a judge, Holmes became a hero to the Progressives by seemingly supporting reforms to the economic system and the right to free speech. As Louis Menand explains, however, Holmes's "fundamental concern" in the postwar struggle between capital and labor "was almost always to permit all parties the democratic means to attempt to make their interests prevail." Holmes, Menand argues, "did not defend the interests of labor because he wished to see those interests prevail. He defended them because he believed that every social interest should have its chance. He believed in experiment." Such a belief echoed Holmes's view of the war. In November 1862 he called the Confederacy "a great civilized nation." A month later he assured his father that he had no doubts about "the right of our cause." "But," he postulated, "if it is true that we represent civilization wh. is in its nature, as well as slavery, diffusive & aggressive, and if civ. & progress are the better things why they will conquer in the long run, we may be sure." The future jurist already believed, therefore, that all sides ought to have their ideas and mettle tested.[35]

This lesson from the war stuck with Justice Holmes throughout his legal career. He rarely concerned himself with other memories from the conflict. Louis Menand observes that Holmes "read almost every other kind of book imaginable" but "could not bear to read histories of the Civil War." The lesson that Holmes learned from the conflict, Menand concludes, was that "certitude leads to violence." Ideologies, unshakable beliefs, Holmes thought, could cause enormous devastation in pursuit of national progress. As an example, he pointed to a group with which he had some familiarity: the abolitionists.[36] Although he sympathized with capitalists, he stayed true to his conscience in his postwar career. He ruled based on what he believed best for the society and not in the interests of political supporters. President Theodore Roosevelt thought a grateful Holmes, whom he had just placed on the Supreme Court, would rule in favor of his legislative agenda. When Justice Holmes, instead, voted his conscience, the president, according to one scholar, "emphatically expressed his displeasure."[37] Influenced by his wartime ordeal, Justice Holmes remained true to the dictates of good character: he supported what he believed best for society and damned the consequences.

New Brahmins who had hoped that a better nation would emerge from the Civil War encountered one disappointment after another. The world they envisioned as young men had not come about. In their youth, they had dreamed of a temporal American empire linking the past and present through the ideas of nationalism and free labor. But, by the turn of the twentieth century, the surviving New Brahmins lived to see the United States take on the role of a colonial power with its annexation of the Philippines. Charles Francis Adams, Jr., in particular, opposed annexation and joined an anti-imperialist movement. The United States, by joining the world's colonial nations, would violate the old New England–centric vision of a shining light that *inspired* rather than assimilated other nations into a democratic fellowship. By the spring of 1899, Adams had to concede defeat as the anti-imperialist movement had failed to gain the support it needed from either politicians or the public. Adams deemed "the mistake" irreversible. Now, Adams argued, the New Brahmins needed to turn their attention to making certain that the management of the new territories remained free from corruption. Unable to prevent annexation, Adams continued to emphasize the importance of character and hoped that good leadership would govern and elevate the new American subjects.[38]

Looking back on the years between the end of the Civil War and the end of the nineteenth century, Charles Francs Adams, Jr., concluded that the character of the American people had faltered. On March 6, 1899, he committed the following to his diary: "A man today who doesn't yield himself to every passing craze, actually loses all influence; he is looked upon as unsympathetic, unpatriotic, and a 'pessimist.'"[39] The passions of the moment as well as the fashions of the mob seemed to have crowded out men of principle. The postwar era had proven most unwelcoming to men of character.

Reconciliation

At the dawn of the twentieth century, New Brahmins looked longingly back at their youthful days when they had proven their character and saved the Union. For some, the war was more than just a historic event in which they had taken part. It also represented the greatest achievement of their lives. Although he did not read histories written about the war, Oliver Wendell Holmes, Jr., one biographer noticed, rarely missed an opportunity "to signalize the dates of the Battles of Ball's Bluff and Antietam, at both of which he had been wounded, by some such note as '31 years and one day after Antietam,' 'Antietam was 65 years ago yesterday,' 'We are celebrating Antietam, where if a bullet had gone one eighth of an inch differently the chances are that I should not be writing to you.'"[40] The old veterans might have boasted of their ability to resist popular trends, but when it came to reconciliation, they swam with rather than against the currents.

Many powerful forces converged to affect the course of Reconciliation. On the one hand, the class and ethnic tensions that emerged alongside the birth of industrial America forced bewildered northerners to find refuge in romanticized visions of the old southern plantation. They longed for a more peaceful time and saw an idealized image on the front porch of a planter's home. Meanwhile, they feared that the nation had lost its character because of the material comforts of the age. Looking for heroes, they turned to the past, when Union and Confederate soldiers had once waged a titanic battle and proudly emerged, having demonstrated their valor. "The soldier's willingness to risk all for a cause he believed noble (even if he was mistaken)," Jackson Lears writes, "seemed a powerful antidote to the self-seeking calculus governing commerce." In one of his most famous speeches, Oliver Wendell Holmes, Jr., told an 1884 crowd that "through our great good fortune, in our youth our hearts were touched with fire. . . . While we . . . do not pretend to undervalue the worldly rewards of ambition, we have seen with our own eyes beyond and above the gold fields the snowy heights of honor, and it is for us to bear the report to those who come after us." "Holmes's language," Lears observes, "captured some key elements in the developing cult of martial virtue" as he contrasted its masculine qualities with material comfort. Both the men who wore the blue and the men who wore the grey had proved their worth and could ascend to the "snowy heights of honor."[41] Reconciliation came at a cost that most white Americans, New Brahmins among them, appeared all too willing to pay. The celebration of Union and Confederate manhood and courage marginalized contentious issues like race. Reconciliationists promoted the idea that the war had been a tragedy that allowed national unity to blossom from the comparable sacrifices made by men on both sides, rather than a conflict over slavery, race, and expansion. African Americans, their plight, and their ongoing struggles had no room in this celebratory vision.[42]

While they embraced some reconciliationist impulses, the New Brahmins certainly did not accept all elements of the Lost Cause mythology and objected to certain southern claims. The war, after all, had been the defining moment of their lives and they jealously guarded the memory of their accomplishments. These findings support recent historical scholarship that suggests a more complicated image of sectional reconciliation. Joshua L. Chamberlain, for example, never condoned the notion implied by the name "War between the States," rejecting the claim that the rebels had fought for a just cause. The conflict, he maintained to the end, "was a war in the name of certain States to destroy the political existence of the United States." When veterans of the 15th Alabama, one of the units that faced the 20th Maine at Little Round Top, attempted to place their monument on the field, Chamberlain objected to their proposed site, engaging in a lengthy debate that refuted the Alabamians' claim about how far up the contested hill they had gotten. In 1896 Joseph H. Twichell disagreed with a proposal that "an ivy from the grave of Robert Lee, a good man, but the historic representative of an infamous cause, shall be planted on this campus to climb the walls of ever loyal Yale." While they granted that Confederates fought bravely, New Brahmins did not forget that, as rebels, their enemies had attempted to destroy the Union.[43]

As they entered the twilight of their years, New Brahmins seemed ever more drawn to reaffirming their prior beliefs about character. In the 1890s Charles Francis Adams, Jr., judged himself a failure in the civilian world and took up the task of writing history. Contending with the rocky legacy of Reconstruction and the curtailment in the 1890s of blacks' civil rights, Adams reiterated his claims that blacks still needed white supervision and considerable character education before they could become equal members of society. He argued that "there is not an instance in all recorded history, from the earlier precedent . . . where a so-called inferior race or community has been elevated in its character, or made self-sustaining and self-governing,—or even put on the way to that result,— through a condition of dependency or tutelage." Adams contended that "race elevation, the capacity in a word of political self-support, cannot be imparted through tutelage." Looking for historical examples, he pointed to the British colonization of India, arguing that "after three rounded centuries of British rule, the Hindostanese,—the natives of India,—in spite of all material, industrial and educational improvements,—roads, schools, justice and peace,—are in 1900 less capable of independent and ordered self-government than they were in the year 1600." Part of this situation stemmed from the fact that the "native Indian dynasties—those natural to the Hindoos—have disappeared; accustomed to foreign rule, the people have no rulers of their own, nor could they rule themselves." Remove British leadership, he warned, and "chaos would inevitably ensue." Adams contrasted British failure in India with America's alternative policy toward "the so-called inferior races." The United States, he pointed out, had adopted a "'Hands-off and Walk-alone' doctrine" when it came to its neighbors Mexico and Haiti. Mexico, "though republican in name and form only, is self-governing in reality." Meanwhile, the United States had not intervened in Haiti because of "the belief that, in the long run and grand result, the inhabitants of Haiti will best work out their problem, if left to work it out themselves." It was better for Haiti to "suffer self-caused misfortune for centuries, as did England before," he argued, "than that a precedent should be created for the frequent violation of a great principle of natural development."[44] In Adams's understanding of history, people that became too dependent required *centuries* to develop their independence. African Americans in this forecast had a long road to travel.

In assessing the character of one prominent Confederate, however, Adams discovered acclaim for himself. Invited to speak before the Phi Beta Kappa Society at the University of Chicago in June 1902, Adams used the occasion to revive Robert E. Lee's reputation. "Was Robert E. Lee a traitor?" he asked, answering, "Technically, I think he was indisputably a traitor to the United States." He then spent the remainder of his lengthy speech explaining the mitigating circumstances. In history, Adams claimed, "there is treason and treason, as there are traitors and traitors. And . . . if Robert E. Lee was a traitor, so also, and undisputedly, were George Washington, Oliver Cromwell, John Hampton, and William of Orange."[45]

Adams's larger point, however, concerned the matter of a man's conscience. Lee, he argued, proved his character by acting in the manner he considered consistent with his beliefs. "From generation to generation," he observed of antebellum southerners, "they had grown up indoctrinated with the gospel, or heresy, of State Sovereignty, and it was as much part of their moral and intellectual being as was clanship of the Scotch highlanders." Force of circumstance had bred the southern politicians who led their section into war. Adams described these men as "masterful in temper, clear of purpose, with a firm grasp on principle, a high sense of honor, and a moral perception developed on its peculiar lines." Despite these qualities, "they were not practical men." Because they "did not see things as they really were," these men made bad decisions. Their recourse, he noted, "was to the sword." That, Adams concluded, had been the mistake of the South's ruling class. Once the die had been cast, other men had to act in a manner consistent with their consciences. Comparing three prominent Virginians, Winfield Scott, George H. Thomas, and Robert E. Lee, Adams declared that each "acted conscientiously, impelled by the purest sense of loyalty, honor, and obligation, taking that course which, under the circumstances and according to his lights, seemed to him right." By acting in accordance with his conscience, doing his duty to the utmost, and, when the time came, seeking peace rather than wage a hopeless and bloody guerrilla war, Robert E. Lee demonstrated all the positive qualities that Adams sought. Lee, he concluded, "will typify historical appreciation of all that goes to make up the loftiest type of character."[46]

Adams received high praise for his speech. One sign of its popularity in the former Confederacy came several years later when Washington and Lee University in Lexington, Virginia, invited him to speak on the occasion of Robert E. Lee's centennial birthday in January 1907. Delivering his oration in Lee Chapel, Adams opened by stating, "The older I have grown and the more I have studied and seen, the greater in my esteem, as an element of strength in a people, has Character become." "With Character," he claimed, "a race will become great." He proclaimed Robert E. Lee "essentially a Man of Character." Perhaps swept up by the moment or perhaps having changed his mind since giving a similar speech in Chicago just five years earlier, Adams pronounced that placed in "similar conditions I would myself have done exactly what Lee did." Indeed, by acting as his conscience dictated, Lee presented Adams with a way to absolve all Confederates. "I maintain," Adams told the audience, "that every man in the eleven States . . . whichever way he decided, if only he decided honestly, putting self-interest behind him, he decided right." He then pivoted to criticize the people he blamed most for the war and postwar issues: radicals. Condemning Radical Reconstruction, Adams thought that "slave confiscation, and reconstruction under African rule" imposed on the region "was distinctly unworthy" of "the high precedent set at Appomattox." Adams had dissociated racial issues and slavery from the war and, instead, populated the conflict with noble men of character.[47] While on the Lexington campus Adams might have noticed the symbolic reunion of northern and southern men of letters. While Harvard and Washington College had sent their sons to fight against one another in the war, now a graduate of the former had come to praise the character of the past head of the latter. Reunion and reconciliation had taken place on a green college lawn.

Joshua L. Chamberlain, meanwhile, took to writing about the past with as much relish as he took to soldiering. One scholar has suggested that Chamberlain felt frustrated by "civilian life's failure to offer many moments of heroic duty," and so he "turned back toward the time when life was more generous." Chamberlain thus mustered his considerable writing talents to produce sweeping reminiscences, pregnant with symbolism. He used the Confederate surrender at Appomattox, where he had presided over the ceremonies, to describe the reconciliation between honorable men. As the first Confederate troops marched up to the federal position to stack their arms, Union soldiers surprised their longtime adversaries by saluting them. Gen. John B. Gordon, who rode "at the head of the column, riding with heavy spirit and downcast face," understood the meaning of the Union action, wheeled "superbly, making with himself and his horse one uplifted figure," dropped "the point of his sword to the boot toe," and gave "word for his successive brigades to pass us with the same position of the manual,—honor answering honor." "On our part," Chamberlain remembered, "not a sound of trumpet more, nor roll of drum; not a cheer, nor word nor whisper of vain-glorying, nor motion of man standing again at the order, but an awed stillness rather, and breath-holding, as if it were the passing of the dead!"[48]

In Adams's Washington and Lee speech and Chamberlain's final musings, these New Brahmins demonstrated another key power of character: it absolved the rebels of their crimes. By defining the actions of Confederates like John B. Gordon and Robert E. Lee as honorable in a northern sense, New Brahmins claimed victory over their southern adversaries. In their own minds, not only had a New England–centric vision of America triumphed in the war, but a northern definition of honor had won as well. They demonstrated their magnanimity by extending their definition of character to cover the actions of their former adversaries. Under the umbrella of character, men of honor in both the North and South reunited.

Epilogue

How should we view the lives of the New Brahmins? What should we remember of their contributions? First and foremost, one must acknowledge that in a time of national crisis, they lived by the code they professed. Taught to embrace their role as society's leaders and tasked with using their elevated status for the betterment of others, the New Brahmins, when the war broke out, acted in a manner befitting their position. Although many of their parents merely seem to have paid lip service to the lofty ideals that their sons learned in moral philosophy classes, the young men themselves fully embraced their role and behaved like men of character. At least two factors contributed to this. First, their belief in the New England–centric narrative of American history that viewed industry and free labor as the cornerstones of the republic prompted them to fight what they considered an alien and alternate vision for the nation—that is, the Confederate, proslavery version. Second, their self-conception as men of character pressured them to join in the war effort. Perhaps struggling with what being a man of character in peacetime entailed, they found that wartime service gave them an easier way of demonstrating their inner qualities. It was, indeed, easier to prove one's character by training, inspiring, and leading men into combat than by rising in the ranks of politics, business, or other peacetime professions. Facing the dangers of the battlefield and the temptations of camp life with determination showed character.

Heading into the conflict, guided by character, the New Brahmins also viewed the Confederacy through that lens. They criticized the character of southern leaders but admired the richness of the region they traversed as invaders. Imposing their understanding of American nationalism on the South, they thought a hearty application of northern industry would set the region back on the right track. Encountering southerners, they pitied poor whites and seemed unimpressed by enslaved blacks. The solution, they argued, was education with an emphasis on developing character in both groups. Blacks, however, had a longer road to travel to achieve the level of character attained by white Americans. Encountering southern homes and witnessing the bravery of southern soldiers on the battlefield affected the New Brahmins in a way they did not expect. They learned, through conflict, to see character in the men who opposed them across the field of battle. This recognition of their enemies' character aided the process of postwar reconciliation.

When the war ended, the New Brahmins that survived resumed their leadership roles in civilian life. They faced again the same problems that plagued them before the war. That is, demonstrating one's character in wartime was, apparently, easier than maintaining it in the pursuit of financial or political goals. Yet the New Brahmins did their best to live as men of character by engaging in education, law, business, and politics. Some succeeded while others faltered. Samuel C. Armstrong, for example, fulfilled his goal of imposing a character-based education on southern blacks. That, of course, came at a price for the freed people themselves. Other New Brahmins who did not fulfill their postwar goals had expected that upon returning from the war as heroes their leadership in reforming the nation's character would be embraced by a grateful public. But Gilded Age Americans seemed uninterested in tackling the scourges of complacency, soft money, high tariffs, and government corruption.

Perhaps one ought to pity the New Brahmins who survived the war for, in most cases, their crowning achievements took place when they were in their twenties and thirties. For many, their success in the armed forces, made possible by the rigid discipline that the service demanded and the command authority to impose their will on subordinates, could not be replicated in civilian life. Joshua L. Chamberlain longed to return to military service. While serving as governor of Maine, he offered his services to the king of Prussia during the Franco–Prussian War, declaring his willingness to resign his civilian post. When the Spanish–American War broke out, he offered to serve his country yet again.[1] No one, however, recalled him to the front lines of battle.

For their part, colleges celebrated the return of their alumni and commemorated their fallen sons. By their war service, college graduates had, after all, demonstrated that their alma maters produced selfless and patriotic individuals. The men honored both themselves and their institutions. Memorials such as plaques, stained glass windows, and even enormous structures—Bowdoin's and Harvard's Memorial Halls, for example—dotted the architecture of the postwar campuses. Collections of letters and memorial biographies flooded the presses as the schools claimed credit for having produced so many heroes for the republic.

Meanwhile, college histories published in the late nineteenth century celebrated the sacrifice and bravery of the young sons of these schools who had proven their worth to society and seemingly justified the continued existence of the institutions that had shaped them. "Prior to the late Rebellion," Henry S. Burrage wrote in his memorial to Brown men who fought in the Civil War, "it was a matter of speculation among us, whether, if opportunity offered, the young men of this generation would emulate the heroism of their patriotic ancestors. In those tranquil times, and to our inexperienced minds, the history of the great struggle for national independence seemed like a romance. Our civil war has at length solved the problem." Burrage cited the life and sacrifice of Sullivan Ballou, placing him "among the first to prove that devotion to their country had not withered in the hearts of American youth."[2]

The war represented a formative period of development for northern gentlemen. It provided them with an opportunity to demonstrate the personal skills they had cultivated behind college walls. The national crisis demanded the action of the nation's leadership class, and New Brahmins girded on their armor, marched to war, and displayed the strength of their character to both the troops they led and the soldiers they confronted. By looking at the formation of these men's nationalistic ideas and understanding their sense of honor, students of nineteenth-century America gain a better grasp of what motivated such an important group of individuals who fought valiantly to preserve and lead the Union. For the men who came home, civilian life never held the same exhilaration that they remembered from the conflict. They returned to their peacetime worlds and attempted as best they could in various fields to stay true to their cherished code of character. Knowing what lay inside them as well as their capacity for leadership, these individuals often looked to their youth and the war to catch a glimpse of their character in its prime. Joshua L. Chamberlain, reflecting on the conflict, concluded that "war is for the participants a test of character; it makes bad men worse and good men better."[3]

Acknowledgments

I am a long way from the New England states I used to cover. These two lanes have taken us blowing from town to town, southwestward, looking for a place to land. Too distant from the rejuvenating waves of the sea, I find myself seeking inspiration in an enchanted New Mexican desert. There is an undeniable and haunting beauty to this place: barren and yet vibrant, empty and yet alive. The ancient, blackened volcanic rocks and lava flows have oozed their way across the land. The sandstone cliffs rise above the desert floor. When the wind is still, a bird's chirp echoes across the valley. From the top of the bluffs, watching storms forming somewhere far away, one imagines that maybe there is a place over the rise where the sands turn into gold. And one road stretches through the landscape, snaking toward unknown destinations and beckoning with its promise. Past, present, and future blur somewhere beyond the horizon.

It has been a long journey to get here and I have accumulated debts that no man can repay. I acknowledge generous funding from the Sherman David Spector of the Class of 1950 Fellowship for Graduate Study in History and Teaching awarded by the Bowdoin College Department of History. At my alma mater, I'd like to thank Caroline Moseley, Kathy Petersen, Dan Hope, and Richard Lindermann at the George J. Mitchell Department of Special Collections and Archives. Thanks also to Matthew Thomson of the Bowdoin class of 2006 who shared his research on the Fessenden family with me. I am grateful for research aid received from the following institutions' libraries: Amherst College, Dartmouth College (especially Peter Carini), the Library of Congress, the Maine State Archives, Wesleyan University, Williams College, Yale University, and the University of Virginia.

In Boston, Conrad E. Wright, director of research at the Massachusetts Historical Society, saw potential in the project early on and supported my endeavors. I acknowledge generous financial support from the Massachusetts Historical Society and the New England Research Fellowship Consortium for funding early research trips. This consortium of outstanding libraries and repositories holds remarkable collections in some of the best research facilities in the nation. I owe a great deal to the support of the following individuals:

Peter Drummey and Rakashi Chand at the Massachusetts Historical Society; Nicholas Noyes, Jamie Kingman Rice, and Bill Barry at the Maine Historical Society; Stephen Z. Nonack at the Boston Athenaeum; Richard C. Malley at the Connecticut Historical Society; the staffs of Houghton Library and the Harvard University Archives; and the Historical Society of Pennsylvania.

The stars burn bright on the desert highway at night. I have been blessed by the inspiration, guidance, and support of numerous scholars. At Bowdoin College, Patrick J. Rael served as my adviser and mentor through my undergraduate years and cheered me on with complete faith in my abilities long after I graduated. He made me a much more complete historian. I am enormously indebted to Gary W. Gallagher, who took a chance on me. His mentorship and support mean more to me than he knows. I thank also Edward L. Ayers—"Superman," as one graduate student called him—for always providing encouragement, inspiration, and boundless energy. At the University of Virginia, I thank Joseph F. Kett, Alon Confino, Gabriel N. Finder, Peter Onuf, and Matthew Hedstrom. I am also thankful for the generous time and knowledge of scholars at various institutions around the nation. Joan Waugh introduced me to Charlie Lowell and has provided her time and support over the years. Lorien Foote, whose scholarship I greatly admire, has become a friend. I also thank Paul Cimbala and Andrew L. Slap, the former and present editors, respectively, of Fordham's "The North's Civil War" series, who have shepherded the project from start to finish. Their professional insight and knowledge have made this a much stronger work. I also wish to thank Peter Carmichael, Michael A. Morrison, C. Dallett Hemphill, Glenn W. LaFantasie, John R. Neff, and the press's anonymous readers for their advice for corrections. The professional staff at Fordham University Press, particularly Fredric Nachbaur, Will Cerbone, and Eric Newman, deserve particular thanks for their diligence and support. I also commend copyeditor Nicholas Taylor for his sharp eye and good suggestions. I assume all responsibilities for any shortcomings of this volume. All these individuals have given me all that I could ask for, and should the results fall short of expectations the fault does not lie with them.

Traveling around the country for research, I have called on the aid of numerous friends. These fleeting moments of reunion and revelry are far too brief and sporadic, but I am reminded that we should take the good times as they go. Lin Chen and Ken Thompson allowed me to make their home in Cambridge, Massachusetts, a base of operations for two summers. Thanks to John A. Meyers for always welcoming me to Boston and providing immeasurable support and entertainment over the years. Thanks to my old friend Zach West, who knows that although we have our own roads to ride and chances to take, we remain inseparable. Lela Stanley, Alexis Rea, and David Butler always found time to see me in D.C. Thanks also to Brian Calabrese, Ed and Nancy Langbein, and the Schofield clan. Special thanks also to my parents-in-law, Bill and Andrea Ostrofsky, who welcomed me into their family and home.

The intellectual and friendly community in Charlottesville contributed greatly to this project. The cohort of hardy graduate students there provided not just food for thought but many enjoyable moments through graduate school. Allison Robbins has become a trusted and beloved comrade in arms. I also thank Rob Rakove (for adventures, culinary and otherwise, in many galaxies), Cynthia L. Nicoletti, Michael J. Callahan, Amanda R. Mushal, Phillip Haberkern, Jason Eldred, Sean P. Nalty, M. Keith Harris, Adam Jortner, Andrew Torget, William Kurtz, Kathryn Meier, Rachel Shelden, and Kathleen Miller.

At Angelo State, I thank for their encouragement and support *mi hermano* John E. Klingemann, Kenna Archer, Arnoldo DeLeón, David Dewar, Angela Howell, D. D. Norton, Jason Pierce, Gary Pumphrey, the late Joe Zheng, and Christine Lamberson, who urges me to treat myself every now and then. I thank my friends at East Tennessee State University, Henry Antkiewicz, Dale Schmidt, Emmett Essin, Steve Fritz, Steve Nash, and Doug Burgess, who welcomed me into their fellowship and coffee club with open arms. Thanks to my writing companion Julie Mujic for her encouragement, for keeping me on track, and for holding me accountable for research goals. And a huge thank-you to Brian J. Maxson, whose correspondences remind me of what is most important in life and to keep pushing ahead.

Longer than I have worked on this project, my parents have supported and provided all I could ask. Without them none of this would be possible. Thank you simply isn't enough.

And finally, for Kathryn, who walked with me out on the wire. She has been my constant for twelve years, and in that time we have been tested by all the challenges that come with a long-distance relationship. But over river and highway, across the airwaves, the plains, the deserts, and the empty skies, her voice has always come clear and true, reassuring, comforting, and sustaining me. She deserves much more than this. Through the years we have laughed, cried, sang, traveled, and dreamed. There are many turns yet in the road, many vistas that will unravel before our eyes as we cross the dark desert. All I can promise is that someday we'll get to that place where we really want to go and we'll walk in the sun.

El Malpais, New Mexico
March 2015

Notes

Introduction

1. Charles Russell Lowell, *Life and Letters of Charles Russell Lowell*, ed. Edward Waldo Emerson (1907; repr., Columbia: University of South Carolina, 2005), xliii–xliv.

2. Wilder Dwight, *Life and Letters of Wilder Dwight, Lieut.-Col. Second Mass. Inf. Vols.*, ed. Elizabeth A. Dwight (Boston: Ticknor and Fields, 1868), 4–5.

3. Oliver Wendell Holmes, *Elsie Venner* (London: Routledge, Warne, and Routledge, 1861), 14; Edmund Wilson, *Patriotic Gore: Studies in the Literature of the American Civil War* (New York: Oxford University Press, 1962), 783.

4. Phillip S. Paludan, one of the most thorough students of northern society in the war, has called his attempt to write about the changing society "a daunting task." The war, he reminded readers, "happened to over twenty million people [in the northern states] who lived in a society divided by race, culture, occupations, age and sex." On the issue of slavery's connection to honor, Edward L. Ayers has argued, "Slavery generated honor. There seems little reason to doubt . . . that had the South not made the 'unthinking decision' to adopt slavery the region would have followed a path of cultural development similar to that of the rest of North America." In his own study of southern honor, Kenneth S. Greenberg agreed, noting that "the language of honor used by Southern gentlemen was embedded in a slave society." Phillip Shaw Paludan, *A People's Contest: The Union and Civil War, 1861–1865* (1988; repr., Lawrence: University Press of Kansas, 1996), x; Edward L. Ayers, *Vengeance and Justice: Crime and Punishment in the Nineteenth-Century American South* (New York: Oxford University Press, 1984), 26–27; Kenneth S. Greenberg, *Honor and Slavery: Lies, Duels, Noses, Masks, Dressing as a Woman, Gifts, Strangers, Humanitarianism, Death, Slave Rebellions, the Proslavery Argument, Baseball, Hunting, and Gambling in the Old South* (Princeton, N.J.: Princeton University Press, 1996), xi.

5. Eric Foner, *Free Soil, Free Labor, Free Men: The Ideology of the Republican Party before the Civil War* (1970; repr., New York: Oxford University Press, 1995), 29. See also Chapter 1 for a full discussion of the term "character."

6. Richard F. Miller, "Brahmins under Fire: Peer Courage and the Harvard Regiment," *Historical Journal of Massachusetts* 30, no. 1 (2002): 76.

7. James M. McPherson, *For Cause and Comrades: Why Men Fought in the Civil War* (New York: Oxford University Press, 1997), 22–23.

8. Bertram Wyatt-Brown, *Southern Honor: Ethics and Behavior in the Old South* (New York, 1983), xv, 14; *Honor and Violence in the Old South* (New York: Oxford University Press, 1986), 14; and *The Shaping of Southern Culture: Honor, Grace, and War, 1760s–1890s* (Chapel Hill: University of North Carolina Press, 2001), xii; Kenneth S. Greenberg, "The Nose, the Lie, and the Duel in the Antebellum South," *American Historical Review* 95 (February 1990): 58; for an examination of how honor influenced

the culture of southern colleges, see Robert F. Pace, *Halls of Honor: College Men in the Old South* (Baton Rouge: Louisiana State University Press, 2004).

    Later on, Wyatt-Brown clarifies, "it was not that inward virtues were wholly absent. Rather, virtue and valor, apart from social utility, simply were unimportant." More recently, Stephen W. Berry II has argued that young southern men served in the war "because . . . they believed in themselves," and this confidence stemmed from the support they drew from their personal lives. According to Berry, scholars know a lot about the South's "hypermasculinized culture" but little of "the men living in and through this culture" and, as such, "men are denied a measure of their humanity." Such an imbalanced understanding, Berry suggests, "results from the nature of the sources. . . . Men of the nineteenth century were encouraged to cloak their hearts and stifle their doubts, to so carefully groom their public persona as to become it. The result is a staggering amount of evidence dedicated to the public, external, and projected aspects of men's lives and significantly less dedicated to the private, internal, and introspective." Wyatt-Brown, *Honor and Violence in the Old South*, 30; Stephen W. Berry II, *All That Makes a Man: Love and Ambition in the Civil War South* (New York: Oxford University Press, 2003), 10–11.

    9. Wyatt-Brown, *Honor and Violence*, 19, 22; Greenberg, *Honor and Slavery*, 15–16.

    10. Amy S. Greenberg, *Manifest Manhood and the Antebellum American Empire* (New York: Cambridge University Press, 2005), 12. Stephen Berry has also noted differences in northern and southern conceptions of manhood. "In the North," he writes, "boys were encouraged to pattern themselves after what might be called *civilized manhood*. Men were supposed to exemplify and embody the *effects* of civilization, underscoring their self-possession and self-restraint by holding up to the world a paragon of gentlemanly conduct, abstemious habits, and Christian rectitude." Identifying the South's pattern as one of *"civilizing* manhood," Berry explains, "Southern men were obliged not merely to affect Civilization but to cause it, the emphasis falling on not merely the composition but the imposition of the self" (*All That Makes a Man*, 34).

    11. Foote uses the southern definition of honor in her study, defining the term in a traditional sense as "a man's self-worth . . . based on public reputation and the respect of others." She also suggests that scholars have had a difficult time identifying honor in the North "because there were various methods that men employed to defend honor," and "some northern men used the language of dueling without any intent to defend honor." Ayers, *Vengeance and Justice*, 19–20, 22–24; Patrick Rael, *Black Identity and Black Protest in the Antebellum North* (Chapel Hill: University of North Carolina Press, 2002), 130; Lorien Foote, *The Gentlemen and the Roughs: Manhood, Honor, and Violence in the Union Army* (New York: New York University Press, 2010), 6, 77–79, 96, 104–5.

    12. George M. Fredrickson, *The Inner Civil War: Northern Intellectuals and the Crisis of the Union* (1965; repr., New York: Harper and Row, 1968), 8–35, 72–73, 151–56, 162, 175. Anne C. Rose, studying Americans from both the North and the South born between 1815 and 1837, also argues that the war came at the right time for wandering Victorians seeking to fill a spiritual void. However, Rose argues that romanticism survived the bloody conflict. See *Victorian America and the Civil War* (New York: Cambridge University Press, 1992), xi, 2–5, 17–20, 235–36.

13. See Peter J. Parish, "Confidence and Anxiety in Victorian America," in *The North and the Nation in the Era of the Civil War*, ed. Adam I. P. Smith and Susan-Mary Grant (New York: Fordham University Press, 2003), 1–21; George B. Forgie, *Patricide in the House Divided: A Psychological Interpretation of Lincoln and His Age* (New York: Norton, 1979).

14. Many Americans of the 1850s subscribed to these fears about government corruption stemming from the spoils system. See Mark W. Summers, *The Plundering Generation: Corruption and the Crisis of the Union, 1849–1861* (New York: Oxford University Press, 1987).

15. "In its initial appearance," historian Joyce Appleby writes, "republicanism referred to a body of ideas said to have animated the men of the revolutionary generation. Drawn from the vivid polemics of the English opposition, republican ideology filled Americans with a horror of arbitrary power and a fear of the incipient corruption of the British Constitution." These concerns continued to influence American political thought into the nineteenth century. Andrew L. Slap has argued that men who attended nineteenth-century colleges were "more likely than most to be familiar with both the classical Roman and Revolutionary concepts of republicanism." Joyce Appleby, "Republicanism and Ideology," *American Quarterly* 37, no. 4 (1985): 461; Andrew L. Slap, *The Doom of Reconstruction: The Liberal Republicans in the Civil War Era* (New York: Fordham University Press, 2006), xxii–xxiii. For older works on republicanism, see Bernard Bailyn, *The Ideological Origins of the American Revolution* (Cambridge, Mass.: Belknap Press of Harvard University Press, 1967); and Gordon S. Wood, *The Creation of the American Republic, 1776–1787* (Chapel Hill: University of North Carolina Press, 1969). For historiographical discussions of the term, see Joyce Appleby, "Liberalism and the American Revolution," *New England Quarterly* 49, no. 1 (1976): 3–26; and "Republicanism in Old and New Contexts," *William and Mary Quarterly* 43, no. 1 (1986): 20–34; Daniel T. Rodgers, "Republicanism: The Career of a Concept," *Journal of American History* 79, no. 1 (1992): 11–38.

16. Mary Kelley, *Learning to Stand and Speak: Women, Education, and Public Life in America's Republic* (Chapel Hill: University of North Carolina Press, 2008), 81. According to Helen Lefkowitz Horowitz, in 1800 a mere 2 percent of young men attended college. In 1840, there were 16,233 students in 173 institutions of higher learning nationwide. By 1880, the number had risen to 85,378 students (less than 2 percent of Americans between eighteen and twenty-one) at 591 schools. Indeed, it was not until the turn of the twentieth century when these proportions and numbers began to rise. The age ranges for students in the nineteenth century varied from teenagers to men in their thirties. The youngest were sons of the wealthiest citizens while the older students were from poorer families. Helen Lefkowitz Horowitz, *Campus Life: Undergraduate Cultures from the End of the Eighteenth Century to the Present* (Chicago: University of Chicago Press, 1987), 4–5.

17. These numbers are approximations calculated from Robert S. Fletcher and Malcolm O. Young, eds., *Amherst College: Biographical Record of the Graduates and Non-graduates, Centennial Edition, 1821–1921* (Amherst, Mass.: Amherst College, 1927).

18. These numbers are approximations calculated from *General Catalogue of Bowdoin College and the Medical School of Maine: A Biographical Record of Alumni and Officers, 1794–1950* (Brunswick, Maine: Bowdoin College, 1950).

19. Peter Dobkin Hall, *The Organization of American Culture, 1700–1900: Private Institutions, Elites, and the Origins of American Nationality* (New York: New York University Press, 1984), 161–62.

20. For a discussion of New England's distinctive qualities, see Nina Silber and Mary Beth Sievens, eds., *Yankee Correspondence: Civil War Letters between New England Soldiers and the Home Front* (Charlottesville: University of Virginia Press, 1996), 3–11. On the concern southern parents had about northern influences on their children, see John McCardell, *The Idea of a Southern Nation: Southern Nationalists and Southern Nationalism, 1830–1860* (New York: Norton, 1979), Chapter 5; and Lorri Glover, *Southern Sons: Becoming Men in the New Nation* (2007; repr., Baltimore: Johns Hopkins University Press, 2010), 51–53, 77–81.

21. Karen Halttunen, *Confidence Men and Painted Women: A Study of Middle-Class Culture in America, 1830–1870* (New Haven, Conn.: Yale University Press, 1982), xv–xvi, 1–9; Thomas Augst, *The Clerk's Tale: Young Men and Moral Life in Nineteenth-Century America* (Chicago: University of Chicago Press, 2003), 4. Historian George Forgie has noted the "paradox of prosperity" for antebellum Americans: "That Americans in the post-heroic period were jubilant and self-congratulatory about their economic good fortune has never been in doubt, but that they were at the same time uneasy with this prosperity is also clear. Prosperity was not only the forcing house of mediocrity—it could generate also greed, selfishness, corruption, self-indulgence, love of luxury, enervation, effeminacy, and boredom." When young men entered the working world, E. Anthony Rotundo has observed, they had to contend with the temptations of alcohol, gambling, and sex. These young men faced great challenges even in their attempts to restrain their behavior and to combat doubts about their ability to succeed in the turbulent and unstable working world of men. Forgie, *Patricide in the House Divided*, 73–74; E. Anthony Rotundo, *American Manhood: Transformations in Masculinity from the Revolution to the Modern Era* (New York: Basic Books, 1993), 59, 61, 71–74, 174–75.

22. According to Peter Dobkin Hall, college graduates "came to regard collegiate affiliation and society membership as important indicators of character and trustworthiness and, hence, credit-worthiness and employability." Degrees from colleges signified "more than the mastery of a body of knowledge" and served as "a credential of a more general kind of trustworthiness and breadth of purpose." Hall, *Organization of American Culture*, 172–75.

23. John J. Pullen, *Patriotism in America: A Study of Changing Devotions, 1770–1970* (New York: American Heritage Press, 1971), 52; Charles Russell Lowell to Anna Jackson Lowell, May 13, 1861, in Lowell, *Life and Letters of Charles Russell Lowell*, 206.

24. Earl Hess, *The Union Solider in Battle: Enduring the Ordeal of Combat* (Lawrence: University Press of Kansas, 1997), 133–34. For an excellent discussion of the class breakdown between officers and enlisted men as well as a look at their interactions, see Foote, *The Gentlemen and the Roughs*.

25. For an excellent study of Whig culture see Daniel Walker Howe, *The Political Culture of the American Whigs* (Chicago: University of Chicago Press, 1979). In study-

ing the "political culture of northern Democrats," Jean H. Baker concluded that the "nineteenth-century family imprinted political behavior," with the father being a partisan recruiter. Not all the men considered here were Whigs; however, as historian Yonatan Eyal has observed, members of the Democratic Party's Young America movement during the 1840s and 1850s became more tolerant of Whig ideas, supporting economic growth and innovation. Jean H. Baker, *Affairs of Party: The Political Culture of Northern Democrats in the Mid-Nineteenth Century* (1983; repr., New York: Fordham University Press, 1998); Yonatan Eyal, *The Young America Movement and the Transformation of the Democratic Party, 1828–1861* (New York: Cambridge University Press, 2007), 2–6.

26. Joseph Allan Frank, *With Ballot and Bayonet: The Political Socialization of American Civil War Soldiers* (Athens: University of Georgia Press, 1998), 3–4, 35; James M. McPherson, *What They Fought For, 1861–1865* (1994; repr., New York: Anchor Books, 1995), 35. Ever since Bell Irvin Wiley launched the genre with his classic works *The Life of Johnny Reb: The Common Soldier of the Confederacy* (1943) and *The Life of Billy Yank: The Common Soldier of the Union* (1952), historians have eagerly joined in the study. In so doing, however, they have continued to perpetuate the idea that they could advance our understanding of the men who fought the Civil War by seeking out the most common aspects of their experiences. This is a mistake. Wiley himself noticed that Union camps were diverse environments, filled with "persons of many nationalities, races, creeds and occupations" who "observe great variations in dress, habits, temperament, education, wealth and social status." Given this variety of backgrounds and prewar experiences, how could historians hope to find the oft-sought-after "common soldier"? Focusing on one particular class may help address the criticism that many studies of Civil War soldiers reach broad conclusions that do not represent the diversity of individuals who fought in the armies. James M. McPherson admitted that his sample of over a thousand men was "biased toward the groups most likely to be moved by patriotic and ideological motives: officers, slaveholders, professional men, the middle class, and 1861–62 volunteers rather than post-1862 conscripts, substitutes, and bounty men." Earl J. Hess's excellent study of Union soldiers, *Liberty, Virtue, and Progress*, also reaches broad and often generalized findings, not necessarily representative of all elements of northern society. Bell Irvin Wiley, *The Life of Johnny Reb: The Common Soldier of the Confederacy* (1943; repr., Baton Rouge: Louisiana State University Press, 1992); and *The Life of Billy Yank: The Common Soldier of the Union* (1952; repr., Baton Rouge: Louisiana State University Press, 1994), 296; McPherson, *For Cause and Comrades*, 101; Earl J. Hess, *Liberty, Virtue, and Progress: Northerners and Their War for the Union* (New York: New York University Press, 1988).

27. Paul Quigley has made a similar argument. "Existing works on Confederate nationalism," he argues, "have largely overlooked the fact that southerners' engagement with nationalism was an ongoing process that did not begin from nothing in 1861. The prewar background is essential for understanding wartime nationalism." See *Shifting Grounds: Nationalism and the American South, 1848–1865* (New York: Oxford University Press, 2012), 8.

28. McPherson, *For Cause and Comrades*, 17–19; Susan-Mary Grant, *North over South: Northern Nationalism and American Identity in the Antebellum Era* (Lawrence:

University Press of Kansas, 2000), 8–9. See also Hess, *Liberty, Virtue, and Progress*. Wartime may have sparked new effort by individuals and associations to lay "the groundwork for the cultural and ideological American nation-state" by redefining the nature of the federal government and emphasizing the nation's "mythical aura," but these ideas were not absent from antebellum thinkers' conceptions of nationhood. See Peter J. Parish, "The Distinctiveness of American Nationalism," in *The North and the Nation in the Era of the Civil War*, ed. Smith and Grant; Melinda Lawson, *Patriot Fires: Forging a New American Nationalism in the Civil War North* (Lawrence: University Press of Kansas, 2002), 2, 11–12.

29. These conclusions support Gary W. Gallagher's argument that the idea of "Union" motivated federal soldiers. Wrapped up in the term were ideas about the maintenance of democratic governments and a preservation of the founders' legacy. "The citizens who labored to save the Union," Gallagher wrote, "subscribed to a vision of their nation built on free labor, economic opportunity, and a broad political franchise they considered unique in the world." See *The Union War* (Cambridge, Mass.: Harvard University Press, 2011), 2, 6, 34.

30. Peter S. Carmichael, *The Last Generation: Young Virginians in Peace, War, and Reunion* (Chapel Hill: University of North Carolina Press, 2005), 10–11, 48–49, 149. Stephen Berry also discovered a level of anxiety in young southerners during the 1850s. "More educated than their fathers," southern sons "were also under more pressure to live up to the version of civilized patriarchy that had become so integral to the South's sense of self and to its defense against the North." Most southern college graduates, he notes, "went out into the world armed only with unachievable ideals and dreams of greatness so lofty they had little practical application." Berry, *All That Makes a Man*, 31–32, 36.

31. Henry Livermore Abbott (Harvard, 1860), Charles Francis Adams, Jr. (Harvard, 1856), Samuel Chapman Armstrong (Williams, 1862), Francis Channing Barlow (Harvard, 1855), William Francis Bartlett (Harvard, 1862), Charles Pickering Bowditch (Harvard, 1863), Nathaniel Bowditch (Harvard Scientific School, non-grad 1861), John Marshall Brown (Bowdoin, 1860), Joshua Lawrence Chamberlain (Bowdoin, 1852), Charles Peleg Chandler (Bowdoin, 1854), George Clary (Dartmouth, 1852), Benjamin William Crowninshield (Harvard, 1858), Caspar Crowninshield (Harvard, 1860), Wilder Dwight (Harvard, 1853), Francis Fessenden (Bowdoin, 1858), James Deering Fessenden (Bowdoin, 1852), Samuel Fessenden (Bowdoin, 1861), James Abram Garfield (Williams, 1856), John Chipman Gray (Harvard, 1859), Franklin Aretas Haskell (Dartmouth, 1854), Oliver Wendell Holmes, Jr. (Harvard, 1861), Theodore James Holmes (Yale, 1853), Charles Henry Howard (Bowdoin, 1859), Oliver Otis Howard (Bowdoin, 1850), Luther Clark Howell (Amherst, 1864), Thomas Hamlin Hubbard (Bowdoin, 1857), Thomas Worcester Hyde (Bowdoin, 1861), Charles Russell Lowell (Harvard, 1854), William Thompson Lusk (Yale, non-grad 1859), Theodore Lyman (Harvard, 1855), Charles Porter Mattocks (Bowdoin, 1862), William McArthur (Bowdoin, 1853), Charles Fessenden Morse (Harvard Scientific School, 1858), Samuel Edward Nichols (Amherst, 1865), John Buttrick Noyes (Harvard, 1858), Uriah Nelson Parmelee (Yale, non-grad 1863), Christopher Pennell (Amherst, non-grad 1863), William Elmer Potter (Harvard Law, 1861), John Read (Harvard, 1862), Paul Joseph Revere (Harvard, 1852),

James Clay Rice (Yale, 1854), William Dwight Sedgwick (Harvard, 1851), Robert Gould Shaw (Harvard, non-grad 1860), Frazer Augustus Stearns (Amherst, 1863), Joseph Hopkins Twichell (Yale, 1859), Stephen Minot Weld (Harvard, 1860), William Wheeler (Yale, 1855), Theodore Winthrop (Yale, 1848), Eri Davidson Woodbury (Dartmouth, 1863).

32. Susan-Mary Grant, for example, relied on travel narratives and other publications in *North over South*, Chapter 4. Daniel Walker Howe has noted the importance of oratory in nineteenth-century America, referring to it as "oral literature." Oratory, wrote Howe, "included not only political oratory and ministers' sermons but also lyceum addresses, public dialogues or 'conversations,' lawyers' oral arguments (a form of entertainment in the courthouse-centered county seats), and commemorative orations, such as those marking college commencements or Washington's Birthday." Howe, *Political Culture of the American Whigs*, 25–27. See also Kenneth Cmiel, *Democratic Eloquence: The Fight over Popular Speech in Nineteenth-Century America* (New York: William Morrow, 1990). For a more detailed discussion of the elements of nationalism and the importance of the print revolution see Benedict Anderson, *Imagined Communities: Reflections on the Origin and Spread of Nationalism* (1983; repr., New York: Verso, 2006).

33. Lowell, "The Reverence Due from the Old to the Young," in *Life and Letters of Charles Russell Lowell*, 9–11.

1. "A Stage with Curtains Drawn": New England College Students and Their World

1. William Hyde Appleton, essay, May 3, 1864, "The Functions of Colleges in Our Democracy," Records of the Class of 1864, Harvard University Archives, Harvard University, Cambridge, Massachusetts (repository hereafter cited as HUA).

2. Ibid.

3. Carl F. Kaestle, *Pillars of the Republic: Common Schools and American Society, 1780–1860* (New York: Hill and Wang, 1983), 3–7; quoted in Henry Steele Commager, *The Era of Reform, 1830–1860* (New York: D. Van Nostrand Company, 1960), 134–35.

4. Steven Mintz, *Huck's Raft: A History of American Childhood* (Cambridge, Mass.: Belknap Press of Harvard University, 2004), 90–91; Hess, *Liberty, Virtue, and Progress*, 13; Baker, *Affairs of Party*, 71–72.

5. Rodney Hessinger, *Seduced, Abandoned, and Reborn: Visions of Youth in Middle-Class America, 1780–1850* (Philadelphia: University of Pennsylvania Press, 2005), 2–10, 69–73.

6. David F. Allmendinger, Jr., *Paupers and Scholars: The Transformation of Student Life in Nineteenth-Century New England* (New York: St. Martin's Press, 1975), 3.

7. Mary Kelley has studied "the role schooling at female academies and seminaries played in mediating" the process of "this transformation in individual and social identities." Education was "decisive" in the process of "recasting women's subjectivity and the felt reality of their collective experience." Female students used their schooling to redefine "themselves and their relationship to civil society." Women who "led the movement . . . into the world beyond their households" as writers, educators, and

reformers, Kelley contends, were educated at academies and the seminaries (women's colleges did not fully emerge until after the Civil War). Indeed, women's schools in this era had many similar goals to their male counterparts. Female students wrote essays, published papers, delivered speeches at commencement, and participated in literary and debate societies. "In concert with the cultivation of mental faculties," Kelley wrote, "students were taught to envision themselves as historical actors who had claim to rights and obligations of citizenship." See *Learning to Stand and Speak*, 1–2, 16–17, 81.

8. Allmendinger, *Paupers and Scholars*, 3–4. In arguing that the Civil War changed American colleges, Michael David Cohen nicely summarizes the changing nature of these institutions of higher learning from the colonial through the antebellum period. See *Reconstructing the Campus: Higher Education and the American Civil War* (Charlottesville: University of Virginia Press, 2012), 2–6.

9. George P. Schmidt, *The Liberal Arts College: A Chapter in American Cultural History* (1957; repr., Westport, Conn.: Greenwood Press, 1975), 24–25, 27–32, 40; Daniel Walker Howe, "Classical Education in America," *Wilson Quarterly* 35 (Spring 2011): 31.

New Englanders moved westward founding Beloit and Carleton Colleges. Princeton produced many Scotch-Irish Presbyterians who moved across the Appalachians into Ohio and southern states, establishing, along the way, Hampden-Sydney, Dickinson, Davidson, Oglethorpe, and Miami. Smaller denominations also founded schools. Episcopalians established Geneva, Kenyon, and Trinity Colleges while the Lutherans founded Gettysburg and Muhlenberg Colleges, and Methodists founded, among others, Madison (Colgate) and Columbian (George Washington) Universities.

10. E. Merton Coulter, *College Life in the Old South: As Seen at the University of Georgia* (1928; repr., Athens: University of Georgia Press, 1973), xi. As Lorri Glover has pointed out, southerners had a different purpose concerning education: "In the minds of southern aristocrats . . . the ultimate value of a university education derived from its capacity to promote public status. Intellectual edification, although a useful consequence, was seldom the primary purpose of attending college." "Southerners," Glover concludes, "emphasized the reputation enjoyed rather than the knowledge acquired by a man of education, and they prized preparation for future leadership more than scholastics." Jennifer R. Green, meanwhile, argues that military academies offered the sons of nonelite southern families an opportunity to obtain a higher education. Like their northern counterparts, the graduates from these military academies entered professional careers. See Glover, *Southern Sons*, 41; Jennifer R. Green, "'Stout Chaps Who Can Bear the Distress': Young Men in Antebellum Military Academies," in *Southern Manhood: Perspectives on Masculinity in the Old South*, ed. Craig Thompson Friend and Lorri Glover (Athens: University of Georgia Press, 2004), 175.

11. Ronald Story, *The Forging of an Aristocracy: Harvard and the Boston Upper Class, 1800–1870* (Middletown, Conn.: Wesleyan University Press, 1980), 91–108 (Henry Adams quoted on p. 97); Richard F. Miller, "Brahmin Janissaries: John A. Andrew Mobilizes Massachusetts' Upper Class for the Civil War," *New England Quarterly* 75 (June 2002): 208. To be fair, some schools tried to diversify their undergraduate populations as well. Yale in 1827 opened an additional dining hall, which served meals that cost 20 percent less than the regular board plan. This essentially created two dining halls, which separated students by their wealth. Princeton and Brown followed in 1831

and 1832, respectively. Such approaches, however, might not have been the best strategy to encourage admission. See Frederick Rudolph, *The American College and University* (New York: Knopf, 1965), 205–6; Miller, "Brahmins under Fire," 77–78.

12. William Whiting Richards, essay and exhibition oration, May 1, 1855, "Universities in Republics," Records of the Class of 1855, HUA.

13. Quoted in Donald G. Tewksbury, *The Founding of American Colleges and Universities before the Civil War: With Particular Reference to the Religious Influence Bearing upon the College Movement* (New York: Teachers College, Columbia University, 1932), 5; Allmendinger, *Paupers and Scholars*, 1–2. Allmendinger's study concerns only the ten New England colleges that awarded degrees before 1825, which included Bowdoin, Brown, Dartmouth, Harvard, Middlebury, Vermont, Waterville (Colby), Williams, and Yale. His study, therefore, neglects Trinity, Wesleyan, Norwich, Holy Cross, and Tufts, though the he claims that "including the five newer institutions would have altered my generalizations in no significant way" (23n).

14. Allmendinger, *Paupers and Scholars*, 9, 11–12; Eri D. Woodbury to his father, July 17, 1863, Eri Davidson Woodbury Letters, 1858 May 13–1866 August 13, Francestown, N.H., to A.J. and Henry Woodbury, Rauner Special Collections Library, Dartmouth College (repository hereafter cited as DCL; collection hereafter cited as Woodbury Letters, DCL).

15. Cohen, *Reconstructing the Campus*, 8; Baker, *Affairs of Party*, 106–7; Wilson Smith, *Professors and Public Ethics: Studies of Northern Moral Philosophers before the Civil War* (Ithaca, N.Y.: Cornell University Press, 1956), 8–9; D. H. Meyer, *The Instructed Conscience: The Shaping of the American National Ethic* (Philadelphia: University of Pennsylvania Press, 1972), vii, 4–5, 12, 63–69; quoted in David M. Tucker, *Mugwumps: Public Moralists of the Gilded Age* (Columbia: University of Missouri Press, 1998), 1. Lorri Glover has argued that "higher education was the centerpiece" of elite southern boys' "transformation into 'southern men.'" See "'Let Us Manufacture Men': Educating Elite Boys in the Early National South," in *Southern Manhood*, ed. Friend and Glover, 22.

16. James A. Berlin, *Writing Instruction in Nineteenth-Century American Colleges* (Carbondale: Southern Illinois University Press, 1984), 56.

17. Joshua Lawrence Chamberlain to Nehemiah Cleaveland, October 14, 1859, Joshua Lawrence Chamberlain Collection, M27, George J. Mitchell Department of Special Collections and Archives, Bowdoin College, Brunswick, Maine (repository hereafter cited as BCL; collection hereafter cited as Chamberlain Collection, BCL). Lorri Glover has observed that, for the early republic period, at least, "universities provided the proving grounds on which young southern men could adopt these behaviors and thereby move from boyhood to refined manhood." One of Glover's "biggest surprises in reading advice to college students [from their parents] is the infrequency with which relatives discussed classes, books, or ideas." See "Let Us Manufacture Men," 29.

18. Howe, "Classical Education in America," 32; Ethan S. Rafuse, "'To Check . . . the Very Worst and Meanest of Our Passions': Common Sense, 'Cobbon Sense,' and the Socialization of Cadets at Antebellum West Point," *War in History* 16 (September 2009): 407, 418, 424.

19. Wilder Dwight, essay, March 11, 1852, "Whether Education Should Aim to Develop All the Faculties Equally or to Foster Individual Peculiarities of Taste and Intellect?" Dwight Family Papers, Massachusetts Historical Society, Boston, Massachusetts (repository hereafter cited as MHS; collection hereafter cited as Dwight Papers, MHS); Edward Savage, essay, July 28, 1860, "The American Scholar in the Old World," Commencement Parts Records, 1771–, DCL (collection hereafter cited as Commencement Parts, DCL).

20. Lucius Henry Buckingham, essay and commencement oration, July 16, 1851, "Female Education," Records of the Class of 1851, HUA; Horowitz, *Campus Life*, 12–13; William Gardner Colburn, essay and commencement oration, July 18, 1860, "College Life a Rehearsal," Records of the Class of 1860, HUA.

21. John Deering, Jr., to "William," September 17, 1860, Student Journals, Letters, and Scrapbooks, BCL; William Wheeler to Theodosia Davenport Wheeler, February 23, 1852, in Wheeler, *Letters of William Wheeler of the Class of 1855*, Y.C. (Cambridge, Mass.: H. O. Houghton and Company, 1875), 4; Luther Clark Howell to sister Bell, undated, Luther Clark Howell Papers, Department of Special Collections and Archives, Amherst College Library, Amherst College, Amherst, Massachusetts (repository hereafter cited as ACL; collection hereafter cited as Howell Papers, ACL).

22. Quoted in Horowitz, *Campus Life*, 61; Samuel Chapman Armstrong to C. C. Armstrong, July 18, 1862, in Samuel Chapman Armstrong, *Personal Memories and Letters of General S. C. Armstrong*, ed. Helen W. Ludlow (Hampton, Va.: Hampton Institute, 1898), 1:225, in Samuel Chapman Armstrong Collection, Williams College Archives and Special Collections, Sawyer Library, Williams College, Williamstown, Massachusetts (repository hereafter cited as WCL).

23. Despite his efforts, Ballou remained dependent on aid. After one of his benefactors suffered some financial losses, Ballou had to leave Brown. Ballou eventually struck a deal with the National Law School, in Ballston, New York, where he taught rhetoric and elocution while beginning his own studies in law. John M. Pellicano, *"Well Prepared To Die": The Life of Brigadier General James Clay Rice* (Fredericksburg, Va.: John M. Pellicano, 2007), 15, 20–22; Robin Young, *For Love and Liberty: The Untold Civil War Story of Major Sullivan Ballou and His Famous Love Letter* (New York: Thunder's Mouth Press, 2006), 22, 29, 37, 64, 71; Henry Sweetser Burrage, *Brown University in the Civil War: A Memorial* (Providence, R.I.: Providence Press Company, 1868), 94–95.

24. George Lafayette Hayes to his father, [undated] November 1850, Student Journals, Letters, and Scrapbooks, BCL.

25. John A. Carpenter, *Sword and Olive Branch: Oliver Otis Howard* (1964; repr., New York: Fordham University Press, 1999), 2–3; Willard M. Wallace, *Soul of the Lion: A Biography of Joshua L. Chamberlain* (1960; repr., Gettysburg, Pa.: Stan Clark Military Books, 1995), 22; Young, *For Love and Liberty*, 66–67; Leah A. Strong, *Joseph Hopkins Twichell: Mark Twain's Friend and Pastor* (Athens: University of Georgia Press, 1966), 11.

26. John Deering, Jr., to "William," Bowdoin College, October 17, 1860, Student Journals, Letters, and Scrapbooks, BCL; Benjamin W. Crowninshield, journal entry, December 18, 1856, in Benjamin W. Crowninshield, *A Private Journal, 1856–1858* (Cambridge, Mass.: Riverside Press, 1941), 13.

27. Brooks Mather Kelley, *Yale: A History* (New Haven, Conn.: Yale University Press, 1974), 209; Oliver Otis Howard to Eliza Howard Gilmore, October 3, 1846, Oliver Otis Howard Papers, BCL (collection hereafter cited as Howard Papers, BCL).

28. Benjamin W. Crowninshield, journal entry, November 17, 1856, in Crowninshield, *A Private Journal*, 2.

29. Oliver Otis Howard to Eliza Howard Gilmore, June 22, 1847, Howard Papers, BCL; Benjamin W. Crowninshield, journal entries, October 27, 1857, December 11, 1856, and April 13, 1858, in Crowninshield, *A Private Journal*, 83, 10, 125; William A. Stearns, *Adjutant Stearns* (1862; repr., Charlestown, Mass.: Acme Bookbinding, 2004), 61; Caleb P. Wickersham, essay, August 5, 1846, "Claims of Nat. Hist.," Commencement Orations Collection, 1833-55, Special Collections and Archives, Wesleyan University Library, Wesleyan University, Middletown, Connecticut (repository hereafter cited as WUL; collection here after cited as Commencement Orations, WUL).

30. Stearns, *Adjutant Stearns*, 21-22, 58; Charles H. Howard to Oliver Otis Howard, March 22, 1857, Howard Papers, BCL; Pellicano, *"Well Prepared To Die,"* 23-24.

For more on the effects of the Second Great Awakening, see Paul E. Johnson, *A Shopkeeper's Millennium: Society and Revivals in Rochester, New York, 1815-1837* (1978; New York: Hill & Wang, 1994) and Steven E. Woodworth, *While God is Marching On: The Religious World of Civil War Soldiers* (Lawrence: University Press of Kansas, 2001), especially part 1.

31. Anders Stephanson, *Manifest Destiny: American Expansion and the Empire of Right* (New York: Hill and Wang, 1995), xi, 51-54.

32. Isaac Parker, essay, July 28, 1853, "The British Colonies in America," Commencement Parts, DCL; C. B. Ford, essay, August 2, 1854, "Monuments the Precursors of National Ruin," Commencement Orations, WUL.

33. Chauncey Nye, journal entry, May 18, 1850, Chauncey Nye Journal, 1850-55, vol. 1, DCL; Edwin Alonso Thomas to his parents, June 23, 1852, Student Letters, DCL.

34. Joseph Emerson Smith to Samuel E. Smith, July 25, 1852, Smith Brothers Student Letters, BCL; Samuel Fessenden to William Pitt Fessenden, May 14, 1860, and May 18 or 21, 1860, Fessenden Collection, BCL.

35. William Wheeler to Theodosia Davenport Wheeler, March 15, 1852, in Wheeler, *Letters of William Wheeler*, 6; Benjamin W. Crowninshield, journal entries, December 15, November 18, November 20, November 28, December 3, December 7, December 8, 1856, June 26, November 16, May 16 and 17, 1857, in Crowninshield, *A Private Journal*, 12, 2, 3, 5, 6-7, 8, 9, 60-61, 87, 48-50.

36. Wilder Dwight to William Dwight, June 15, 1850, Dwight Papers, MHS.

37. William G. Hammond, diary entries, August 10 and 12, 1847, in William Gardiner Hammond, *Remembrance of Amherst: An Undergraduate's Diary, 1846-1848*, ed. George F. Whicher (New York: Columbia University Press, 1946), 168, 174.

2. "The Great People of the Future": American Civilization and National Character

1. Wilder Dwight essay, November 1851, "The Americans a Practical People: How Far Is This Character True, and How Far Is It Justly a Reproach?" Dwight Papers, MHS.

2. Wilder Dwight, November 23, 1850, "An Adventurer Returning from California," Dwight Papers, MHS.

3. Elizabeth Amelia Dwight, "Wilder Dwight," in Thomas Wentworth Higginson, ed., *Harvard Memorial Biographies* (Cambridge, Mass.: Sever and Francis, 1867), 1:252–56.

4. Greenberg, *Manifest Manhood*, 11–12, 21, 51, 261. Such a proposal is similar to historian Anders Stephanson's "wider sense" of Manifest Destiny. This version, which was articulated by Woodrow Wilson, according to Stephanson, emphasized "the providentially assigned role of the United States to lead the world to new and better things." In Wilson's understanding, the United States "had been allowed to see the light and was bound to show the way for the historically retrograde." Stephanson noted that one of the ways this ideology was spread was through the developing of the United States "into an exemplary state *separate* from the corrupt and fallen world, letting others emulate it as best they can." See *Manifest Destiny*, xii.

5. Parish, "Distinctiveness of American Nationalism," 58–63; for works that suggest that Civil War–era Americans understood their relationship to the nation-state through familial or local connections, see Reid Mitchell, *The Vacant Chair: The Northern Soldier Leaves Home* (New York: Oxford University Press, 1993), 14–15; and Paludan, *People's Contest*, 12–14. Such ideas are in line with work on European nationalism. Alon Confino, for example, has argued that German nationalism should be viewed as an extension of local identification. See Confino, *The Nation as a Local Metaphor: Württemberg, Imperial Germany, and National Memory, 1871–1918* (Chapel Hill: University of North Carolina Press, 1997).

6. Foner, *Free Soil, Free Labor, Free Men*, 9; William R. Taylor, *Cavalier and Yankee: The Old South and American National Character* (1961; repr., New York: Oxford University Press, 1993), 15–18; Grant, *North over South*, 1–4.

7. Harlow W. Sheidley, *Sectional Nationalism: Massachusetts Conservative Leaders and the Transformation of America, 1815–1836* (Boston: Northeastern University Press, 1998), xi–xii, 87, 118–19. Joanne Melish has demonstrated that New Englanders attempted to create "a triumphant narrative of a historically free, white New England" as a way to portray free African Americans as innately inferior. Joanne Pope Melish, *Disowning Slavery: Gradual Emancipation and "Race" in New England, 1780–1860* (Ithaca, N.Y.: Cornell University Press, 1998), 1–7.

8. Joseph A. Conforti, *Imagining New England: Explorations of Regional Identity from the Pilgrims to the Mid-Twentieth Century* (Chapel Hill: University of North Carolina Press, 2001), 123–25, 150, 188–89; Stephanson, *Manifest Destiny*, 4, 29–30.

9. Eric Foner, *The Fiery Trial: Abraham Lincoln and American Slavery* (New York: W. W. Norton, 2010), 70–72. Meanwhile, as Stephen Berry points out, southerners of the same generation did not concede that their vision of the future stood in opposition to progress. Rather, "they believed they were—alongside their Northern brethren at first, better than their Northern brethren ultimately—building a Civilization." In fact, part of southern manhood stemmed from one's ability to "contribute" to the "attainment" of "a perfect Civilization." See *All That Makes a Man*, 26–27.

10. Conforti, *Imagining New England*, 172; Sheidley, *Sectional Nationalism*, xi–xii, 87, 118–19. As Daniel Walker Howe has observed, most Whig interpretations of history

viewed the American Revolution as the "climax of history." See *Political Culture of the American Whigs*, 70.

11. Thomas M. Allen, *A Republic in Time: Temporality and Social Imagination in Nineteenth-Century America* (Chapel Hill: University of North Carolina Press, 2008), 13.

12. William P. Leeman, "George Bancroft's Civil War: Slavery, Abraham Lincoln, and the Course of History," *New England Quarterly* 81 (September 2008): 463; Sacvan Bercovitch, *The Rites of Assent: Transformations in the Symbolic Construction of America* (New York: Routledge, 1993), 174; Howe, *Political Culture of the American Whigs*, 73–74.

13. Daniel Avery Whedon, July 17, 1845, "Intellect—a Transformation," Commencement Orations, WUL; Robert Treat Paine, essay and exhibition oration, May 1, 1855, "The Moral Progress of Nations," Records of the Class of 1855, HUA; Joshua Hall, essay, July 31, 1851, "The Comparative Happiness of Society the 16th Century and in the 19th," Commencement Parts, DCL.

14. Stephanson, *Manifest Destiny*, 6, 10.

15. John Davis Long, essay and commencement oration, July 15, 1857, "The Body of Liberties," Records of the Class of 1857, HUA; Hermann Jackson Warner, essay and Commencement Day oration, July 17, 1850, "Political Life," Records of the Class of 1850, HUA.

16. Benjamin Shurtleff Savage, "The Characteristics of the New Englander," Public Exhibition of the Senior and Junior Classes of Bowdoin College, May 16, 1848, Records of the Class of 1848, BCL.

17. John Allard, essay, July 27, 1854, "The Wealth of New England in Her Mountains and Rivers," Commencement Parts, DCL.

18. As Sacvan Bercovitch has written of George Bancroft's historical interpretation, "The fathers were not English. They were *New* English, the English-speaking founders of a new kind of community, and what they initiated the Revolutionary sons fulfilled." See Bercovitch, *Rites of Assent*, 177.

19. Edwin Clowes Rushmore, essay, August 5, 1846, "Political Morality," Commencement Orations, WUL; George Miller Hobbs, essay and commencement oration, July 17, 1850, "Civilization in the Pacific," Records of the Class of 1850, HUA.

20. Silas Hardy, essay, July 26, 1855, "The Relation of the American Colonies to Each Other before the Revolution," Commencement Parts, DCL; Leander Collamore, essay, July 31, 1856, "The Ballads of the American Revolution," Commencement Parts, DCL; Francis Balch, essay and exhibition oration, October 19, 1858, "A Citizen of a Free Country Who Feels No Interest in Politics," Records of the Class of 1859, HUA.

21. Baker, *Affairs of Party*, 80–84; David Noyes, essay, July 30, 1857, "National Amusements," Commencement Parts, DCL; John Marshall Brown essay, undated, "The Influence of History and Legendary Lore upon Natural Scenery and Art," John Marshall Brown Collection, Maine Historical Society, Portland, Maine (repository hereafter cited as MeHS; collection hereafter cited as Brown Collection, MeHS). As Len Travers has pointed out in his study of Fourth of July celebrations during the early republic, by the nation's Jubilee in 1826 "Independence Day was clearly losing its immediacy and its power to persuade Americans of their homogeneity." Instead, the cohesive message was becoming more "diffused, and . . . drowned out" in the face of expansion and "budding sectional issues." More recently, Mark Neely has argued that

Fourth of July celebrations were not political in nature. Thomas A. Chambers observes that battlefield tourism "did not fully develop until fifty years after the Declaration of Independence" and grew from Americans' attempts to imitate European grand tours. The development of internal improvements in the young republic—turnpikes, railroads, and canals—also increased tourism at historic sites. John F. Sears notes that places like Saratoga Springs in New York attracted the first tourists seeking healthy remedies for their ailments. See Len Travers, *Celebrating the Fourth: Independence Day and the Rites of Nationalism in the Early Republic* (Amherst: University of Massachusetts Press, 1997), 10; Mark E. Neely, Jr., *Lincoln and the Triumph of the Nation: Constitutional Conflict in the American Civil War* (Chapel Hill: University of North Carolina Press, 2011), 9–11; Thomas A. Chambers, *Memories of War: Visiting Battlegrounds and Bonefields in the Early American Republic* (Ithaca, N.Y.: Cornell University Press, 2012), 3–9; John F. Sears, *Sacred Places: American Tourist Attractions in the Nineteenth Century* (New York: Oxford University Press, 1989), 3; for a description of the early development of American tourism, see Richard H. Gassan, *The Birth of American Tourism: New York, the Hudson Valley, and American Culture, 1790–1830* (Amherst: University of Massachusetts Press, 2008).

22. William E. Potter Diary, September 12, 1859, University Archives, Department of Rare Books and Special Collections, Princeton University Library, Princeton, New Jersey (collection hereafter cited as Potter Diary, PUL).

23. Charles Gilman Connor, essay and exhibition oration, "Contemporaneous Expositions of the Constitution," Records of the Class of 1854, HUA; Willard S. Heath, essay, July 29, 1858, "Necessity of a Liberal Spirit in American Statesmen," Commencement Parts, DCL; Edwin Coleman Hand essay, undated (ca. 1852–56), "The Perpetuity of Our Government," Unpublished Manuscripts in Alumni Biographical Files and Class Shelves, Edwin C. Hand Civil War Papers, ACL.

24. Paine, "Moral Progress of Nations"; Thomas B. Fox, Jr., essay, undated, "'For Forms of Government Let Fools Contest; Whare'er Is Best Administered, Is Best.' Pope. Is This True?" Thomas Bayley Fox, Jr., Papers, MHS; Warner, "Political Life."

25. Charles Cushing Mitchell, essay and exhibition oration, October 15, 1850, "The Punishment of Political Offenders," Records of the Class of 1851, HUA; J. T. Graham, essay, August 1, 1855, "Liberty," Commencement Orations, WUL; James Morss Chase, essay and Commencement Day oration, July 17, 1850, "A New People," Records of the Class of 1850, HUA.

26. David Pulsifer Kimball, essay and commencement oration, July 16, 1856, "The Influence of the New World upon the Old," Records of the Class of 1856, HUA; Frederick B. Dodge, essay, July 28, 1860, "The Moral Element in Political Revolutions," Commencement Parts, DCL.

27. David Waldstreicher, *In the Midst of Perpetual Fetes: The Making of American Nationalism, 1776–1820* (Chapel Hill: University of North Carolina Press, 1997), 141–42.

28. The nation, historian George Forgie has observed, was often compared to a growing youth, especially when contemporaries considered the issue of territorial expansion. Robert Lemelin, meanwhile, has used travel narratives to explain how Americans conceived of the character of each section. Northerners, he notes, compared themselves to southerners, minority races, and different ethnic groups that they

encountered. See Forgie, *Patricide in the House Divided*, 103; Robert Lemelin, *Pathway to the National Character, 1830–1861* (Port Washington, N.Y.: Kennikat Press Corps, 1974), 102–3, 109–24.

29. Charles Augustus Gregory, essay and exhibition oration, October 17, 1854, "The Last Census," Records of the Class of 1855, HUA; F. D. Hodgson, essay, August 3, 1853, "Elements of National Character," Commencement Orations, WUL.

30. Franklin Aretas Haskell, essay, February 13, 1858, "The American Character," Franklin Aretas Haskell Papers, 1858-63, DCL (collection hereafter cited as Haskell Papers, DCL).

31. Leonard Case Alden, essay, July 17, 1861, "National Character Elevated by National Affliction," Records of the Class of 1861, HUA.

32. Parish, "Distinctiveness of American Nationalism," 61–63; James M. McPherson, *Is Blood Thicker Than Water? Crises of Nationalism in the Modern World* (New York: Vintage, 1999), 29–36; Reginald Horsman, *Race and Manifest Destiny: The Origins of American Racial Anglo-Saxonism* (Cambridge, Mass.: Harvard University Press, 1981), 1, 4–5. Peter Parish has observed that by the 1850s, Americans accepted an "ethnic nationalism" that separated them from other races. See "Partisanship and the Construction of Nationalism," in *The North and the Nation in the Era of the Civil War*, ed. Smith and Grant, 114–15.

33. John H. Morse, essay, July 28, 1853, "California and Australia in Their Relations to General Civilization," Commencement Parts, DCL.

34. Burrill Porter, essay, July 31, 1856, "The Mingling of Races," Commencement Parts, DCL. James McPherson has noted that Americans "defined their nationality in accordance" with the ideas of "civic nationalism" and "ethnic nationalism." He pointed out that "American civic nationalism" could be "identified not only with citizenship, but also with ideals of liberty, republicanism, manhood suffrage, equality of opportunity, and the absence of rigid class lines," while "ethnic nationalism" revolved around a group identity "shared by . . . people united among themselves and distinguished from others by one or more of the following factors: language; religion; culture; and . . . a belief in the common genetic or biological descent of the group." Americans, McPherson observed, "remained confident of their ability to absorb European nationalities into American civic nationality." See *Is Blood Thicker Than Water?* 29–36.

35. Porter, "Mingling of Races"; Daniel Swan Preston, essay and exhibition oration, October 19, 1858, "Science as a Peacemaker," Records of the Class of 1859, HUA.

36. Henry Conant Prentiss, essay and exhibition oration, May 2, 1854, "Perishing Races," Records of the Class of 1854, HUA. According to Amy S. Greenberg, antebellum American expansionists argued that "a higher law, or natural destiny" connected America's fate with the rest of the continent, and this helped justify "the flouting of international law." They used "the same justifications that enabled Americans at home to displace and exterminate Native Americans in the name of destiny" (*Manifest Manhood*, 86.)

37. Allard, "Wealth of New England in Her Mountains and Rivers." As Thomas A. Chambers has argued, America's "relative youth became an asset." Despite not having Europe's "ancient ruins and cultivated scenery," the "wild and unsettled scenery" of America "provoked more than reflections upon a specific castle's legend or an associated

poem." Its "untrammeled mountains and ancient forests" helped America strike "the perfect balance between historical associations and unspoiled wilderness." John F. Sears, meanwhile, points out that Americans visited Niagara Falls, "a waterfall rather than a cathedral, but as one of God's grandest, if not *the* grandest of His creations." The falls, along with sites such as Mammoth Cave, "whose scale Europe could not match, offered tourists samples of the magnificence of Nature in the New World." When American tourists wanted "refined landscapes that reflected the progress of America in meeting European standards of culture," however, they ventured to the Connecticut and Hudson River Valleys. While New England students used their descriptive skills to praise their home region, American travelers in Central America, as Amy Greenberg has noted, helped promote the beauty of that part of the continent, whetting expansionists' appetites. See Chambers, *Memories of War*, 9; Sears, *Sacred Places*, 6, 49; Greenberg, *Manifest Manhood*, 59–67.

38. Alexander Ingram, essay, July 29, 1858, "The Pacific Railroad," Commencement Parts, DCL; Franklin Aretas Haskell, essay, February 13, 1858, "The American Character," Haskell Papers, DCL.

39. Gregory, "Last Census."

40. Henry Pickering, essay, October 16, 1860, "The Causes and Results of Modern Emigration," Records of the Class of 1861, HUA.

41. H. R. Tarbell, essay, July 29, 1852, "The Shores of the Pacific," Commencement Parts, DCL; George Miller Hobbs, essay and commencement oration, July 17, 1850, "Civilization in the Pacific," Records of the Class of 1850, HUA.

42. William Dwight Sedgwick to William Minot, Jr., February 11, 1855, Charles Sedgwick Papers, MHS (collection hereafter cited as Sedgwick Papers, MHS).

43. William Wirt Burrage, essay and commencement oration, July 16, 1856, "Our 'Manifest Destiny,'" Records of the Class of 1856, HUA; Ingram, "Pacific Railroad."

44. Stephen Goodhue Emerson, essay, July 17, 1861, "The Plebs," Records of the Class of 1861, HUA.

45. Joseph Charles Augustus Wingate, "The Right to Labor for Remunerative Wages," Commencement Parts, May 1851, Records of the Class of 1851, BCL.

46. Thomas Emerson, essay and exhibition oration, May 6, 1856, "Industrial Interests a Protest against War," Records of the Class of 1856, HUA. As Amy S. Greenberg has noted, "Restrained men . . . condemned the values of the aggressive expansionists as antiquated and retrograde." The martial men, meanwhile, viewed foreign territories as "an exceptional sphere for manly activity, a place where martial men could express their talents" (*Manifest Manhood*, 21, 51, 261).

47. Theodore French, essay, July 29, 1852, "The Mutual Responsibilities of Nations," Commencement Parts, DCL; Burrage, "Our 'Manifest Destiny.'"

48. Parker, "British Colonies in America," Commencement Parts, DCL; Thomas Weston Ritche, essay, July 27, 1848, "The Prospects of British America," Commencement Parts, DCL. Ritchie, who was from Canada, admitted to his fondness of being British even as he foresaw the relationship between England and Canada coming to an end.

49. Herbert Sleeper, July 17, 1861, "The Progress of California and of Australia Compared," Records of the Class of 1861, HUA. Amy S. Greenberg has observed that "Manifest Destiny was much more than simple political rhetoric. Even in the 1850s it

resonated as a deeply held belief among many ordinary Americans." The idea of America's spread, therefore, had lasting and widespread appeal. See *Manifest Manhood*, 79.

50. Burrage, "Our 'Manifest Destiny.'"

51. Zebina Thomas Dean, essay, August 5, 1846, "Constitution of the United States," Commencement Orations, WUL.

52. Russell Duncan, *Where Death and Glory Meet: Colonel Robert Gould Shaw and the 54th Massachusetts Infantry* (Athens: University of Georgia Press, 1999), 12–13, 18.

53. Wilder Dwight essay, March 18, 1852, "Iphigenia in Tauris Complains That the Condition of Women Is Lamentable. How Much Has Their Condition Been Improved in Two Thousand Years? How Much Remains to Be Done? And How Far Will Iphigenia's Complaint Always Be True," Dwight Papers, MHS. Kristin Hoganson has demonstrated how proslavery advocates, in their attempts to discredit the Garrisonian abolitionists, criticized race reformers for wishing to upend social gender structures as well as racial ones. See "Garrisonian Abolitionists and the Rhetoric of Gender, 1850–1860," *American Quarterly* 45 (December 1993): 558–59.

54. Gregory, "Last Census."

55. Potter Diary, July 4, 1860, and December 21, 1859, PUL.

56. Quoted in Theodore Winthrop, *Life in the Open Air, and Other Papers*, ed. George W. Curtis (Boston: Ticknow and Fields, 1863), iii–iv.

57. George Clary essay, August 1851, "Reformers," George Clary Papers, Connecticut Historical Society, Hartford, Connecticut (collection hereafter cited as Clary Papers, CHS); Osgood Johnson, essay, July 29, 1852, "The Slow Progress of Useful Revolutions," Commencement Parts, DCL.

58. Johnson, "Slow Progress of Useful Revolutions." Not all New Brahmins, of course, detested abolitionists. Oliver Wendell Holmes, Jr., for example, contributed money to the Anti-slavery Society and served as one of Wendell Phillips's bodyguards at an event in the midst of the secession crisis. See Louis Menand, *The Metaphysical Club: A Story of Ideas in America* (2001; repr., New York: Farrar, Straus and Giroux, 2002), 30–31.

59. Potter Diary, May 31 and June 1, 1860, PUL. In another instance, Potter tried to attend a memorial for John Brown. His attempt to join in the event was not to honor the abolitionist martyr but rather to observe the "miserable fanatics holding the meeting," for they presented a "phase of human nature we wished to study" (Potter Diary, December 3, 1860, PUL).

60. David Quigg, essay, July 26, 1855, "The Relation of the New States to the Old," Commencement Parts, DCL.

61. Samuel Craft Davis, essay, October 21, 1862, "National Vitality," Records of the Class of 1863, HUA.

3. To Act Like Men: Building Character in the New Brahmins

1. Oliver Otis Howard to Eliza Howard Gilmore, April 18, 1849, and August 16, 1848; Oliver Otis Howard to Eliza Howard Gilmore, March 26, 1849, Howard Papers, BCL. Howard later attended the United States Military Academy at West Point after graduating from Bowdoin.

2. Oliver Otis Howard to Eliza Howard Gilmore, March 14, 1848, Howard Papers, BCL.

3. Oliver Otis Howard to Rowland Bailey Howard, March 25, 1846, and June 29, 1848, Howard Papers, BCL.

4. James Marten has noted that antebellum and wartime children's magazines "sought to cultivate principles designed to ensure order and social responsibility: hard work, obedience, generosity, humility, and piety. . . . Works of fiction and nonfiction alike stressed character and framed the world in moral terms, assuring readers that patriotism and unselfishness together would guarantee individual success and national honor." See *Lessons of War: The Civil War in Children's Magazines* (Wilmington, Del.: Scholarly Resources, 1999), xii–xiii. See also Marten, *The Children's Civil War* (Chapel Hill: University of North Carolina Press, 1998), 23–24.

5. J. A. Mangan and James Walvin, eds., *Manliness and Morality: Middle-Class Masculinity in Britain and America, 1800–1940* (New York: St. Martin's Press, 1987), 1, 4–5; Greenberg, *Manifest Manhood*, 11–12. In addition, see E. Anthony Rotundo, "Learning about Manhood: Gender Ideals and the Middle-Class Family in Nineteenth-Century America," in *Manliness and Morality*, ed. Mangan and Walvin, 38–40. For a discussion of different class ideals of masculinity, see Elliott J. Gorn, *The Manly Art: Bare-Knuckle Prize Fighting in America* (1986; repr., Ithaca, N.Y.: Cornell University Press, 2010). Different circumstances also affected perceptions and actions relating to one's manhood. Stephen Kantrowitz has noted how black and white abolitionists chose different paths to combat slavery because of their racial differences. Meanwhile John Stauffer, writing about male and female New England authors in the 1860s, notes how "a crisis of manhood during the war led to a backlash against feminine virtues and a masculinization of culture after the war." See Stephen Kantrowitz, "Fighting Like Men: Civil War Dilemmas of Abolitionist Manhood," and John Stauffer, "Embattled Manhood and New England Writers, 1860–1870," both in *Battle Scars: Gender and Sexuality in the American Civil War*, ed. Catherine Clinton and Nina Silber (New York: Oxford University Press, 2006), 19–40, 120–39.

6. Joseph Kett argued that character was "not a set of doctrines or even a code of behavior." This study argues for a more expansive definition and proposes that the term might indeed include the elements that Kett rejected. See *Rites of Passage: Adolescence in America, 1790 to the Present* (New York: Basic Books, 1977), 107.

7. Hall, *Organization of American Culture*, 174.

8. Wyatt-Brown, *Southern Honor*, xv, 14. Certain attributes signified honor as a southern cultural phenomenon. For instance, it could be distinguished from simple "manliness" and "masculinity" because it "embraced hierarchy—especially about race." Slavery, Wyatt-Brown contended, was also "sustained by notions of honor" (*Shaping of Southern Culture*, xii).

9. Greenberg, "The Nose, the Lie, and the Duel in the Antebellum South," 58.

10. Glover, *Southern Sons*, 3.

11. Friend and Glover conclude that, "at their core, these two sets of values [honor and mastery] differed. Honor was externally presented for public consumption; mastery was internally realized for personal fulfillment." In a separate essay, Glover noted the similarities between northern and southern masculine identity and education in

the early republic. The institution of slavery, however, drove the young men of the two sections apart. Friend and Glover, *Southern Manhood*, ix–x; Glover, "Let Us Manufacture Men," 22–23.

12. David S. Reynolds, *John Brown, Abolitionist* (New York: Knopf, 2005), 333; Greenberg, *Honor and Slavery*, 91.

13. Ralph Waldo Emerson, *Essays: Second Series*, vol. 2 (1844; repr., Boston: Houghton Mifflin, 1883), 90–91, 96, 103. Character was not a term unique to the antebellum period. It was used in the early days of the republic, linked to honor, and served as the basis by which men—particularly politicians—evaluated one another. It was in this early republic world of political intrigue that historian Joanne B. Freeman defined "character" as "personality with a moral dimension referring to the mixture of traits, vices, and virtues that determined a person's social worth." Thomas Augst, another scholar of masculine identity in the nineteenth century, noted that character referred "less to a standardized type of nature than to a special sum of moral habits and qualities that singles out an individual for esteem and emulation." See Joanne B. Freeman, *Affairs of Honor: National Politics in the New Republic* (New Haven, Conn.: Yale University Press, 2001), xx; Augst, *Clerk's Tale*, 25.

14. Kett, *Rites of Passage*, 105; John Foster, *Essay on Decision of Character* (Burlington, Vt.: Chauncey Goodrich, 1830), 11, 32, 57, 60–61.

15. Ozias Cornwall Pitkin, essay, July 29, 1847, "Influence of Early Studies upon the Future of Character," Commencement Parts, DCL; Robert Carter Pitman, essay, August 4, 1845, "Portraiture of Character—Cardinal Wolsey—Character, Not Success, the Object of Life," Commencement Orations, WUL.

16. Charles Russell Lowell, essay and exhibition performance, "Affectation," Records of the Class of 1854, HUA; Charles Cutler, essay, July 29, 1852, "The Advantages of Asserting the Duties Rather Than the Rights of Man," Commencement Parts, DCL. As Lorri Glover has observed, southern parents valued traits in their sons that they attempted to dissuade in their enslaved laborers. Parents hoped to see "initiative, vitality, accomplishment" in their youth but "deplored attributes deemed less manly and associated with slaves—docility, self-doubt, and reticence." "In short," Glover concludes, "what white parents wanted in their sons they feared in their slaves, and vice versa" (*Southern Sons*, 26).

17. Levi Little, essay, July 27, 1854, "Men of the Right Sort," Commencement Parts, DCL.

18. Edwin C. Griswold, essay, August 4, 1847, "Mental Servitude," Commencement Orations, WUL.

19. Oliver Otis Howard to Eliza Howard Gilmore, October 24, 1846, Howard Papers, BCL.

20. Samuel Chapman Armstrong to Richard Baxter Armstrong, April 21, 1861, in Armstrong, *Personal Memories and Letters of General S. C. Armstrong*, 1:145.

21. G. G. Smith, "College Secret Societies," *Williams Quarterly* 8, no. 4 (1861): 270–72. Although the fraternity system attracted many students, others were repelled by the notions of exclusiveness and created anti-secret societies in response. At Williams College in 1834, students formed the anti-secret Social Fraternity. Ironically, this anti-secret fraternity adopted the model of secret societies and became the national Delta

Upsilon fraternity. As a result "Neutrals" emerged as an alternative to both the secret and the anti-secret societies. One study estimates that, of the graduates of Williams between 1833 and 1872, 42 percent of the men had been members of a fraternity. Society membership may be a useful gauge to delineate between the different groups in a college. According to one scholar studying the Williams College sample, only 131 men from the secret fraternities as opposed to 413 from the neutrals or anti-secret societies became pastors. Perhaps even more dramatically, "in Amherst's class of 1851 all but two of the fourteen members of the anti-secret society became ministers or college professors, but Delta Kappa Epsilon produced no ministers and only one professor" (Horowitz, *Campus Life*, 61–62).

22. Henry George Spaulding, essay and exhibition oration, October 18, 1859, "Individualism," Records of the Class of 1860, HUA.

23. J. S. Griffing, essay, August 4, 1852, "The Moulding Process," Commencement Orations, WUL.

24. Addison Brown, essay and exhibition oration, May 4, 1852, "Unsuccessful Great Men," Records of the Class of 1852, HUA.

25. Augst, *Clerk's Tale*, 32, 58, 134; Hessinger, *Seduced, Abandoned, and Reborn*, 139. Philip N. Racine, editor of Charles Mattocks's papers, argued that "Bowdoin College played the pivotal roll in the forming of Charles's character." See Mattocks, *"Unspoiled Heart": The Journal of Charles Mattocks of the 17th Maine*, ed. Philip N. Racine (Knoxville: University of Tennessee Press, 1994), xv.

26. Pitkin, "Influence of Early Studies upon the Future Of Character"; Arthur McArthur, Jr., to William McArthur, June 25, 1848, McArthur Family Papers, BCL (collection hereafter cited as McArthur Papers, BCL). Historian Larry M. Logue has pointed out that self-discipline was a key trait that Americans sought to cultivate going back to the colonial period. He notes its prominence for individuals seeking "to deal with the demands of wage employment" in the antebellum era. See *To Appomattox and Beyond: The Civil War Soldier in War and Peace* (Chicago: Ivan R. Dee, 1996), 5–7.

27. Potter Diary, April 11 and June 13, 1860, PUL.

28. Joshua Lawrence Chamberlain to Benjamin Galen Snow, May 5, 1848, Chamberlain Collection, BCL.

29. John Deering, Jr., journal entry, January 29, 1861, Student Journals, Letters, and Scrapbooks, BCL.

30. Oliver Otis Howard to Eliza Howard Gilmore, November 1, 1846, Howard Papers, BCL; William Wheeler to Theodosia Davenport Wheeler, March 15, 1852, in Wheeler, *Letters of William Wheeler*, 6; John Deering, Jr., journal entry, August 1, 1861, Student Journals, Letters, and Scrapbooks, BCL.

31. Arthur McArthur, Sr., to Charles McArthur, December 11, 1859, McArthur Papers, BCL. Elite southern parents also hoped to set their children on the right track by promoting proper influences. As Lorri Glover explains, "Along with their northern contemporaries, southerners adopted John Locke's perspective on parenting: children represented a 'tabula rasa.' Character was not inherent in Locke's conception, but rather externally molded. Experiences and education determined character, so boys needed to enjoy proper influences and avoid the insidious, and they needed to do so in early childhood" (*Southern Sons*, 24).

32. Wilder Dwight to Howard Dwight, December 1850, Dwight Papers, MHS.

33. Harriet Sears Crowninshield to Caspar Crowninshield, November 16, 1854, Crowninshield–Magnus Papers, 1834–1965, MHS (collection hereafter cited as Crowninshield–Magnus Papers, MHS).

34. Alpheus Spring Packard, Sr., to Arthur McArthur, Jr., February 15, 1848, McArthur Papers, BCL; Henry I. Bowditch to Nathaniel Bowditch, February 27, 1860, Nathaniel Bowditch Memorial Collection, MHS (collection hereafter cited as Bowditch Memorial, MHS). Such ideas pervaded the antebellum world. In 1808 Supreme Court Justice Thomas Todd told his son, whom he sent to the College of William and Mary, "You are now laying the foundation on which your future prospects thro life depend, the more solid the foundation, the greater certainty in supporting & rearing the superstructure. This period is to form your character—habits of industry & study are now easily acquired and pursued, which will become familiar & easy & last you forever—If on the contrary; you now neglect them, you will fall into idleness, which begets sloth, that engenders dissipation & finally all energy of thought, of Character, & of respectability is forever gone, no exertion can produce a reformation and you will sink into contempt & misery" (quoted in Glover, *Southern Sons*, 37).

35. Wilder Dwight, college essay, June 2, 1853, "Whether Conscientious Scruples Ought Always to Be Held Paramount to the Law of the Land?" Dwight Papers, MHS. Jennifer R. Green has noted how southern men who received their educations at military schools "presented their ideal of a true man as a man of letters, a man with knowledge of the world around him." See "Stout Chaps Who Can Bear Distress," 182.

36. Hammond, diary entry, October 22, 1847, in Hammond, *Remembrance of Amherst*, 191; Pitkin, "Influence of Early Studies upon the Future Of Character"; Spaulding, "Individualism"; James Coolidge Carter, essay and Class Day oration, June 21, 1850, "Class Day Oration," Records of the Class of 1850, HUA; John Gillespie Baker, essay, July 30, 1846, "The Scholar and the People," Commencement Parts, DCL; Edwin Grover, essay and commencement oration, July 15, 1857, "The Influence of Science and Learning on the Popular Opinions of Their Day," Records of the Class of 1857, HUA.

37. Wilder Dwight, May 26, 1851, "No Man Can at the Same Time Court Applause, and Demand a Place among the Generous and Devoted Benefactors of His Race," Dwight Papers, MHS.

38. F. A. Loomis, essay, August 4, 1852, "Influence," Commencement Orations, WUL; Eli Converse Bruce, essay, July 27, 1846, "Beneficence," Commencement Orations, WUL; Potter Diary, June 13, 1860, PUL.

39. Griswold, "Mental Servitude."

40. Francis Balch, essay and exhibition oration, October 19, 1858, "A Citizen of a Free Country Who Feels No Interest in Politics," Records of the Class of 1859, HUA.

41. James Elijah Latimer, essay, August 2, 1848, "The Loneliness of Genius"; C. F. Gerry, essay, 1851, "Genius"; Daniel Martindale, essay, August 5, 1846, "The Failure of Great Men"; G. W. Wendell, essay, August 4, 1852, "Influence of Speculative Minds," Commencement Orations, WUL.

42. George Whittemore, essay and exhibition oration, May 5, 1857, "The Passion of Applause Inconsistent with True Public Spirit," Records of the Class of 1857, HUA. George Forgie has observed that no word in the "eulogistic vocabulary" for George

Washington "was more frequently used than 'character.' Two of the most famous speeches ever given about the first president are titled 'The Character of Washington.' People reached for the word as though it explained him—in fact, insisted that it did explain him" (*Patricide in the House Divided*, 26–28).

43. William Weeks, essay, July 25, 1861, "The Prince of Wales at the Tomb of Washington," Commencement Parts, DCL; Solomon Lincoln, essay and commencement oration, July 15, 1857, "Knowledge and Wisdom," Records of the Class of 1857, HUA. Southerners also looked to Washington as "the archetype of manly character." New Englander Daniel Webster, who had graduated from Dartmouth College, offered the New Brahmins another model to emulate. Webster employed the language of character in his public life and also used George Washington as the perfect model of character. Glover, *Southern Sons*, 11; Howe, *Political Culture of the American Whigs*, 218.

44. F. A. Loomis, "Influence"; Wilder Dwight, June 17, 1852, "Whether Dr. Franklin Is a Good Model of Character," Dwight Papers, MHS; Addison Brown, essay and commencement oration, July 11, 1852, "Henry Clay," Records of the Class of 1852, HUA.

45. J. T. Dickinson, "Speeches of Daniel Webster," August 3, 1853, Commencement Orations, WSC; William Thompson, essay, July 28, 1860, "The Advantages of Living in Periods Commonly Called Calamitous," Commencement Parts, DCL; Alden, "National Character Elevated by National Affliction," Records of the Class of 1861, HUA; Wilder Dwight, October 21, 1852, "The Advantages of Living at Periods Commonly Considered Calamitous," Dwight Papers, MHS.

46. William Dwight Sedgwick to William Minot, Jr., February 11, 1855, Sedgwick Papers, MHS; Samuel Chapman Armstrong to Richard Baxter Armstrong, April 21, 1861, in Armstrong, *Personal Memories and Letters of General S. C. Armstrong*, 1:145. New Brahmins probably did not realize that young southern men shared the same problems of living up to idealized notions and examples. "Any college student," Stephen Berry writes, "experiences some despondency when he turns finally to the problems of building a career and raising a family. These problems were exacerbated, however, by the antebellum system that almost monomaniacally stressed the glorious histories of the world's great men—even as the opportunity for glory began to fade." The South's cultural ideals "instilled" in its children "an unconscious and irresolvable resentment of standards for manhood that could not reasonably be met" (*All That Makes a Man*, 38, 41–42).

47. Dwight, "No Man Can at the Same Time Court Applause," Dwight Papers, MHS; Robert McGonegal, essay, August 2, 1848, "Conscience in Public Men," Commencement Orations, WUL.

48. McGonegal, "Conscience in Public Men."

49. Warner, "Political Life," Records of the Class of 1850, HUA. How college students reacted to politicians and politics in the 1850s is similar to how George Forgie's "sentimentalists" tried to "restore the Republic to its early virtue." The subjects of Forgie's study saw both the nation and its people as being worse off in the 1850s, "in the sense that the earlier world was simpler and (so it seemed) characterized by fraternal regard" (*Patricide in the House Divided*, 194–95).

50. Albert Hale, essay, May 7, 1861, "Rotation in Office," Records of the Class of 1861, HUA.

51. Stearns, *Adjutant Stearns*, 48–49.
52. Cutler, "Advantages of Asserting the Duties Rather Than the Rights of Man."
53. Grover, "Influence of Science and Learning on the Popular Opinions of Their Day."
54. Daniel F. Pond, essay, August 2, 1848, "The Scholar," Commencement Orations, WUL; Howe, *Political Culture of the American Whigs*, 300–301.
55. Griswold, "Mental Servitude."
56. Charles Gilman Connor, essay and exhibition oration, "Contemporaneous Expositions of the Constitution," Records of the Class of 1854, HUA.
57. G. Warrington, "Jefferson and Hamilton," *Amherst College Magazine* 9 (November 1861): 143–46.
58. James A. Garfield to Burke A. Hinsdale, July 12, 1861, in Garfield, *Wild Life of the Army: Civil War Letters of James A. Garfield*, ed. Frederick D. Williams (East Lansing: Michigan State University Press, 1964), 20–21.
59. Potter Diary, March 20, 1861, PUL.
60. Robert Treat Paine, essay and commencement oration, July 18, 1855, "The Man of Purpose," Records of the Class of 1855, HUA; James Jackson Lowell, essay and exhibition oration, October 20, 1857, "Loyalty," Records of the Class of 1858, HUA.
61. James Coolidge Carter, essay and Class Day oration, June 21, 1850, "Class Day Oration," Records of the Class of 1850, HUA.

4. "To Put Those Theories into Practice": Secession and the Crisis of Character

1. Walter Stone Poor to Joshua Lawrence Chamberlain, October 13, 1861, container no. 1, "General Correspondence, February 5, 1848–February 2, 1873," Papers of Joshua Lawrence Chamberlain, Library of Congress, Washington, D.C. (collection hereafter cited as Chamberlain Papers, LC).
2. Joshua Lawrence Chamberlain to Israel Washburn, July 14, 1862, Records Relating to the Career of Joshua Lawrence Chamberlain, Maine State Archives, Augusta, Maine; Alice Rains Trulock, *In the Hands of Providence: Joshua L. Chamberlain and the American Civil War* (Chapel Hill: University of North Carolina Press, 1992), 8.
3. Joshua Lawrence Chamberlain to Israel Washburn, August 8, 1862, in Chamberlain, *Through Blood and Fire: Selected Civil War Papers of Major General Joshua Chamberlain*, ed. Mark Nesbitt (Mechanicsburg, Pa.: Stackpole Books, 1996), 14; Trulock, *In the Hands of Providence*, 9–12.
4. Rowland B. Howard to Oliver Otis Howard, November 10, 1860, Howard Papers, BCL.
5. Potter Diary, December 28, 1860, and January 3, 1861, PUL; Charles Russell Lowell to Henry Lee Higginson, December 28, 1860, in Lowell, *Life and Letters of Charles Russell Lowell*, 192; Charles Henry Howard to Oliver Otis Howard, January 2, 1861 (mistakenly written as 1860), Howard Papers, BCL.
6. Oliver Otis Howard to Eliza Howard Gilmore, December 31, 1860, Howard Papers, BCL; Potter Diary, January 1 and January 4, 1861, PUL.

7. Charles H. Howard to Rodelphus Gilmore, December 15, 1860, in Howard, *We Are in His Hands Whether We Live or Die: The Letters of Brevet Brigadier General Charles Henry Howard*, ed. David K. Thomson (Knoxville: University of Tennessee Press, 2013), 35; Luther Clark Howell to Sidney Howell, January 24, 1861, Howell Papers, ACL; Charles Russell Lowell to John M. Forbes, February 11, 1861, and Charles Russell Lowell to Anna Jackson Lowell, January 27, 1861, both in Lowell, *Life and Letters of Charles Russell Lowell*, 195, 192–93. Seward, who had remained on the sidelines for much of the crisis, finally broke his silence when he addressed the U.S. Senate on January 12. According to Russell McClintock, Seward aimed to help keep the border states firmly in the Union. The New York senator called on "Congress to advocate repeal of the Northern states' personal liberty laws, send to the states a constitutional amendment forbidding any future amendment that gave Congress authority to interfere with slavery in the states, pass a law against invasions of states such as John Brown's, and construct two Pacific railroads, one North and one South." Russell McClintock, *Lincoln and the Decision for War: The Northern Response to Secession* (Chapel Hill: University of North Carolina Press, 2008), 121.

8. Rowland Bailey Howard to Oliver Otis Howard, January 20, 1861, Howard Papers, BCL.

9. William Wheeler to H. N. C., April 6, 1861, in Wheeler, *Letters of William Wheeler*, 275–76.

10. Potter Diary, February 21, March 5, and March 7, 1861, PUL; Charles Russell Lowell to Anna Jackson Lowell, March 28, 1861, in Lowell, *Life and Letters of Charles Russell Lowell*, 196; Robert Gould Shaw to his sister Susanna, April 5, 1861, in Shaw, *Blue-Eyed Child of Fortune: The Civil War Letters of Colonel Robert Gould Shaw* (Athens: University of Georgia Press, 1992), 71.

11. William Wheeler to H. N. C., April 14, 1861, in Wheeler, *Letters of William Wheeler*, 276–77.

12. Christopher Pennell to Lewis Pennell, April 21, 1861, Alumni Biographical Files, ACL (collection hereafter cited as Pennell Papers, ACL); Luther Clark Howell to his brother, August 2, 1861, and Luther Clark Howell to sister Clara, October 17, 1861, both in Howell Papers, ACL.

13. Robert G. Poirier, *"By the Blood of Our Alumni": Norwich University Citizen Soldiers in the Army of the Potomac* (Mason City, Iowa: Savas, 1999), 158–59.

14. Luther Clark Howell to brother Sidney, April 21, 1861, Howell Papers, ACL; William Wheeler to L. R. P., May 5, 1861, in Wheeler, *Letters of William Wheeler*, 282; quoted in Theodore Winthrop, *The Life and Poems of Theodore Winthrop*, ed. Laura Winthrop Johnson (New York: Henry Holt and Company, 1884), 284. After the war, Oliver Wendell Holmes, Jr., apparently "carefully erased every connection between his experiences as a soldier and his views as an abolitionist." "This," Louis Menand argues, "is not because he changed those views. It is because he changed his view of the nature of views" (*Metaphysical Club*, 38).

15. *A Memorial of Paul Joseph Revere and Edward H. R. Revere* (1874; repr., Clinton, Mass.: W. J. Coulter Press, 1913), 51; Sullivan Ballou to "Charlie" (perhaps Charles Parkhurst), unspecified date, in Young, *For Love and Liberty*, 359.

16. Frazar Augustus Stearns to William Augustus Stearns, December 29, 1861, in Stearns, *Adjutant Stearns*, 82; Charles Russell Lowell to Charles E. Perkins, June 7, 1861, in Russell, *Life and Letters of Charles Russell Lowell*, 210–11; William Dwight Sedgwick to A. Tellkampf, quoted in L. T. Sedgwick, "William Dwight Sedgwick," in Higginson, *Harvard Memorial Biographies*, 1:170.

17. Christopher Pennell to Lewis Pennell, April 21, 1861, Pennell Papers, ACL; F. J. Child, "James Jackson Lowell," in Higginson, *Harvard Memorial Biographies*, 1:400; William Wheeler to Theodosia Davenport Wheeler, May 9, 1861, in Wheeler, *Letters of William Wheeler*, 283; Stearns, *Adjutant Stearns*, 64–65.

18. Potter Diary, April 3, 1861, PUL.

19. Sullivan Ballou to Sarah Ballou, July 19, 1861, in Young, *For Love and Liberty*, 624–26; Charles Francis Adams, Jr., to Henry Adams, December 10, 1861, in Charles Francis Adams, Sr., Charles Francis Adams, Jr., and Henry Adams, *A Cycle of Adams Letters, 1861–1865*, ed. Worthington Chauncey Ford (Boston: Houghton Mifflin, 1920), 1:79; George Clary to Timothy Clary, April 24, 1861, Clary Papers, CHS; Charles G. Loring, Jr., "William Oliver Stevens," in Higginson, *Harvard Memorial Biographies*, 1:140.

20. Charles Francis Adams, Jr., to Henry Adams, undated, January 1862, Charles Francis Adams, Jr., to Charles Francis Adams, Sr., June 10, 1861, Charles Francis Adams, Jr., to Charles Francis Adams, Sr., November 26, 1861, all in Adams et al., *A Cycle of Adams Letters*, 1:103, 10, 73; Mary Robbins Revere to unknown recipient, undated (1863), Paul Joseph Revere Papers, MHS (collection hereafter cited as Revere Papers, MHS).

21. John Barrett Hubbard to John Hubbard, October 20, 1861, quoted in Emma Hubbard to Thomas H. Hubbard, October 22, 1861, and Thomas H. Hubbard to John Hubbard, October 27, 1861, Hubbard Family Papers, BCL (collection hereafter cited as Hubbard Papers, BCL); Charles Francis Adams, Jr., to Henry Adams, August 23, 1861, in Adams et al., *A Cycle of Adams Letters*, 1:30. Although sibling rivalry seems like a reasonable explanation for this behavior, Andy DeRoche has argued that, among his sample of Maine soldiers, at least, familial concerns weighed heavily on Civil War volunteers. Soldiers faced a difficult choice when forced to decide between their family and their nation. Some soldiers, he noted, "responded to this dilemma by advocating that each family supply only one or two soldiers and retain a similar number of males at home to help mothers and sisters keep the family intact." See "Blending Loyalties: Maine Soldiers Respond to the Civil War," *Maine History* 35, no. 3 (1996): 126, 129.

22. Frazar Augustus Stearns to William Augustus Stearns, October 3, 1861, and Frazar Augustus Stearns to his stepmother, October 6, 1861, both in Stearns, *Adjutant Stearns*, 74–75, 78; Christopher Pennell to Lewis Pennell, April 29, 1861, Pennell Papers, ACL. The belief that educated men ought to set an example for others to follow continued to motivate men well into the war. In November 1863 Theodore Holmes observed that there was "a general stupor among our young men that must be broken up if our government ever succeeds in crushing the Rebellion. No one thinks of any personal duty in the matter." He declared that the bounty men were "mostly gone." Referring to himself, he noted, "Some of us must go who can not well go—who have important work to do at home." And yet he still thought that it was his "duty to set the example."

I can do nothing whatever in the way of exhorting others to enlist while I stay at home myself. I am anxious to convince others as well to convince myself that I am willing to sacrifice all that I ask others to sacrifice." Theodore J. Holmes to Mr. Goldsmith, November 24, 1863, in Theodore James Holmes Papers, Manuscripts and Archives, Yale University Library, New Haven, Connecticut (collection hereafter cited as Holmes Papers, YUL).

23. Foote, *The Gentlemen and the Roughs*, 119; Charles Pickering Bowditch to Jonathan Ingersoll Bowditch, July 28, 1861, and Charles Pickering Bowditch to Jonathan Ingersoll Bowditch, August 5, 1862, in Bowditch, "War Letters of Charles P. Bowditch," *Massachusetts Historical Society Proceedings* 57 (October 1923–June 1924): 415, 416.

24. Thomas H. Hubbard to John Hubbard, September 21, 1862, Hubbard Papers, BCL; Henry Livermore Abbott to Josiah Gardner Abbott, May, 1861, in Henry Livermore Abbott, *Fallen Leaves: The Civil War Letters of Major Henry Livermore Abbott*, ed. Robert Garth Scott (Kent, Ohio: Kent State University Press, 1991), 31–32; William Wheeler to Theodosia Davenport Wheeler, April 27, 1861, in Wheeler, *Letters of William Wheeler*, 281; Christopher Pennell to Lewis Pennell, April 21, 1861, Pennell Papers, ACL; Robert Gould Shaw to Francis G. Shaw, May 7, 1861, in Robert Gould Shaw, *Letters/RGS*, ed. Sarah Blake Shaw (Cambridge, Mass.: University Press, 1864), 31.

25. William Lewis Haskell to Jacob Hale Thompson, July 28, 1861, Alumni Biographical Files, BCL; William Wheeler to Theodosia Davenport Wheeler, May 11, 1861, in Wheeler, *Letters of William Wheeler*, 284; Theodore Winthrop to Elizabeth Winthrop, May 10, 1861, in Winthrop, *The Life and Poems of Theodore Winthrop*, 287–88; Theodore Winthrop to George W. Curtis, May 15, 1861, in Ellsworth Eliot, Jr., *Theodore Winthrop* (New Haven, Conn.: Yale University Library), 27–28.

26. William Thompson Lusk to Cousin Lou (Mrs. Henry G. Thompson), June 27, 1861, in Lusk, *War Letters of William Thompson Lusk, Captain, Assistant Adjutant-General, United States Volunteers 1861–1863, Afterward M.D., LL.D.* (New York: privately printed, 1911), 47.

27. James Abram Garfield to Harry, April 17, 1861, in Garfield, *Wild Life of the Army*, 9; Joshua Lawrence Chamberlain to Israel Washburn, Jr., July 17, 14, 1862, in Chamberlain, *Through Blood and Fire*, 12, 9–10.

28. Thomas Hamlin Hubbard to John Hubbard, July 28, 1861, Hubbard Papers, BCL; Stearns, *Adjutant Stearns*, 47, 64. Chamberlain accepted the position of lieutenant colonel in the 20th Maine Volunteer Regiment in early August 1862 (Wallace, *Soul of the Lion*, 36).

29. James Abram Garfield to J. Harrison Rhodes, April 17, 1861, and James Abram Garfield to Eliza Ballou Garfield, August 30, 1861, in Garfield, *Wild Life of the Army*, 9, 33; Samuel E. Nichols to Alpheus Nichols, July 4, 1862, in Samuel Edmund Nichols, *"Your Soldier Boy Samuel": Civil War Letters of Lieut. Samuel Edmund Nichols, Amherst, '65 of the 37th Regiment Massachusetts Volunteers*, ed. Charles Sterling Underhill (Buffalo, N.Y.: privately printed, 1929), 15–16; P. A. M. Taylor, "A New England Gentleman: Theodore Lyman III, 1833–1897," *Journal of American Studies* 17, no. 3 (1983): 377–79; William Howard Fessenden to William Pitt Fessenden, September 17, 1864, Fessenden Collection, BCL; Charles A. Jellison, *Fessenden of Maine, Civil War Senator* (Syracuse, N.Y.: Syracuse University Press, 1962), 150.

30. William Wheeler to Theodosia Davenport Wheeler, August 4, 1863, in Wheeler, *Letters of William Wheeler*, 417; Pellicano, "Well Prepared To Die," 132; quoted in Wilson, *Patriotic Gore*, 748.

31. Stearns, *Adjutant Stearns*, 67–68; Thomas H. Hubbard to John and Sarah H. B. Hubbard, January 1, 1865, Hubbard Papers, BCL.

32. Benjamin William Crowninshield to Paul Joseph Revere, August 16, 1862, Revere Papers, MHS; Charles Pickering Bowditch to Jonathan Ingersoll Bowditch, July 22, 1861, and Jonathan Ingersoll Bowditch to Charles Pickering Bowditch, July 24, 1861, in Bowditch, "War Letters of Charles P. Bowditch," 414–15.

33. Charles Pickering Bowditch to Jonathan Ingersoll Bowditch, August 5, 1862, in Bowditch, "War Letters of Charles P. Bowditch," 416–18.

34. Charles Pickering Bowditch to Jonathan Ingersoll Bowditch, August 6, 1862, in Bowditch, "War Letters of Charles P. Bowditch," 418. In response to this letter, Jonathan I. Bowditch responded, "The *tone* and spirit of your letters I cannot too much praise." He acknowledged that his son had "stated the case as well as it could be." Regardless, Bowditch's father wished that he would finish his college courses and reiterated, "I do not think that the country needs your services yet." "I hope you will *cheerfully* acquiesce in the decision I have been compelled to arrive at, because I should be extremely sorry to cause you any unhappiness," he noted. Jonathan Ingersoll Bowditch to Charles Pickering Bowditch, August 8, 1862, in Bowditch, "War Letters of Charles P. Bowditch," 419.

35. Charles Pickering Bowditch to Jonathan Ingersoll Bowditch, circa August 9, 1862, and Charles Pickering Bowditch to Lucy Nichols Bowditch, August 14, 1862, both in Bowditch, "War Letters of Charles P. Bowditch," 419–20.

36. Charles Francis Adams, Jr., to Charles Francis Adams, Sr., May 27, 1861, in Adams et al., *A Cycle of Adams Letters*, 1:5; quoted in Edward Chase Kirkland, *Charles Francis Adams, Jr., 1835–1915: The Patrician at Bay* (Cambridge, Mass.: Harvard University Press, 1965), 22; Henry Livermore Abbott to Caroline Abbott, July 11, 1861, in Abbott, *Fallen Leaves*, 33–35. For a history of the 20th Massachusetts Regiment, which boasted large numbers of Harvard graduates, see Richard F. Miller, *Harvard's Civil War: The History of the Twentieth Massachusetts Volunteer Infantry* (Lebanon, N.H.: University Press of New England, 2005). Jordan Ross studied how some elite soldiers—Henry L. Abbott, Charles Bowditch, and William Wheeler—explained their reasons for enlisting, and observed, "The similarity of these three expressions of self-contempt is remarkable." "Self-contempt" may be a rather harsh way of describing these men's feelings. Although the men did express dissatisfaction with their peacetime accomplishments, they made their self-assessment in the middle of a war in which they strongly wished to participate. Compared to wartime service, their professional occupations would have seemed quite boring. See Ross, "Uncommon Union: Diversity and Motivation among Civil War Soldiers," *American Nineteenth Century History* 3, no. 1 (2002): 28.

37. John Hubbard, Sr., to John Hubbard, Jr., October 23, 1861, and Hubbard, Sr., to Thomas Hamlin Hubbard, November 4, 1861, Hubbard Papers, BCL.

38. Christopher Pennell to Lewis Pennell, April 29, 1861, Pennell Papers, ACL.

39. Joan Waugh, "'It Was a Sacrifice We Owed': The Shaw Family and the Fifty-Fourth Massachusetts Regiment," in *Hope and Glory: Essays on the Legacy of the Fifty-*

Fourth Massachusetts Regiment, ed. Martin H. Blatt, Thomas J. Brown, and Donald Yacovone (Amherst: University of Massachusetts Press, 2001), 64–71; Olivia Bowditch to Nathaniel Bowditch, February 23, 1862, Olivia Bowditch to Nathaniel Bowditch, March 6, 1862, Olivia Bowditch to Nathaniel Bowditch, April 11, 1862, Henry I. Bowditch to Nathaniel Bowditch, April 21, 1862, and Henry I. Bowditch to Nathaniel Bowditch, October 28, 1862, Bowditch Memorial, MHS.

40. Historians have used soldiers' rank to address questions about class representation. Richard F. Miller has noted that, with regard to the 20th Massachusetts Volunteers (the "Harvard Regiment"), "Military rank dovetailed nicely with the civilian social hierarchy already familiar to the gentlemen officers. In fact, rank provided a means of enforcing class distinctions that were unavailable in civilian life." McPherson, *What They Fought For*, 35; Miller, "Brahmins under Fire," 85.

41. John Hubbard to John Barrett Hubbard, September 14, 1862, Hubbard Papers, BCL.

42. Thomas H. Hubbard to John B. Hubbard, November 18, 1861, and Thomas H. Hubbard to Sarah H. B. Hubbard, August 10, 1862, Hubbard Papers, BCL; John C. Gray, Jr., to his mother, May 17, 1863, in John C. Gray, Jr., and John C. Ropes, *War Letters, 1862–1865* (Boston: Houghton Mifflin, 1927), 111; Thomas B. Fox, "George Whittemore, Jr.," in Higginson, *Harvard Memorial Biographies*, 1:383.

43. George Beaman Kenniston, diary entry, September 14, 1861, Alumni Biographical Files, BCL; William Thompson Lusk to Elizabeth Freeman Lusk, December 7, 1862, and William Thompson Lusk to Elizabeth Freeman Lusk, December 23, 1862, in Lusk, *War Letters of William Thompson Lusk*, 242, 258; John B. Noyes to George Dana Noyes, January 14, 1862, John B. Noyes to George Dana Noyes, May 25, 1862, and John B. Noyes to George Rapall Noyes, July 11, 1862, John Buttrick Noyes Civil War Letters, Houghton Library, Harvard University, Cambridge, Massachusetts (repository hereafter cited as HUL; collection hereafter cited Noyes Letters, HUL).

44. Thomas H. Hubbard to Sarah H. B. Hubbard, November 11, 1861, Hubbard Papers, BCL; Thomas W. Hyde to Annie Hayden, October 1, 1862, Thomas W. Hyde Papers, BCL.

45. Charles Peleg Chandler to Sarah Wheeler Chandler, May 20, 1862, Chandler Family Papers, BCL (collection hereafter cited as Chandler Papers, BCL); Franklin A. Haskell to undisclosed recipient, October 31, 1863, in Haskell, *Haskell of Gettysburg: His Life and Civil War Papers*, ed. Frank L. Byrne and Andrew T. Weaver (Kent, Ohio: Kent State University Press, 1989), 226; Theodore J. Holmes Journal, April 29, 1864, Holmes Papers, YUL; Oliver Wendell Holmes, Jr., quoted in Menand, *Metaphysical Club*, 56; James Deering Fessenden to William Pitt Fessenden, April 13, 1863, Fessenden Collection, BCL. After the bloody Overland Campaign of 1864, Oliver Wendell Holmes, Jr., did resign from the army after three years of service in which he had been seriously wounded several times. He explained, "I have been coming to the conclusion ... that my duty has changed—I can do a disagreeable thing or face a great danger coolly enough when I *know* it is a duty—but a doubt demoralizes me as it does any nervous man—and now I honestly think the duty of fighting has ceased for me—

ceased because I have laboriously and with much suffering of mind and body *earned* the right . . . to decide for myself how I can best do my duty to myself to the country and, if you choose, to God" (quoted in Menand, *Metaphysical Club*, 56–57).

46. Joshua Lawrence Chamberlain to Joshua Chamberlain, Sr., February 12, 1865, Joshua L. Chamberlain Letterbook, Joshua L. Chamberlain Collection, Pejepscot Historical Society, Brunswick, Maine (collection hereafter cited as Chamberlain Collection, PHS); Joshua Lawrence Chamberlain to Joshua Chamberlain, Sr., February 20, 1865, Chamberlain Collection, BCL.

47. Luther Clark Howell to his sister Bell, March 17, 1865, Howell Papers, ACL; Joshua Lawrence Chamberlain to Frances Caroline Adams Chamberlain, October 25, 1862, Chamberlain Papers, LC; Joseph Hopkins Twichell to Edward Twichell, June 12, 1862, in Joseph Hopkins Twichell, *The Civil War Letters of Joseph Hopkins Twichell: A Chaplain's Story*, ed. Peter Messent and Steve Courtney (Athens: University of Georgia Press, 2006), 140; George Clary to unknown recipient, undated, Clary Papers, CHS; Samuel E. Nichols to Betsey Richardson Nichols, November 7, 1862, in Nichols, *"Your Solider Boy Samuel,"* 44; Charles Russell Lowell to Josephine Shaw, July 3, 1863, in Lowell, *Life and Letters of Charles Russell Lowell*, 271. These individuals support Lorien Foote's conclusion that the war "did not shatter ideals of courage among a core set of volunteers. Men who valued honor when the war began continued to value honor throughout the war" (*The Gentlemen and the Roughs*, 141).

5. Marching into "Rebeldom": The Failure of Southern Character

1. Samuel C. Armstrong to C. C. Armstrong, March 8, 1864, in Armstrong, *Personal Memories and Letters of General S. C. Armstrong*, 2:368–70.

2. Samuel C. Armstrong to Clara Armstrong, March 29, 1864, in ibid., 2:371–73.

3. Samuel C. Armstrong to Clara Armstrong, April 1, 1864, in ibid., 2:375. For the experiences and stories of other northerners in the South during the war, particularly reformers and investors, see Willie Lee Rose, *Rehearsal for Reconstruction: The Port Royal Experiment* (1964; repr., Athens: University of Georgia Press, 1999); and Eric Foner, *Reconstruction: America's Unfinished Revolution, 1863–1877* (1988; repr., New York: Perennial Classics, 2002).

4. John D. Cox, *Traveling South: Travel Narratives and the Construction of American Identity* (Athens: University of Georgia Press, 2005), 165–67; Union soldier's observations quoted in Joseph T. Glatthaar, *The March to the Sea and Beyond: Sherman's Troops in the Savannah and Carolinas Campaigns* (New York: New York University Press, 1985), 39–40. For other sources on northern soldiers in the South, see Stephen V. Ash, *When the Yankees Came: Conflict and Chaos in the Occupied South, 1861–1865* (Chapel Hill: University of North Carolina Press, 1995); Mark Grimsley, *The Hard Hand of War: Union Military Policy toward Southern Civilians, 1861–1865* (New York: Cambridge University Press, 1995); Jacqueline Glass Campbell, *When Sherman Marched North from the Sea: Resistance on the Confederate Home Front* (Chapel Hill: University of North Carolina Press, 2003).

5. Wiley, *Life of Billy Yank*, 96. Wiley discusses the northerners in the South throughout Chapter 4 ("In Dixie Land").

6. Reid Mitchell, *Civil War Soldiers* (1988; repr., New York: Penguin, 1997), 23, 90–91. New Englanders especially distinguished the difference between their homes and what they saw in the South (Silber and Sievens, *Yankee Correspondence*, 10).

7. Joshua Lawrence Chamberlain to Frances Caroline Adams Chamberlain, November 3, 1862, in Chamberlain, *Through Blood and Fire*, 31.

8. Paul J. Revere to unknown recipient, May 19, 1862, Revere Papers, MHS; George Clary to Sarah Clary, May 12, 1862, and George Clary to Timothy Clary, May 20, 1863, Clary Papers, CHS; John Marshall Brown to Ellen G. B. Clifford, November 3, 1863, Brown Collection, MeHS; William Thompson Lusk to Elizabeth Freeman Lusk, November 9, 1861, in Lusk, *War Letters of William Thompson Lusk*, 97; Theodore J. Holmes Journal, September 29, 1864, Holmes Papers, YUL; Thomas Hamlin Hubbard to Sarah Hodge Barrett Hubbard, October 11, 1864, Hubbard Papers, BCL; William Wheeler to unspecified recipient, June 15, 1862, and William Wheeler to "Auntie," July 23, 1862, in Wheeler, *Letters of William Wheeler*, 338, 340.

9. Charles Peleg Chandler to Sarah Wheeler Chandler, December 18, 1861, Chandler Papers, BCL; Charles Francis Adams, Jr., to Charles Francis Adams, Sr., September 5, 1863, in Adams et al., *A Cycle of Adams Letters*, 2:78; William Wheeler to unspecified recipient, April 1, 1864, in Wheeler, *Letters of William Wheeler*, 445–46.

10. Stephen Minot Weld, Jr., to Stephen Minot Weld, Sr., March 10, 1862, in Stephen Minot Weld, *War Diary and Letters of Stephen Minot Weld, 1861–1865* (Cambridge, Mass.: Riverside Press, 1912), 69; Nathaniel Bowditch to Olivia Bowditch, May 23, 1862, Bowditch Memorial, MHS.

11. George Clary to Sarah Clary, May 12, 1862, George Clary to Eliza Clary, May 14, 1862, and George Clary to Eliza Clary, February 16, 1864, Clary Papers, CHS.

12. William Thompson Lusk to Elizabeth Freeman Lusk, July 19, 1861, in Lusk, *War Letters of William Thompson Lusk*, 52; John B. Noyes to George Dana Noyes, October 23, 1861, Noyes Letters, HUL; Stephen Minot Weld, Jr., to Stephen Minot Weld, Sr., March 10, 1862, in Weld, *War Diary and Letters of Stephen Minot Weld*, 71; Theodore J. Holmes Journal, May 28, 1864, and September 21, 1864, Holmes Papers, YUL.

13. Charles Peleg Chandler to Sarah Wheeler Chandler, April 12, May 13, and May 20, 1862, Chandler Papers, BCL; Uriah N. Parmelee to his mother, May 20, 1862, Samuel Spencer Parmelee Papers, 1845–1911, Manuscripts Reading Room, David M. Rubenstein Rare Book and Manuscript Library, Duke University, Durham, North Carolina; Charles H. Howard to Rodelphus Gilmore, December 13, 1863, in Howard, *We Are In His Hands Whether We Live or Die*, 135.

14. Charles Fessenden Morse to unspecified recipient, March 5, 1862, in Morse, *Letters Written during the Civil War, 1861–1865* (Boston: privately printed, 1898), 40; William Wheeler to "M," March 27, 1862, in Wheeler, *Letters of William Wheeler*, 322; Mattocks, journal entry, June 26 and July 16, 1863, in Mattocks, *"Unspoiled Heart,"* 43, 55; John B. Noyes to George Rapall Noyes, July 21, 1863, Noyes Letters, HUL.

15. Joshua Lawrence Chamberlain to Frances Caroline Adams Chamberlain, October 25, 1862, Chamberlain Papers, LC.

16. James Abram Garfield to Lucretia Garfield, February 23, 1862, in James A. Garfield, *Crete and James: Personal Letters of Lucretia and James Garfield*, ed. John Shaw (East Lansing: Michigan State University Press, 1994), 127.

17. William Thompson Lusk to Elizabeth Freeman Lusk, November 9, 1861, in Lusk, *War Letters of William Thompson Lusk*, 97; Caspar Crowninshield to unspecified recipient, May 18, 1862, Crowninshield–Magnus Papers, MHS.

18. Charles Francis Adams, Jr., to Abigail Brooks Adams, February 2, 1862, in Adams et al., *A Cycle of Adams Letters*, 1:111–12; Caspar Crowninshield to his mother, January 16, 1862, Crowninshield–Magnus Papers, MHS.

19. Charles Peleg Chandler to Sarah Wheeler Chandler, September 28, 1861, Chandler Papers, BCL; William Wheeler to unspecified recipient, November 12, 1863, in Wheeler, *Letters of William Wheeler*, 432.

20. Charles P. Chandler to Sarah W. Chandler, September 28, 1861, Chandler Papers, BCL; John Read to Bill Read, August 29, 1863, and John Read to Sarah Goodwin Atkins Read, December 3, 1863, John Read Papers, HUL.

21. John C. Gray, Jr., to his mother, November 16, 1862, in Gray and Ropes, *War Letters*, 25; Charles H. Howard to Eliza Gilmore, March 13, 1862, in Howard, *We Are in His Hands Whether We Live or Die*, 59–60; Pellicano, "Well Prepared To Die," 67–68.

22. William Wheeler to unspecified recipient, April 1, 1864, in Wheeler, *Letters of William Wheeler*, 445.

23. Quoted in Sedgwick, "William Dwight Sedgwick," in Higginson, *Harvard Memorial Biographies*, 1:172; William Wheeler to unspecified recipient, November 12, 1863, in Wheeler, *Letters of William Wheeler*, 432–33; Charles H. Howard to Rodelphus Gilmore, March 20, 1864, in Howard, *We Are in His Hands Whether We Live or Die*, 159.

24. William Wheeler to "Auntie," July 23, 1862, in Wheeler, *Letters of William Wheeler*, 339; Charles Peleg Chandler to Sarah Wheeler Chandler, September 14, 1861, Chandler Papers, BCL.

25. Charles Peleg Chandler to Sarah Wheeler Chandler, September 18, 1861, Chandler Papers, BCL; Thomas H. Hubbard to Sarah H. B. Hubbard, February 19, 1865, Hubbard Papers, BCL.

26. Charles H. Howard to Rodelphus Gilmore, April 19, 1861, in Howard, *We Are in His Hands Whether We Live or Die*, 43.

27. Joseph Hopkins Twichell to Edward Twichell, May 2 and May 9, 1862, and July 15, 1863, in Twichell, *Civil War Letters of Joseph Hopkins Twichell*, 121, 126, 255; Samuel Chapman Armstrong to C. C. Armstrong, September 17, 1862, in Armstrong, *Personal Memories and Letters of General S. C. Armstrong*, 2:243; Samuel E. Nichols to Sophronia Nichols, September 24, 1862, in Nichols, *"Your Solider Boy Samuel,"* 27; Mattocks, journal entry, May 1, 1863, in Mattocks, *"Unspoiled Heart,"* 9; Francis C. Barlow to Almira Barlow, July 7, 1863, in Francis Channing Barlow, *Fear Was Not in Him: The Civil War Letters of Major General Francis C. Barlow, U.S.A.*, ed. Christian G. Samito (New York: Fordham University Press, 2004), 164; Frank A. Haskell to unspecified recipient, July 16, 1863, in Haskell, *Haskell of Gettysburg*, 184.

28. Joseph Hopkins Twichell to Edward Twichell, July 9, 1862, in Twichell, *Civil War Letters of Joseph Hopkins Twichell*, 164.

29. Henry Livermore Abbott to Josiah Gardner Abbott, June 6, 1862, in Abbott, *Fallen Leaves*, 129; Charles Fessenden Morse to unspecified recipient, September 26, 1862, in Morse, *Letters Written during the Civil War*, 92; William Wheeler to unspecified recipient, November 12, 1863, in Wheeler, *Letters of William Wheeler*, 432–33;

Woodbury Diary, February 14 and March 28, 1864, Woodbury Letters, DCL; Theodore J. Holmes, October 2, 1864, Holmes Papers, YUL.

30. Charles Peleg Chandler to Sarah Wheeler Chandler, May 14, 1862, and Charles Peleg Chandler to Sarah Wheeler Chandler, "late evening," May 14, 1862, Chandler Papers, BCL; Charles Fessenden Morse to unspecified recipient, July 15, 1864, in Morse, *Letters Written during the Civil War*, 176–77.

31. William Wheeler to Theodosia Davenport Wheeler, June 12, 1862, in Wheeler, *Letters of William Wheeler*, 337.

32. Charles Fessenden Morse to unspecified recipient, July 15, 1864, in Morse, *Letters Written during the Civil War*, 178.

33. Charles Peleg Chandler to Sarah Wheeler Chandler, September 28, 1861, Chandler Papers, BCL; George Clary to Timothy Clary, May 25, 1862, Clary Papers, CHS; Joseph Hopkins Twichell to unspecified recipient, November 24, 1862, in Twichell, *Civil War Letters of Joseph Hopkins Twichell*, 190.

34. Nathaniel Bowditch to Olivia Bowditch, February 16, 1862, Bowditch Memorial, MHS; Robert Gould Shaw to Sarah Blake Sturgis Shaw, March 28, 1862, in Shaw, *Blue-Eyed Child of Fortune*, 186; Luther Clark Howell to sister Clara, July 10, 1862, Howell Papers, ACL.

35. John C. Gray to John C. Ropes, November 13, 1862, and John C. Gray to his mother, May 2, 1863, and April 11, 1864, in Gray and Ropes, *War Letters*, 24, 97, 314–15.

36. Joseph Hopkins Twichell to Edward Twichell, August 5, 1861, in Twichell, *Civil War Letters of Joseph Hopkins Twichell*, 53; John B. Noyes to George Rapall Noyes, May 14, 1863, Noyes Letters, HUL; William Francis Bartlett to Harriet Plummer Bartlett, March 24, 1863, in William Francis Bartlett, *Memoir of William Francis Bartlett*, ed. Francis Winthrop Palfrey (Boston: Houghton, Osgood and Company, 1879), 79.

37. William Thompson Lusk to Cousin Lou (Mrs. Henry G. Thompson), September 21, 1861, and William Thompson Lusk to Elizabeth Freeman Lusk, undated (1861), in Lusk, *War Letters of William Thompson Lusk*, 84, 88–89.

38. William Thompson Lusk to Elizabeth Freeman Lusk, November 13, 1861, in ibid., 101; John B. Noyes to Martha Wilson Noyes Tindell, February 22, 1862, Noyes Letters, HUL.

39. George Clary to Timothy Clary, August 6 and September 10, 1862, Clary Papers, CHS; Charles Francis Adams, Jr., to Henry Adams, April 6, 1862, in Adams et al., *A Cycle of Adams Letters*, 1:125.

40. Charles Francis Adams, Jr., to Henry Adams, April 6, 1862, in Adams et al., *A Cycle of Adams Letters*, 1:131; Caspar Crowninshield to unspecified recipient, May 18, 1862, Crowninshield–Magnus Papers, MHS.

41. John C. Gray, Jr., to Elizabeth Gray, June 2, 1863, in Gray and Ropes, *War Letters*, 122; Charles Francis Adams, Jr., to Henry Adams, April 6, 1862, in Adams et al., *A Cycle of Adams Letters*, 1:129–30.

42. Charles P. Chandler to Sarah W. Chandler, September 28, 1861, Chandler Papers, BCL; Charles Francis Adams, Jr., to Henry Adams, September 18, 1864, in Adams et al., *A Cycle of Adams Letters*, 2:195.

43. Charles Fessenden Morse to unspecified recipient, October 15, 1863, in Morse, *Letters Written during the Civil War*, 149–50.

44. Theodore Lyman notebook entries, September 7 and December 11, 1863, and May 7, 1864, in Lyman, *Meade's Army: The Private Notebooks of Lt. Col. Theodore Lyman*, ed. David W. Lowe (Kent: Kent State University Press, 2007), 30, 79–80, 142.

45. James A. Garfield to Lucretia Garfield, May 27, 1862, and May 6, 1863, in Garfield, *Wild Life of the Army*, 102, 267.

46. Charles Francis Adams, Jr., to Charles Francis Adams, Sr., March 11, 1862, in Adams et al., *A Cycle of Adams Letters*, 1:117–18; Caspar Crowninshield to unspecified recipient, May 30, 1863, Crowninshield-Magnus Papers, MHS.

6. The Character to Command

1. Thomas W. Hyde, *Following the Greek Cross; or, Memories of the Sixth Army Corps*, ed. Eric J. Mink (1894; repr., Columbia: University of South Carolina Press, 2005), 99–105; Thomas W. Hyde to Eleanor Davis Hyde, September 24, 1862, in Thomas Worcester Hyde, *Civil War Letters* (n.p., privately printed, John H. Hyde, 1933), 49–53.

2. For works about the "common soldier" of the Civil War see Wiley, *Life of Johnny Reb*, and *Life of Billy Yank*; James I. Robertson, Jr., *Soldiers Blue and Gray* (Columbia: University of South Carolina Press, 1988); Mitchell, *Civil War Soldiers*; McPherson, *What They Fought For*, and *For Cause and Comrades*.

3. See Foote, *The Gentlemen and the Roughs*. Works that look at the experiences of different ethnic groups during the war include Christian G. Samito, *Becoming American under Fire: Irish Americans, African Americans, and the Politics of Citizenship during the Civil War Era* (Ithaca, N.Y.: Cornell University Press, 2009); Susannah J. Ural, *Civil War Citizens: Race, Ethnicity, and Identity in America's Bloodiest Conflict* (New York: New York University Press, 2010).

4. Gerald F. Linderman, *Embattled Courage: The Experience of Combat in the American Civil War* (New York: Free Press, 1987), 7–17, 21, 61; Hess, *Union Soldier in Battle*, 75. Joseph Allan Frank expanded on the concept of courage and defined it as "a purposely political act, used to attain transcendental ends like saving freedom and republican government in the world. It was inspired, defined, nurtured, and demanded of virtuous citizens by the democratic polity." In short, antebellum events influenced wartime perceptions and actions (*With Ballot and Bayonet*, 21). For works that consider northerners' ideology see Hess, *Liberty, Virtue, and Progress*; and Mitchell, *Vacant Chair*.

5. Miller, "Brahmins under Fire," 76, 87; Lorien Foote, "Rich Man's War, Rich Man's Fight: Class, Ideology, and Discipline in the Union Army," *Civil War History* 51, no. 3 (2005): 269–87; Frank, *With Ballot and Bayonet*, 18; Foote, *The Gentlemen and the Roughs*, 1. According to historian Wiley Sword, regular soldiers "were too often regarded as the dregs of society, unable to find more gainful employment among civil pursuits, hence, misfits, morons, or malcontents, mindful only of a firm guiding hand. Regular army practices, such as placing a sergeant with a fixed, leveled bayonet behind a deployed battle line to prevent the men from running away in combat, carried over into the volunteer service. The regulars were noted more for their discipline than for their spirit; thus spread a belief that the American volunteer soldier needed not spirit but discipline to achieve the greatest prowess in combat." See *Courage under Fire:*

Profiles in Bravery from the Battlefields of the Civil War (New York: St. Martin's Press, 2007), 14.

6. Other historians have also made this observation. Philip Racine, for example, noticed that Charles Mattocks "seems never to have fraternized with most of his men." This led some to observe that he "seemed aloof with a too highly developed sense of propriety." Mattocks was, in fact, "more comfortable with educated people, in particular officers from Maine and New England." Furthermore, Mattocks went "out of his way to mention the colleges his messmates attended" to his mother. Racine suggested that this need to be in the company of educated men might be one of "necessity . . . for Charles Mattocks was a man of the mind" (Mattocks, *"Unspoiled Heart,"* xix–xx). See also Miller, "Brahmins under Fire," 87–88; and Foote, "Rich Man's War, Rich Man's Fight," 276.

7. Henry Livermore Abbott to Josiah Gardner Abbott, May 1861, in Abbott, *Fallen Leaves*, 30; Richard A. Sauers and Martin H. Sable, *William Francis Bartlett: Biography of a Union General in the Civil War* (Jefferson, N.C.: McFarland, 2009), 13, 54; Stephen Minot Weld, Jr., to Stephen Minot Weld, Sr., April 25, 1862, in Weld, *War Diary and Letters of Stephen Minot Weld*, 102.

8. His fellow Harvard graduate, Adams explained, returned to "first principles" in all his army duties: "The object of discipline is obedience; the end of fighting is victory, and he naturally and instinctively sweeps away all the forms, rules and traditions which, . . . in the hands of incompetent men, ultimately usurped the place of the ends they were calculated to secure." He greatly admired Barlow for his ability to see through the "forms" for the "principles," that is, the ultimate goals of the conflict. "I am more disposed to regard Barlow as a military genius than any man I have yet seen," he concluded. Charles Francis Adams, Jr., to Henry Adams, June 22, 1864, in Adams et al., *A Cycle of Adams Letters*, 2:167–68.

9. Thomas H. Hubbard to John Hubbard, August 3, 1862, Hubbard Papers, BCL; William Wheeler to "M," January 26, 1862, in Wheeler, *Letters of William Wheeler*, 305; John B. Noyes to George Dana Noyes, August 1, 1863, Noyes Letters, HUL; Francis Channing Barlow to his mother and brothers, May 8, 1863, Francis Channing Barlow to Charles Dalton, June 2, 1863, Francis Channing Barlow to his mother, June 7, 1863, and Francis Channing Barlow to unknown recipient, undated, in Barlow, *Fear Was Not in Him*, 130, 138, 140, 165; Theodore Lyman, notebook entry, September 5, 1863, in Lyman, *Meade's Army*, 28.

10. Charles H. Howard to Rowland Howard, March 3, 1865, in Howard, *We Are In His Hands Whether We Live or Die*, 187; Joseph T. Glatthaar, *Forged in Battle: The Civil War Alliance of Black Soldiers and White Officers* (Baton Rouge: Louisiana State University Press, 1990), 13–14, 38–50. Altruistic acts alone did not motivate these men's service in the USCT. Charles Francis Adams, Jr., for example, attached himself to a black regiment in an attempt to bolster his career. For more on Adams's tortured Civil War career and his relationship with African American troops, see Michael De Gruccio, "Manhood, Race, Failure, and Reconciliation: Charles Francis Adams, Jr., and the American Civil War," *New England Quarterly* 81 (December 2008): 636–75.

11. Joshua Lawrence Chamberlain to "Loring," August 11, 1862, in Chamberlain, *Through Blood and Fire*, 15; Thomas H. Hubbard to John Hubbard, October 27, 1861,

Hubbard Papers, BCL; Charles H. Howard to Rowland Howard, March 3, 1865, in Howard, *We Are In His Hands Whether We Live or Die*, 187. Lorien Foote has noted how elites "believed it was their duty as officers to provide for the needs of their enlisted men and they worked long hours to ensure the men were properly fed and housed" (*The Gentlemen and the Roughs*, 122).

12. Quoted in Robert Francis Engs, *Educating the Disfranchised and Disinherited* (Knoxville: University of Tennessee Press, 1999), 37; Thomas W. Hyde to Eleanor Davis Hyde, June 23, 1864, in Hyde, *Civil War Letters*, 143.

13. Joseph Hopkins Twichell to Edward Twichell, April 22, 1861, in Twichell, *Civil War Letters of Joseph Hopkins Twichell*, 16, 18; John B. Noyes to George Rapall Noyes, July 31, 1863, Noyes Letters, HUL.

14. Nathaniel Bowditch to Ned Bowditch (brother), February 13, 1863, Bowditch Memorial, MHS; Pellicano, "Well Prepared To Die," 46, 59; Thomas W. Hyde to Eleanor Davis Hyde, July 13, 1862, in Hyde, *Civil War Letters*, 39; Theodore Winthrop to George W. Curtis, May 5, 1861, in Eliot, *Theodore Winthrop*, 24; Joshua Lawrence Chamberlain to Frances Caroline Adams Chamberlain, October 25, 1862, Chamberlain Papers, LC. Lorien Foote has observed how middle- and upper-class northerners "embraced the notion of professionalism" and, upon entering the armed forces, "believed it was their responsibility to assume the duties and attitudes of the military profession" (*The Gentlemen and the Roughs*, 168).

15. John B. Noyes to George Rapall Noyes, July 11, 1862, Noyes Letters, HUL; Charles Mattocks to Martha Dyer, March 27, 1864, in Mattocks, *"Unspoiled Heart,"* 111; Theodore Winthrop to George W. Curtis, May 5, 1861, in Eliot, *Theodore Winthrop*, 25.

16. William Dwight Sedgwick to Elizabeth B. D. Sedgwick, August 28, 1861, Sedgwick Papers, MHS; Charles H. Howard to Eliza Gilmore, March 13, 1862, in Howard, *We Are In His Hands Whether We Live or Die*, 60.

17. Caspar Crowninshield, diary entry August 1861, 4–5, Caspar Crowninshield Diaries, 1861–62, MHS; Thomas H. Hubbard to John and Sarah H. B. Hubbard, January 1, 1865, Hubbard Papers, BCL.

18. Foote, "Rich Man's War, Rich Man's Fight," 286. At the same time, the officers also needed to obey army regulations and behave accordingly. "Army regulations," writes Foote, "required officers to maintain the character of a gentleman," and they equated "gentlemanly character with temperance and abstinence from profanity and sexual immorality" (*The Gentlemen and the Roughs*, 31).

19. Charles Russell Lowell to Josephine Shaw, September 10, 1863, in Lowell, *Life and Letters of Charles Russell Lowell*, 301; Nathaniel Bowditch to Olivia Bowditch, April 14, 1862, Bowditch Memorial, MHS.

20. Mattocks, journal entry, June 20, 1863, and April 16, 1864, in Mattocks, *"Unspoiled Heart,"* 40, 123. Mattocks's school was not unique. As Lorien Foote has noted, Francis C. Barlow "established schools for commissioned and noncommissioned officers" to teach "methods of teaching drills" ("Rich Man's War, Rich Man's Fight," 278).

21. Charles H. Howard to Eliza Gilmore, July 20, 1863, in Howard, *We Are In His Hands Whether We Live or Die*, 104; Theodore Lyman notebook entry, May 26, 1864, Lowe, ed., *Meade's Army*, 176. As Lorien Foote has observed, a man's social status

modified perceptions of his behavior, and this also influenced the punishments meted out. "Men from the lowest socioeconomic classes who drank," Foote explains, "were denigrated for their lack of manhood, whereas a man from the right social class with the right deportment was free to engage in reckless behavior and indulge in vice without losing his reputation as a gentleman." Mattocks, for example, did not wish to discipline a subordinate from a higher class than his regular men (Foote, *The Gentlemen and the Roughs*, 37–38).

22. Wilder Dwight to Elizabeth Amelia Dwight, September 7, 1861, in Dwight, *Life and Letters of Wilder Dwight*, 97–98; Samuel E. Nichols to unspecified recipients, October 18, 1862, in Nichols, *"Your Solider Boy Samuel,"* 39; Charles H. Howard to Eliza Gilmore, January 14, 1863, in Howard, *We Are In His Hands Whether We Live or Die*, 87; Mattocks, journal entry, April 16, 1864, in Mattocks, *"Unspoiled Heart,"* 124. Southern men, whatever the New Brahmins' observations, bristled at becoming "soulless machines." "The notion that men were interchangeable," writes Stephen Berry, "flew directly in the face of Southerners' self-beliefs. Depersoning was supposed to be a Yankee phenomenon, like soulless machines, soulless men, and the cult of interchangeable parts." To southern soldiers' frustrations, they "found that the loss of self was an impersonal enemy" (*All That Makes a Man*, 177).

23. William Wheeler to "Aunt E.," November 25, 1862, in Wheeler, *Letters of William Wheeler*, 365–66.

24. Joseph Hopkins Twichell to Edward Twichell, November 17, 1861, in Twichell, *Civil War Letters of Joseph Hopkins Twichell*, 84; Nathaniel Bowditch to Olivia Bowditch (mother), December 27, 1861, Bowditch Memorial, MHS; Caspar Crowninshield to unspecified recipient, March 7, 1862, Crowninshield-Magnus Papers, MHS; John B. Noyes to George Dana Noyes, August 1, 1863, Noyes Letters, HUL; Charles Francis Adams, Jr., to Charles Francis Adams, Sr., January 16, 1864, in Adams et al., *A Cycle of Adams Letters*, 2:118–19; William McArthur to Sarah P. M. McArthur, April 26, 1864, McArthur Papers, BCL.

25. Quoted in Bartlett, *Memoir of William Francis Bartlett*, 67; Paul J. Revere to unknown recipient, July 27, 1862, Revere Papers, MHS.

26. Charles Francis Adams, Jr., to Charles Francis Adams, Sr., July 28, 1862, in Adams et al., *A Cycle of Adams Letters*, 1:171; Luther Clark Howell to his sister, August 30, 1862, Howell Papers, ACL.

27. Charles Russell Lowell to Anna Jackson Lowell, February 9, 1863, and Charles Russell Lowell to H. L. Higginson, February 15, 1863, in Lowell, *Life and Letters of Charles Russell Lowell*, 234–35; Charles Fessenden Morse to unspecified recipient, February 8, 1863, in Morse, *Letters Written during the Civil War*, 119–20.

28. Charles Pickering Bowditch to Lucy Nichols Bowditch, August 5, 1863, in Bowditch, "War Letters of Charles P. Bowditch," 428; Charles Russell Lowell to Lt. Col. Russell, July 26, 1863, Charles Russell Lowell to Josephine Shaw, July 28, 1863, Charles Russell Lowell to J. M. Forbes, August 4, 1863, and Charles Russell Lowell to H. L. Higginson, September 14, 1863, in Lowell, *Life and Letters of Charles Russell Lowell*, 285, 288–89, 293, 303–4.

29. George Clary to Eliza Clary, June 2, 1863, Clary Papers, CHS; Charles Pickering Bowditch to Lucy Nichols Bowditch, May 29, 1864, in Bowditch, "War Letters of

NOTES TO PAGES 152–56   233

Charles P. Bowditch," 479; John B. Noyes to George Rapall Noyes, June 23, 1864, Noyes Letters, HUL; Reuben D. Mussey, March 27, 1865, Reuben Delavan Mussey Papers, DCL. Mussey also wrote, "Should I never return" his only regret was "I have not served God and my Country more faithfully."

30. John C. Gray, Jr., to John C. Ropes, August 19, 1863, in Gray and Ropes, *War Letters*, 184; Henry Livermore Abbott to Caroline Livermore Abbott (mother), August 7, 1863, in Abbott, *Fallen Leaves*, 198–99.

31. Charles Francis Adams, Jr., to Charles Francis Adams, Sr., July 22, 1863, Charles Francis Adams, Jr., to Henry Adams, September 18, 1864, and Charles Francis Adams, Jr., to Charles Francis Adams, Sr., November 2, 1864, in Adams et al., *A Cycle of Adams Letters*, 2:52, 195, 215–18. Charles P. Bowditch thought that "the negroes will make very good horsemen, though perhaps not graceful ones. They will be able to stick on a horse's back if they are not able to sit up straight." Charles Pickering Bowditch to Jonathan Ingersoll Bowditch, December 15, 1863, in Bowditch, "War Letters of Charles P. Bowditch," 454.

32. Charles Francis Adams, Jr., to Charles Francis Adams, Sr., June 19, 1864, in Adams et al., *A Cycle of Adams Letters*, 153–54; Luther Clark Howell to his brother, April 15, 1865, Howell Papers, ACL. Larry M. Logue has pointed out that Union soldiers considered self-control an important trait to cultivate but also used it as a way to contrast themselves with black troops (*To Appomattox and Beyond*, 13–14).

33. William Wheeler to "Coz," October 23, 1861, in Wheeler, *Letters of William Wheeler*, 295.

34. Foote, *The Gentlemen and The Roughs*, 57; Henry Livermore Abbott to Josiah Gardner Abbott, February 5, 1862, in Abbott, *Fallen Leaves*, 100; Charles Russell Lowell to Anna Cabot Jackson Lowell, May 13, 1861, in Lowell, *Life and Letters of Charles Russell Lowell*, 205; William Wheeler to Theodosia Davenport Wheeler, June 12, 1862, in Wheeler, *Letters of William Wheeler*, 335.

35. Charles Peleg Chandler to Sarah Wheeler Chandler, May 7, 1862, Chandler Papers, BCL; Robert Gould Shaw to Sarah B. S. Shaw, June 2, 1862, in Shaw, *Letters/RGS*, 158; Charles Francis Adams, Jr., to Charles Francis Adams, Sr., June 18, 1862, in Adams et al., *A Cycle of Adams Letters*, 1:155–56; Eri D. Woodbury to unknown recipient (date not specified), 1865, Woodbury Letters, DCL.

36. Quoted in Foote, *The Gentlemen and the Roughs*, 100; Oliver Wendell Holmes, Jr., to Amelia Jackson Holmes, October 23, 1861, and Holmes, Jr., diary, undated, in Oliver Wendell Holmes, Jr., *Touched with Fire: Civil War Letters and Diary of Oliver Wendell Holmes, Jr., 1861–1864*, ed. Mark DeWolfe Howe (Cambridge, Mass.: Harvard University Press, 1946), 13, 18, 27.

37. Quoted in Richard F. Welch, *The Boy General: The Life and Careers of Francis Channing Barlow* (Madison, N.J.: Fairleigh Dickinson University Press, 2003), 76; quoted in Byrne and Weaver, *Haskell of Gettysburg*, 244. "Upper-class officers," as Lorien Foote has written, "claimed obedience in battle through personal example as well as coercion." Seeing themselves as "natural shepherds of society," the men "had to model the manly behavior they sought to instill." Battle served a dual purpose for the men: "a measuring stick of their own character but also as an essential tool to inspire appropriate battle discipline in their men" (*The Gentlemen and the Roughs*, 125).

38. Charles Peleg Chandler to Sarah Wheeler Chandler, June 26, 1862, Chandler Papers, BCL; quoted in Chamberlain, *Through Blood and Fire*, 130.

39. Taylor, "New England Gentlemen," 380; William Wheeler to "L. R. P.," September 30, 1862, and William Wheeler to "L. R. P.," November 19, 1863, in Wheeler, *Letters of William Wheeler*, 357, 434; Thomas W. Hyde to Eleanor Davis Hyde, May 27, 1862, in Hyde, *Civil War Letters*, 15; T. W. Higginson, "Samuel Henry Eells," 1:391, and Joseph Willard, "Sidney Willard," 1:247, in Higginson, *Harvard Memorial Biographies*. According to Wiley Sword, soldiers commonly became too preoccupied with their duties to worry in battle (*Courage under Fire*, 37–38).

40. Frank A. Haskell to undisclosed person, July 16, 1863, in Haskell, *Haskell of Gettysburg*, 162.

41. Frank A. Haskell to his brothers and sisters, September 22, 1862, in Haskell, *Haskell of Gettysburg*, 48; Henry Livermore Abbott to Josiah Gardner Abbott, November 7, 1861, in Abbott, *Fallen Leaves*, 73–74.

42. Oliver Wendell Holmes, Jr., to Amelia Holmes, December 12 and 14, 1862, in Holmes, *Touched with Fire*, 74, 76; Luther Clark Howell to his sister Clara, June 22, 1864, Howell Papers, ACL.

43. Joshua Lawrence Chamberlain to Frances Caroline Adams Chamberlain, July 17, 1863, Chamberlain Papers, LC.

44. Frazar Augustus Stearns to "All," February 19, 1862, in Stearns, *Adjutant Stearns*, 96; Charles H. Howard to Rowland Howard, May 8, 1863, and Charles H. Howard to Eliza Gilmore, May 17, 1863, in Howard, *We Are In His Hands Whether We Live or Die*, 97, 99.

45. Charles Fessenden Morse to unspecified recipient, June 3, 1862, in Morse, *Letters Written during the Civil War*, 65; Charles Mattocks to Martha Dyer, May 10, 1863, in Mattocks, *"Unspoiled Heart,"* 31.

46. Joseph Hopkins Twichell to Edward Twichell, June 25, 1862, in Twichell, *Civil War Letters of Joseph Hopkins Twichell*, 148; Charles Peleg Chandler to Sarah Wheeler Chandler, May 11, 1862, Chandler Papers, BCL; Charles H. Howard to Rodelphus Gilmore, September 21, 1862, in Howard, *We Are In His Hands Whether We Live or Die*, 71–72.

7. Character Triumphant: Reconstruction, Reform, and Reconciliation

1. John C. Gray, Jr., to John C. Ropes, April 21, 1865, in Gray and Ropes, *War Letters*, 470; Oliver Otis Howard to Elizabeth Anne Waite Howard, April 18, 1865, Howard Papers, BCL; Joshua Lawrence Chamberlain to Frances Caroline Adams Chamberlain, April 19, 1865, Chamberlain Collection, PHS; Charles Henry Howard to unnamed brother (likely Oliver Otis Howard), April 22, 1865, Howard Papers, BCL.

2. Thomas Hubbard to Emma Hubbard, April 18, 1865, Hubbard Papers, BCL; Mark Perry, *Conceived in Liberty: Joshua Chamberlain, William Oates, and the American Civil War* (New York: Viking, 1997), 299.

3. Leslie Butler, *Critical Americans: Victorian Intellectuals and Transatlantic Liberal Reform* (Chapel Hill: University of North Carolina Press, 2007), 3, 4, 6. In selecting her subjects, Butler did not specifically limit her sample by the men's ages, wartime ser-

vice, or level of education. Her primary list of intellectuals includes Charles Francis Adams, Jr., Henry Adams, George William Curtis, Charles W. Eliot, Richard Watson Gilder, Thomas Wentworth Higginson, William Dean Howells, William James, James Russell Lowell, Charles Eliot Norton, Moorfield Storey, and Mark Twain.

4. John G. Sproat, *"The Best Men": Liberal Reformers in the Gilded Age* (New York: Oxford University Press, 1968), 6, 9, 60; Tucker, *Mugwumps*, 38; Nancy Cohen, *The Reconstruction of American Liberalism, 1865–1914* (Chapel Hill: University of North Carolina Press, 2002), 221; Slap, *Doom of Reconstruction*, xi–xii, xxi, 216, 238. Slap also convincingly demonstrates that John Sproat's use of the term "best men" to describe the reformers was a creation of the 1872 Liberal Republican Party and perpetuated by historians. The reformers, therefore, are more complicated than the out-of-touch elites that Sproat portrayed in his book.

5. Charles Francis Adams, Jr., to Charles Francis Adams, Sr., July 16, 1862, in Adams et al., *A Cycle of Adams Letters*, 1:165; John C. Gray, Jr., to John C. Ropes, April 21, 1865, in Gray and Ropes, *War Letters*, 470–71; Lyman quoted in Taylor, "New England Gentleman," 375.

6. John C. Gray, Jr., to his father, May 14, 1865, in Gray and Ropes, *War Letters*, 486–87.

7. Perry, *Conceived in Liberty*, 312, 318–19, 332–33.

8. Luther Clark Howell to his sister Clara, March 6, 1866, and Luther Clark Howell to "Friend Day," September 7, 1866, Howell Papers, ACL.

9. Oliver O. Howard, *Autobiography of Oliver Otis Howard* (New York: Baker & Taylor, 1908), 2:213; Foner, *Reconstruction*, 157.

10. Allan Peskin, *Garfield* (Kent, Ohio: Kent State University Press, 1978), 255; for a detailed description of events during Presidential Reconstruction and the early phase of Radical Reconstruction see Foner, *Reconstruction*, Chapters 5 and 6.

11. Mary Atwater Neely to James A. Garfield, March 14, 1873, quoted in James A. Padgett, "Reconstruction Letters from North Carolina: Part X Letters of James Abram Garfield," *North Carolina Historical Review* 21, no. 2 (1944): 146–47.

12. Howard, *Autobiography*, 2:195, 391, 452–53. Howard apparently objected to naming the institution after himself, but the committee overseeing the process dismissed his protests (Carpenter, *Sword and Olive Branch*, 170).

13. Robert F. Engs, *Freedom's First Generation: Black Hampton, Virginia, 1861–1890* (1979; repr., New York: Fordham University Press, 2004), 74, 83, 87–89, 158 (Armstrong quoted on 74).

14. Jeremy Wells, "Up from Savagery: Booker T. Washington and the Civilizing Mission," *Southern Quarterly* 42, no. 1 (2003): 54–55, 60–62; Engs, *Educating the Disfranchised and Disinherited*, 76, 152.

15. Perry, *Conceived in Liberty*, 343–45.

16. Quoted in Peskin, *Garfield*, 253; Allan Peskin, "President Garfield and the Southern Question: The Making of a Policy That Never Was," *Southern Quarterly* 16, no. 4 (1978): 379–81.

17. Howard, *Autobiography*, 2:375–76, 385; Cohen, *Reconstruction of American Liberalism*, 83–84.

18. Perry, *Conceived in Liberty*, 348–49.

19. Robert H. Wiebe, *The Search for Order, 1877–1920* (1967; repr., New York: Hill and Wang, 1968), 6; Peskin, *Garfield*, 329–30.

20. Tucker, *Mugwumps*, 38; Kirkland, *Charles Francis Adams*, 162–64.

21. Joshua Lawrence Chamberlain, *The Grand Old Man of Maine: Selected Letters of Joshua Lawrence Chamberlain, 1865–1914*, ed. Jeremiah E. Goulka (Chapel Hill: University of North Carolina Press, 2004), xxxi–xxxvi.

22. Sauers and Sable, *William Francis Bartlett*, 156–59, 163–65.

23. Richard F. Welch, *The Boy General: The Life and Careers of Francis Channing Barlow* (Madison, N.J.: Fairleigh Dickinson University Press, 2003), 227–28; Adams quoted in Kirkland, *Charles Francis Adams*, 163. As Robert Wiebe notes, by this point in Grant's presidency, "Never had so many citizens held their government in such low regard." Such an opinion partially stemmed from "the extraordinary experiments in reconstructing the former Confederate States" (*Search for Order*, 5).

24. Welch, *Boy General*, 225–36.

25. Joshua Lawrence Chamberlain to Carl Schurz, April 5, 1877, in Chamberlain, *Grand Old Man of Maine*, 80–81; Chamberlain quoted in Trulock, *In the Hands of Providence*, 518n57.

26. Quoted in Perry, *Conceived in Liberty*, 362–63, 414–15. For an overview of Lost Cause ideology see Gary W. Gallagher, *Causes Won, Lost, and Forgotten: How Hollywood and Popular Art Shape What We Know about the Civil War* (Chapel Hill: University of North Carolina Press, 2008), 17–24; and Joan Waugh, *Ulysses Grant: American Hero, American Myth* (Chapel Hill: University of North Carolina Press, 2009), 185–86.

27. Justus D. Doenecke, *The Presidencies of James A. Garfield and Chester A. Arthur* (1981; repr., Lawrence: University Press of Kansas, 1988), 11.

28. Garfield quoted in Howard V. Young, Jr., "James A. Garfield and Hampton Institute," in *Stony the Road: Chapters in the History of Hampton Institute*, ed. Keith L. Schall (Charlottesville: University Press of Virginia, 1977), 40–41.

29. Doenecke, *Presidencies of James A. Garfield and Chester A. Arthur*, 22–24; Allan Peskin, "Garfield and Hayes: Political Leaders of the Gilded Age," *Ohio History* 77 (April 1968): 124; Peskin, *Garfield*, 261–63.

30. Perry, *Conceived in Liberty*, 349–53; Wallace, *Soul of the Lion*, 223; Taylor, "New England Gentleman," 387–89.

31. Strong, *Joseph Hopkins Twichell*, 87; Welch, *Boy General*, 241.

32. Wiebe, *Search for Order*, 60; Edward N. Saveth, "History of an Elite," *History of Education Quarterly* 28, no. 3 (1988): 368–71.

33. Thomas K. McCraw, *Prophets of Regulation: Charles Francis Adams, Louis D. Brandeis, James M. Landis, Alfred E. Kahn* (Cambridge, Mass.: Belknap Press of Harvard University Press, 1984), 55; Sproat, *"Best Men,"* 164; Slap, *Doom of Reconstruction*, 99–106.

34. Susan D. Carle, "Lawyers' Duty to Do Justice: A New Look at the History of the 1908 Canons," *Law and Social Inquiry* 24, no. 1 (1999): 1–7, 18, 27. Carle suggests that perhaps lawyers' liberal arts educations and professional law degrees affected their positions on this matter.

35. Menand, *Metaphysical Club*, 64, 66–67; Wilson, *Patriotic Gore*, 749–50.

36. Wilson, *Patriotic Gore*, 753; Menand, *Metaphysical Club*, 61–62.

37. Wilson, *Patriotic Gore*, 785. On Holmes's sympathy with capitalists, see Menand, *Metaphysical Club*, 65.

38. Paul C. Nagel, "Reconstruction, Adams Style," *Journal of Southern History* 52, no. 1 (1986): 7–8; Adam Cooke, "'An Unpardonable Bit of Folly and Impertinence': Charles Francis Adams, Jr., American Anti-imperialists, and the Philippines," *New England Quarterly* 83, no. 2 (2010): 318–19, 327–28. Amy Greenberg has observed that after the Civil War, restrained men continued to oppose expansionists who wished to annex Hawaii. Their argument remained similar to their antebellum one: America's "religious, social and economic system," not just its military might, would "exert control over the Western Hemisphere, and the world" (*Manifest Manhood*, 271).

39. Quoted in Cooke, "Unpardonable Bit of Folly and Impertinence," 328.

40. Wilson, *Patriotic Gore*, 758.

41. Nina Silber, *The Romance of Reunion: Northerners and the South, 1865–1900* (Chapel Hill: University of North Carolina Press, 1997), 2–11; Jackson Lears, *Rebirth of a Nation: The Making of Modern America, 1877–1920* (2009; repr., New York: Harper Perennial, 2010), 29–30. Historian Reid Mitchell has also pointed out that the children of the postwar generation feared that they might not measure up to their parents' achievements. Reid Mitchell, "Soldiering, Manhood, and Coming of Age: A Northern Volunteer," in *Divided Houses: Gender and the Civil War*, ed. Catherine Clinton and Nina Silber (New York: Oxford University Press, 1992), 53.

42. David W. Blight, "Quarrel Forgotten or a Revolution Remembered? Reunion and Race in the Memory of the Civil War, 1875–1913," in *Union and Emancipation*, ed. David W. Blight and Brooks D. Simpson (Kent, Ohio: Kent State University Press, 1997), 157, 171; David W. Blight, *Race and Reunion: The Civil War in American Memory* (Cambridge, Mass.: Belknap Press of Harvard University Press, 2002), prologue, Chapters 4–5, 8–10.

43. Perry, *Conceived in Liberty*, 397, 415–19; Strong, *Joseph Hopkins Twichell*, 39. Many scholars have also challenged the myth of an easy reconciliation, pointing to contentious issues between Union and Confederate veterans such as the causes for which they fought, burial, the role of African American soldiers, and blacks' acceptance into veterans organizations. See John R. Neff, *Honoring the Civil War Dead: Commemoration and the Problem of Reconciliation* (Lawrence: University Press of Kansas, 2005); Caroline E. Janney, *Remembering the Civil War: Reunion and the Limits of Reconciliation* (Chapel Hill: University of North Carolina Press, 2013); Barbara A. Gannon, *The Won Cause: Black and White Comradeship in the Grant Army of the Republic* (Chapel Hill: University of North Carolina Press, 2014); and M. Keith Harris, *Across the Bloody Chasm: The Culture of Commemoration among Civil War Veterans* (Baton Rouge: Louisiana State University Press, 2014).

44. Charles Francis Adams, Jr., "An Undeveloped Function," lecture, Annual Meeting of the American Historical Association, December 27, 1901, in *Lee at Appomattox, and Other Papers* (1902; repr., Freeport, N.Y.: Books for Library Press, 1970), 324–27, 331–34.

45. Charles Francis Adams, Jr., "Shall Cromwell Have a Statue?" lecture, Beta Illinois Chapter of the Phi Beta Kappa Society, University of Chicago, June 17, 1902, in *Lee at Appomattox*, 381–82. The process of reconciling with the South actually started early

in the Adams household. Charles's brother, John Quincy Adams II, had opposed Radical Reconstruction and, in 1868, traveled to Columbia, South Carolina. There, he lauded Robert E. Lee and criticized black suffrage. See Nagel, "Reconstruction, Adams Style," 4–7.

46. Adams, "Shall Cromwell Have a Statue?" 393, 395–96, 407, 429.

47. In his lecture in Chicago, Adams had concluded that, "confronted with the question, what would I have done in 1861 had positions have reversed, and Massachusetts taken the course then taken by Virginia, I found the answer already recorded. I would have gone with the Union, and against Massachusetts." Nagel, "Reconstruction, Adams Style," 10–13; De Gruccio, "Manhood, Race, Failure, and Reconstruction," 72–73; Charles Francis Adams, Jr., *Lee's Centennial: An Address by Charles Francis Adams, Delivered at Lexington, Virginia, Saturday, January 19, 1907, on the Invitation of the President and Faculty of Washington and Lee University* (Boston: Houghton, Mifflin and Company, 1907), 1–2, 7, 8, 65; Adams, "Shall Cromwell Have a Statue?" 417.

48. Chamberlain, *Grand Old Man of Maine*, xx; Joshua Lawrence Chamberlain, *The Passing of the Armies: An Account of the Final Campaign of the Army of the Potomac, Based upon Personal Reminiscences of the Fifth Army Corps* (1915; repr., Gettysburg, Pa.: Stan Clark Military Books, 1994), 261.

Epilogue

1. Joshua Lawrence Chamberlain to Wilhelm I, July 20, 1870, in Chamberlain, *Grand Old Man of Maine*, 33; Perry, *Conceived in Liberty*, 413.

2. Burrage, *Brown University in the Civil War: A Memorial*, 93. Families, reform movements, and other institutions also celebrated the heroic dead. See, for example, the essays in Martin Blatt, Thomas Brown, and David Yacovone, eds., *Hope and Glory: Essays on the Legacy of the Fifty-Fourth Massachusetts Regiment* (2001; repr., Amherst: University of Massachusetts Press, 2009).

3. Chamberlain, *Passing of the Armies*, 386.

Bibliography

Primary Sources

Amherst College Library (Amherst College Archives and Special Collections), Amherst, Massachusetts
    Alumni Biographical Files
        Christopher Pennell
    Amherst College Magazine
    Unpublished Manuscripts in Alumni Biographical Files and Class Shelves
        Edwin C. Hand Civil War Papers
    Luther Clark Howell Papers
Bowdoin College Library (George J. Mitchell Department of Special Collections and Archives), Brunswick, Maine
    Alumni Biographical Files
        George Beaman Kenniston Diary
        William Lewis Haskell
    Chandler Family Papers
    Charles Henry Howard Collection
        Class Records
    Class of 1848
    Class of 1851
    Fessenden Collection
    Hubbard Family Papers
    Joshua Lawrence Chamberlain Collection
    McArthur Family Papers
    Oliver Otis Howard Papers
    Smith Brothers Student Letters
    Student Journals, Letters, and Scrapbooks
        Galen Clapp Moses
        John Deering, Jr.
    Thomas W. Hyde Papers
Connecticut Historical Society, Hartford, Connecticut
    George Clary Papers
Dartmouth College Library (Rauner Special Collections Library), Hanover, New Hampshire
    Chauncey Nye Journal, 1850–55
    Commencement Parts Records, 1771–
    Dartmouth Œstrus
    D. G. Wild Diary

Eri Davidson Woodbury Letters, 1858–66
Franklin Aretas Haskell Papers, 1858–63
Reuben Delavan Mussey Papers
Student Letters
Duke University Manuscript Library, Durham, North Carolina
Samuel Spencer Parmelee Papers, 1845–1911
Harvard University Archives, Cambridge, Massachusetts
General information about Harvard commencement, Class Day, and exhibitions in academic years (Class Records):
1849/1850
1850/1851
1851/1852
1852/1853
1853/1854
1854/1855
1855/1856
1856/1857
1858/1859
1859/1860
1860/1861
1862/1863
1863/1864
Houghton Library, Harvard University, Cambridge, Massachusetts
John Buttrick Noyes Civil War Letters
John Read Papers
Robert Gould Shaw Letters to His Family and Other Papers
Library of Congress, Washington, D.C.
Joshua Lawrence Chamberlain Papers
Maine Historical Society, Portland, Maine
John Marshall Brown Collection
Maine State Archives, Augusta, Maine
Records Relating to the Career of Joshua Lawrence Chamberlain
Massachusetts Historical Society, Boston, Massachusetts
Caspar Crowninshield Diaries, 1861–62
Charles Sedgwick Papers
Crowninshield-Magnus Papers, 1834–1965
Dwight Family Papers
Nathaniel Bowditch Memorial Collection
Paul Joseph Revere Papers
Pejepscot Historical Society, Brunswick, Maine
Joshua L. Chamberlain Collection
Princeton University Library (University Archives, Department of Rare Books and Special Collections), Princeton, New Jersey
William E. Potter Diary

University of Virginia, Special Collections, Charlottesville, Virginia
   Papers of Theodore Winthrop, 1856–77
Wesleyan University Special Collections and Archives, Middletown, Connecticut
   Commencement Orations Collection, 1833–55
Williams College Archives and Special Collections, Williamstown, Massachusetts
   Samuel Chapman Armstrong Collection
   Williams Quarterly
Yale University Library (Manuscripts and Archives), New Haven, Connecticut
   Theodore James Holmes Papers

Published Primary Sources

Abbott, Henry Livermore. *Fallen Leaves: The Civil War Letters of Major Henry Livermore Abbott*. Edited by Robert Garth Scott. Kent, Ohio: Kent State University Press, 1991.
Adams, Charles Francis, Jr. "Shall Cromwell Have a Statue?" In *Lee at Appomattox, and Other Papers*. 1902. Reprint, Freeport, N.Y.: Books for Library Press, 1970.
———. "An Undeveloped Function." In *Lee at Appomattox, and Other Papers*. 1902. Reprint, Freeport, N.Y.: Books for Library Press, 1970.
Adams, Charles Francis, Jr. *Lee's Centennial: An Address by Charles Francis Adams, Delivered at Lexington, Virginia, Saturday, January 19, 1907, on the Invitation of the President and Faculty of Washington and Lee University*. Boston: Houghton, Mifflin and Company, 1907.
Adams, Charles Francis, Sr., Charles Francis Adams, Jr., and Henry Adams. *A Cycle of Adams Letters, 1861–1865*. 2 vols. Edited by Worthington Chauncey Ford. Boston: Houghton Mifflin, 1920.
Armstrong, Samuel Chapman. *Personal Memories and Letters of General S. C. Armstrong*. 5 vols. Edited by Helen W. Ludlow. Hampton, Va.: Hampton Institute, 1898.
Barlow, Francis Channing. *Fear Was Not in Him: The Civil War Letters of Major General Francis C. Barlow, U.S.A*. Edited by Christian G. Samito. New York: Fordham University Press, 2004.
Bartlett, William Francis. *Memoir of William Francis Bartlett*. Edited by Francis Winthrop Palfrey. Boston: Houghton, Osgood and Company, 1879.
Bowditch, Charles Pickering. "War Letters of Charles P. Bowditch." *Massachusetts Historical Society Proceedings* 57 (October 1923–June 1924): 414–95.
Brown, Francis H. *Harvard University in the War of 1861–1865: A Record of Services Rendered in the Army and Navy of the United States by the Graduates and Students of Harvard College and the Professional Schools*. Boston: Cupples, Upham, and Company, 1886.
Brown University. *Historical Catalogue of Brown University*. Providence, R.I.: Brown University, 1914.
Chamberlain, Joshua Lawrence. *The Grand Old Man of Maine: Selected Letters of Joshua Lawrence Chamberlain, 1865–1914*. Edited by Jeremiah E. Goulka. Chapel Hill: University of North Carolina Press, 2004.

———. *The Passing of the Armies: An Account of the Final Campaign of the Army of the Potomac, Based upon Personal Reminiscences of the Fifth Army Corps*. 1915. Reprint, Gettysburg, Pa.: Stan Clark Military Books, 1994.
———. *Through Blood and Fire: Selected Civil War Papers of Major General Joshua Chamberlain*. Edited by Mark Nesbitt. Mechanicsburg, Pa.: Stackpole Books, 1996.
Crowninshield, Benjamin W. *A Private Journal, 1856–1858*. Cambridge, Mass.: Riverside Press, 1941.
Dwight, Wilder. *Life and Letters of Wilder Dwight, Lieut.-Col. Second Mass. Inf. Vols.* Edited by Elizabeth A. Dwight. Boston: Ticknor and Fields, 1868.
Emerson, Ralph Waldo. *Essays: Second Series*. Vol. 2. 1844. Reprint, Boston: Houghton Mifflin, 1883.
Fletcher, Robert S., and Malcolm O. Young, eds. *Amherst College: Biographical Record of the Graduates and Non-graduates, Centennial Edition, 1821–1921*. Amherst, Mass.: Amherst College, 1927.
Foster, John. *Essay on Decision of Character*. Burlington, Vt.: Chauncey Goodrich, 1830.
Garfield, James A. *Crete and James: Personal Letters of Lucretia and James Garfield*. Edited by John Shaw. East Lansing: Michigan State University Press, 1994.
———. *The Wild Life of the Army: Civil War Letters of James A. Garfield*. Edited by Frederick D. Williams. East Lansing: Michigan State University Press, 1964.
General Catalog of Bowdoin College and the Medical School of Maine: A Biographical Record of Alumni and Officers, 1794–1950. Brunswick, Maine: Bowdoin College, 1950.
Gray, John C., Jr., and John C. Ropes. *War Letters, 1862–1865*. Boston: Houghton Mifflin, 1927.
Hall, Edward Winslow. *Third General Catalogue of Colby College, Waterville, Maine, 1820–1906*. Waterville, Maine, 1909.
Hammond, William Gardiner. *Remembrance of Amherst: An Undergraduate's Diary, 1846–1848*. Edited by George F. Whicher. New York: Columbia University Press, 1946.
Harvard University. *Twenty-Fifth Annual Report of the President of Harvard College to the Overseers, Exhibiting the State of the Institution for the Academical Year 1849–50*. Cambridge, Mass.: Metcalf and Company, 1851.
———. *Twenty-Sixth Annual Report of the President of Harvard College to the Overseers, Exhibiting the State of the Institution for the Academical Year 1850–51*. Cambridge, Mass.: Metcalf and Company, 1852.
———. *Twenty-Seventh Annual Report of the President of Harvard College to the Overseers, Exhibiting the State of the Institution for the Academical Year 1851–52*. Cambridge, Mass.: Metcalf and Company, 1853.
———. *Twenty-Eighth Annual Report of the President of Harvard College to the Overseers, Exhibiting the State of the Institution for the Academical Year 1852–53*. Cambridge, Mass.: Metcalf and Company, 1854.
———. *Twenty-Ninth Annual Report of the President of Harvard College to the Overseers, Exhibiting the State of the Institution for the Academical Year 1853–54*. Cambridge, Mass.: Metcalf and Company, 1855.
———. *Thirtieth Annual Report of the President of Harvard College to the Overseers, Exhibiting the State of the Institution for the Academical Year 1854–55*. Cambridge, Mass.: Metcalf and Company, 1856.

———. *Thirty-First Annual Report of the President of Harvard College to the Overseers, Exhibiting the State of the Institution for the Academical Year 1855–56*. Cambridge, Mass.: Metcalf and Company, 1857.

———. *Thirty-Second Annual Report of the President of Harvard College to the Overseers, Exhibiting the State of the Institution for the Academical Year 1856–57*. Cambridge, Mass.: Metcalf and Company, 1858.

———. *Thirty-Third Annual Report of the President of Harvard College to the Overseers, Exhibiting the State of the Institution for the Academical Year 1857–58*. Cambridge, Mass.: Metcalf and Company, 1859.

———. *Thirty-Fourth Annual Report of the President of Harvard College to the Overseers, Exhibiting the State of the Institution for the Academical Year 1858–59*. Cambridge, Mass.: Welch, Bigelow, and Company, 1860.

———. *Thirty-Fifth Annual Report of the President of Harvard College to the Overseers, Exhibiting the State of the Institution for the Academical Year 1859–60*. Cambridge, Mass.: Welch, Bigelow, and Company, 1860.

———. *Thirty-Sixth Annual Report of the President of Harvard College to the Overseers, Exhibiting the State of the Institution for the Academical Year 1860–61*. Cambridge, Mass.: Welch, Bigelow, and Company, 1862.

———. *Thirty-Seventh Annual Report of the President of Harvard College to the Overseers, Exhibiting the State of the Institution for the Academical Year 1861–62*. Cambridge, Mass.: Welch, Bigelow, and Company, 1863.

———. *Thirty-Eighth Annual Report of the President of Harvard College to the Overseers, Exhibiting the State of the Institution for the Academical Year 1862–63*. Cambridge, Mass.: Welch, Bigelow, and Company, 1864.

———. *Thirty-Ninth Annual Report of the President of Harvard College to the Overseers, Exhibiting the State of the Institution for the Academical Year 1863–64*. Cambridge, Mass.: Welch, Bigelow, and Company, 1865.

———. *Fortieth Annual Report of the President of Harvard College to the Overseers, Exhibiting the State of the Institution for the Academical Year 1864–65*. Cambridge, Mass.: Welch, Bigelow, and Company, 1866.

Haskell, Franklin Aretas. *Haskell of Gettysburg: His Life and Civil War Papers*. Edited by Frank L. Byrne and Andrew T. Weaver. Kent, Ohio: Kent State University Press, 1989.

Higginson, Thomas Wentworth, ed. *Harvard Memorial Biographies*. 2 vols. Cambridge, Mass.: Sever and Francis, 1867.

Hodges, Almon D., Jr. *The Civil War Journal of Almon D. Hodges, Jr*. Edited by Stephen Z. Nonack. Boston: Boston Athenaeum, 2003.

Holmes, Oliver Wendell, Jr. *Touched with Fire: Civil War Letters and Diary of Oliver Wendell Holmes, Jr., 1861–1864*. Edited by Mark DeWolfe Howe. Cambridge, Mass.: Harvard University Press, 1946.

Holmes, Oliver Wendell, Sr. *Elsie Venner*. London: Routledge, Warne, and Routledge, 1861.

Howard, Charles H. *We Are in His Hands Whether We Live or Die: The Letters of Brevet Brigadier General Charles Henry Howard*. Edited by David K. Thomson. Knoxville: University of Tennessee Press, 2013.

Howard, Oliver O. *Autobiography of Oliver Otis Howard*. 2 vols. New York: Baker & Taylor, 1908.

Hyde, Thomas Worcester. *Civil War Letters*. Privately printed, John H. Hyde, 1933.

———. *Following the Greek Cross; or, Memories of the Sixth Army Corps*. Edited by Eric J. Mink. 1894. Reprint, Columbia: University of South Carolina Press, 2005.

Lowell, Charles Russell. *Life and Letters of Charles Russell Lowell*. Edited by Edward Waldo Emerson. 1907. Reprint, Columbia: University of South Carolina, 2005.

Lusk, William Thompson. *War Letters of William Thompson Lusk, Captain, Assistant Adjutant-General, United States Volunteers 1861–1863, Afterward M.D., LL.D.* New York: privately printed, 1911.

Lyman, Theodore. *Meade's Army: The Private Notebooks of Lt. Col. Theodore Lyman*. Edited by David W. Lowe. Kent, Ohio: Kent State University Press, 2007.

Mattocks, Charles. *"Unspoiled Heart": The Journal of Charles Mattocks of the 17th Maine*. Edited by Philip N. Racine. Knoxville: University of Tennessee Press, 1994.

A Memorial of Paul Joseph Revere and Edward H. R. Revere. 1874. Reprint, Clinton, Mass.: W. J. Coulter Press, 1913.

Morse, Charles Fessenden. *Letters Written during the Civil War, 1861–1865*. Boston: privately printed, 1898.

Nichols, Samuel Edmund. *"Your Soldier Boy Samuel": Civil War Letters of Lieut. Samuel Edmund Nichols, Amherst, '65 of the 37th Regiment Massachusetts Volunteers*. Edited by Charles Sterling Underhill. Buffalo, N.Y.: privately printed, 1929.

Phisterer, Frederick. *The Army in the Civil War*. Vol. 13 of *Statistical Record of the Armies of the United States*. New York: Charles Scribner's Sons, 1885.

Shaw, Robert Gould. *Blue-Eyed Child of Fortune: The Civil War Letters of Colonel Robert Gould Shaw*. Edited by Russell Duncan. Athens: University of Georgia Press, 1992.

———. *Letters/RGS*. Edited by Sarah Blake Shaw. Cambridge, Mass.: University Press, 1864.

Stearns, William Augustus. *Adjutant Stearns*. 1862. Reprint, Charlestown, Mass.: Acme Bookbinding, 2004.

Twichell, Joseph Hopkins. *The Civil War Letters of Joseph Hopkins Twichell: A Chaplain's Story*. Edited by Peter Messent and Steve Courtney. Athens: University of Georgia Press, 2006.

Wheeler, William. *Letters of William Wheeler of the Class of 1855, Y.C.* Cambridge, Mass.: H. O. Houghton and Company, 1875.

Winthrop, Theodore. *The Life and Poems of Theodore Winthrop*. Edited by Laura Winthrop Johnson. Henry Holt and Company, 1884.

———. *Life in the Open Air, and Other Papers*. Edited by George W. Curtis. Boston: Ticknor and Fields, 1863.

Yale University. *Obituary Record of Graduates of Yale College Deceased from July 1859 to July 1870: Presented at the Annual Meetings of the Alumni, 1860–70*. New Haven, Conn.: Tuttle, Morehouse & Taylor, 1870.

———. *Obituary Record of Graduates of Yale University Deceased during the Academical Year Ending in June 1905, Including the Record of a Few Who Died Previously, Hitherto Unreported*. 1905.

BIBLIOGRAPHY

Secondary Works: Books

Allen, Thomas M. *A Republic in Time: Temporality and Social Imagination in Nineteenth-Century America*. Chapel Hill: University of North Carolina Press, 2008.
Allmendinger, David F., Jr. *Paupers and Scholars: The Transformation of Student Life in Nineteenth-Century New England*. New York: St. Martin's Press, 1975.
Anderson, Benedict. *Imagined Communities: Reflections on the Origin and Spread of Nationalism*. 1983. Reprint, New York: Verso, 2006.
Ash, Stephen V. *When the Yankees Came: Conflict and Chaos in the Occupied South, 1861–1865*. Chapel Hill: University of North Carolina Press, 1995.
Augst, Thomas. *The Clerk's Tale: Young Men and Moral Life in Nineteenth-Century America*. Chicago: University of Chicago Press, 2003.
Ayers, Edward L. *Vengeance and Justice: Crime and Punishment in the Nineteenth-Century American South*. New York: Oxford University Press, 1984.
Bailyn, Bernard. *The Ideological Origins of the American Revolution*. Cambridge, Mass.: Belknap Press of Harvard University Press, 1967.
Baker, Jean H. *Affairs of Party: The Political Culture of Northern Democrats in the Mid-Nineteenth Century*. 1983. Reprint, New York: Fordham University Press, 1998.
Bercovitch, Sacvan. *The Rites of Assent: Transformations in the Symbolic Construction of America*. New York: Routledge, 1993.
Berlin, James A. *Writing Instruction in Nineteenth-Century American Colleges*. Carbondale: Southern Illinois University Press, 1984.
Berry, Stephen W., II. *All That Makes a Man: Love and Ambition in the Civil War South*. New York: Oxford University Press, 2003.
Blatt, Martin, Thomas Brown, and David Yacovone, eds. *Hope and Glory: Essays on the Legacy of the Fifty-Fourth Massachusetts Regiment*. 2001. Reprint, Amherst: University of Massachusetts Press, 2009.
Blight, David. *Race and Reunion: The Civil War in American Memory*. Cambridge, Mass.: Belknap Press of Harvard University Press, 2002.
Buell, Thomas B. *The Warrior Generals: Combat Leadership in the Civil War*. New York: Three Rivers Press, 1997.
Bundy, Carol. *The Nature of Sacrifice: A Biography of Charles Russell Lowell, Jr., 1835–64*. New York: Farrar, Straus and Giroux, 2005.
Burrage, Henry Sweetser. *Brown University in the Civil War: A Memorial*. Providence, R.I.: Providence Press Company, 1868.
Butler, Leslie. *Critical Americans: Victorian Intellectuals and Transatlantic Liberal Reform*. Chapel Hill: University of North Carolina Press, 2007.
Calhoun, Charles C. *A Small College in Maine: Two Hundred Years of Bowdoin*. Brunswick, Maine: Bowdoin College, 1993.
Carmichael, Peter S. *The Last Generation: Young Virginians in Peace, War, and Reunion*. Chapel Hill: University of North Carolina Press, 2005.
Campbell, Jacqueline Glass. *When Sherman Marched North From the Sea: Resistance on the Confederate Home Front*. Chapel Hill: University of North Carolina Press, 2003.
Carpenter, John A. *Sword and Olive Branch: Oliver Otis Howard*. 1964. Reprint, New York: Fordham University Press, 1999.

Chambers, Thomas A. *Memories of War: Visiting Battlegrounds and Bonefields in the Early American Republic.* Ithaca, N.Y.: Cornell University Press, 2012.

Chapman, George T. *Sketches of the Alumni of Dartmouth College from the First Graduation in 1771 to the Present Time, with a Brief History of the Institution.* Cambridge, Mass.: Riverside Press, 1867.

Chase, Henry, ed. *Representative Men of Maine: A Collection of Portraits with Biographical Sketches of Residents of the State Who Have Achieved Success and Are Prominent in Commercial Industrial, Professional and Political Life, to Which Is Added the Portraits and Sketches of All the Governors since the Formation of the State.* Portland, Maine: Lakeside Press, 1893.

Cmiel, Kenneth. *Democratic Eloquence: The Fight over Popular Speech in Nineteenth-Century America.* New York: William Morrow, 1990.

Cohen, Michael David. *Reconstructing the Campus: Higher Education and the American Civil War.* Charlottesville: University of Virginia Press, 2012.

Cohen, Nancy. *The Reconstruction of American Liberalism, 1865–1914.* Chapel Hill: University of North Carolina Press, 2002.

Colby, Elbridge. *Theodore Winthrop.* New York: Twayne, 1965.

Commager, Henry Steele. *The Era of Reform, 1830–1860.* New York: D. Van Nostrand Company, 1960.

Confino, Alon. *The Nation as a Local Metaphor: Württemberg, Imperial Germany, and National Memory, 1871–1918.* Chapel Hill: University of North Carolina Press, 1997.

Conforti, Joseph A. *Imagining New England: Explorations of Regional Identity from the Pilgrims to the Mid-Twentieth Century.* Chapel Hill: University of North Carolina Press, 2001.

Coulter, E. Merton. *College Life in the Old South: As Seen at the University of Georgia.* 1928. Reprint, Athens: University of Georgia Press, 1973.

Cox, John D. *Traveling South: Travel Narratives and the Construction of American Identity.* Athens: University of Georgia Press, 2005.

Doenecke, Justus D. *The Presidencies of James A. Garfield and Chester A. Arthur.* 1981. Reprint, Lawrence: University Press of Kansas, 1988.

Duncan, Russell. *Where Death and Glory Meet: Colonel Robert Gould Shaw and the 54th Massachusetts Infantry.* Athens: University of Georgia Press, 1999.

Eliot, Ellsworth, Jr. *Theodore Winthrop.* New Haven, Conn.: Yale University Library, 1938.

Engs, Robert F. *Educating the Disfranchised and Disinherited.* Knoxville: University of Tennessee Press, 1999.

———. *Freedom's First Generation: Black Hampton, Virginia, 1861–1890.* 1979. Reprint, New York: Fordham University Press, 2004.

Eyal, Yonatan. *The Young America Movement and the Transformation of the Democratic Party, 1828–1861.* Cambridge, U.K.: Cambridge University Press, 2007.

Foner, Eric. *The Fiery Trial: Abraham Lincoln and American Slavery.* New York: Norton, 2010.

———. *Free Soil, Free Labor, Free Men: The Ideology of the Republican Party before the Civil War.* 1970. Reprint, New York: Oxford University Press, 1995.

———. *Reconstruction: America's Unfinished Revolution, 1863–1877.* 1988. Reprint, New York: Perennial Classics, 2002.
Foote, Lorien. *The Gentlemen and the Roughs: Manhood, Honor, and Violence in the Union Army.* New York: New York University Press, 2010.
Forgie, George B. *Patricide in the House Divided: A Psychological Interpretation of Lincoln and His Age.* New York: Norton, 1979.
Frank, Joseph Allan. *With Ballot and Bayonet: The Political Socialization of American Civil War Soldiers.* Athens: University of Georgia Press, 1998.
Fredrickson, George M. *The Inner Civil War: Northern Intellectuals and the Crisis of the Union.* 1965. Reprint, New York: Harper and Row, 1968.
Freeman, Joanne B. *Affairs of Honor: National Politics in the New Republic.* New Haven, Conn.: Yale University Press, 2001.
Friend, Craig T., and Lorri Glover, eds. *Southern Manhood: Perspectives on Masculinity in the Old South.* Athens: University of Georgia Press, 2004.
Fuller, Corydon Eustathius. *Reminiscences of James A. Garfield: With Notes Preliminary and Collateral.* Cincinnati, Ohio: Standard Publishing, 1887.
Gallagher, Gary W. *Causes Won, Lost, and Forgotten: How Hollywood and Popular Art Shape What We Know about the Civil War.* Chapel Hill: University of North Carolina Press, 2008.
———. *The Union War.* Cambridge, Mass.: Harvard University Press, 2011.
Gannon, Barbara A. *The Won Cause: Black and White Comradeship in the Grand Army of the Republic.* Chapel Hill: University of North Carolina Press, 2014.
Gassan, Richard H. *The Birth of American Tourism: New York, the Hudson Valley, and American Culture, 1790–1830.* Amherst: University of Massachusetts Press, 2008.
Glatthaar, Joseph T. *Forged in Battle: The Civil War Alliance of Black Soldiers and White Officers.* Baton Rouge: Louisiana State University Press, 1990.
———. *The March to the Sea and Beyond: Sherman's Troops in the Savannah and Carolinas Campaigns.* New York: New York University Press, 1985.
Glover, Lorri. *Southern Sons: Becoming Men in the New Nation.* 2007. Reprint, Baltimore: Johns Hopkins University Press, 2010.
Gorn, Elliott J. *The Manly Art: Bare-Knuckle Prize Fighting in America.* 1986. Reprint, Ithaca, N.Y.: Cornell University Press, 2010.
Grant, Susan-Mary. *North over South: Northern Nationalism and American Identity in the Antebellum Era.* Lawrence: University Press of Kansas, 2000.
Greenberg, Amy S. *Manifest Manhood and the Antebellum American Empire.* New York: Cambridge University Press, 2005.
Greenberg, Kenneth S. *Honor and Slavery: Lies, Duels, Noses, Masks, Dressing as a Woman, Gifts, Strangers, Humanitarianism, Death, Slave Rebellions, the Proslavery Argument, Baseball, Hunting, and Gambling in the Old South.* Princeton, N.J.: Princeton University Press, 1996.
Grimsley, Mark. *The Hard Hand of War: Union Military Policy toward Southern Civilians, 1861–1865.* New York: Cambridge University Press, 1995.
Hall, Peter Dobkin. *The Organization of American Culture, 1700–1900: Private Institutions, Elites, and the Origins of American Nationality.* New York: New York University Press, 1984.

Halttunen, Karen. *Confidence Men and Painted Women: A Study of Middle-Class Culture in America, 1830–1870.* New Haven, Conn.: Yale University Press, 1982.
Harris, M. Keith. *Across the Bloody Chasm: The Culture of Commemoration among Civil War Veterans.* Baton Rouge: Louisiana State University Press, 2014.
Hemphill, C. Dallett. *Bowing to Necessities: A History of Manners in America, 1620–1860.* New York: Oxford University Press, 1999.
Hess, Earl J. *Liberty, Virtue, and Progress: Northerners and Their War for the Union.* New York: New York University Press, 1988.
———. *The Union Soldier in Battle: Enduring the Ordeal of Combat.* Lawrence: University Press of Kansas, 1997.
Hessinger, Rodney. *Seduced, Abandoned, and Reborn: Visions of Youth in Middle-Class America, 1780–1850.* Philadelphia: University of Pennsylvania Press, 2005.
Horowitz, Helen Lefkowitz. *Campus Life: Undergraduate Cultures from the End of the Eighteenth Century to the Present.* Chicago: University of Chicago Press, 1987.
Horsman, Reginald. *Race and Manifest Destiny: The Origins of American Racial Anglo-Saxonism.* Cambridge, Mass.: Harvard University Press, 1981.
Howe, Daniel Walker. *The Political Culture of the American Whigs.* Chicago: University of Chicago Press, 1979.
Janney, Caroline E. *Remembering the Civil War: Reunion and the Limits of Reconciliation.* Chapel Hill: University of North Carolina Press, 2013.
Jellison, Charles A. *Fessenden of Maine, Civil War Senator.* Syracuse, N.Y.: Syracuse University Press, 1962.
Johnson, Paul E. *A Shopkeeper's Millennium: Society and Revivals in Rochester, New York, 1815–1837.* 1978. Reprint, New York: Hill and Wang, 1994.
Kaestle, Carl F. *Pillars of the Republic: Common Schools and American Society, 1780–1860.* New York: Hill and Wang, 1983.
Kelley, Brooks Mather. *Yale: A History.* New Haven, Conn.: Yale University Press, 1974.
Kelley, Mary. *Learning to Stand and Speak: Women, Education, and Public Life in America's Republic.* Chapel Hill: University of North Carolina Press, 2008.
Kett, Joseph F. *Rites of Passage: Adolescence in America, 1790 to the Present.* New York: Basic Books, 1977.
Kirkland, Edward Chase. *Charles Francis Adams, Jr., 1835–1915: The Patrician at Bay.* Cambridge, Mass.: Harvard University Press, 1965.
LaFantasie, Glenn W. *Gettysburg Heroes: Perfect Soldiers, Hallowed Ground.* Bloomington: Indiana University Press, 2008.
Lawson, Melinda. *Patriot Fires: Forging a New American Nationalism in the Civil War North.* Lawrence: University Press of Kansas, 2002.
Lears, Jackson. *Rebirth of a Nation: The Making of Modern America, 1877–1920.* 2009. Reprint, New York: Harper Perennial, 2010.
Lemelin, Robert. *Pathway to the National Character, 1830–1861.* Port Washington, N.Y.: Kennikat Press, 1974.
Linderman, Gerald F. *Embattled Courage: The Experience of Combat in the American Civil War.* New York: Free Press, 1987.
Logue, Larry M. *To Appomattox and Beyond: The Civil War Soldier in War and Peace.* Chicago: Ivan R. Dee, 1996.

Bibliography

Lord, John King. *A History of Dartmouth College, 1815–1909.* Concord, N.H.: Rumford Press, 1913.
Mangan, J. A., and James Walvin, eds. *Manliness and Morality: Middle-Class Masculinity in Britain and America, 1800–1940.* New York: St. Martin's Press, 1987.
Marten, James. *The Children's Civil War.* Chapel Hill: University of North Carolina Press, 1998.
———, ed. *Lessons of War: The Civil War in Children's Magazines.* Wilmington, Del.: Scholarly Resources, 1999.
McCardell, John. *The Idea of a Southern Nation: Southern Nationalists and Southern Nationalism, 1830–1860.* New York: Norton, 1979.
McClintock, Russell. *Lincoln and the Decision for War: The Northern Response to Secession.* Chapel Hill: The University of North Carolina Press, 2008.
McCraw, Thomas K. *Prophets of Regulation: Charles Francis Adams, Louis D. Brandeis, James M. Landis, Alfred E. Kahn.* Cambridge, Mass.: Belknap Press of Harvard University Press, 1984.
McPherson, James M. *For Cause and Comrades: Why Men Fought in the Civil War.* New York: Oxford University Press, 1997.
———. *Is Blood Thicker Than Water? Crises of Nationalism in the Modern World.* New York: Vintage, 1999.
———. *What They Fought For, 1861–1865.* 1994. Reprint, New York: Anchor Books, 1995.
Melish, Joanne Pope. *Disowning Slavery: Gradual Emancipation and "Race" in New England, 1780–1860.* Ithaca, N.Y.: Cornell University Press, 1998.
Menand, Louis. *The Metaphysical Club: A Story of Ideas in America.* 2001. Reprint, New York: Farrar, Straus and Giroux, 2002.
Meyer, D. H. *The Instructed Conscience: The Shaping of the American National Ethic.* Philadelphia: University of Pennsylvania Press, 1972.
Miller, Richard F. *Harvard's Civil War: The History of the Twentieth Massachusetts Volunteer Infantry.* Lebanon, N.H.: University Press of New England, 2005.
Mintz, Steven. *Huck's Raft: A History of American Childhood.* Cambridge, Mass.: Belknap Press of Harvard University, 2004.
Mitchell, Reid. *Civil War Soldiers.* 1988. Reprint, New York: Penguin, 1997.
———. *The Vacant Chair: The Northern Soldier Leaves Home.* New York: Oxford University Press, 1993.
Montague, W. L. *Biographical Record of the Non-graduate Members of Amherst College during Its First Half Century, 1821–1871.* Amherst, Mass., 1881.
Moore, Frank, ed. *Heroes and Martyrs: Notable Men of the Time: Biographical Sketches of the Military and Naval Heroes, Statesmen and Orators, Distinguished in the American Crisis of 1861–62.* New York: G. P. Putnam, 1862.
Neely, Mark E., Jr. *Lincoln and the Triumph of the Nation: Constitutional Conflict in the American Civil War.* Chapel Hill: University of North Carolina Press, 2011.
———. *The Union Divided: Party Conflict in the Civil War North.* Cambridge, Mass.: Harvard University Press, 2002.
Neff, John R. *Honoring the Civil War Dead: Commemoration and the Problem of Reconciliation.* Lawrence: University Press of Kansas, 2005.

Pace, Robert F. *Halls of Honor: College Men in the Old South*. Baton Rouge: Louisiana State University Press, 2004.
Paludan, Phillip Shaw. *A People's Contest: The Union and Civil War, 1861–1865*. 1988. Reprint, Lawrence: University Press of Kansas, 1996.
Parish, Peter J. *The North and the Nation in the Era of the Civil War*. Edited by Adam I. P. Smith and Susan-Mary Grant. New York: Fordham University Press, 2003.
Pellicano, John M. *"Well Prepared To Die": The Life of Brigadier General James Clay Rice*. Fredericksburg, Va.: John M. Pellicano, 2007.
Perry, Mark. *Conceived in Liberty: Joshua Chamberlain, William Oates, and the American Civil War*. New York: Viking, 1997.
Peskin, Allan. *Garfield*. Kent, Ohio: Kent State University Press, 1978.
Poirier, Robert G. *"By the Blood of Our Alumni": Norwich University Citizen Soldiers in the Army of the Potomac*. Mason City, Iowa: Savas, 1999.
Posner, Richard, ed. *The Essential Holmes: Selections from the Letters, Speeches, Judicial Opinions, and Other Writings of Oliver Wendell Holmes, Jr.* Chicago: University of Chicago Press, 1992.
Pullen, John J. *Patriotism in America: A Study of Changing Devotions, 1770–1970*. New York: American Heritage Press, 1971.
Quigley, Paul. *Shifting Grounds: Nationalism and the American South, 1848–1865*. New York: Oxford University Press, 2012.
Rael, Patrick. *Black Identity and Black Protest in the Antebellum North*. Chapel Hill: University of North Carolina Press, 2002.
Reynolds, David S. *John Brown, Abolitionist*. New York: Knopf, 2005.
Ring, Elizabeth. *The McArthurs of Limington, Maine: The Family in America a Century Ago, 1783–1917*. Falmouth, Maine: Kennebec River Press, 1992.
Robertson, James I., Jr. *Soldiers Blue and Gray*. Columbia: University of South Carolina Press, 1988.
Rose, Anne C. *Victorian America and the Civil War*. New York: Cambridge University Press, 1992.
Rose, Willie Lee. *Rehearsal for Reconstruction: The Port Royal Experiment*. 1964. Reprint, Athens: University of Georgia Press, 1999.
Rotundo, E. Anthony. *American Manhood: Transformations in Masculinity from the Revolution to the Modern Era*. New York: Basic Books, 1993.
Rudolph, Frederick. *The American College and University*. New York: Knopf, 1965.
Samito, Christian G. *Becoming American under Fire: Irish Americans, African Americans, and the Politics of Citizenship during the Civil War*. Ithaca, N.Y.: Cornell University Press, 2009.
Schmidt, George P. *The Liberal Arts College: A Chapter in American Cultural History*. 1957. Reprint, Westport, Conn.: Greenwood Press, 1975.
Sauers, Richard A., and Martin H. Sable. *William Francis Bartlett: Biography of a Union General in the Civil War*. Jefferson, N.C.: McFarland, 2009.
Sears, John F. *Sacred Places: American Tourist Attractions in the Nineteenth Century*. New York: Oxford University Press, 1989.
Sheidley, Harlow W. *Sectional Nationalism: Massachusetts Conservative Leaders and the Transformation of America, 1815–1836*. Boston: Northeastern University Press, 1998.

Shepherd, Jack. *The Adams Chronicles: Four Generations of Greatness*. Boston: Little, Brown and Company, 1975.
Silber, Nina. *The Romance of Reunion: Northerners and the South, 1865–1900*. Chapel Hill: University of North Carolina Press, 1997.
Silber, Nina, and Mary Beth Sievens, eds. *Yankee Correspondence: Civil War Letters between New England Soldiers and the Home Front*. Charlottesville: University of Virginia Press, 1996.
Slap, Andrew L. *The Doom of Reconstruction: The Liberal Republicans in the Civil War Era*. New York: Fordham University Press, 2006.
Smith, Wilson. *Professors and Public Ethics: Studies of Northern Moral Philosophers before the Civil War*. Ithaca, N.Y.: Cornell University Press, 1956.
Sproat, John G. *"The Best Men": Liberal Reformers in the Gilded Age*. New York: Oxford University Press, 1968.
Stephanson, Anders. *Manifest Destiny: American Expansion and the Empire of Right*. New York: Hill and Wang, 1995.
Story, Ronald. *The Forging of an Aristocracy: Harvard and the Boston Upper Class, 1800–1870*. Middletown, Conn.: Wesleyan University Press, 1980.
Strong, Leah. *Joseph Hopkins Twichell: Mark Twain's Friend and Pastor*. Athens: University of Georgia Press, 1966.
Summers, Mark W. *The Plundering Generation: Corruption and the Crisis of the Union, 1849–1861*. New York: Oxford University Press, 1987.
Sword, Wiley. *Courage under Fire: Profiles in Bravery from the Battlefields of the Civil War*. New York: St. Martin's Press, 2007.
Taylor, William R. *Cavalier and Yankee: The Old South and American National Character*. 1961. Reprint, New York: Oxford University Press, 1993.
Tewksbury, Donald G. *The Founding of American Colleges and Universities before the Civil War: With Particular Reference to the Religious Influence Bearing upon the College Movement*. New York: Teachers College, Columbia University, 1932.
Tomlinson, Everett T., and Paul G. Tomlinson. *A Leader of Freemen: The Life Story of Samuel Chapman Armstrong, Brevet Brigadier-General, U.S.A.* Philadelphia, PA: American Sunday-School Union, 1917.
Travers, Len. *Celebrating the Fourth: Independence Day and the Rites of Nationalism in the Early Republic*. Amherst: University of Massachusetts Press, 1997.
Trulock, Alice Rains. *In the Hands of Providence: Joshua L. Chamberlain and the American Civil War*. Chapel Hill: University of North Carolina Press, 1992.
Tucker, David M. *Mugwumps: Public Moralists of the Gilded Age*. Columbia: University of Missouri Press, 1998.
Tyler, William S. *A History of Amherst College, during the Administrations of Its First Five Presidents from 1821 to 1891*. New York: Frederick H. Hitchcock, 1895.
Ural, Susannah J. *Civil War Citizens: Race, Ethnicity, and Identity in America's Bloodiest Conflict*. New York: New York University Press, 2010.
Waldstreicher, David. *In the Midst of Perpetual Fetes: The Making of American Nationalism, 1776–1820*. Chapel Hill: University of North Carolina Press, 1997.
Wallace, Willard M. *Soul of the Lion: A Biography of General Joshua L. Chamberlain*. 1960. Reprint, Gettysburg, Pa.: Stan Clark Military Books, 1995.

Waugh, Joan. *Ulysses Grant: American Hero, American Myth*. Chapel Hill: University of North Carolina Press, 2009.

Welch, Richard F. *The Boy General: The Life and Careers of Francis Channing Barlow*. Madison, N.J.: Fairleigh Dickinson University Press, 2003.

Weld, Stephen Minot. *War Diary and Letters of Stephen Minot Weld, 1861–1865*. Cambridge, Mass.: Riverside Press, 1912.

Wiebe, Robert H. *The Search for Order, 1877–1920*. 1968. Reprint, New York: Hill and Wang, 1967.

Wiley, Bell Irvin. *The Life of Billy Yank: The Common Soldier of the Union*. 1952. Reprint, Baton Rouge: Louisiana State University Press, 1994.

———. *The Life of Johnny Reb: The Common Soldier of the Confederacy*. 1943. Reprint, Baton Rouge: Louisiana State University Press, 1992.

Wilson, Edmund. *Patriotic Gore: Studies in the Literature of the American Civil War*. New York: Oxford University Press, 1962.

Wilson, Major L. *Space, Time, and Freedom: The Quest for Nationality and the Irrepressible Conflict, 1815–1861*. Westport, Conn.: Greenwood Press, 1974.

Wood, Gordon S. *The Creation of the American Republic, 1776–1787*. Chapel Hill: University of North Carolina Press, 1969.

Woodworth, Steven E. *While God Is Marching On: The Religious World of Civil War Soldiers*. Lawrence: University Press of Kansas, 2001.

Wyatt-Brown, Bertram. *Honor and Violence in the Old South*. New York: Oxford University Press, 1986.

———. *The Shaping of Southern Culture: Honor, Grace, and War, 1760s–1890s*. Chapel Hill: University of North Carolina Press, 2001.

———. *Southern Honor: Ethics and Behavior in the Old South*. New York: Oxford University Press, 1983.

Young, Robin. *For Love and Liberty: The Untold Civil War Story of Major Sullivan Ballou and His Famous Love Letter*. New York: Thunder's Mouth Press, 2006.

Articles and Chapters

Appleby, Joyce. "Liberalism and the American Revolution." *New England Quarterly* 49, no. 1 (1976): 3–26.

———. "Republicanism and Ideology." *American Quarterly* 37, no. 4 (1985): 461–73.

———. "Republicanism in Old and New Contexts." *William and Mary Quarterly* 43, no. 1 (1986): 20–34.

Blight, David W. "Quarrel Forgotten or a Revolution Remembered? Reunion and Race in the Memory of the Civil War, 1875–1913." In *Union and Emancipation*, edited by David W. Blight and Brooks D. Simpson. Kent, Ohio: Kent State University Press, 1997.

Bowdoin College. "Obituary Record of the Graduates of Bowdoin College Including the Bowdoin Medical School for the Year Ending 1 June 1917." *Bowdoin College Bulletin* 74 (May 1917): 421–22.

Carle, Susan D. "Lawyers' Duty to Do Justice: A New Look at the History of the 1908 Canons." *Law and Social Inquiry* 24, no. 1 (1999): 1–44.

Cohen, Daniel A. "The Passions of Lieutenant Pennell." *Amherst* (Fall 1978): 2–5, 24–28.
Cooke, Adam. "'An Unpardonable Bit of Folly and Impertinence': Charles Francis Adams, Jr., American Anti-imperialists, and the Philippines." *New England Quarterly* 83, no. 2 (2010): 313–38.
De Gruccio, Michael. "Manhood, Race, Failure, and Reconciliation: Charles Francis Adams, Jr., and the American Civil War." *New England Quarterly* 81 (December 2008): 436–75.
DeRoche, Andy. "Blending Loyalties: Maine Soldiers Respond to the Civil War." *Maine History* 35, no. 3 (1996): 124–39.
Foote, Lorien. "Rich Man's War, Rich Man's Fight: Class, Ideology, and Discipline in the Union Army." *Civil War History* 51 (2005): 269–87.
Glover, Lorri. "'Let Us Manufacture Men': Educating Elite Boys in the Early National South." In *Southern Manhood: Perspectives on Masculinity in the Old South*, edited by Craig Thompson Friend and Lorri Glover. Athens: University of Georgia Press, 2004.
Green, Jennifer R. "'Stout Chaps Who Can Bear the Distress': Young Men in Antebellum Military Academies." In *Southern Manhood: Perspectives on Masculinity in the Old South*, edited by Craig Thompson Friend and Lorri Glover. Athens: University of Georgia Press, 2004.
Greenberg, Kenneth S. "The Nose, the Lie, and the Duel in the Antebellum South." *American Historical Review* 95 (February 1990): 57–74.
Hoganson, Kristin. "Garrisonian Abolitionists and the Rhetoric of Gender, 1850–1860." *American Quarterly* 45 (December 1993): 558–95.
Howe, Daniel Walker. "Classical Education in America." *Wilson Quarterly* 35 (Spring 2011): 31–36.
Kantrowitz, Stephen. "Fighting Like Men: Civil War Dilemmas of Abolitionist Manhood." In *Battle Scars: Gender and Sexuality in the American Civil War*, edited by Catherine Clinton and Nina Silber. New York: Oxford University Press, 2006.
Leeman, William P. "George Bancroft's Civil War: Slavery, Abraham Lincoln, and the Course of History." *New England Quarterly* 81 (September 2008): 462–88.
McLachlan, James. "The *Choice of Hercules*: American Student Societies in the Early 19th Century." In *The University in Society*, 2 vols., edited by Lawrence Stone. Princeton, N.J.: Princeton University Press, 1974.
Miller, Richard F. "Brahmin Janissaries: John A. Andrew Mobilizes Massachusetts' Upper Class for the Civil War." *New England Quarterly* 75 (June 2002): 204–34.
———. "Brahmins under Fire: Peer Courage and the Harvard Regiment." *Historical Journal of Massachusetts* 30, no. 1 (2002): 75–109.
———. "The Trouble with Brahmins: Class and Ethnic Tensions in Massachusetts' 'Harvard Regiment.'" *New England Quarterly* 76 (March 2003): 38–72.
Mitchell, Reid. "Soldiering, Manhood, and Coming of Age: A Northern Volunteer." In *Divided Houses: Gender and the Civil War*, ed. Catherine Clinton and Nina Silber. New York: Oxford University Press, 1992.
Nagel, Paul C. "Reconstruction, Adams Style." *Journal of Southern History* 52, no. 1 (1986): 3–18.
Padgett, James A. "Reconstruction Letters from North Carolina: Part X Letters of James Abram Garfield." *North Carolina Historical Review* 21, no. 2 (1944): 139–57.

Parish, Peter J. "Confidence and Anxiety in Victorian America." In *The North and the Nation in the Era of the Civil War*, edited by Adam I. P. Smith and Susan-Mary Grant. New York: Fordham University Press, 2003.

———. "The Distinctiveness of American Nationalism." In *The North and the Nation in the Era of the Civil War*, edited by Adam I. P. Smith and Susan-Mary Grant. New York: Fordham University Press, 2003.

———. "Partisanship and the Construction of Nationalism." In *The North and the Nation in the Era of the Civil War*, edited by Adam I. P. Smith and Susan-Mary Grant. New York: Fordham University Press, 2003.

Peskin, Allan. "Garfield and Hayes: Political Leaders of the Gilded Age." *Ohio History* 77 (April 1968): 111–25.

———. "President Garfield and the Southern Question: The Making of a Policy That Never Was." *Southern Quarterly* 16, no. 4 (1978): 375–86.

Rafuse, Ethan S. "'To Check . . . the Very Worst and Meanest of Our Passions': Common Sense, 'Cobbon Sense,' and the Socialization of Cadets at Antebellum West Point." *War in History* 16 (September 2009): 406–24.

Rodgers, Daniel T. "Republicanism: The Career of a Concept." *Journal of American History* 79, no. 1 (1992): 11–38.

Ross, Jordan. "Uncommon Union: Diversity and Motivation among Civil War Soldiers." *American Nineteenth Century History* 3, no. 1 (2002): 17–44.

Rotundo, E. Anthony. "Learning about Manhood: Gender Ideals and the Middle-Class Family in Nineteenth-Century America." In *Manliness and Morality: Middle-Class Masculinity in Britain and America, 1800–1940*, edited by J. A. Mangan and James Walvin. New York: St. Martin's Press, 1987.

Saveth, Edward N. "History of an Elite." *History of Education Quarterly* 28, no. 3 (1988): 367–86.

Stauffer, John. "Embattled Manhood and New England Writers, 1860–1870." In *Battle Scars: Gender and Sexuality in the American Civil War*, edited by Catherine Clinton and Nina Silber. New York: Oxford University Press, 2006.

Taylor, P. A. M. "A New England Gentleman: Theodore Lyman III, 1833–1897." *Journal of American Studies* 17, no. 3 (1983): 367–90.

Thayer, Ezra Ripley, Samuel Williston, and Joseph H. Beale. "John Chipman Gray." *Harvard Law Review* 28 (April 1915): 539–49.

Waugh, Joan. "'It Was a Sacrifice We Owed': The Shaw Family and the Fifty-Fourth Massachusetts Regiment." In *Hope and Glory: Essays on the Legacy of the Fifty-Fourth Massachusetts Regiment*, edited by Martin H. Blatt, Thomas J. Brown, and Donald Yacovone. Amherst: University of Massachusetts Press, 2001.

Wells, Jeremy. "Up from Savagery: Booker T. Washington and the Civilizing Mission." *Southern Quarterly* 42, no. 1 (2003): 53–74.

Wyatt-Brown, Bertram. "Andrew Jackson's Honor." *Journal of the Early Republic* 17 (Spring 1997): 1–36.

Young, Howard V., Jr. "James A. Garfield and Hampton Institute." In *Stony the Road: Chapters in the History of Hampton Institute*, edited by Keith L. Schall. Charlottesville: University Press of Virginia, 1977.

Index

1st Massachusetts Cavalry, 104, 144
1st U.S. Sharp Shooters, 145
2nd Massachusetts, 140, 141, 162
5th Massachusetts Cavalry, 153
6th Massachusetts, 105
7th Maine, 137
7th Squadron, Rhode Island Cavalry ("College Cavaliers"), 93
9th Army Corps, 152
9th United States Colored Troops, 171
11th Army Corps, 142, 147–48, 160, 162
15th Alabama, 184
17th Maine, 119, 160
20th Maine, 87, 159, 184
20th Massachusetts ("Harvard Regiment"), 104, 140, 141, 162, 224*n*40
45th New York, 144
49th Massachusetts, 141
54th Massachusetts, 7, 151

Abbott, Henry Livermore, 99, 104, 141, 158, 202*n*31, 223*n*36; on African American soldiers, 153; on the death of Robert Gould Shaw, 153; eager for battle, 155–56; interaction with Confederate soldiers, 128
Abolitionists, 5, 55, 57, 105, 151, 213*n*53, 214*n*5
Adams, Charles Francis, Jr., 141, 142, 183, 202*n*31, 230*n*8, 230*n*10, 235*n*3; on African American soldiers, 134, 150, 153–54; anti-imperialist movement and, 182–83; description of combat, 155; distrust of radicals, 167–68; election of 1876 and, 177; on the future of African Americans, 134–36, 185; on the future of the postwar South, 133–34, 185; interaction with African Americans, 132–33; Liberal Republican movement and, 175; motivation to volunteer, 96–97, 98, 104; reconciliation and, 185–87, 188, 238*n*47; reformist campaigns of, 181; relationship with soldiers, 149; views of the South/white southerners, 117, 121
Adams, Charles Francis, Sr., 104
Adams, Henry, 22, 97, 235*n*3
Adams, John Quincy, 79, 81
Adams, John Quincy II, 237–38*n*45
African American soldiers, 112, 130, 134–36, 150–54, 161; reconciliation and, 184, 237*n*43; United States Colored Troops (USCT), 142
Alden, Leonard C., 46, 76–77
Allard, John, 41, 49
Allmendinger, David F., 205*n*13
American Bar Association, 181
Ames, Adelbert, 145, 178
Amherst College, 9, 13, 23, 30, 34, 93, 99, 216*n*21
Antietam, Battle of (1862), 1, 93, 108, 120, 137–38, 161, 183
Appleby, Joyce, 199*n*15
Appleton, William H., 19
Armstrong, Samuel Chapman, 9, 112–13, 179, 190, 202*n*31; on commanding soldiers, 144; education and, 171–73, 179; Hampton Institute and, 172–73, 179; Reconstruction and, 169; view of Confederate soldiers, 127; at Williams College, 27, 67, 77, 112
Augst, Thomas, 215*n*13
Ayers, Edward L., 6, 197*n*4

Baker, Jean H., 200–1*n*25
Baker, John G., 72

Balch, Francis, 42, 74
Ball's Bluff, Battle of (1861), 156, 183
Ballou, Sullivan, 27, 28, 94, 96, 191, 206n23
Barlow, Francis Channing, 141, 148, 162, 180, 202n31, 230n8, 231n20; in combat, 156; election of 1876 and, 177–78; on immigrant soldiers, 142; view of Confederate soldiers, 127
Bartlett, William Francis, 131, 141, 150, 176–77, 202n31
Bancroft, George, 39, 209n18
Beloit College, 204n9
Bercovitch, Sacvan, 209n18
Berlin, James A., 25
Berry, Stephen W. II, 198n8, 202n30, 208n9, 218n46, 232n22
Black Codes, 170
Blaine, James Gillespie, 178, 180
Bowditch, Charles Pickering, 98, 102–3, 202n31, 223n36, 233n31; on the death of Robert Gould Shaw, 151
Bowditch, Henry Ingersoll, 71, 106
Bowditch, Jonathan I., 103, 144, 223n34
Bowditch, Nathaniel, 71, 105–6, 117, 147, 202n31; reaction to slavery, 130; relationship with soldiers, 149
Bowditch, Olivia, 105–6
Bowdoin College, 9, 13, 21, 25, 29, 30, 32, 190, 205n13, 216n25
Brahmins. See Holmes, Oliver Wendell, Sr.
Brown, Addison, 68, 76
Brown, John (abolitionist), 64, 119
Brown, John Marshall, 43, 116, 202n31
Brown University, 21, 191, 204–5n11, 205n13
Bruce, Eli, 73
Buchanan, James, 89–90
Buckingham, Lucius, 26
Bull Run, Battle of First (1861), 100, 102
Bull Run, Battle of Second (1862), 109, 157
Bureau of Refugees, Freedmen, and Abandoned Lands, 169–70
Burr, Aaron, 75–76
Burrage, Henry S., 191
Burrage, William, 51, 53
Butler, Leslie, 165–66, 234–35n3

Carleton College, 204n9
Carmichael, Peter, 12–13
Carter, James C., 72, 84–85
Cedar Creek, Battle of (1864), 1
Chamberlain, Joshua Lawrence, 100, 120, 143, 178, 190, 191, 202n31; African Americans' civil rights and, 178; ambition of, 109–10, 169, 180; Bowdoin College and, 28, 69, 87, 175–76; combat experience, 159; Congressional Medal of Honor, 162; "Drill rebellion" (1874) and, 175–76; educational philosophy of, 25; history of the Civil War and, 174–75, 184, 187–88; learning to be a soldier, 145; on Abraham Lincoln's death, 163, 164; motivating troops, 156–57; motivation to volunteer/continue fighting, 86–87, 109–10; political career of, 180; reconciliation and, 187–88; Reconstruction and, 169, 173, 178; views of the South, 115–16
Chambers, Thomas A., 210n21, 211–12n37
Chancellorsville, Battle of (1863), 156, 160
Chandler, Charles Peleg, 202n31; Confederate prisoners and, 128–29; description of combat, 155, 160–61; motivating troops, 156; motivation to volunteer/continue fighting, 109; reaction to raids/confiscation of property, 125–26; reaction to slavery, 116–17, 130, 134; views of the South/white southerners, 116–19, 122–23
character, 214n6, 215n13; college experience and, 2–3, 10, 61–63, 65–68; conscience/Conscientious actions, 71–84; definition of, 1–2, 62–65; dignity, 6; exemplary characters (from history), 75–76, 78–80, 83–84; formation of, 2–3, 10, 61–73; individuality, 61–63, 65–68, 78; leadership and, 32–33, 58–59, 71–85, 88–89, 98–99, 106, 111, 138–39, 143–62; military life and, 125, 138–39, 143–62; national character, 35, 45–52, 88, 91–92; proving one's, 87–89, 99, 111, 138–62, 189–90; respectability,

6; self-control/discipline, 68–71, 146–48, 154–62, 216n26, 233n32; southern honor (compared to), 5–6, 64, 114, 198n11, 214n8; subsumes southern honor, 165, 176–77, 184, 186–88
Chase, James, 44
children's literature, 214n4
Clary, George, 57, 96, 110, 116, 118, 202n31; reaction to slavery, 130; view of African Americans, 132, 152
Clay, Henry, 76
Clemens, Samuel Langhorne. *See* Twain, Mark
Cohen, Michael David, 204n8
Cohen, Nancy, 166
Colburn, William G., 26
Collamore, Leander, 42
College of the Holy Cross, 205n13
colleges and universities, 2–3, 9–10, 14–15, 20–25, 62–63, 71–73, 97, 191; Civil War's effects on, 204n8; college compositions, 6, 14, 31–32, 60, 62–63; college life, 21, 28–29, 31–33, 69–70, 77; cost, 27–28; curriculum, 22, 24, 71–73; disciplinary problems, 21; guaranteeing character of graduates, 63, 71–73, 200n22; moral philosophy courses, 24–26, 71–73, 189; population of, 9, 21, 199n16; religious life, 30; secret societies (fraternities), 33, 66–67, 215–16n21; social class, 20–25, 71–73, 140–41
Columbian (George Washington) University, 204n9
Confederate States of America, 37, 95–96, 189, 201n27
Congressional Medal of Honor, 13, 162
Connecticut State Legislature, 25
Connor, Charles, 43, 82–83
Constitutional Union Party (election of 1860), 11
corruption (political), 79, 83–84, 199n14
courage (scholarly debate of), 139–40, 154, 229n4
Crowninshield, Benjamin William, 28, 29, 30, 33, 102, 202n31

Crowninshield, Caspar, 71, 121–22, 146, 149, 202n31; view of enslaved laborers, 133, 136
Curtis, George William, 235n3
Cutler, Charles, 66, 80

Dartmouth College, 13, 24, 31, 93, 205n13
Davidson College, 204n9
Davis, Samuel C., 60
Day, Jeremiah, 25
Dean, Zebina, 55
Deering, John Jr., 27, 28, 69, 70
Democratic Party, 11, 79, 81, 200–1n25
DeRoche, Andy, 221n21
Dickinson, J. T., 76
Dickinson College, 204n9
Dodge, Frederick, 44
duty, 4–5
Dwight, Elizabeth A., 1
Dwight, Howard, 70
Dwight, Wilder, 1, 35, 71–72, 73, 77, 78, 202n31; on choosing good associates, 70; conception of the United States, 35; defines a "well educated man," 26; discipline of troops, 148; Harvard College pride, 33–34; national character of Americans, 35; on reformers, 55–56; on selflessness and Benjamin Franklin, 76

education, 20, 25–26, 180–81; American population and, 9; founding generation and, 20–22, 59; social class and, 20–23, 59; as solution to the South's problems, 124, 134, 171–73, 189; women's education, 203–4n7
elections: of 1852, 32; of 1860, 32, 89; of 1872, 175; of 1876, 177; of 1884, 180
Eliot, Charles W., 235n3
Ells, Samuel H., 157
Emerson, Edward Waldo, 1
Emerson, Ralph Waldo, 64–65
Emerson, Stephen G., 52
Emerson, Thomas, 53
Eyal, Yonatan, 201n25

Fessenden, James Deering, 109, 202*n*31
Fessenden, Samuel, 32, 109, 202*n*31
Fessenden, William Howard, 100–1
Fessenden, William Pitt, 32, 109, 173
Fifteenth Amendment, 173
Foote, Lorien, 6, 98, 139, 140–41, 146, 154, 198*n*11, 225*n*47, 231*nn*11,14,18, 231–32*n*21, 233*n*37
Ford, C. B., 31
Forgie, George, 200*n*21, 210*n*28, 217–18*n*42, 218*n*49
Fort Pillow, Tennessee, 152, 154
Fort Sumter, South Carolina, 83, 92
Fort Wagner, South Carolina, 151–52
Foster, John, 65
Fourteenth Amendment, 172, 173
Fourth of July celebrations, 209–10*n*21
Fox, Thomas B. Jr., 44
Franco-Prussian War (1870–1871), 190
Frank, Joseph Allan, 229*n*4
Franklin, Benjamin, 76
Fredericksburg, Battle of (1862), 159
Fredrickson, George M., 7
Freedmen's Bureau. *See* Bureau of Refugees, Freedmen, and Abandoned Lands
Freeman, Joanne B., 215*n*13
French, Theodore, 53
Friend, Craig, 214–15*n*11

Gallagher, Gary W., 202*n*29
Garfield, James Abram, 9, 83, 100, 179–80, 202*n*31; and African Americans, 135, 179; political career of, 179–80; Reconstruction and, 170, 173–74, 175; on the South's leaders, 120–21; at Williams College, 27
Garrison, William Lloyd, 38, 58
gender: manhood/masculinity, 6, 36–37, 62–64, 98, 154, 184, 198*nn*8,10, 200*n*21, 214*n*5, 233*n*37; "restrained" *versus* "martial" men, 212*n*46, 237*n*38
Geneva College, 204*n*9
Gerry, C. F., 75
Gettysburg, Battle of (1863), 158, 159, 184
Gettysburg College, 204*n*9

Gilder, Richard Watson, 235*n*3
Glover, Lorri, 63–64, 204*n*10, 205*nn*15,17, 214–15*n*11, 215*n*16, 216*n*31
Gordon, George H., 141
Gordon, John B., 187, 188
Graham, J. T., 44
Grant, Susan-Mary, 12
Grant, Ulysses S., 19, 173, 174–75, 176, 177, 236*n*23
Gray, John Chipman, 107, 123, 202*n*31; African American soldiers and, 152–53; distrust of radicals, 168; on postwar issues, 168; reaction to enslaved laborers, 131, 133; view of the 54th Massachusetts, 152–53
Greeley, Horace, 175
Green, Jennifer R., 204*n*10, 217*n*35
Greenberg, Amy S., 6, 36–37, 211*n*36, 212*nn*37,46, 212–13*n*49, 237*n*38
Greenberg, Kenneth S., 5, 63, 64, 197*n*4
Gregory, Charles A., 45, 50, 56
Griffing, J. S., 67
Griswold, Edwin, 66, 74, 82
Grover, Edwin, 72–73, 80

Hale, Albert, 79
Hall, Joshua, 40
Hall, Peter Dobkin, 200*n*22
Hamilton, Alexander, 82–83
Hammond, William G., 34, 72
Hampden-Sydney College, 204*n*9
Hampton Normal and Agricultural Institute/University, 172, 179
Hand, Edwin C., 43
Hardy, Silas, 42
Harpers Ferry, 112, 116, 119–20
Harvard College/Harvard University, 9, 13, 21–23, 29, 33–34, 190, 205*n*13; students who fought in the Civil War, 4, 19, 190
Haskell, Franklin Aretas, 45–46, 49–50, 109, 202*n*31; combat experience of, 158; on leading soldiers in combat, 156; view of Confederate soldiers, 127
Haskell, William Lewis, 99

Hawthorne, Nathaniel, 5
Hayes, George L., 28
Hayes, Rutherford Birchard, 177, 178
Heath, Willard, 43
Henry, Patrick, 78
Hess, Earl, 10, 140, 201*n*26
Higginson, Thomas Wentworth, 235*n*3
historical sites, 118–20
Hobbs, George, 51
Hodgson, F. D., 45
Hoganson, Kristin, 213*n*53
Holmes, Oliver Wendell, Jr., 101, 103, 109, 159, 182, 183, 184, 202*n*31, 224–25*n*45; anti-slavery support, 213*n*58, 220*n*14; description of combat, 156; postwar career of, 181–82
Holmes, Oliver Wendell, Sr.: "Brahmin caste of New England," 2; *Elsie Venner*, 2
Holmes, Theodore James, 109, 116, 118, 128, 202*n*31, 221–22*n*22
Horowitz, Helen Lefkowitz, 199*n*16
Howard, Charles Henry, 90, 119, 123, 124, 146, 160, 161, 202*n*31; African American soldiers and, 142, 143; Bowdoin College and, 30; enforcement of discipline in the ranks, 147–48; on Abraham Lincoln's death, 163; Reconstruction and, 169; view of southerners, 126
Howard, Oliver Otis, 61–62, 90, 142, 146, 147–48, 160, 202*n*31, 213*n*1, 235*n*12; Bowdoin College and, 28, 29, 61, 66–67, 70; Congressional Medal of Honor, 162; education and, 171; on Abraham Lincoln's death, 163; Reconstruction and, 169–70, 174
Howard, Rowland Bailey, 61–62, 89, 91
Howard University, 171
Howe, Daniel Walker, 203*n*32, 208–9*n*10
Howell, Luther C., 27, 91, 93–94, 110, 159, 202*n*31; opinion of the postwar South, 169; reaction to slavery, 131; view of African American soldiers, 150–51, 154
Howells, William Dean, 235*n*3

honor: northern (*see* character); southern, 2, 4–5, 64, 114, 197*n*4, 214–15*n*11
Hubbard, John, Sr., 104–5, 106–7
Hubbard, John Barrett, 97, 104, 107
Hubbard, Thomas Hamlin, 100, 104, 143, 146, 202*n*31; dislike of immigrant soldiers, 141; interaction with southerners, 126; on Abraham Lincoln's death, 163–64; military rank and, 107; motivation to volunteer in the war, 97, 98–99, 102, 108; postwar career, 181; views of the South, 116
Hunter, David, 150
Hyde, Thomas Worcester, 108, 144, 157, 202*n*31; Battle of Antietam, 137–38; Congressional Medal of Honor, 162

immigrants: in the Union Army, 3–4, 141–42
industrial education, 172
Ingram, Alexander, 49, 51–52
intellectuals: in northern society, 7, 31
Irvin, William, 137–38

Jackson, Andrew, 79, 81, 89–90
Jacksonian Era, 7, 22
James, William, 235*n*3
Jefferson, Thomas, 83
Johnson, Andrew, 170, 173
Johnson, Osgood, 57–58

Kantrowitz, Stephen, 214*n*5
Kelley, Mary, 203–4*n*7
Kenniston, George, 107
Kenyon College, 204*n*9
Kett, Joseph, 63, 214*n*6
Kimball, David, 44
Ku Klux Klan, 173–74

Latimer, James, 74–75
Lears, Jackson, 184
Lee, Robert Edward, 184–87, 188
Lee, William Henry Fitzhugh "Rooney," 33
Lemelin, Robert, 210*n*28
Liberal reformers, 165–67, 174

Liberal Republicans, 11, 167, 175, 176, 235*n*4
Liberty Party, 38
Lincoln, Abraham, 38, 89, 90, 91, 92, 111, 163, 168
Lincoln, Solomon, 75
Linderman, Gerald F., 139
Little, Levi, 66
Little Round Top. *See* Gettysburg, Battle of (1863)
Logue, Larry M., 216*n*26, 233*n*32
Long, John D., 40
Loomis, F. A., 75–76
Lost Cause Ideology, 184
Lowell, Charles Russell, 1, 18, 110, 202*n*31; on the death of Robert Gould Shaw, 151–52; eager for battle, 155; individualism, 66; motivation to fight/volunteer, 94; qualification for commission, 10; on secession crisis, 90, 91, 92; self-discipline and, 147; view of the 54th Massachusetts, 151
Lowell, James Jackson, 84, 95
Lowell, James Russell, 235*n*3
Lusk, William Thompson, 202*n*31; military rank and, 107–8; motivation to volunteer/fight, 99; view of African Americans, 131–32; views of the South/white southerners, 116, 118, 121
Lyman, Theodore, 100, 148, 202*n*31; on African American soldiers, 134–35; on combat experience, 157; critical of radicals, 168; on immigrant soldiers, 142; political career of, 180

Macy, George N., 141
Madison (Colgate) University, 204*n*9
Manifest Destiny, 31, 37, 208*n*4, 211*n*36, 212–13*n*49; Metaphysical Manifest Destiny, 36, 43–44, 53–54, 60
Mann, Horace, 20
manhood/masculinity. *See* gender
Marten, James, 214*n*4
Martindale, Daniel, 75
Massachusetts Board of Railroad Commissioners, 181

Mattocks, Charles Porter, 119, 202*n*31, 215*n*25, 230*n*6, 232*n*21; Congressional Medal of Honor, 162; disciplining troops under his command, 145, 147, 148; view of Confederate soldiers, 127
McArthur, Arthur, Jr., 68–69
McArthur, Arthur, Sr., 70
McArthur, Charles, 70
McArthur, William, 149, 202*n*31
McCraw, Thomas, 181
McGonegal, Robert, 78
McPherson, James M., 201*n*26, 211*n*34
Melish, Joanne, 208*n*7
Menand, Louis, 182, 220*n*14
Miami University, 204*n*9
Middlebury College, 21, 205*n*13
military academies, 204*n*10, 217*n*35
Miller, Richard F., 224*n*40
Mintz, Steven, 20
Mitchell, Charles, 44
Mitchell, Donald G., 29
Mitchell, Reid, 237*n*41
Morse, Charles Fessenden, 119, 160, 202*n*31; on African American soldiers, 134, 151; interaction with Confederate soldiers, 128–29
Morse, John H., 47
Muhlenberg College, 204*n*9
Mussey, Reuben Delavan, 142, 152

nationalism (American), 3, 12, 35–44, 53–54, 94–96, 114–15, 118–20, 201–2*n*28, 208*n*5, 211*n*34
nationalism (Confederate), 201*n*27, 208*n*9
Neely, Mark, 209–10*n*21
New Brahmins, 1–2; ambition and, 106–11; American exceptionalism and, 32–33, 39–41, 43–44, 53–54; American Revolution and, 42–44, 96–97, 104–5, 118–19; character and (*see* character); character-based education for freed people, 171–73, 190; Civil War and, 8, 18, 189; combat and, 137–38, 154–162, 233*n*37; education, 8, 13, 71–73, 106,

180–81; "ethnic nationalism" *versus* "civic nationalism," 46–47, 211*nn*32,34; Federalists (view of), 82; free labor and, 1, 3, 13, 16, 36–38, 41, 49–53, 56–57, 60, 113, 115–17, 189; generational conflict with parents, 88, 101–6; gentlemen (view of selves as), 4, 71–73, 87–88, 98, 125, 231*n*18; leadership and, 32–33, 45, 71–85, 97–99, 102, 106–11, 137–162, 164; Liberal reformers/Liberal Republicans and, 167, 175; Manifest Destiny and, 31, 35–38; military rank and, 89, 106–11, 224*n*40; moderate political and social beliefs of, 3, 11, 55, 78–84, 168; motivation to volunteer in the war, 86–111; national character and, 45–47, 52, 87, 91–92, 164; nationalism and, 32–33, 36–44, 46–47, 88, 94–96, 114–15, 118–20, 189; as officers, 10, 13, 137–62, 231*nn*11,14; political beliefs, 6, 8, 11, 31–32, 38, 78–84; postwar activities/careers, 165, 167–83, 190; qualifications for officers' commissions, 10; racial and ethnic beliefs of, 3–4, 16, 36, 40–41, 46–48, 57–58, 141–42, 150–54, 161, 164, 169; Reconciliation and, 165, 176–77, 183–88; Reconstruction and, 164, 166–78; reform movements and, 54–55, 57–58, 167; secession and, 59, 85, 86–92; social class, 11–12, 22–23, 58–59, 71–73, 140–41, 224*n*40, 231–32*n*21; Union (conceptions of), 3–4, 12, 31, 35, 36–44, 49–57, 60, 94–96, 202*n*29; Union Army and, 3–4, 89, 125; United States Constitution and, 43, 56, 58; views of African Americans, 3–4, 54–55, 57–58, 150–54, 161, 164, 169–70, 189–90; views of antebellum society, 8, 32–33; views of Confederate soldiers, 126–29; views of slavery and enslaved laborers, 13, 16, 36, 41, 52–53, 54–57, 60, 90, 114–15, 119–20, 130–36, 164, 189; views of the South and southerners, 3, 41, 112–36, 189; George Washington (view of), 42–43, 75, 119, 145, 217–18*n*42, 218*n*43; the West and, 13, 36, 47, 49–52, 81; Whig interpretation of history and, 8, 36, 39–40, 201*n*25, 208–9*n*10

New England (region), 21, 49, 208*n*7
New England–centric ideas, 3, 12, 36–41, 45, 49, 60, 95–96, 114–18, 164, 179, 189, 208*n*7
Nichols, Samuel Edmund, 100, 110, 148, 202*n*31; view of Confederate soldiers, 127
Norton, Charles Eliot, 235*n*3
Norwich University, 93, 205*n*13
Noyes, David, 42–43
Noyes, John Buttrick, 119–20, 144, 145, 202*n*31; class and ethnic makeup of unit, 141–42; desire for promotion and rank, 108; relationship with soldiers, 149; view of African Americans, 131, 132, 152; view of the South, 118
Nullification Crisis, 82

Oglethorpe College, 204*n*9
oratory, 203*n*32

Packard, Alpheus Spring, Sr., 71
Paine, Robert, 40, 43–44, 84
Paludan, Phillip Shaw, 197*n*4
Parish, Peter, 211*n*32
Parker, Isaac, 31, 53–54
Parmelee, Uriah Nelson, 119, 202*n*31
patronage. *See* corruption (political)
Pennell, Christopher, 93, 95, 97–98, 99, 105, 202*n*31
Petersburg, Virginia, 152
Phillips, Wendell, 58
Pickering, Henry, 50–51
Pierce, Franklin, 32, 177
Pitkin, Ozias, 65, 68, 72
Pitman, Robert, 65
Pond, Daniel, 81
Poor, Walter S., 86
Port Hudson, Louisiana, 152
Porter, Burrill, 47–48

Potter, William Elmer, 69, 73–74, 83, 202*n*31; on the Confederate States of America, 95–96; historical sites and, 43; Abraham Lincoln (views of and hopes for), 92; on reformers (abolitionists), 58, 213*n*59; on secession, 89–90; slavery (views of), 56
Prentiss, Henry, 48
Preston, Daniel, 48
Princeton University, 21, 204*nn*9,11
Progressive Movement, 181–82
Pullen, John, 10

Quigg, David, 59
Quigley, Paul, 201*n*27

Racine, Philip, 230*n*6
Rael, Patrick, 6
Read, John, 122–23, 202*n*31
Reconciliation, 176–77, 183–88, 237*n*43
Reconstruction, 167–78; Congressional/Radical Reconstruction, 170–71; Presidential Reconstruction, 170, 173
Republican Party, 11, 81, 175
Republicanism, 199*n*15
Revere, Paul Joseph, 94, 97, 102, 116, 150, 202*n*31
Rice, James Clay, 27, 30–31, 101, 123, 144, 203*n*31
Richards, William, 22
Ritchie, Thomas W., 54
Roosevelt, Theodore, 182
Ropes, Henry, 155–56
Rose, Anne C., 198*n*12
Ross, Jordan, 223*n*36
Rotundo, E. Anthony, 200*n*21
Rushmore, Edwin, 41–42
Rutgers University, 21

Saratoga Springs, New York, 210*n*21
Savage, Benjamin S., 40–41
Savage, Edward, 26
Schurz, Carl, 178
Scott, Winfield, 186
Sears, John F., 210*n*21, 212*n*37

secession. *See* New Brahmins: secession and
Second Great Awakening, 30
Sedgwick, William Dwight, 51, 77, 94–95, 124, 145–46, 203*n*31
Seward, William Henry, 90–91, 220*n*7
Shaw, Robert Gould, 7, 33, 92, 105, 142, 203*n*31; 54th Massachusetts and, 151; description of combat, 155; family's abolitionism and, 55; motivation to volunteer in the war, 99; reaction to secession, 92; reaction to slavery, 130–31
Sheridan, Philip Henry, 174
Shiloh, Battle of (1862), 157
Slap, Andrew L., 166, 199*n*15, 235*n*4
slavery, 74, 80, 88, 95–96, 119–20, 189; cause of the South's lack of development, 16–17, 116–17; as the cause of the war, 90; effect on southerners, 123–24, 129–36; essential to southern honor, 2, 197*n*4, 214*n*8; free labor in competition with, 37–38, 52–53; New England-centric vision of the future and, 16, 37–38, 41, 45; restricting spread of, 13, 49, 95; threat to the Union, 54–57
Sleeper, Herbert, 54
social class, 11–12, 22–23, 58–59, 71–73, 140–41
Society of the Army of the Potomac, 174
South, the (region), 112–136; civilization of, 3, 113–18, 208*n*9; leadership class of, 3, 22, 113–18, 120–24, 148–49, 189, 202*n*30, 205*nn*15,16,17, 216*n*31, 218*n*46; physical landscape/descriptions of, 112–20, 189, 226*n*6; slaveholders, 59–60, 112–18, 120–24; southerners, 59, 112–36, 189, 198*nn*8,10, 204*n*10, 232*n*22
Smith, Joseph Emerson, 32
Spanish-American War (1898), 190
Sparks, Jared, 33
Spaulding, Henry, 67, 72
spoils system. *See* corruption (political)
Sproat, John G., 235*n*4

INDEX

Stauffer, John, 214*n*5
Stearns, Frazer Augustus, 30, 79–80, 94, 95, 97, 98, 100, 102, 203*n*31; attributes unit's success to good leadership, 159
Stearns, William, 97
Stephanson, Anders, 40, 208*n*4
Stephens, Alexander Hamilton, 95, 170
Stevens, William O., 96
Storey, Moorfield, 235*n*3
Sword, Wiley, 229*n*5, 234*n*39

Tarbell, H. R., 51
Thomas, Edwin, 32
Thomas, George Henry, 186
Thompson, William, 76
Tilden, Samuel J., 177
Todd, Thomas, 217*n*34
tourism/travel narratives, 210*n*21, 210–11*n*28, 211–12*n*37
Travers, Len, 209*n*21
Trinity College, 204*n*9, 205*n*13
Tufts College (University), 205*n*13
Twain, Mark, 235*n*3
Twichell, Joseph Hopkins, 28, 110, 160, 180, 184–85, 203*n*31; immigrant soldiers and, 144; reaction to slavery, 130; relationship with soldiers, 149; view of African Americans, 131; view of Confederate soldiers, 126–28

Union. *See* New Brahmins: Union (conceptions of)
Union Army: characteristics of soldiers in, 10–11, 229*n*5; motivation of soldiers, 139–40, 201*n*26, 221*n*21; social class in, 140–41
Union College, 21
United States Military Academy at West Point, 25–26, 213*n*1
University of Vermont, 205*n*13

Ware, John, 33
Warner, Hermann, 40, 78–79

Warren, Gouverneur Kemble, 174–75
Warrington, George, 83
Washburn, Israel, Jr., 86
Washington, Booker Taliaferro, 172
Washington and Lee University, 186, 188
Waterville (Colby) College, 205*n*13
Webster, Daniel, 76, 218*n*43
Weeks, William, 75
Weld, Stephen Minot, 117–18, 141, 203*n*31
Wells, Jeremy, 172
Wesleyan University, 14, 30, 205*n*13
Whedon, Daniel, 39–40
Wheeler, William, 27, 33, 70, 154, 155, 203*n*31, 223*n*36; on combat experience, 157; disapproval at invasion of private property, 125; immigrant soldiers and, 141; interaction with Confederate soldiers, 128, 148–49; motivation to volunteer/fight, 94, 95, 99, 101; reaction to southerners, 122–24, 129, 148–49; on secession, 91–93; views of the South, 116, 117
Whig Party, 6, 11, 32, 81, 201*n*25
Whittemore, George, 75, 107
Wickersham, Caleb P., 30
Wiebe, Robert H., 236*n*23
Wiley, Bell Irvin, 201*n*26
Willard, Sidney, 157
Williams College, 9, 13, 21, 205*n*13, 215–16*n*21
Williamsburg, Battle of (1862), 155, 160
Wilson, Edmund, 2
Wilson, Thomas Woodrow, 208*n*4
Wingate, Joseph, 52
Winthrop, Theodore, 56–57, 94, 99, 144–45, 203*n*31
Woodbury, Eri Davidson, 24, 128, 155, 162, 203*n*31
Woods, Leonard, 70
Wyatt-Brown, Bertram, 5, 63, 198*n*8

Yale University, 9, 13, 23, 25, 28, 29, 185, 204*n*11, 205*n*13; Yale Report of 1828, 25

THE NORTH'S CIVIL WAR
Andrew L. Slap, series editor

Anita Palladino, ed., *Diary of a Yankee Engineer: The Civil War Story of John H. Westervelt, Engineer, 1st New York Volunteer Engineer Corps.*

Herman Belz, *Abraham Lincoln, Constitutionalism, and Equal Rights in the Civil War Era.*

Earl J. Hess, *Liberty, Virtue, and Progress: Northerners and Their War for the Union.* Second revised edition, with a new introduction by the author.

William L. Burton, *Melting Pot Soldiers: The Union's Ethnic Regiments.*

Hans L. Trefousse, *Carl Schurz: A Biography.*

Stephen W. Sears, ed., *Mr. Dunn Browne's Experiences in the Army: The Civil War Letters of Samuel W. Fiske.*

Jean H. Baker, *Affairs of Party: The Political Culture of Northern Democrats in the Mid-Nineteenth Century.*

Frank L. Klement, *The Limits of Dissent: Clement L. Vallandigham and the Civil War.* With a new introduction by Steven K. Rogstad.

Lawrence N. Powell, *New Masters: Northern Planters during the Civil War and Reconstruction.*

John A. Carpenter, *Sword and Olive Branch: Oliver Otis Howard.*

Thomas F. Schwartz, ed., *"For a Vast Future Also": Essays from the* Journal of the Abraham Lincoln Association.

Mark De Wolfe Howe, ed., *Touched with Fire: Civil War Letters and Diary of Oliver Wendell Holmes, Jr.* With a new introduction by David Burton.

Harold Adams Small, ed., *The Road to Richmond: The Civil War Letters of Major Abner R. Small of the 16th Maine Volunteers.* With a new introduction by Earl J. Hess.

Eric A. Campbell, ed., *"A Grand Terrible Dramma": From Gettysburg to Petersburg: The Civil War Letters of Charles Wellington Reed.* Illustrated by Reed's Civil War sketches.

Herbert Mitgang, ed., *Abraham Lincoln: A Press Portrait.*

Harold Holzer, ed., *Prang's Civil War Pictures: The Complete Battle Chromos of Louis Prang.*

Harold Holzer, ed., *State of the Union: New York and the Civil War.*

Paul A. Cimbala and Randall M. Miller, eds., *Union Soldiers and the Northern Home Front: Wartime Experiences, Postwar Adjustments.*

Mark A. Snell, *From First to Last: The Life of Major General William B. Franklin.*

Paul A. Cimbala and Randall M. Miller, eds., *An Uncommon Time: The Civil War and the Northern Home Front.*

John Y. Simon and Harold Holzer, eds., *The Lincoln Forum: Rediscovering Abraham Lincoln.*

Thomas F. Curran, *Soldiers of Peace: Civil War Pacifism and the Postwar Radical Peace Movement.*

Kyle S. Sinisi, *Sacred Debts: State Civil War Claims and American Federalism, 1861–1880.*

Russell L. Johnson, *Warriors into Workers: The Civil War and the Formation of Urban-Industrial Society in a Northern City.*

Peter J. Parish, *The North and the Nation in the Era of the Civil War.* Edited by Adam L. P. Smith and Susan-Mary Grant.

Patricia Richard, *Busy Hands: Images of the Family in the Northern Civil War Effort.*

Michael S. Green, *Freedom, Union, and Power: The Mind of the Republican Party During the Civil War.*

Christian G. Samito, ed., *Fear Was Not In Him: The Civil War Letters of Major General Francis S. Barlow, U.S.A.*

John S. Collier and Bonnie B. Collier, eds., *Yours for the Union: The Civil War Letters of John W. Chase, First Massachusetts Light Artillery.*

Grace Palladino, *Another Civil War: Labor, Capital, and the State in the Anthracite Regions of Pennsylvania, 1840–1868.*

Christian B. Keller, *Chancellorsville and the Germans: Nativism, Ethnicity, and Civil War Memory.*

Sidney George Fisher, *A Philadelphia Perspective: The Civil War Diary of Sidney George Fisher.* Edited and with a new Introduction by Jonathan W. White.

Robert M. Sandow, *Deserter Country: Civil War Opposition in the Pennsylvania Appalachians.*

Craig L. Symonds, ed., *Union Combined Operations in the Civil War.*

Harold Holzer, Craig L. Symonds, and Frank L. Williams, eds., *The Lincoln Assassination: Crime and Punishment, Myth and Memory.* A Lincoln Forum Book.

Earl F. Mulderink III, *New Bedford's Civil War.*

David G. Smith, *On the Edge of Freedom: The Fugitive Slave Issue in South Central Pennsylvania, 1820–1870.*

George Washington Williams, *A History of the Negro Troops in the War of the Rebellion, 1861–1865.* Introduction by John David Smith.

Randall M. Miller, ed., *Lincoln and Leadership: Military, Political, and Religious Decision Making.*

Andrew L. Slap and Michael Thomas Smith, eds., *This Distracted and Anarchical People: New Answers for Old Questions about the Civil War–Era North.*

Paul D. Moreno and Johnathan O'Neill, eds., *Constitutionalism in the Approach and Aftermath of the Civil War.*

Steve Longenecker, *Gettysburg Religion: Refinement, Diversity, and Race in the Antebellum and Civil War Border North.*

Harold Holzer, Craig L. Symonds, and Frank L. Williams, eds., *Exploring Lincoln: Great Historians Reappraise Our Greatest President.* A Lincoln Forum Book.

Lorien Foote and Kanisorn Wongsrichanalai, eds., *So Conceived and So Dedicated: Intellectual Life in the Civil War–Era North.*

William B. Kurtz, *Excommunicated from the Union: How the Civil War Created a Separate Catholic America.*

Kanisorn Wongsrichanalai, *Northern Character: College-Educated New Englanders, Honor, Nationalism, and Leadership in the Civil War Era.*

www.ingramcontent.com/pod-product-compliance
Lightning Source LLC
Chambersburg PA
CBHW030436300426
44112CB00009B/1034